Studying the Media

An Introduction

Second Edition

Tim O'Sullivan
Brian Dutton
Philip Rayner

A member of the Hodder Headline Group
LONDON
Co-published in the USA by Oxford University Press, Inc., New York

First published in Great Britain in 1994
Second edition published in 1998 by
Arnold, a member of the Hodder Headline Group
338 Euston Road, London NW1 3BH

http://www.arnold publishers.com

Co-published in the United States of America by
Oxford University Press, Inc.,
198 Madison Avenue, New York, NY 10016

British Library Cataloguing in Publication Data
A catalogue entry for this book is available from the British Library

Library of Congress Cataloging-in-Publication Data
A catalog record for this book is available from the Library of Congress

ISBN 0 340 67685 X

2 3 4 5 6 7 8 9 10

Production Editor: Julie Delf
Production Controller: Rose James
Design: Pentacor

Composition by Saxon Graphics Ltd, Derby
Printed and bound in India by Ajanta Offset & Packagings Ltd.

Contents

Contents

Acknowledgements

We would like to thank the many people who have directly and indirectly helped with the development and production of this book. The processes involved in producing this second edition, like the first, would have made an interesting case study and many of these processes began 'at home'. As a result, our thanks go first to the everyday support from our families and partners.

In addition, we also wish to acknowledge:

Colleagues, students and friends, past and present, inside and outside the institutions we work in.

Lesley Riddle, Elena Seymenliyska, Julie Delf and the team at Arnold, who managed the initial project with patience and enthusiasm, and then came back for more.

Arthur Parker, Roberta Harries, Mike Edwards, Ivor Hicks, Jill Nelmes and Jude Brigley, past and present Media Studies Officers and Examiners at the Welsh Joint Education Committee.

Val Bond, Jim Taylor, Len Masterman and members of the Northern Examinations and Assessment Board Media Studies Subject Committee.

The British Film Institute and their continuing work in the field of Media Education

Jarrod Cripps, Paul Hickinbotham and Barbara Hind, for photographic work.

Liz Hornby and Francis Lewis, for editorial work.

The *Newbury Weekly News*.

The School of Humanities Research Committee, the Department of English, Media and Cultural Studies, and the British Cinema and Television Research Group, De Montfort University, Leicester.

The authors and publishers would also like to acknowledge the following for permission to use copyright material in this book:

The Advertising Association for figure 5.5; AGB Television/BARB for figure 1.4; the Audit Bureau of Circulation for figure 5.4; Gianpaolo Barbieri for figure 3.12; BBC Picture Archives for figure 6.14; Steve Bell for figure 4.1; BFI for figure 6.15; Bodleian Library for figures 6.2, 6.3, and 6.4; British Advertising Association for figure 1.12; British Phonographic Industries for figures 5.13 and 5.15; the

Central Office for Information for figure 4.4; Channel 5 for figure 6.24; Cinema Advertising Association for figures 1.7 and 1.8; Cinema and Video Industry Audience Research for figure 4.7; Comedia for figure 5.6; the Commission for Racial Equality for figures 9.1 and 9.2; Coty for figures 2.13 and 3.16; Jarrod Cripps for figures 1.3, 1.16, 1.17, 6.23, 7.3, 7.11, 7.12, 7.13, and 8.4; Cyberia Internet Cafe for figure 7.9; E.P. Dutton & Co for figures 6.6, 6.7, 6.8, and 6.9; EMAP Elan Ltd for figure 3.13; Express Newspapers for figures 3.2 and 3.4b; the *Fiji Times* for figure 7.15; Gallup for figure 5.17; The *Guardian* for figures 3.5, 3.23, 4.2, 5.2, 5.8, 6.19, and 6.20; Heinemann for figure 9.3; Paul Hickinbotham for figures 1.5, 1.9, 1.13, 1.15, 1.18, 1.20, 1.23, 1.24, 4.11, 4.13, 5.14, 5.16, 5.21, 7.1, 7.2, 7.5, and 7.17; Barbara Hind for figure 7.18; HMSO for figures 1.14b and 1.14c; Houghton for figures 2.3 and 2.4; Hovis, Collett, Dickenson, Pearce and Partners Ltd for figure 3.1; Hulton Getty Pictures Collection Ltd for figure 6.13; Hutchinson for figure 4.5; the *Independent* for figures 2.7, 2.8a, and 2.8b; the *Independent on Sunday* for figure 3.30; the Independent Television Commission for figure 1.10; International Broadcasting and Audience Research Library for figures 7.14; IPC Magazines for figure 3.19; John Brown Publishing Ltd for figure 3.7; KICK FM Ltd for figures 5.25 and 5.26; the Kobal Collection for figures 2.14, 2.16, 2.17, 2.18, 2.19, 2.20, 2.21, 2.22a, 2.22b, 3.8, 3.9, 3.14, 3.17, 3.18, 3.21, 3.22, 3.26, 3.27, 3.29, and 5.19; John Libbey for figure 6.21; Longman for figure 1.21; Lowe Howard Spink for figure 2.12; Macmillan for figure 8.2; the Mirror Group for figures 2.9, 3.6b, and 5.3; National Readership Surveys Ltd for figure 1.14a; the *New Statesman and Society* for figure 5.20; the *Newbury Weekly News* for figures 5.23 and 5.24; NOP for figure 4.3; The *Observer* Newspaper for figures 3.25 and 6.18; Our Price Video for figures 4.9a and 4.9b; *Over Land and Sea* for figure 5.10; Pacemaker Press International for figure 2.6; Pan Books for figure 2.5; Pandora Press for figure 4.6; Policy Studies Institute for figure 1.6; Polity Press for figure 4.10; the *Post Courier* for figure 7.16; the Press Complaints Commission for figure 5.7; the *Radio Times* for figures 3.3, 6.10, and 6.11; Rainey Kelly Campbell Roalfe for figure 3.15; Reckitt & Coleman Products for figure 2.15; Red Flannel Films for figure 5.12; Routledge Ltd for figure 5.18; Sage Publications Ltd for figure 4.8; the *Sun* for figures 3.4a, 3.6 a, 3.6c, and 3.10; TBWA Ltd for figure 3.20; *Television Week* for figures 9.4, 9.5, 9.6, and 9.7; *The Times* for figure 6.1; *TV Times* for figure 6.17; Virgin Direct for figure 2.10; Vodafone Group Services for figure 2.11; *The Voice* for figure 3.28; Wendy Wallace for figure 3.24; *The Water in Majorca* for figure 5.11; West Ham United Football Club for figure 5.9; and Yves Saint Laurent for figure 3.11.

As with the first edition, every effort has been made to trace copyright holders of material produced in this book. Any rights not acknowledged here, will be acknowledged in subsequent editions if notice is given to the publisher.

Preface

In the last fifteen years, media studies has become a well-known and established subject in many schools, colleges and universities. This development has been rapid, and, if somewhat against the grain of educational policy and press opinion in the period,[1] the subject has proved to be popular and worthwhile for many students and teachers.

It may be mocked by Education Secretary John Patten as 'cultural Disneyland for the weaker minded' and regarded with suspicion even by journalists and broadcasters, but media studies is the boom subject of the nineties.
D. Macleod, The Guardian, 8 November 1993

This book is the product of our combined experience of learning and teaching about the media in a variety of different contexts and syllabuses – GCSE, A-level, BTEC, GNVQ, undergraduate and postgraduate courses – over the last twenty years. These diverse experiences, in secondary, further and higher educational settings, have provided the main impetus for the book and we hope that this second edition continues to have a wide application and will prove generally useful for a range of post-16 courses in media studies, including A-level, BTEC and GNVQ, as well as providing introductory reading for undergraduate courses.

As practised teachers, we recognised the need for a book addressed directly to students, which would provide an *accessible and stimulating introduction* to the systematic study of the media. The book covers key areas of study relevant to A-level students but will also be useful in a number of other courses of study and investigation. It provides a *foundation framework* to build upon, and a range of activities and suggestions for further

[1] See: O'Sullivan, T. 'What Lies between Mechatronics and Medicine? The Critical Mass of Media Studies'. *Soundings*, Issue 5, Spring 1997, pp. 211–21.

reading is an important component of each chapter. These have been fully updated for the second edition.

At the turn of the century, media studies continues to be a broad-ranging and fast-moving field of enquiry. This has forced us to be selective, and while we have tried to use relevant and current examples wherever possible, it is in the nature of the subject that some of these will become dated fairly quickly. There is no one right way to use or read the book, although we have reorganised this second edition according to feedback from readers and users of the first edition and changes in the organisation of syllabuses. As a result, this second edition follows a slightly different sequence from the first. This sequence may and should be varied, however, according to your own specific interests and focus; each chapter continues to provide a relatively self-contained discussion and analysis, but there are a number of key themes which recur throughout the book as a whole.

The first chapter begins by examining the presence of the media in our everyday lives. *Media saturation* is outlined and discussed, and this provides a central theme which is revisited regularly in later sections. Chapter 2 explores *forms of media output* and develops an analytical framework for studying media texts in detail. This emphasis is, in turn, extended in chapter 3, which examines key questions surrounding debates over forms of *media representation and realism*. Chapter 4 is devoted to the study of *media audiences*, and the relationships between audiences and media output. Chapter 5 discusses some of the central characteristics of *media institutions* in the current period, and, using case studies, focuses on some of the major determinants of media industries and organisations. Chapter 6 focuses on *media histories*, looking at the growth and development of key media institutions and audiences from the nineteenth century to the present day. Chapter 7 addresses issues surrounding change in the current period, in particular examining key developments in *new media technologies* and the emergence of global or *worldwide media networks*. Chapter 8 looks at forms of *media practice* and emphasises the value and importance of practical production work and professional contacts within the context of media studies as a whole. Finally, the concluding chapter offers a guide to *researching and investigating* the media.

Media studies in particular and media education more generally have now reached an important and critical stage of development. The momentum and dynamics of rapid growth continue to be interwoven with some major issues; the precarious position of the subject within the National Curriculum and educational policy, debates over the most appropriate direction and rationale for the subject, and public perceptions of the subject area all contribute to this critical state. This book seeks to introduce some of the most important areas of study and the principal analytical approaches and questions which currently comprise the subject area. In the twenty-first century, the significance of the systematic study of the media will not diminish, although its form and focus may have to change to keep up with changes within and across the media themselves. If this book enables you to ask the right kinds of question about the media and to keep pace with their relationships within modern social and cultural life, then it will have worked. However, the real test of the book lies in its use and application. We welcome any responses to, or comments about, the book, or any suggestions you might have for subsequent editions. Please write to us via the publishers, or contact us via the following sign of the times: http:\\www.arnoldpublishers.com

Tim O'Sullivan
Brian Dutton
Philip Rayner
January 1998

Note

A Glossary of essential media-related words and expressions is provided towards the end of the book.

1

The mass media and modern culture

Media saturation

It is important to begin a book like this by noting the commanding presence and power of the mass media in modern public and private life. Those of us who live in western and other highly industrialised societies inhabit cultures and worlds which have been described as *media saturated*. This fact of modern life provides the major rationale for media studies. This chapter aims to introduce and frame some of the key issues at stake in this idea and to provide you with a range of arguments and suggestions for developing relevant project work.

Initially, you should start your study of the mass media by systematically considering and taking stock of your own patterns of **media involvement** and use. Throughout the chapter you will encounter a range of material which may help you to start to identify distinctive aspects of your own personal forms of media involvement. You will also find different forms of data presented which index some of the larger-scale social patterns of

Fig. 1.1
Source: Tim O'Sullivan

Fig. 1.2
Source: Tim O'Sullivan

ACTIVITY 1.1

Keep a diary for one week, noting your daily involvements with different media. Analyse the patterns and habits which emerge as a result. When do you tend to use different media and for what kinds of purpose? How do you use different media?

Tunstall (1983) makes a distinction between primary, secondary and tertiary forms of media consumption. *Primary* involvement occurs when the television programme, magazine, newspaper or radio broadcast is the exclusive and focused activity. *Secondary* types of involvement are those forms of media consumption and use which accompany other activities; for instance, listening to the radio or music while doing other forms of work at home. The *tertiary* category of use is in one sense the weakest and least intensive relationship, where, for example, the TV or radio set is on in the background, or in another room in the household. As Tunstall notes:

> Tertiary could literally mean that one listens to the sound through the wall, while awaiting the next item; or tertiary might refer to glancing back and forth at a newspaper, opened at the TV schedule or the sports fixtures ... one might be glancing at the television with its sound turned down, listening to radio news-on-the-hour, while inspecting the schedules in the newspaper.
>
> *Tunstall (1983), p.135*

Using these distinctions, you should be able to arrive at a rough estimate of the number of hours in the week you spend in differing forms of media involvement and consumption. You may also want to consider use of video, visits to the cinema and other 'out-of-home' forms of media consumption. How does the tape cassette player, the personal computer or the telephone fit into this picture?

Fig. 1.3
Source: Jarrod Cripps

media involvement and use which characterise current trends and dimensions. These will also enable you to locate and compare your own media-related experience in the current context.

The results of this type of research generally provide evidence at the personal level for our extensive, patterned, everyday involvements with the mass media. In many ways we are reliant and dependent upon regular contact with the mass media for information, opinion, entertainment, ideas and a range of other resources, which are deeply bound up with our continuing attempts to maintain a coherent sense of 'who' and 'where' we think we are. Michael Real (1996) has recently drawn attention to the importance of what he calls *ritual interaction* with modern media. By this he means that forms of media consumption – reading, watching, listening and so on – are particular ways of creatively participating in the life of modern culture. This active participation operates to express aspects of collective identity and to bind individuals into the society and culture as a whole. We should begin by noting, then, that the nature of cultural experience in modern societies has been profoundly affected by the development of systems of mass communication. Indeed, many writers have argued that modern societies and cultures require such systems and that what we understand as modern life would be impossible without specialised institutions which are generically referred to as the *mass media*. Books, magazines, adverts, newspapers, radio and television programmes, films and videos, computer networks or games, records, tapes or CDs occupy a central and pivotal role in our lives, providing a continuous and rapidly expanding flow of information and leisure facilities.

All the time in the world?

One of the first ways in which we can start to get a grip on the notion of 'media saturation' is to consider the amounts of time that we spend in media-related activities, largely in forms and practices of media consumption – reading, watching or listening. At a general level, these activities account for considerable proportions of our non-sleep, discretionary time. If we start by taking that most domestic of media, television, recent measures of TV viewing in the UK based on data collected in 1993, 1994 and 1995 (see figure 1.4) indicate that the average number of hours per week spent watching TV was just over 25. These data do not include time spent in timeshifting, watching material recorded off-air by VCR, watching pre-recorded videos or watching other,

ACTIVITY 1.2

Write a short summary of the measurements of weekly television viewing contained in figure 1.4. Which groups appear to watch the least and the most amounts of TV? How would you account for these differences? How might these patterns of viewing time be distinctive in terms of choice of programme types?

| | Weekly hours viewed | | |
	1993	1994	1995
Age			
Children	19.2	18.4	18.1
Adults 16–24	19.7	19.3	19.1
Adults 25–34	25.1	24.3	24.2
Adults 35–44	24.4	24.0	24.0
Adults 45–54	25.4	25.2	25.3
Adults 55–64	30.0	29.5	29.8
Adults 65+	35.7	35.9	35.8
Sex			
Men	25.2	24.8	24.9
Women	28.7	28.4	28.3
Social class			
Individuals AB	19.8	20.5	20.1
Individuals C1	24.0	23.6	23.4
Individuals C2	26.4	25.6	25.6
Individuals DE	30.1	29.1	29.3
All population (Individuals)	25.7	25.2	25.1

Fig. 1.4
Television viewing 1993–95
Source: AGB Television

cable, satellite or digital services. The figures do point to some significant differences in patterns of viewing. We do not all watch the average amount. Our age, our gender and social class are factors which all appear to have important implications for our amounts of viewing. And we don't all choose to watch the same programmes. Summaries of the types of television programmes watched indicate that the average diet of television for those in the 16–24 age range for instance, is made up of about 30 per cent drama, 20 per cent light entertainment, 17 per cent films, 11 per cent documentaries and features, 10 per cent sport, 6 per cent news, and 6 per cent children's programmes.

Longer-term monitoring points to a decrease in average amounts of time spent watching conventional, terrestrial broadcast TV. In 1995, for instance, in spite of longer broadcasting hours, viewers watched an average of just over 25 hours per week, compared to over 27 hours in the mid 1980s. This average long-term decrease has been the source of considerable concern in recent years on the part of the BBC and ITV television companies who have had to recognise that video, cable and satellite services have started to make significant inroads into what was previously their exclusive territory (see chapter 6, p. 259 for further discussion). The availability of Channel 5 and of digital terrestial services in 1998 will further complicate

Fig. 1.5
Source: Paul Hickinbotham

matters. However, for our purposes here, we should note that it is 'normal' to spend between three and four hours per day in the company of a television set which is switched on. To put this another way, we spend on average over one full 24-hour day per week continuously in the presence of TV. Commenting on the patterns of time spent with television in Britain and America in the 1980s, one study has suggested:

> If in such countries a typical viewer's total viewing during the year were laid end to end, it would fill two months, the whole of January and February say, for 24 hours each day! Although that may be hard to accept, it may be harder still to think of our imaginary television viewer having the set totally switched off throughout the other ten months of the year.
>
> *Barwise and Ehrenberg (1988), p. 20*

Clearly, not all media demand and get the same kinds of time and attention as the changing face of television but they fit into the 'media-mix' of modern times. Listening to radio, for example, is estimated on average in the late 1990s to account for about 20 additional hours per week, across an expanding range, if not always diversity, of radio stations and their services (see figure 6.16, p. 252). Behind these averages, radio listening, like television viewing, varies by age and other social factors. For media relationships which take us outside the household, average weekly attendances at cinemas in the UK have increased since the mid 1980s, although this development perhaps needs to be plotted against a historical slump in attendance which commenced in the 1950s, reaching an all-time low of 54 million admissions in 1984. In recent years, the recovery of cinema-going has been quite dramatic, with annual admissions more than doubling within ten years. We now make an average of two visits per year to the cinema, although there are significant variations according to age, and we do not all choose to watch the same films (see chapter 4, p. 141).

In general, we should note that the kind of data in these figures is based on *averages*, large-scale estimates of media con-

---

ACTIVITY 1.3

Look at the statistical patterns and measures of cinema attendance contained in figures 1.6, 1.7 and 1.8. What do they suggest about cinema-going in the UK? Make some initial notes about what you think they indicate and how they can be interpreted. (These will form the basis for later activities in chapter 9.)

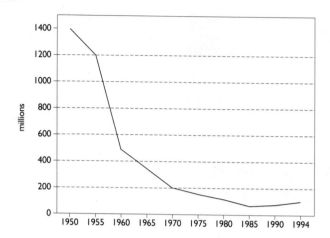

Fig. 1.6
UK cinema admissions 1950–94
Source: Cultural Trends 1994:23 © Policy
Studies Institute

sumption which, as we have seen, on closer scrutiny may vary considerably in the context of different lifestyles and their associated dimensions of age, gender, class, affluence and other significant historical factors. In addition, some of the key assumptions concerning the ability of this kind of data to 'measure' accurately what counts as average 'television viewing' or 'radio listening' have quite rightly been called into question in recent years. The set may be on, for instance, but whether and how people listen and view varies considerably (this is a theme which is developed in more detail in chapters 4 and 9). In spite of these important reservations, however, it remains the case that we continue to spend large and perhaps increasing proportions of our time in a range of media-related activities. In order to gain access to this time and attention, advertisers spend very large amounts of money and this 'fuels' and influences many sectors of media production. In 1994, for example, over £10 billion was spent on advertising in the UK, with an interesting spread of expenditure across the different media and advertising sectors. Commercial television claims over 25 per cent of the total with about 50 per cent going to local newspapers, national papers and magazines. Direct mail takes the lion's share of the remainder, with commercial radio taking about 3 per cent and cinema about 1 per cent of the total (See figure 5.5 for further data and discussion.)

Hardware and commodities

In order to participate in these activities, we need access to certain media technologies or commodities (see figure 1.10). You cannot watch TV if you do not have one available to you, cannot rent and view videos if you do not have a VCR, cannot read certain magazines if you do not buy them, and so on.

	Number of screens	Average number of admissions per screen (thousands)
1955	4 483	264
1960	3 034	165
1965	1 993	167
1970	1 553	128
1971	1 510	121
1972	1 531	106
1973	1 600	89
1974	1 590	90
1975	1 576	80
1976	1 562	68
1977	1 547	70
1978	1 563	81
1979	1 582	71
1980	1 576	65
1981	1 528	58
1982	1 439	45
1983	1 303	49
1984	1 246	43
1985	1 251	56
1986	1 229	59
1987	1 215	62
1988	1 250	62
1989	1 424	62
1990	1 552	57
1991	1 642	57
1992	1 805	54
1993	1 848	61
1994	1 919	64

Note: Data only related to those cinemas which take advertising, covered by the Cinema Advertising Association. It is estimated that by 1992 this included all but between 30 and 40 cinemas in the UK

Fig. 1.7
UK cinemas: number of screens and average admissions, 1955–94
Source: Cinema Advertising Association

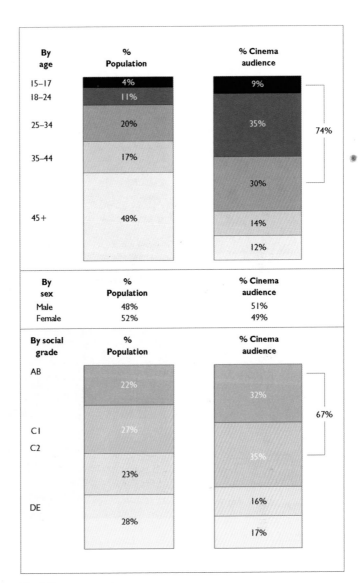

Fig. 1.8
Cinema audience profile, 1995
Source: CAA/NRS Jan–Dec 1995

Fig. 1.9
Source: Paul Hickinbotham

	1988 %	1989 %	1990 %	1991 %	1992 %	1993 %	1994 %	1995 %
Video recorder	58	70	75	72	77	80	83	84
Teletext	25	30	41	40	46	49	55	60
Compact disc	n/a	n/a	n/a	22	29	27	35	37
Home computer	18	26	22	22	30	29	29	27
Video games	10	11	11	12	17	20	23	23
Satellite TV dish	*	2	4	8	10	12	14	15
Video camera	2	3	4	5	9	10	11	14
Nicam digital stereo television set	n/a	n/a	n/a	5	6	7	10	10
Cable TV	1	2	1	3	3	3	7	6
Widescreen television	n/a	n/a	n/a	n/a	n/a	n/a	7	6
Cable phone	n/a	n/a	n/a	n/a	n/a	1	5	6
Video disc player	1	2	2	2	3	2	4	5
Have one or more of these	67	77	81	80	83	86	89	91
Have none of these	33	23	19	20	17	14	11	9

Note: * Less than 0.5%
n/a Not asked

Fig 1.10

Home entertainment equipment in the home (all TV viewers)
Source: Independent Television Commission, 1995

Fig 1.11
Source: Tim O'Sullivan

	Total	Action/ Adventure	Comedy	Drama	Thriller	Children/ Family	Horror	Sci-fi
Male	51	55	49	46	54	44	50	58
Female	49	45	51	54	46	56	50	42
AB	18	16	18	20	19	15	15	13
C1	26	27	26	28	29	21	25	24
C2	28	28	28	27	26	33	28	32
DE	28	29	28	25	26	32	32	31
4–15	19	17	26	10	8	45	11	15
16–24	20	20	19	20	24	10	24	22
25–34	27	27	24	31	33	20	30	29
35–54	27	30	26	30	28	21	28	28
55+	6	6	5	9	7	4	7	6

Fig. 1.12
Demographic breakdown of video renters (percentages)
Source: MVR/British Video Association

ACTIVITY 1.4

Since the early 1980s, the personal stereo (or the Walkman to give it its Sony tradename) has had a significant impact on the ways in which music and other audio material are consumed. Do you have or have you used a Walkman? How have they changed or developed the standard cassette player or CD player? Carry out some informal interviews with people who regularly use (or perhaps don't use) a Walkman to ascertain how they use them and what they think of them. Discuss the results of these interviews. What do they tell us about the historical development and use of the personal stereo? For detailed development of this activity you will find it useful to consult: Du Gay *et al.* (1997) *Doing Cultural Studies: The Story of the Sony Walkman*, Open University/Sage.

Fig 1.13
Source: Paul Hickinbotham

Another way of indexing the 'media saturation' of contemporary culture, then, is to examine available evidence which charts either the diffusion or the developing 'spread' of media hardware or the circulation of particular media products. Of all households in Britain in the 1990s, 96 per cent have at least one colour television and more than half of these are 'multiset' homes, with a number of televisions in different locations, in the main living room, in bedrooms or in the kitchen. Statistically and culturally, it is abnormal to live without a TV. More than 80 per cent of households in Britain now have at least one video cassette recorder and about a quarter of these are used regularly each week to replay at least one rented video

	All adult %	Men %	Women%
Newspapers			
any national morning	57.9	62.4	53.6
any regional morning/evening	29.6	31.4	27.9
any regional evening	25.0	26.6	23.6
any national/regional Sunday	66.6	68.9	64.6
any regional Sunday	2.0	2.4	1.6
any local free	61.1	60.4	61.8
any local paid	31.2	31.2	31.3
Consumer & special interest			
any general weekly	43.1	45.5	40.9
any women's weekly	29.3	13.3	44.3
any general monthly	48.2	56.5	40.4
any women's monthly	35.3	20.9	48.9

Fig. 1.14a

Broad readership patterns in relation to the population, Jan–Dec 1995

Notes: Estimated population 15+ 45 500 000. Unweighted sample: all adults 38 724 000, men 16 840 000, women 21 884 000

Source: National Readership Surveys (NRS Ltd), Jan–Dec 1995

	Percentage of adults reading each newspaper in 1990			Percentage of each age group reading each newspaper in 1990				Readership[1] (millions)	
	Males	Females	All adults	15–24	25–44	45–64	65 and over	1971	1990
Daily newspapers									
Sun	25	20	23	29	24	21	16	8.5	10.2
Daily Mirror	22	17	19	20	18	21	18	13.8	8.7
Daily Mail	10	9	9	7	8	11	11	4.8	4.2
Daily Express	10	8	9	7	7	10	11	9.7	3.9
Daily Star	8	5	6	8	8	5	3		2.8
Daily Telegraph	6	4	5	3	4	7	7	3.6	2.3
Today	5	3	4	5	5	3	1		1.7
Guardian	4	2	3	3	4	3	1	1.1	1.3
The Times	3	2	3	2	3	3	2	1.1	1.2
Independent	3	2	2	3	3	2	1		1.1
Financial Times	2	1	2	1	2	2	–	0.7	0.7
Any daily newspaper[2]	69	59	64	63	62	68	63		
Sunday newspapers									
News of the World	31	28	29	37	32	27	21	15.8	13.2
Sunday Mirror	22	19	21	23	21	21	17	13.5	9.3
People	17	15	16	15	16	18	15	14.4	7.4
Mail on Sunday	13	11	12	14	14	13	7		5.6
Sunday Express	10	9	10	6	7	13	14	10.4	4.4
Sunday Times	9	7	8	8	9	8	4	3.7	3.5
Sunday Telegraph	5	4	4	3	3	6	5	2.1	1.9
Observer	5	4	4	4	5	4	3	2.4	1.8
Independent on Sunday	3	2	3	3	3	2	1		1.2
Any Sunday newspaper[3]	74	69	71	73	70	75	67		

1 Defined as the average issue readership and represents the number of people who claim to have read or looked at one or more copies of a given publication during a period equal to the interval at which the publicatiom appears.

2 Includes the above newspapers plus the *Daily Record*.

3 Includes the above newspapers plus the *Sunday Post*, *Sunday Mail*, *Scotland on Sunday* and *Sunday Sport*.

Fig. 1.14b

Reading of national newspapers: by sex and age, 1971 and 1990
Source: HMSO, 1992

	Percentage of adults reading each newspaper in 1990			Percentage of each age group reading each newspaper in 1990				Readership¹ (millions)		Readers per copy
	Males	Females	All adults	15–24	25–44	45–64	65 and over	1971	1990	1990
General magazines										
Radio Times	18	19	19	20	20	18	17	9.5	8.5	2.9
TV Times	18	19	19	21	19	18	15	9.9	8.4	3.0
Reader's Digest	14	13	13	8	13	17	14	9.2	6.1	3.9
What Car	7	1	4	6	5	3	1		1.8	12.2
National Geographic	5	3	4	4	4	4	2	1.1	1.7	–
Exchange and Mart	5	2	3	5	4	3	1		1.5	8.2
Women's magazines²										
Woman's Own	3	16	10	10	11	9	8	7.2	4.3	4.2
Bella	3	15	10	12	11	8	6		4.3	–
Woman's Weekly	2	11	7	4	5	9	10	4.7	3.1	2.6
Woman	2	11	7	6	8	6	5	8.0	3.0	3.2
Best	2	11	6	9	8	5	3		2.9	3.1
Prima	2	10	6	7	8	5	2		2.6	3.0

1 Defined as the average issue readership and represents the number of people who claim to have read or looked at one or more copies of a given publication during a period equal to the interval at which the publicatiom appears.

2 The age analysis for women's magazines includes male readers.

Fig. 1.14c

Reading of the most popular magazines: by sex and age, 1971 and 1990
Source: HMSO, 1992

film. Figure 1.12 summarises the video rental market. Radios are very widely available in the UK: there are more than one and a half radio sets per head of population for use in the home, at work and in the car. Recent years have seen important changes in the patterns of musical consumption: compact discs, for example, have overtaken LPs, although cassettes continue to account for over a third of all items sold (see figure 5.13, p. 187). Their continued success may partly be explained by the increase in ownership of personal stereos.

What about the circulation of newspapers and magazines? The broad readership patterns are summarised in figures 1.14a–c. In 1996, the most widely read daily national newspaper in Great Britain was the *Sun*, which was read regularly by one quarter of all men and about one fifth of all women (see figure 5.4, p. 167). The net total readership and sales of newspapers has declined in the postwar period, as have magazine circulations, although the period from the late 1980s onwards has seen some important developments at the level of production techniques and shifts in patterns of marketing and readership. However, in the late 1990s over 60 per cent of men and over 50 per cent of women regularly read a national daily paper. Nearly half of all women regularly read a women's weekly magazine and over half of the population of men read a general monthly magazine. The *Reader's Digest* continues to achieve the highest circulation of all UK magazines, closely followed by *Take A Break* and a number of new and old titles competing for the weekly television schedules market.

These kinds of data, concerning either the time we spend with different media or the 'reach', frequency or diffusion of certain forms of media activity, offer important, if not altogether unproblematic, measures of the 'media saturation' of modern cultures. They indicate that some forms of media consumption are indeed very widespread activities and they accord well with a predominant way of thinking about the *mass* media in terms of numbers – statistical profiles or percentages of readership, attendance, sales or ratings. These kinds of numerical expression are important, but they are always open to a range of interpretations and can be misleading (see chapter 9). They are frequently used as historical evidence, to point to the growth, for example, of new media forms from the development of popular print media in the nineteenth century, through to current shifts in broadcasting and other emergent electronic media networks. Here, the data are often rather uncritically held to map or transparently measure the declines or shifts in the 'popularity' of certain cultural forms and practices or the 'inevitability' of new technologies. These issues deserve further discussion and they are developed in a number of subsequent chapters (see especially chapters 6, 7 and 9).

For now, a key general point to note is that our own personal, private patterns of media consumption and use are parts of wider social and cultural relationships and structures. Our individual media relations and choices are parts of a 'bigger picture', which operates outside of our own individual determination or control. The kinds of data introduced in this discussion should most importantly suggest that the mass media are amongst the most central social institutions which *constitute* modern life. In order to develop further the theme of 'media saturation', we need to move on from asking questions about the basic scale and scope of media activities, to consider in more detail what is at stake in the time, money, contact and attention we regularly and routinely give to the media.

Situation and mediation

We all inhabit particular situations. These are defined not only in the geographical sense of specific place, territory and location

Fig. 1.15
Source: Paul Hickinbotham

Fig. 1.16
Source: Jarrod Cripps

Fig 1.17
Source: Jarrod Cripps

Fig. 1.18
Source: Paul Hickinbotham

Fig. 1.19
Source: Tim O'Sullivan

but also in terms of the patterns of culture, the 'dialects' and the social relationships which distinguish them. Our identities are fundamentally linked with this idea of personal place, culture and biography. Much of a sense of identity and belonging is rooted in and derived from the immediate, familiar surroundings of place and from networks of regular, face-to-face contacts with family or friends in school, college, workplace, home and so on. Through these networks of direct interpersonal communication we both participate in and are a part of a *situated culture*. We may hear or relay news of recent events in the neighbourhood, likewise rumours, gossip, stories or jokes. We may attend and participate in local events, entertainments, family ceremonies or other rituals. These cultures of situation are primarily *oral*, that is, communicated by word-of-mouth relationships, and although they have important historical and generational dimensions, they tend to be limited and defined in relation to a particular locale, often within the private sphere of the household. In certain ways they embody elements of pre-industrial cultures, based on relatively small-scale forms of social interaction and groupings and derived from the immediate, face-to-face environment and its daily experience and rituals.

We know these cultures to be distinctive, but they are also bound by a number of limiting factors. Of these, perhaps the most obvious is physical space. We do not know about events and issues occurring beyond the immediate horizons of the known situation or locale – that is, we do not know in the direct, experiential or first-hand sense. Since the mid nineteenth century, however, we have increasingly learned to live not only in our situated culture, but also in a *culture of mediation*, whereby specialised social agencies – the press, film and cinema, radio and television broadcasting – developed to supply and cultivate larger-scale forms of public communication, mediating news and other forms of culture into the situation. 'Our' immediate private worlds co-exist with the mediated 'world out there'. In the late 1990s, for instance, television is named by about 70 per cent of the UK population as their principal source of world news. Sources of local news, however, feature first local newspapers, then television followed by radio. The growth of these media was both a product of and a response to larger-scale social networks or collectivities. They also embodied certain applications of developing technologies and the growth of commercial markets in expanding forms of social and public communication.

This juxtaposition and contrast between social formations *without* mass media and those *with* mass-mediated culture has been explored in a number of significant ways. Writing in the 1960s, Marshall McLuhan, for example, pointed to the ways in which modern media have 'shrunk' the world – by regularly 'transporting' or 'networking' us around the globe – effortlessly, as we don't have to move from the room. He identified the potential for modern media systems and technologies to establish what he called 'the global village', to connect the myriad of situated cultures into one, ideal, face-to-face planet-wide totality (for development of this idea, see discussion of globalisation in chapter 7). Another important way in which this distinction has been employed is in the definition of *mass communication*, which is held to be distinctively different from the direct and face-to-face forms and relations of interpersonal communication.

Identifying the 'mass media'

In general terms, communication is understood, often somewhat mechanistically, as the successful transmission and reception of meaningful 'messages'. These are often expressed in language and speech but may be conveyed by means of other symbolic systems in accordance with shared rules or codes, signs or symbols (see chapter 2). Much communication in everyday life takes place in the situated context of direct face-to-face interaction, between people who are physically present and involved in a dialogue or conversation, more or less continuously reciprocating or providing 'feedback' for the other participants involved. In the case of mass communication, the nature of the communicative relationship appears to be quite different and conventionally four main differences are identified (see Thompson, 1995, and McQuail, 1994, for further discussion).

First of all, there is an *institutional break* or *gap* between the participants in the communicative relationship. In crude terms, the 'senders' of mass-mediated messages do not have the same meaningful, tangible or direct forms of feedback relationship with the 'receivers' – the audiences. This is not to say that people do not regularly shout at their television screens or radios, argue about a film they have just seen or disagree with the editor of their magazine or newspaper. It is, however, to say that such responses are rarely heard or received in such direct and unmediated ways by those 'senders'. It is in the nature of the relationship that they cannot be. Admittedly, there are specialised systems for feedback – viewers' or readers' letters, faxes, e-mails or phone calls, for example – but these differ in a number of ways from those which characterise face-to-face interaction.

Fig. 1.20
Source: Paul Hickinbotham

Partly because of this, mass-mediated culture tends to be 'one-way': it is directed either at unknown 'people out there', in general, or at specified 'target' groups. Not only are there issues here concerning the people who receive mass-mediated information and the position that this relationship places them in, but also this situation raises problems for those who 'send' or produce the programmes, films, newspapers and so on. *Who* are they talking to? Or rather, who do they think they are talking to? To overcome this problem of not knowing who their actual audiences or readers might be, media producers often have to work to imaginary, generalised constructs or stereotypes – the 'general public', the 'person (historically, usually a man) in the street', 'young people', the 'busy housewife' and the 'active career woman', are some conventional examples (the concept stereotype is discussed in more detail in chapter 3). These constructs allow media producers to select and 'shape' their products with the aim of establishing credible and engaging forms of communication and discourse with large numbers of people whom they cannot see or know and whose situation they may not share.

Part of this separation is the result of a related but second distinction. Most commonly, mass media or mass communications are defined in terms of *specialised technologies*, and indeed the technical means of exchange of direct, interpersonal forms of interaction and those characteristic of mass-mediated culture differ considerably. How for instance does the telephone, the radio or the television intervene in communication between people? As noted above, media technologies have traditionally tended to reinforce a one-way system of communication *from* media producers *to* media audiences, giving rise to what one writer has described as an 'asymmetrical and unbalanced' relationship between participants (McQuail, 1975, p.167). There is a long tradition of attempts to change or challenge this 'one-sidedness' and some of the assumptions which have often accompanied it. Some of these initiatives have often been classed together as 'alternative media' (see chapter 5 for further discussion). Many would argue, in the late 1990s, that the development of the Internet and other computer networks have important implications for this traditional model of how the media *have* worked.

There are other, additional issues worth considering here, however. These concern the ways in which mass communications are made available in material, physical forms. Unlike the transient, ephemeral nature of much face-to-face interaction – here, then gone, as with conversations, gestures, and so on – mass communications have tended to be inscribed or stored in physical and reproducible forms or texts: the book, the film, the video, the disc, the tape, the newspaper, the comic, the computer file, and so on. The material forms of communication have had consequences for the nature and forms of the message itself, giving, for example, a permanency or reproducibility which is not conventionally found in everyday, direct, interpersonal interaction. This technical ability to record and reproduce messages and many varied forms of information results in a *historical permanence – a record*. A good example here is to be found in the history of photography and film, where various writers have noted the impact that the technical ability to capture, hold and socially distribute visual records has had on the modern sense of 'history'. In this context, it has been argued that our sense of the 'modern world' is very much bound up with the period that first saw the emergence of film and photographic records (Chanan, 1995), and which subsequently has encompassed the historical 'immediacy' of forms of broadcasting coverage.

A third distinctive feature of mass media or mass communication is derived from this characteristic of technical reproducibility. Media messages differ from interpersonal forms of communication in that their potential *scale and availability* are greatly extended 'outwards', across space, time, population and public culture. This means, for example, that events taking place in specific national, regional or local locations can receive 'worldwide' distribution and, with the intervention of satellite technologies, 'live' or simultaneous forms of global coverage or mediation. Audiences for major sporting spectaculars, such as the Olympic Games or other international 'mega' events – environmental disasters or political or terrorist crises, for example – are frequently calculated in billions.

Having noted, however, that mass communications are potentially available across time, space and population, this does not mean that they are available in an unrestricted fashion – 'open to all'. On the contrary, access to such potential tends to be regulated in a number of important and decisive ways, notably by the operation of commercial markets (Can you afford it?) and legal or statutory forms of control, which may differ significantly from one national or cultural context to another.

The fourth and final factor which is used to distinguish mass communication from interpersonal forms of direct, face-to-face interaction relates to this last point. In general it makes sense to understand media messages as particular forms of modern *commodity*. Despite the tendency to talk in terms of media 'messages', we need to bear in mind that mass communications are distributed as products or services, commodities which are developed and sold according to the dynamics of

ACTIVITY 1.5

As a group, draw up two lists. On the first, list as many forms of *communication* as you can think of. On the second, list only forms of *mass communication* and *mass media*. When you have drawn up the lists, note down the key differences between them and the general features that distinguish them.

On the first list, you may expect to find all sorts of entries: speaking, writing, hieroglyphics, tom-toms, smoke signals, Morse Code, music, art, theatre, gesture, mime, facial expression, body language, semaphore, walkie-talkies, CB radio, teaching, sermons, railways, roads, telephones, telex, satellite, letters, nudging, winking, the Post Office, war, photocopies, snapshots, architecture, clothes, hairstyles, handshakes, etc.

The second list is likely to be much shorter, and no matter what else appears in it, you are likely to find that only a very few candidates get unanimous agreement about their status as mass media. These are: television, radio, cinema, newspapers. In addition, people may mention publishing, popular music, advertising, theatre, music, video, telephones, speech, photography, magazines, the music industry, the Internet, teletext ...

Some important differences might be that those on your second list all:

- reach large numbers of people;
- employ high technology;
- are modern;
- involve large-scale commercial corporations and finance;
- are state-controlled or -regulated;
- are centrally produced but privately consumed;
- are cooperative, not individual forms of communication;
- are popular (widespread and/or well liked).

In fact, once such a set of characteristics has been found, it is quite easy to think of things that fulfil these criteria but are *not* mass media as commonly understood – religion and education being clear examples.

Further, there are things like music, photography, pictures, drama, advertising, speech and printing that appear in more than one of the mass media. Are these *forms* of communication, or *media* in their own right?

Working with lists generated in this way does serve one useful purpose, beyond showing that there's no *single* definition of the media.

That is, despite their plurality and the differences between them, the media are nevertheless *socially recognised*; everyone agrees that they include TV, radio, cinema, newspapers. After discussion, most will agree that music and publishing (magazines and books) should be included, as well as advertising. Usually, people will express their recognition of mass media most easily by reference to a *technological apparatus*, which explains why TV, radio, cinema and the press recur. But people are less used to thinking of the media as *social and commercial institutions* – although they can recognise one when they see it in the shape of the advertising and music industries, or popular magazines and books.

Adapted from: Hartley, Goulden and O'Sullivan (1985), vol.1, p.12

supply and demand of commercial markets (see chapter 5). Profitability continues to be a decisive factor in shaping the available forms of mass communication. Indeed, at a basic level, we can understand modern media as specialised, industrialised agencies involved in and dependent upon the commercial supply and the cultivation of demands for diverse forms of information, communication and entertainment commodities.

While an index of media saturation is gained, as we have suggested, by examining the patterns of time, involvement and attention routinely accorded to varying forms of media, the kinds of data outlined in this introductory section are really only starting points for further analysis. As the presence of successive mass media, from newspapers to film to radio and TV, have become accepted as everyday 'facts of life' and social existence, so, it is argued, we have become socially and culturally more *dependent* upon them. Limited, to an extent, by the particular confines of our respective situations, we have learned to rely on different media, in particular for news and information about the wider public sphere, the world and large-scale social processes. Around the increasingly private, domestic presence of forms of public, mediated culture, a series of central debates and arguments has been developed. These lie at the heart of media studies.

The power of the media?

It has now become somewhat of a cliché to suggest that the media collectively act to provide their audiences with 'windows on the world' or with 'definitions of social reality'. Implicit in this kind of claim is the idea that the media act as powerful agencies capable of shaping and directing public and private understandings of the world and awareness of its social, economic, moral, cultural, technological and political affairs. In this manner, the media have been termed 'consciousness industries', involved in the manufacture or management of the public sphere, of consensus and consent. That is, in providing images, interpretations and explanations of events occurring in the wider world, the modern media do not simply and neutrally provide information about that world but actively encourage us to see and understand it in particular ways and in certain terms. Rather than faithfully 'mirroring' the external world and its 'reality', it is argued that the media have come to play an increasingly central role in constructing and interpreting the nature of that world according to certain values, ideological frameworks and cultural principles. For those engaged in the systematic study of the mass media, this recognition has resulted in a general and sustained focus upon questions of *media representation* – how and in what terms do the media *re-present* aspects of society and social process to their audiences. This theme is explored in more detail in chapter 3.

For now, it is worth noting that questions of media saturation encompass some major issues which are bound up with arguments about the social or political consequences of our relationships with and dependence upon mediated culture (see, for useful discussion, Tolson, 1996). There are key questions here which concern not only the nature of the images and versions of the world which are now, as one writer has noted 'as easily available as water, gas or electricity' (Hood, 1980). We also need, perhaps now more than ever, to ask about the ways in which such images and accounts are produced, and under what kinds of conditions: controlled and formed in response to what kinds of social and political forces. We need to analyse the relations between the controls over the mediation of information and entertainment to people and the dispositions of political power more generally. We also need to study in detail the diverse ways in which different everyday cultures respond to, interact with and resist the presence of media saturation.

Many have argued that the case for this type of investigation has become more urgent, given the post-1950s growth in the management and manufacture of information, the development of new media and the increasing penetration of the media into both private and public spheres. It has been suggested, for example, that we now inhabit an *information* and *consumer* society, where the manufacture and dissemination of information has become an essential facet of modern democratic and commercial processes. The media and cultural industries now encompass multinational corporations, government agencies and departments, political parties, advertisers, public relations firms and many other forms of corporate, private and public organisation.

These are locked into increasingly sophisticated complexes and networks of information gathering, management, manipulation and distribution in the specific sphere of institutionalised politics, for example, elections have virtually ceased to have a social significance for the general public, outside of their construction and mediation as 'media events' (see Negrine, 1994, Seymour-Ure, 1991, Franklin, 1994, McNair, 1995).

Given these and related developments in the levels and dynamics of media saturation in the modern period, it is not surprising that the media have attracted considerable public debate and criticism. We now briefly consider some of the dominant concerns that have accompanied the growth of media saturation.

Mediation and social concern

As the modern media have developed, so have a number of competing claims about their social significance and impact. In historical terms, the various media have often operated both to condense and to relay anxieties and fears about the nature of change in a rapidly changing world. As such they have often been singled out as if they are the sole cause of particular tendencies in society and culture. This is a debate we shall return to in later chapters. For now, however, it is worth noting some of the predominant concerns which have regularly and recurrently structured public and private ideas and shaped thinking about the media. Such claims and concerns have, it is important to note, often formed the basis for advocating particular kinds of increased media regulation or control. Many of the concerns of the current period, dealing, for example, with the 'invasion' of privacy by the popular tabloid press, or the anti-social effects of films, video 'nasties' or computer games, have a lengthy heritage, stretching back in form at least to the nineteenth century. Three general themes and areas of concern have recurred, all focusing upon 'effects' that the media are claimed to have had on society.

The first of these concerns the political or persuasive powers of the mass media, particularly in terms of the supposed abilities of the press, film, radio or television to manipulate whole populations' attitudes. George Orwell's novel *Nineteen Eighty-four*, first published in 1949, represents an interesting example of a 'dystopian' vision of a society where control over the masses is in part exerted through the incessant surveillance and propaganda of the 'telescreens'. In the context of the rise of fascism and dictators in a number of European states, and the widespread use of propaganda techniques to apparently manipulate the minds of whole populations prior to and during the Second World War, the media appeared to have enormous political potential. The theme of mass persuasion was also foregrounded, although in slightly modified form, in consideration of the rise of advertising in the 1930s and in the period following the war. This theme of the 'mind-bending' powers of the media is one which still has considerable common currency.

A second recurrent theme can be traced back to the middle of the nineteenth century. This was rooted in a concern for conserving certain traditions, especially in aesthetic and cultural terms, and articulated a general opposition to the 'new' popular media and what was seen as their damaging impact upon long-established cultural values and practices. The popular press and publishing, followed by cinema and, later, radio and television, have all been accused of degrading or debasing cultural traditions and standards, eroding the authentic and replacing it with the 'trivial' and 'vulgar' substitutes of the modern age. Once again, this theme continues to exercise considerable influence in debates about the position and place of the media in the current period. A good example here is the series of debates which have emerged in the context of the future of public service broadcasting in Britain in the 1990s. In an age of shrinking budgets and competition from satellite, video, cable and digital services, the question of what should be at the core of public service provision in the new broadcast market has emerged as a key issue. A significant part of this debate has involved contending definitions of 'quality' and cultural value in broadcast output (see Corner, 1995 for relevant summary and discussion).

The final theme has perhaps been the most influential. It concerns the arguments about the impact or 'effects' of the mass media on social behaviour – in fact, usually anti-social behaviour – and the moral contours of society. The most debated area in this context has been the issue of violence and delinquency, where the media have regularly been held to 'cause' outbreaks of violent or aggressive activity. These incidents have usually been part of wider and regular cycles of social concern, often referred to as 'moral panics', and they continue to make their presence felt in the 1990s.

Culture and mass communication

So far we have introduced a series of themes concerning the presence and the defining characteristics of mass communication in modern social life. We have also noted that the media have been a particularly powerful focus for a number of debates about the nature of modernity. In order to develop these themes further, it is important to consider briefly some general questions about the nature of the interrelations between culture and mass communication.

Culture, as we have suggested, first and foremost concerns the ways in which we understand and relate to social situations. We are socialised into a particular set of cultural orientations, rituals or ways of making sense of the world, and these encompass two particular dimensions. First of all, culture in the general sense refers to the beliefs, values or other frames of reference through which we learn to make sense of our experiences on a daily and ongoing basis. Secondly, definitions of culture usually encompass the various means by which people communicate or articulate a sense of self and situation. This highlights the view that:

> cultures are not primarily collections of objects, but stocks of shared understandings and responses accumulated in the course of confronting a common set of social conditions. They provide a pool of available meanings and modes of expression which people can draw upon to describe and respond to their own particular experiences. Far from being separated from everyday life, therefore, involvement in culture is an integral part of people's continuing attempt to make sense of their situation and to find ways of coming to terms with it, or else of changing it.
>
> *Murdock (1974), p. 90*

What we understand as the mass media are centrally involved and implicated in the production of modern culture. Most modern, technologically advanced societies now encompass a great diversity or plurality of cultures which correspond to the major and varied social groupings of class, gender, ethnicity, generation, and so on. Since the mid nineteenth century, the growth of the mass media has undoubtedly assisted in processes whereby certain forms of cultural differentiation have taken place – various media have responded to the particular needs or values of particular cultural groups – particularly when they represent commercially viable forms of investment. However, at the same time, the media have also been involved in the consolidation of forms of centralised, non-specific, 'public', national cultures which have purported to transcend particular sectional interests or differing points of view and to allow for forms of democratic exchange. The writer Jurgen Habermas has referred, in this context, to the *public sphere* of modern communication systems, central to the development of public opinion, which he sees as changing for the worse in the current period (see Webster, 1995, for further discussion). In part, one's view of this dilemma is dependent upon whichever perspective or model of mass communication and its dynamics one adopts.

Traditional perspectives on 'mass' communication have tended to emphasise a singular, mechanistic, process model. In these terms, 'messages' are sent to 'the mass'. At its crudest, this assumes a central, unitary 'sender', technically capable of transmitting a message to a large-scale 'mass' population, who react, as to a common stimulus, with virtually identical responses. The shortcomings of this notion are many, and we will suggest throughout this book that you consider viewing 'mass' or modern communication as part of a set of cultural 'circuits', composed of relations between forms of *media production, media texts*

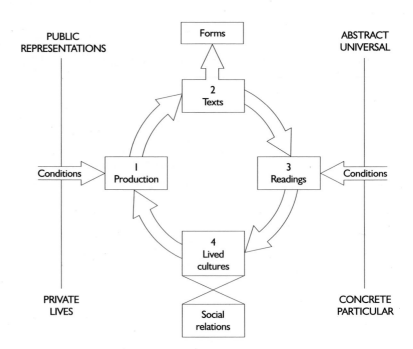

Fig. 1.21
Cultural circulation
Source: R. Johnson, in D. Punter (ed.),
Introduction to Contemporary Cultural Studies,
p. 284, Longman, 1986

and media reception. In particular, it is important to avoid the tendency to cut the media off from their social, commercial and historical contexts. There are significant social and cultural conditions which surround both the composition of the screen, the page, the programme and so on, and their reception by diverse audiences, their readers, listeners and viewers.

The 'map' of cultural circulation in figure 1.21 usefully summarises the major relationships at stake in the study of the media. The diagram suggests a circuit or cycle in the production, circulation and reception of cultural products. For our purposes it can usefully be applied to virtually any form of media. Its strength lies in the manner in which it directs our attention to a 'holistic', encompassing mode of enquiry. You will note that the circuit links moments and conditions of production to the texts and forms so produced, to the readings or forms of reception they may activate, which link in turn to the contexts of lived or situated cultures and wider social relations, which are both directly and indirectly implicated in the circuit.

From popular culture to postmodernism

For some writers, the study of the media can be dismissed as a valid area of enquiry, precisely because it embraces the study of popular culture. Often implicit in this view is the idea that popular culture is something we all know about already and that it is something rather simplistic or of little worth. It is impossible to study the modern media without encountering a series of debates about popular culture. The twentieth-century growth in media industries has been accompanied by a rapid expansion in many multiplying forms of cultural output – films, music,

ACTIVITY 1.6

The framework outlined in figure 1.21 will be examined in more detail in the chapters that follow. As a way of opening up some of the issues initially, you will find it useful to note down one or two examples of contemporary media texts or output that you are familiar with. Work round the circuit noting some of the conditions or questions which may shape or have consequences for your chosen cases. What do you know about the circumstances surrounding production? How is your chosen example produced? How does that production process have consequences for the form of the text? How do audiences and users make sense of the output, under what conditions and with what particular or general results?

magazines, adverts, and so on. These have, in turn, often stimulated related developments, 'cross-overs' or 'spin-offs', in the form of stars, celebrities or merchandising campaigns for instance. There is little doubt that these developments have added to and massively expanded the notion of what is popular at any one point in time. But the idea of popular culture contains several issues which go well beyond the purely numerical frequency or prevalence of any current product or practice, trend or fashion.

It is worth asking what we mean when we use the term 'popular'. As Raymond Williams (1976) suggested, the term combines some contradictory ideas and meanings. In historical perspective, he noted that to call something 'popular' was a negative description until the nineteenth century, a bad thing. Positive connotations – the idea that 'popular' could be good – developed from that time onwards. In the modern media age, if something is popular, or part of popular culture, it is understood first of all, to be *widespread*, to be liked by or at least encountered by many people. A prerequisite for this in the modern period has been the development of mass production and distribution systems, industries and technologies devoted to the mass mediation of culture. So, in addition to the idea of 'liked by many', the notion of popular culture also often carries this implication of *mass-produced* culture. Associated with this theme are ideas that popular culture is 'machine-made' for the 'mass' of people and not the elite, not based for example on certain craft traditions and as a result perhaps regarded as rather trashy, contrived, ephemeral and commercial.

In this context of values and tastes, discussions of popular culture inevitably also bring us into contact with another set of definitions, especially those which have attempted to distinguish between 'high' and 'low' culture. These often pose fundamental questions of cultural value and worth. The accepted definitions of cultural value or excellence have traditionally been associated with dominant or powerful groups and classes in society. Such definitions have often made distinctions between 'high' culture – the educated appreciation of works which are often classical in origin in terms of music, art, theatre, ballet, opera, literature – and 'low' or popular culture. Whilst 'high' culture tends to be equated with the educated discernment, taste and distance of an intellectually refined elite, seeking to universalise its values, 'low' culture is all that is not refined or approved in these terms. It is therefore perceived as 'popular', vulgar, common and easy. Modern media and popular culture in general have often been found wanting from this

ACTIVITY 1.7

Draw up two lists of examples of cultural works or activities that you would label as 'high' culture and 'popular' culture respectively. Try to select a range of examples from different media and cultural forms. What general characteristics divide your examples? Is this division still important or significant today, in the late twentieth century? Summarise some of your general views on popular culture, using your examples.

Fig 1.22
Source: Tim O'Sullivan

standpoint, although to confuse matters somewhat, modern media have also played a significant role in 'popularising' aspects of 'high' or elite culture, for instance Classic FM, Pavarotti, and so on (see Lewis, 1990).

There is a final twist in the debate over popular culture and it brings into play another inflection in the term 'popular'. This emphasises the idea that popular culture is 'of the people', a kind of modern equivalent of folk culture. The importance of this view lies in a stress on popular culture as the modern site, an arena, where all sorts of ideas, images, styles and values can be expressed, articulated and compete for allegiance: where resistance and challenge, especially from less powerful or oppressed groups, can be symbolically advanced, and where dominant or powerful values can be subverted or countered. The extent to which involvement in the consumption of forms of popular culture can be seen as predictably conformist in its outcome and impact, as opposed to unpredictable and resistant, has formed a key area for debate in recent studies of media audiences (see chapter 4). The work of John Fiske (1989a, 1989b) has often been discussed in this context (see also Turner, 1996).

If the study of the media has always involved questions of popular culture, it has more recently also had to deal with claims that modern culture has entered a postmodern phase. For many cultural critics and writers, recent developments in society and culture have led them to suggest that we are currently living in *postmodern times*, experiencing the *postmodern condition*. This idea has been used to describe a number of features of contemporary media culture, including for instance, the style of output of music videos including those shown on MTV, magazine design (*The Face*), films, for instance *Blade Runner*, and the work of David Lynch (notably *Blue Velvet* and *Twin Peaks*), and the films of Quentin Tarantino (*Pulp Fiction* for example). There have been a number of approaches to defining postmodernism drawn from architecture, history, literature and a range of other disciplines and traditions. As Michael Real has suggested:

> When we use postmodernism as a vehicle for exploring media culture, we note certain characteristics of the specific media experience – a sense of irony, bald commercialism, a playful ambiguity, a nostalgic blend of past and present, disparate art styles, a lack of absolutes, and more...
>
> *Real (1996), p. 238*

Fig. 1.23
Source: Paul Hickinbotham

Postmodernism is an unstable and difficult category, but it has been used to refer to a number of developments which relate to themes in this chapter and the rest of the book. These include,

Fig 1.24
Source: Paul Hickinbotham

first, the idea that popular culture and media images saturate and increasingly dominate our sense of identity and reality, that there is no longer a reality outside of popular culture and the media and the fragmenting, increasingly *intertextual* world. This points to the centrality of communication technologies in providing global access to a culture of mass reproduction. Images, copies, simulations or simulacra exist without any longer being tied to an authentic original. As a result, popular culture has eclipsed art and high culture, the simulated and contrived has replaced the real of experience and history. Under conditions of late capitalism, how and what we consume has become more important than what and how we produce.

Secondly, postmodernism implies the domination and prevalence of certain styles, particularly styles of pastiche or collage in art, advertising and architecture for instance. Style is emphasised at the expense of content or substance. These tend to be styles which select, mix together and juxtapose elements borrowed from past styles and influences into new or novel ensembles and cultural products. The word **bricolage** – a kind of 'borrowing' or re-using signs and symbols – has been used to describe this aspect of postmodernism.

Thirdly, time and space, history and place, once secure anchors of identity, have become confused and incoherent entities or spaces. National cultures have become eroded by the forces of global communication networks and their endless, dislocating flows of imagery and information. In postmodern times, one of the key tensions is that which emerges in the tugs between the local situation and the global culture.

Finally, postmodernism is sceptical of any claim to absolute truth: scientific, historical, artistic or political. In the same way that notions of historical time and progress are seen as collapsing and the securities of a sense of place and environment are becoming difficult to sustain, so all-embracing claims to knowledge and large-scale theories are increasingly open to question and doubt.

Summary: public, private and popular

In concluding and reviewing this chapter, we want to suggest that you consider some of the ways in which the historical development of the media has been instrumental in the emergence of what we understand as modern social and cultural life.

Three key aspects of their presence and operation have been noted in the discussion so far.

First, they represent the emergence of large-scale systems of *public* communication, linked to what has been called the *public sphere*. At this level, newspapers and print media from the 1850s, followed by photography in the 1880s, cinema in the 1900s, radio in the 1920s and television in the 1950s, all represent important developments of, and extensions to, public culture. Key themes here concern questions of power, access, representation and mediation.

At the same time, these developments have also had important implications for the *private* sphere and everyday life 'at home'. Radio and television, for example, have accompanied what one writer has called 'the withdrawal into inner space' (Donzelot, 1980), whereby leisure activities have become progressively concentrated in 'the home', the domestic sphere. While important changes might be said to be taking place inside households in the current phase, the private sphere is still 'connected' to the outside world in important and decisive ways via the media and their networks.

Finally, the media and mass communications have interacted with pre-existing cultures, forms and values in a number of significant ways. Of these, perhaps the most central has been in the development of *popular* culture, that 'site of struggle and contest' which, as this discussion has noted, contains a number of contradictory ideas: from 'liked by many' to 'not elite or high culture'; from that of 'the common people' to 'mass-produced' culture, in postmodern times.

These three themes – public, private and popular – will be explored in the chapters that follow. In the next chapter we turn to consideration of the forms and texts which make up media output.

Further reading

Bignall, J. 1997: *Media Semiotics: An Introduction*. Manchester University Press.

Branston, G. and Stafford, R. 1995: *The Media Student's Book*. Routledge.

Burton, G. 1997: *More Than Meets the Eye: An Introduction to Media Studies*. Arnold.

Dutton, B. 1995: *Media Studies: An Introduction*. Longman.

Dutton, B. 1997: *The Media*. Longman.

Eldridge, J., Kitzinger, J. and Williams, K. 1997: *The Mass Media and Power in Modern Britain*. Oxford University Press.

McGuigan, J. 1992: *Cultural Populism*. Routledge.

McQuail, D. 1994: *Mass Communication Theory: An Introduction*. Sage.

McRobbie, A. 1994: *Postmodernism and Popular Culture*. Routledge.

Negrine, R. 1994: *Politics and the Mass Media in Britain*. Routledge.

Nelmes, J.,(ed.), 1996: *An Introduction to Film Studies*. Routledge.

O'Sullivan, T., Hartley, J., Saunders, D., Montgomery, M. and Fiske, J. 1994: *Key Concepts in Communication and Cultural Studies*. Routledge.

O'Sullivan, T. and Jewkes, Y., (eds), 1997: *The Media Studies Reader*. Arnold.

Real, M.R. 1996: *Exploring Media Culture: A Guide*. Sage.

Stevenson, N. 1995: *Understanding Media Cultures: Social Theory and Mass Communication*. Sage.

Thompson, J.B. 1995: *The Media and Modernity*. Polity Press.

Tolson, A. 1996: *Mediations: Text and Discourse in Media Studies*. Arnold.

Trowler, P. 1996: *Investigating the Media*. HarperCollins.

Turner, G. 1996: *British Cultural Studies: An Introduction*. Routledge.

Van Zoonen, L. 1994: *Feminist Media Studies*. Sage.

Watson, J. and Hill A. 1996: *A Dictionary of Communication and Media Studies*. Arnold.

Webster, F. 1995: *Theories of the Information Society*. Routledge.

Useful additional reference sources

British Rate & Data (BRAD). A range of reference publications (including electronic data bases) which are produced annually and bi-monthly and concern all forms of media. Used especially by media planners and advertisers.

Broadcast. The leading weekly news journal on the TV and radio industries in Britain.

Campaign. The leading weekly news magazine for the advertising industry.

Cultural Trends. Annual publication from the Policy Studies Institute which regularly surveys trends in video, cinema, broadcasting and other relevant areas.

The Guardian Media Guide. Edited by Steve Peak and Paul Fisher, published by Fourth Estate for the *Guardian*, this is an annual reference book covering many useful details and addresses concerning the media in Britain.

Social Trends. Annual publication of the Government Statistical Service which details shifts and patterns in demographics. It has useful sections on home, leisure and social and cultural activities.

Press Gazette. The leading weekly paper for all journalists in newspapers, magazines, television and radio.

Sight & Sound. The monthly magazine published by the British Film Institute, devoted to reviews of films and critical discussions of film and television culture.

2

Media forms and analysis

In the first chapter we highlighted the idea that we live in a *media saturated* society where, as part of our everyday lives, we come into contact with a wide variety of media texts and forms of media output. These may include the radio that wakes us up in the morning and the same radio that switches itself off at night after sending us off to sleep. In between we may have read a daily newspaper, watched television either at breakfast or during the evening 'peak' schedule. We could have glanced through a magazine or watched a film, either in the cinema or by renting a video. We might also have listened to some music either being played on the radio by a DJ, on our own hi-fi sytem or individually through a personal stereo. Throughout much of this daily consumption we will have encountered advertising – on the radio, on television, in the magazines or newspapers or on advertising billboards.

As sophisticated western audiences we probably feel comfortable with all these different texts, largely taking them for granted and generally assuming that their meanings are more or less obvious and 'natural'. However the 'meaning' of all these media texts, like language itself, is a social construct that we 'learn' to read and make sense of according to social and cultural codes and conventions.

This chapter will start to explore the relationship between the forms that different media texts take and how we, as audiences, 'construct' the meanings of media texts. In particular there will be an explanantion of the encoding and decoding process of media texts, semiotics, narrative codes and the concept of genre.

We learn to 'read' simple sign systems like traffic signs that tell us when to stop or give way or when we are approaching a

Fig. 2.1
Source: Tim O'Sullivan

roundabout. We learn to 'read' the sequence of red, green and amber lights that tell us when it is safe to proceed across a junction.

We understand the meaning of media texts because we have learnt to 'read' them in the same way that we have learnt to read traffic signs or the words and sequences of letters which make up sentences. For instance :

THE CAT SAT ON THE MAT is a sequence of words that we can make sense of. It is a well-known example of a sentence taken from an early reading book.

THE MAT SAT ON THE CAT however, does not make immediate sense but could have some kind of surreal or *aberrant* meaning.

THE THE ON SAT CAT MAT does not appear to make any conventional sense at all because we are not able to interpret or 'read' any meaning contained in that particular, 'jumbled' sequence of words.

Just as words have to be put into an order that we can recognise and interpret, so media texts work by being put together, or constructed, in particular ways that allow for recognition and interpretation. This process of putting together media texts, assembling them into more or less coherent and meaningful messages, has been referred to as *encoding*.

Semiotics

We live in a world of signs, and communication is only possible by means of signs and sign systems, whether they are letters on a page, sounds or visual images. We can understand visual images because we learn to read them – to *decode* them – in the same way as we do the codes of language: by learning the rules and conventions which govern how the components go together to make up recognisable units of meaning. For instance, we recognise the theme tune to *Newsnight* as somehow being different to other theme tunes, say *Blind Date*, and that it signifies something 'serious'; the images of the title sequence that accompany the theme tune reinforce this notion of 'serious' topicality, referring to the up-to-the-minute world of public events and affairs.

To understand better how these codes work we therefore have to examine sign systems and their conventions or rules. The study of signs and sign systems and their role in the construction and organisation of meaning is called *semiotics*, and it has become influential as one of the main methods for analysing media texts and output.

Semiotics has become an important part of media and cultural studies, due partly to the French writer Roland Barthes, who based his studies of culture on linguistic models developed by earlier writers such as C.S. Pierce and Ferdinand de Saussure. Barthes, however, applied these models to the more general study of cultural and visual signs and their meanings. For example, he suggested that we are likely to 'read' photographs like the two that follow (figures 2.3 and 2.4) by interpreting the various elements within them, rather than by simply reading a fixed and unitary message. A photograph, Barthes claimed, involves a mechanical process where the image – that which is *denoted* – is transferred on to photographic paper, but there is also an expressive, human and cultural process that involves the selection and interpretation of such elements as camera angles, framing, lighting techniques and focus. These extra *connotations* may provide different meanings depending upon the culture, especially the *situated culture* (see chapter 1, p. 14) of both the photographer (the encoder) and the viewer (the decoder) of the photograph. How we read figure 2.3 may be influenced by our knowledge and our particular view of the image of the group that is portrayed in the photograph. One person may see this as a remembrance of the glorious days of the British Raj; others may view it as an elitist and exploitative image from the British imperial past.

According to this view, media texts always have a number of potential meanings or readings; that is, they are *polysemic* – potentially open to many interpretations. An *open* text, for instance, can have many different meanings depending upon the time, place, and the class, gender, occupation and experience of the 'reader'. *Closed* texts, by contrast, strongly encourage or prefer a particular meaning, allowing little space for the reader to produce different ranges of meaning.

Each media text is 'read' and interpreted individually, either alone, for instance in the case of reading a newspaper or magazine, or with members of families or household groups watching a television programme or cinema film. But however private and individualised our media consumption may seem to be, we will draw upon shared codes and conventions to make sense of media output. Often, we make sense of media images and texts by means of what is known as the 'preferred reading'. In order to understand this idea, which is examined also in later chapters, we need to consider the relationships between the encoding and decoding of media texts.

Encoding and decoding

Our individual interpretations of the meaning of media texts are dependent upon a variety of factors all closely linked to the individual viewer; these may include age, gender, social class or ethnic background. Audiences learn to make sense and organise the possible multiple meanings by using a 'grammar' or system of codes and signs that is similar to those which govern written or spoken languages but which also includes other visual and audio dimensions.

To analyse the meanings of media texts we not only have to consider how and under what particular conditions audiences 'read' the particular signs and codes but also to consider both the form and the contexts in which particular texts are produced. These forms are the result of organised production systems which involve processes of *encoding*, the production of the programme, film, page, etc., by the sender or producer and then processes of *decoding*, whereby they are received and read by the audience. For instance, in the nineteenth century naval communication was made possible by semaphore, using combinations of flags that 'meant' different letters of the alphabet (see figure 2.2). One sailor would *encode* a message into a series of flag sequences, with each combination representing a particular letter or phrase. This would then be used to 'signal' to another sailor, on land or on another ship, who would 'read' or *decode* this combination of flags by spelling out the letters that made up the message. Only sailors who were trained could understand the 'code' of the flags and this particular form of communication developed as a result of the specific requirements and conditions of the navy at that time.

With the advent of the Morse Code and developments in telecommunications, things have changed a great deal since the nineteenth century, but the model of encoding and decoding remains useful in analysing forms of media and communication. Whether it is naval semaphore, a television show or a tabloid newspaper, the routines, conditions and practices of production, the *encoding*, will have implications for the *decoding* processes which may vary considerably in terms of predictability. We therefore need to highlight the key stages of communicating meaning, the way meanings are encoded or packaged by

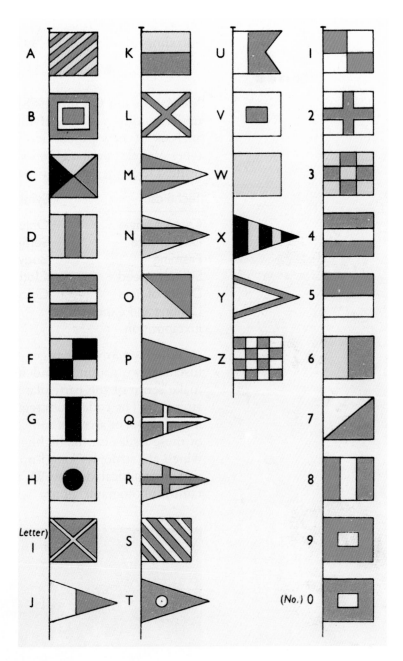

Fig. 2.2
Alphabetical and numeral flags used in naval signalling

'senders' and decoded or unpacked by audiences or 'receivers'.
The possible steps and relations in this encoding and decoding
process become apparent when the meanings of any

media text are analysed. (There is further discussion of the encoding–decoding model in chapter 4.)

Codes

McMahon and Quinn (1988) provide a useful framework for understanding and classifying codes with reference to their analysis of newspapers and magazines. They identify three types of code: *technical, symbolic and written*. For most written or printed texts these categories include the following elements:

Technical:	Symbolic:	Written:
Camera angle	Objects	Headlines
Lens choice	Setting	Captions
Framing	Body language	Speech bubbles
Shutter speed	Clothing	Style
Depth of field	Colour	
Lighting and exposure		
Juxtaposition		

When we *decode* the pages of our magazine or newspaper for instance, we routinely and invisibly draw on these codes to make sense of the particular article or image that catches our attention. The codes both regulate and allow us to make meaningful sense, or arrive at some interpretation of the pages. Some of these issues can be highlighted by considering photographs which are strongly bound up with our own sense of personal and biographical identity. We are all familiar with the idea of the family photograph album whose contents can cover several

Fig. 2.3
Source: Houghton

Fig. 2.4
Source: Houghton

generations of a family but will tend to highlight the positive, the great occasions: marriages, holidays, births, anniversaries. Like soap operas, family photograph albums often appear to represent life with, as it has been described, 'the boring [or unhappy?] bits left out'. Sontag (1977) focuses on the family photograph album as a good illustration of the selective stories families tell about themselves and how their history is a particular form of social construct.

In 'reading' photographs, like the ones contained in family albums, we make use of and draw upon a series of codes embodied in the photographs and the times that they were taken. These codes include the technical codes involved in taking the photographs in the first place – black and white or colour for instance, as well as the codes of dress, colour and posture involved and how these combine to symbolise the occasion depicted.

We quickly learn to 'read' these texts and come to some understanding of their meaning; for instance because the photograph in figure 2.3 is black and white we may understand that it is 'old'. The clothes that the people in the photograph are wearing reinforce this interpretation. Looking more closely we identify some 'clues' about both the uniform and postures of the black servants as well as some of the furniture and general setting. We see that some of the people are sitting and others standing. So we start to piece together an idea about the relationship between the people in the photograph and perhaps develop some notion of the occasion. However, it is likely that only those in the family, or their descendants, will know the exact details of who the people are and where and when the photograph was taken.

Because the photograph in figure 2.4 is in colour and the clothes the people are wearing are clearly signifying a particular, and familiar, social convention, we can 'read' its meaning more easily – a more modern family's wedding with bride, groom, bridesmaid, pageboy and other members of the family. Although the photograph in figure 2.3 probably took longer to take and was more of a technical novelty, the poses of the people look more natural or casual with some of the people appearing to be ignoring the camera and looking elsewhere. This makes it less clear as to whether the camera is recording an everyday event or a special occasion. In figure 2.4 everyone is standing in a formal line looking into the camera and because we recognise the occasion we understand that this is one of the 'formal' wedding photographs that will form part of the 'official' record, or *narrative* (see p. 51) of the event.

As visual and linguistic codes are socially and culturally defined, they can change over time, reflecting change in, for example, social attitudes or opinions, the 'currency' or value of certain images, and the changing position of intended audiences.

Figure 2.5 shows two covers of the same book, *Young Renny* by Mazo de la Roche, one taken from an edition published in 1948 and the other in 1959. How do we 'know' which cover was published earlier and which later? Why have the covers changed over time?

The earlier image is, by today's standards, rather simple with one clear, unambiguous meaning. Technically it is a simple graphic, limited in colours, that reflects the symbolic significance and associations of horse-riding that were prevalent when the book was published.

The later image is more garish and complex and offers a greater variety of possible readings although the general sense of the image is to do with sexual attraction. The ambiguity lies in the posture of the two people, the state of the clothing of the woman and in particular the man who may appear to be rejecting the woman. The caption on the back cover reinforces this ambiguity: 'I thought I was dead to men till you came along'. It sets up a series of questions about what happened in the past of

ACTIVITY 2.1

Look through a family photograph album. How do you make sense of the photographs that it contains? Make a list of all the code systems which you can identify and which you make use of in decoding the images.

How is the family portrayed? What stories do the photographs tell? How do they relate to our own personal experiences of the family and to general ideals about family life?

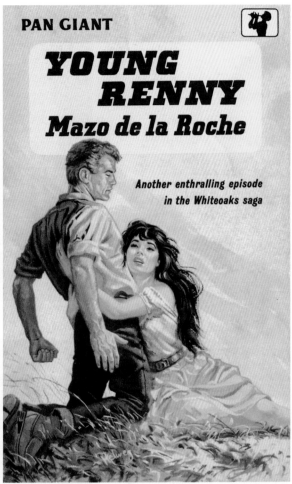

Fig. 2.5
Source: Pan Books

Consider what a cover for *Young Renny* might look like today and try to design your own version.

Consider how the publishers would try to sell the book today and what visual codes and images they might use to promote the book.

the story and what will happen in its future. The publisher hoped that these questions would encourage people to purchase the book in order to find out the answers.

Figures 2.6 and 2.7 show the same event and were taken at the same place at the same time; however, the different angles and *cropping* – cutting the frame of the picture in different ways – offer different meanings. Figure 2.6 is perhaps more closed in its connotative meanings, illustrating in a graphic and emotional manner the view that Sinn Fein representatives were being 'barred' or 'imprisoned' for their views. The *Daily Telegraph* newspaper was criticised by some Members of Parliament for printing this photograph because it was suggested it aided Sinn Fein in its cause and propaganda. Figure 2.7 is more open to a

Fig. 2.6
*'Locked out: Gerry Adams and Martin
McGuinness of Sinn Fein keep watch from
outside the gates as the delegations arrive at
the Northern Ireland talks yesterday.'*
Source: Pacemaker Press International
Ltd/*Daily Telegraph*, 11 June 1996 (original
caption)

Fig. 2.7
*'Outside: Sinn Fein leaders Gerry Adams and
Martin McGuinness on the wrong side of the
wire fence surrounding castle buildings after
they were refused entry to yesterday's talks.'*
Source: *Independent*, 11 June 1996 (original
caption)/Brian Harris

variety of interpretations. Figure 2.6 shows how the cropping of a photograph can 'direct' the viewer towards a particular or *preferred* reading. Cropping is the process by which the 'superfluous' content of a photograph is removed, thereby highlighting only that which the producer considers essential to establish a particular meaning or focus in a defined context.

Anchorage

Often a text is so constructed that the audience is encouraged into understanding one particular meaning, into taking up one particular stance with regard to the issue or event represented. This is often done through a process referred to as *anchorage*, where words are used to direct or 'anchor' the meaning of an image for the reader, encouraging them to a particular reading: for example, as part of an advertisement or by placing a particular caption underneath or next to an image. This resultant, often value-laden meaning has been called the *preferred reading* and is discussed further in chapter 4.

Figure 2.8 demonstrates how the *anchorage* of an image can change its reading. Figure 2.8a shows coverage of the 1990 Poll Tax riots in the *Independent Magazine*. The photograph on its own could be rather ambiguous, but the headline and caption seem to anchor the connotative meaning of the photograph in a clear and explicit manner, one that might be considered to meet the expectations of many of the readers of the *Independent Magazine*. Yet the letter from the woman in the photograph which was published in a subsequent edition of the magazine (figure 2.8b) reveals the 'true' meaning of the picture and caption to be substantially different from its original loading.

The front page of the newspaper used in figure 2.9 is a good example of a text that is made up of several different segments, all contributing to the overall impact and meaning. These

THE MOB'S BRIEF RULE

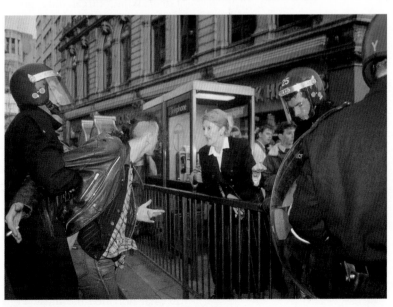

Fig. 2.8(a)
The Poll Tax riot, central London, 6 April 1990
Source: Independent Magazine, 7 April 1990

A West End shopper argues with a protester who is being taken away by the police. Photograph: Richard Smith, KATZ.

EYE-WITNESS

Sir: In last week's article about the poll-tax riot in Trafalgar Square ("The Mob's Brief Rule", 7 April) there is a large photograph labelled "A West End shopper argues with a protestor". The woman in the photograph is me, and I thought you might like to know the true story behind the picture.

I was on my way to the theatre, with my husband. As we walked down Regent Street at about 6.30 pm, the windows were intact and there was a large, cheerful, noisy group of poll-tax protestors walking up from Piccadilly Circus. We saw ordinary uniformed police walking alongside, on the pavement, keeping a low profile. The atmosphere was changed dramatically in moments when a fast-walking, threatening group of riot squad police appeared.

We walked on to the top of Haymarket, where the atmosphere was more tense and more protestors were streaming up Haymarket from the Trafalgar Square end. Suddenly, a group of mounted police charged at full gallop into the rear of the group of protestors, scattering them, passers-by and us and creating panic. People screamed and some fell. Next to me and my husband another group of riot squad police appeared, in a most intimidating manner.

The next thing that happened is what horrified me most. Four of the riot squad police grabbed a young girl of 18 or 19 for no reason and forced her in a brutal manner on to the crowd control railings, with her throat across the top of the railings. Her young male companion was frantically trying to reach her and was being held back by one riot squad policeman. In your photograph I was urging the boy to calm down or he might be arrested; he was telling me that the person being held down across the railings was his girlfriend.

My husband remonstrated with the riot squad policeman holding the boy, and I shouted at the four riot squad men to let the girl go as they were obviously hurting her. To my surprise, they did let her go – it was almost as if they did not know what they were doing.

The riot squad police involved in this incident were *not* wearing any form of identification. Their epaulettes were unbuttoned and flapping loose; I lifted them on two men and neither had any numbers on. There was a sergeant with them, who was numbered, and my husband asked why his men wore no identifying numbers. The sergeant replied that it did not matter as he knew who the men were.

We are a middle-aged, suburban couple who now feel more intimidated by the Metropolitan Police than by a mob. If we feel so angry, how on earth did the young hot-heads at the rally feel?

Mrs R.A. Sare,
Northwood, Middlesex

Fig. 2.8(b)

Source: Independent Magazine, 14 April 1990

DAILY Mirror

Saturday, July 21, 1990   COLOUR NEWSPAPER OF THE YEAR   Average daily sale w/e July 14: 3,931,862 (INCORPORATING THE DAILY RECORD)   22p   CHANNEL ISLANDS 23p

Stephanie is really clued up
—SEE PAGE 11

CAGED!

I'd sooner die than spend 20 years in jail, says drugs girl

● FULL STORY – Page 3

LIKE an animal in a zoo, British drugs girl Karyn Smith clings to the bars that hold her inside the grim walls of a Bangkok jail.

The frightened 18-year-old from Solihull told the Daily Mirror yesterday how she and pal Patricia Cahill, 17, were duped by "a man in a pink Porsche"

into carrying 67lb of heroin through a Thai airport.

And she said shakily: "Patricia says she's going to kill herself – so am I if I have to stay in this place for another 20 years."

PICTURE: ROGER ALLEN

IRA'S BIG BANG ROCKS STOCK EXCHANGE   Pages 4 and 5

Fig. 2.9
Source: The Mirror Group, 21 July 1990

include the overall scale and dominance of the picture and its connotations, combined with a dramatic headline and exclamation mark. The printing of the headline has been reversed so that it is white print on a black background. It is only when reading the other stories on the front page do we understand that this was not in fact the main or lead 'news' story of the day – that was an IRA bomb in London which is what all the other newspapers would have led with. In fact, could this particular story have been run in this form at any time? In what way was it a 'news story'?

Now, taking your own selection of newspaper front pages, use the three categories of codes identified by McMahon and Quinn (p. 36) to analyse how and why the text has been put together as it has. Start by looking at the *technical codes*:

- How is the page laid out – to what effect?
- What typefaces and fonts have been used? Why?
- What can be said about the size and quality of the photographs?
- Have they been cropped? If so, how and why? How do we know that cropping has taken place?
- How do the photographs relate to the rest of the stories and the front page?
- Why have these particular pictures been selected?

Next focus on the *written codes*:

- How does the size of the headline(s) compare with the rest of the page?
- What are the key words and what do they signify?
- What conventions are being used?
- To what extent does the copy meet the expectations set up by the headline(s)?
- Is any information omitted from the copy?
- How does the headline influence the way the reader will approach the story?
- Does/do the caption(s) help anchor the meaning(s)?

Then think about the *symbolic codes*:

- What do the masthead and title of the newspaper signify? How do they achieve this?
- Why are particular graphics used and what do they signify?
- What colours are used and what do they signify?
- Are there any symbolic codes used in the pictures?

Finally consider the front page as a whole:

- How does the overall layout help attract readers?
- Is any particular impression or message given out by the overall 'look' of the front page?
- How is this 'look' created?

Intertextuality

Although various conventions are discussed separately in this chapter, it is important to understand that they are integrated and mixed together in the dynamics of everyday media 'flow'.

Fig. 2.10
Source: Virgin Direct

This mixing, often referred to as *intertextuality*, can create extra layers of associations and meaning, so that a text is often partly understood by what preceded it or what will follow it or even perhaps by references within it to other media texts. A memorable example formed the basis for a television advert for Carling Black Label lager which was set in a laundromat and which referred to a previous Levi jeans advert that itself included a 1960s soul record and 1950s, James Dean imagery. In chapter 5, the *Batman* films and associated images are given as an instance of intertextuality.

In the summer of 1996 the Conservative Party ran a series of posters depicting the Labour Party leader, Tony Blair, with 'demon-like' eyes. These posters attracted considerable controversy which sparked more publicity in the media as well as criticism from the Advertising Standards Authority. Soon after, a series of different texts were produced that referred back to the original Conservative Party posters. These included the front covers of both *Punch* and *Private Eye* magazines as well as the advert for Virgin Direct in figure 2.10. The advert only really works if you are able to refer back to the original Conservative Party poster and the controversy surrounding it.

This process of 'borrowing' signs and features from different texts, sources and styles, usually (as in this case) in a humorous and self-conscious manner, and re-using them in different contexts, is often called *bricolage* and has been defined as a particular characteristic of *postmodern* culture (see chapter 1).

Look, for instance at the Vodafone advert in figure 2.11, which refers the discerning reader back to a set of earlier, historic images and 'adds' these to 'today's' message. In the 'October 1992' advert, the sombre red and brown colours, the woman in the grey coat, the way she is standing and holding the telephone, the manifesto with its 'declaration of rights' and the form of a 'people's charter' are all signs associated with the codes of revolutionary posters of early communist Russia. These associations are trying to create a sense of revolution, of a 'new dawn breaking'. They can only work effectively if the reader can recognise, and decode, these references. The advertisers therefore have to place the adverts where they think readers will recognise and easily understand these 'quotations', in this case the *Independent* or the *Sunday Times*. A bonus for the advertiser may be that if the reader does recognise the references to the earlier texts, he or she may then feel 'informed' or 'special' in some way because of having 'understood' the story, the private joke, and that particular goodwill may then be associated with the product itself.

Fig. 2.11
Source: Vodafone Group Services

In figure 2.12 the *denotative* content – what the image actually shows – is a man standing in front of a glass case bare-footed and with his right hand on his hip. Suspended in the glass case is a hammer that appears to be floating in air. In the top left-hand corner of the page is the trademark sign for Stella Artois Dry and at the bottom of the page is a quote with some words highlighted in bold. Next to this is a name on a green background.

The *connotative* meaning of this image is more difficult, more 'abstract' or subjective, more dependent upon the viewer, their point of view and their ability to 'read' and interpret the

"**THIS IS A RARE** and marvellous example of an art form I'd thought long lost. It has an inner **strength** and a **lightness** of touch that could only be improved by the addition of some cheese & onion crisps."

BRIAN SEWELL

Fig. 2.12
Source: Lowe Howard Spink

various clues that have been encoded in the image. As viewers, we have to make judgements about what the image 'means' and this will depend upon whether we solve the 'puzzle' and recognise Brian Sewell as a 'personality', a famous, idiosyncratic person, an art critic for the *London Evening Standard* who has fairly strong views on modern art, who has a particular voice and who regularly appears on arts programmes on radio and television. The individual viewer's interpretation will also depend on understanding the 'art object' that Brian Sewell is looking at and its similarity to the works of art created by Damien Hurst, the modern British conceptual, and controversial, artist and sculptor. It is only when we start to read the caption at the bottom of the image that we are given clearer clues as to the image's meaning. The language of the quote reads as if it were an art review, but it is only when we come to the words '...some cheese and onion crisps' that we realise that this advertisement is intended to be an irreverent parody and is not taking either Brian Sewell or Damien Hurst-type works of art seriously.

The analysis and interpretation of this image so far, with very few components considered, has taken some time and has already had to work on, and between, a number of codes and levels. As readers, we are given some information but are required to add 'extra' information ourselves for the advertisement to truly work and reveal its full meaning. It can still be understood as an advertisement for Stella Artois Dry even if the viewer has no idea who Brian Sewell is or what is the intended meaning of the advert. However the 'cleverness' of the image lies in its ability to work on multiple levels with multiple meanings, and it is interesting to ask at which level it is most successful as an advertisement for Stella Artois Dry. Do we need to know all the finer details to be persuaded to buy and drink Stella Artois Dry? How do adverts like this one work for the product?

Much of this analysis and interpretation will depend upon the '*situated culture*' of the viewer and it is worth spending a little time considering where the advertising agency would consider placing this advert to reach its potential audience. (In this particular case it came from a 1995 edition of the magazine *Tank Girl* as well as appearing in a range of magazines and Sunday supplements.)

The three categories of codes identified by McMahon and Quinn can be used to analyse particular adverts such as the advertisement for 'exclamation' perfume (figure 2.13).

Start by looking at the *technical* codes:

Fig. 2.13
Source: © Coty

- The advert is a good-quality reproduction with the image in varying shades of blue and white. The clarity of the image allows us to see the detail of the woman's clothing and the 'transparency' of the bubbles.
- The image does not attempt to recreate any sense of 'reality', there are no clues to the context or the situation where the woman is featured. In fact the situation appears to have been deliberately placed in some kind of fantasy, occurring like a dream or in a 'vacuum'.
- It is not immediately clear if the woman is a 'real' person, a model, who has been photographed, or whether (as is perhaps more likely) the whole image is computer-generated to create the bubbles and the giant bottle that the woman is leaning on. Even if the woman is 'real' there has been a process of manipulation, probably by computer, to create the image.
- Other technical details include the shiny floor which 'reflects' back part of the woman and the bottle. The producers of the advert decided that this needed to be included in the overall image; why is it there? What is its purpose? What connotations do the producers think that the shiny sur-

face of the floor and its reflection 'add' to the image? Is it to try and create a sense of realism?

Next consider the *written* codes:

- In this advert there is very little text apart from the 'wavy' (floating like bubbles?) slogan 'make it happen' with its exclamation mark (connecting it with the name of the product?), the name of the product itself and the name of the company. Presumably the producers are confident that there is enough information in the advert for the audience to be able to remember and identify the product in the shop.
- There appears to be no real attempt to inform us about the product except to say that it is called 'exclamation' (without a capital letter at the beginning) and is an 'eau'; 'eau' being written in a larger and different typeface to 'exclamation'. Why is the name 'exclamation' all lower case?
- Is the advert trying to create a sense of 'fun' and 'whackyness', with a youthful 'let it happen' or 'make it happen' feeling? Does it succeed?

Then focus on the *symbolic* codes:

- The way in which the (young, white, blonde) woman is dressed appears to be smart, fashionable and ready for leisure and pleasure. The dress is tight-fitting to show off her figure and to make her appear attractive. She is wearing boots and an ankle-chain, but it is not clear what they are supposed to signify. She is well groomed and appears to be very 'casual', 'free' or 'cool' and gives the impression of being able to do what she wants when she wants.
- The product appears larger-than-life as a support for the woman and as part of the carefree (and unreal) atmosphere that is created. What possible reasons did the producers of the advert have for making the woman lean against the bottle of 'eau'?
- Another major component of the image is the bubbles, although there is nothing for the woman to dip her bubble-blower into; again the producers seem not to be concerned about trying to create any sense of realism. What do the bubbles signify?

Finally, when putting all these constituent parts together, consider the overall meaning created by the advertisement:

- There is a sense of the woman being free, fun-loving and with a couldn't-care-less attitude.

- Are we supposed to identify with the woman? Is there a sense of the advertisement trying to attract women who would like to be like this woman?
- What is being promised by this advert? If you buy this product will you become like this woman?
- Are there any particular values that are being highlighted in this advert? Freedom? Fun? 'Making it happen'? Are these values?
- Much of the power of the advert seems to lie in the apparent coolness and attractiveness of the woman and unrealness of the situation.
- Is this an effective way to try and sell 'eau de toilette'?
- Where would you expect to see this advertisement placed?

It is worth spending some time comparing and contrasting this advert with other adverts for similar products. These adverts are usually aimed at similar audiences and attempt to create a similar sense of freedom and fun. They also often use a similar 'ideal' woman to illustrate their products and perhaps to try to capture the attention of their readers, who may wish to look (and live?) like the women portrayed.

ACTIVITY 2.4

Using the categories of codes listed above, go back to figures 2.12 and 2.13 and analyse the images and their meanings by taking apart all the various components of the adverts. Consider also what is not included in the images: what else might you have expected to have been included? Why is it missing?

Look at other advertisements for beer, lager or other drinks such as tea, coffee or whisky. Try to indentify how the advertisers have 'shaped' the adverts for particular brands to appeal to particular target groups. How have they tried to distinguish themselves from the rest of the competition in their particular sector? Are there any common features amongst the beer and lager adverts?

Narrative codes

All media texts tell us some kind of story and narrative is the way of organising this process of telling stories – how these stories are shaped, structured and then potentially decoded and understood.

Analysing narrative structure follows from the idea that most narratives have a common structure, starting with the establishing of a plot, theme or problem: for instance, the murder by an unknown person at the beginning of a detective series. This is then followed by the development or elaboration of the problem, an enigma, an increase in tension, perhaps with the main suspect being murdered or new characters or 'twists' being introduced. Finally comes the resolution of the plot, theme or situation, in which the problems are conventionally solved. This resolution may happen when the detective 'reveals all' and the murderer is exposed, or when the hero triumphs and marries the heroine. Other well-known forms of resolution include the gunfight in a traditional western or the 'big bang' endings of action adventure films like the James Bond, *Die Hard* or *Rambo* series.

These narratives can be unambiguous and linear, as in traditional storytelling (from 'Once upon a time' to 'and they all lived happily ever after') or factual, as in the news ('The trial continues' or 'These are today's main stories'). Sometimes the narrative structure is altered, chopped up or manipulated and, as a result, the narrative can begin at the end and be presented as a series of flashbacks (as in *Pulp Fiction, D.O.A., Bad Timing* or *Citizen Kane*). Occasionally the narrative is structured as a combination of both 'real time' and flashback, as in a live sports broadcast, where key moments in the development of the narrative of the event are highlighted as action replays or edited highlights.

In advertising there is often a simple before-and-after narrative that says: 'Before it/I was like this, but after using product X, it is/I am like this.' Increasingly the narrative structures of some adverts have been made obscure and the key elements of character, time and narrator deliberately ambiguous or surreal, or have been parodied. One of the most successful of these parodies are the television adverts for Boddington's beer, that 'work' by using the woman's voice, language and characteristics of the perfume and aftershave adverts on television in the late 1980s and early 1990s, but apply them to beer.

Narrator

The meaning of a narrative is often established by means of a narrator – the storyteller – who manages the relationship between the narrative and the audience. For example, 'It was a dark and stormy night and the captain gathered his men together one by one … "Tell us a story, Captain," they said, and so he began … "It was a dark and stormy night…" ' and so on and so on.

Identification is the process by which members of an audience align at least some of their own identity with that of the characters in the text, putting themselves in the characters' place. If the narrative is told in the first person, with 'I' as participant, individual members of the audience are directly drawn into the story and the relationship between the text and the individual may become more subjective as, to varying degrees, they identify with a particular character or performer. Examples include *Adrian Mole* and the 'video diaries' genre of programmes as well as the Raymond Chandler books and films, such as *The Big Sleep* or *Farewell My Lovely*: 'I got up at nine, drank three cups of black coffee, bathed the back of my head with ice-water and read the two morning papers that had been thrown against the apartment door.'

On the other hand, if the narrator is spoken of as 'He/she/it' as reported by an observer or witness, the relationship between text and audience is more detached and objective and, as in news bulletins, documentaries or sports programmes, 'we' the audience are positioned as interested but usually impartial observers: 'Protesters took to the streets of Moscow again today as … ' Sometimes, however, the story is told by a silent, 'invisible' or detached third party represented by just the camera lens as observer. In this case the relationship between text and audience is less clear and each individual has to construct his or her own position or point of view. (There is more detailed discussion on mode of address and point of view in chapter 4.)

Narration

Narration is the act of telling the 'story', and the form which it takes will affect how the narrative is told. One of the main differences between these forms is how *time* is handled; for instance, an eight-hundred-page novel can deal with a time span of many years (*Bleak House*) or a few hours (*Ulysses*), and equally the time taken to read the novel can also vary widely. A thirty-minute radio or television programme can attempt to cover a similar time period but has to do so in a finite, or fixed, time slot. Consumption by the audience is also much more limited, although the video recorder does offer some degree of control and choice. To bridge this difference between the audience's 'real time' and the narrative's 'story time', various conventions are used. One of the most common devices for showing the passing of time used to be the speeding up of the hands of a clock or blowing away the pages of a calendar; today these are both rather clichéd or heavy-handed, and as audiences we accept and understand more sophisticated technical conventions, such as the use of fade-outs or slow mixes from one shot to another, or even a single caption that may say 'two years later'.

Crisell (1994) suggests that in radio, as all the signs and codes are auditory (words, sounds, music and silence) and sequential, then time is the major structuring agent for radio narratives, although the 'meaning' of radio texts is created by the contexts which the words, sounds, music and silences construct.

In order to be convincing, television soap operas often try to blur the gap between real time and story time; for instance, a *Brookside* episode may start in the morning with families meeting over breakfast, follow characters through the day and end with the families meeting again over dinner. By the evening the events being shown on the screen may be happening at the same time as the audience is watching them happen. Events in soap operas may parallel 'real' events and seasons; for instance, Christmas editions of popular soaps often show the characters themselves celebrating Christmas.

We often create the story ourselves by decoding the clues that we are given and then filling in the gaps to create the story. Adverts and title sequences are particularly successful at giving just enough information for us to do this. Television title sequences can be seen as mini-narratives that act as trailers for the coming programme and mark the end of the previous segment, perhaps a commercial break. The use of certain types of image and the importance of music prepare us for the next narrative segment by introducing the character and signposting the type or genre of programme. Title sequences can be seen as a familiar and reassuring element of a programme's popularity which each week repeat the broader narrative of a series. In the television series *Quantum Leap*, each week viewers see the hero suffer again the nuclear accident that now allows him to travel through time. These title sequences are an important part of attracting and maintaining the interest of the audience and can last for several minutes. In *Star Trek* the title sequence has developed its own catch phrase, 'to boldly go where no man has gone before', which has become part of the series' mythology. In America the first commercial break, the next narrative segment, comes directly after this title sequence.

Even the most 'open' of narratives, however, usually has a clear start and finish point, even if the structure within the narrative itself is unclear. A detective or police story that starts with a murder and then recaps the events leading up to it will often start with a title sequence and end with credits. In newspapers the headlines can be seen to mark the start of a particular narrative. The audience is being given a clear marker as to when each narrative is beginning or ending. However, because of the changing social contexts in which we consume media texts, it may be that we are increasingly creating our own narratives, stopping or starting part way through a radio or TV programme, film or magazine or, through the use of the remote control, 'zapping' from one narrative segment to another, heightening intertexuality and creating our own 'synthesis' of narrative structures.

Codes of enigma and action

There are two key codes involved in the sequencing of narratives, the *action* code and the *enigma* code. *Action* codes are often used as a shorthand for advancing the narrative: Tilley (1991) cites as an example the buckling of a gun-belt in the western as a prelude to the gunfight, or the packing of a suitcase which 'signals' confrontation, panic or escape in a crime thriller. Other devices can include the starting of a car engine or the whistle of an approaching train. Increasingly television uses 'flashing blue

Fig. 2.14
Citizen Kane, *1941*
Source: Kobal Collection/Mercury

lights' as action codes in a variety of fictional (*The Bill, Casualty*) and 'real life' (*Crimewatch, 999*) programmes.

The *enigma* code 'explains' the narrative by controlling what, and how much, information is given to the audience. This code is intended to capture the audience's interest and attention by setting up an enigma or problem that is then resolved during the course of the narrative. (Who was the murderer whose hand we saw in the opening sequence? What does 'Rosebud' mean in *Citizen Kane* (figure 2.14)? Why was the phrase 'In space no one can hear you scream' used to promote the film *Alien*?) Headlines in a newspaper serve the same function of summarising the key elements ('Killer dogs foil cops acid party raid') and making a direct appeal to readers, as do the 'trailers' for films and new television or radio programmes: 'Another chance to catch up with *The Old Devils* on BBC1 tonight at 10.15' or '*Cracker* is back in a new and exciting series.'

SALON SMOOTH LEGS WITHOUT THE SALON

Immac

IMMAC'S IMPROVED WAX STRIPS, COMPLETE WITH A UNIQUE VIAL OF SKIN CONDITIONING OIL, GIVE YOU SALON SMOOTH RESULTS, WHEREVER YOU ARE.

Immac

Fig. 2.15
Source: Reckitt & Colman Products

Advertisements are particularly good at using and compressing these enigma codes. They try to arouse the audience's interest but at the same time want to contain and limit what we know. Look at figure 2.15 with its narrative enigma. The advert shows someone being 'saved', but what actually is being saved? The owner of the legs by an unseen (male?) rescuer? Or the hairiness of the model's legs by the use of Immac? Or 'our' legs? The advert tries to create an enigma that aims to attract the reader's attention while at the same time suggesting some kind of parody or joke: 'wherever you are' - even when shipwrecked?

The pleasure of the text

As audiences become more sophisticated and adept at recognising these codes of enigma and action, we begin to perceive patterns and anticipate developments. There is then a 'pleasure of the text', the creation of tension in trying to anticipate what is going to happen and then pleasure at predicting the resolution. We, as audiences, like to be able to recognise what is going to happen, the feeling of being 'in the know' that the promise of familiarity brings. It is this familiarity and continuity that for many of us makes narratives likeable, predictable and understandable. We know what is going to happen because it is the convention of this type of narrative or programme to be resolved in a certain way (the policeman gets his man, the hero and heroine live happily ever after), but we will watch anyway, wanting to confirm our knowingness, our familiarity and understanding of the narrative structure: 'Ah yes! I was right, he is the secret father of her child.'

Part of this pleasure in predicting and recognising what is going to happen lies in an overlap between these fictional narratives and the 'real' narratives of our own lives. In the same way as we recognise our own lives as stories, so we recognise that these fictional stories reflect our own lives (or our projected desires and fantasies), the social world we inhabit and our place in it. The real and the fictional often have common values and attitudes, and perhaps the members of the audience can rewrite their own personal narratives to produce different meanings or different endings.

Equilibrium and disequilibrium

Many writers have suggested that narratives generate a dynamic of equilibrium and disequilibrium. This suggests a model of narrative which starts with equilibrium or 'harmony', a state where all is well, which is then disrupted, often by an outside influence which causes a disequilibrium or tension. For instance, a peaceful American surburban family or community is threatened from outside in many of Steven Spielberg's films (*Close Encounters, E.T., Gremlins, Back to the Future,* etc.) or in David Lynch's *Blue Velvet,* before finally the threat is resolved and replaced by a new equilibrium. In other narratives the disruption may be violent, as in *Alien,* or some of the 'spaghetti westerns'. Some television programme narratives only exist in a world of disequilibrium (*Land of the Giants, The Prisoner* or *My Two Dads*).

The notion of equilibrium highlights questions on the way narratives can speak ideologically about how social order is represented and how equilibrium functions to effect closure within narratives: 'At the end of *The Outlaw Josey Wales* a new community has been created – a sharing and stable community of male and female, young and old, white and red' (Tilley, 1991).

Character functions

In 1928, in a famous analysis of narratives, Vladimir Propp used fairy tales as a basis for his model of over thirty character types,

---

ACTIVITY 2.6

Choose three films that you know well and analyse the ways in which disequilibrium occurs and is managed within the narrative. Compare the two states of equilibrium, the first at the beginning and the second at the end of the film. How has the equilibrium changed? In what ways has it remained the same? Have the characters' positions, status or relationships to each other altered in any significant way?

Study the two film posters in figures 2.16 and 2.17, then consider the following questions:

- What visual and written codes are being used?
- What information do they provide about the films?
- What other information might you have expected but is missing?
- In what ways do these posters create a sense of enigma?
- How are the film producers trying to create a sense of danger or disequilibrium?
- What genre of film do these belong to?
- What are the generic conventions that are at work in these posters?
- What differing representations of 'aliens' do they present?

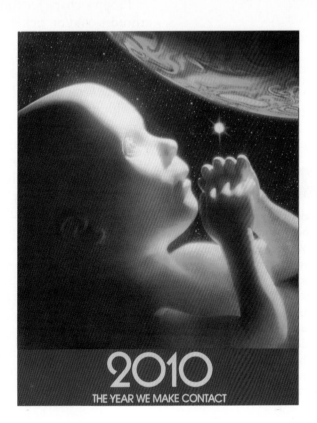

all of whom perform some kind of function in the way narrative is organised and developed. Some of these key character functions include:

- the *hero*, who seeks something;
- the *villain*, who hinders or is in competition with the hero;
- the *donor*, who provides some kind of magic talisman that helps the hero;
- the *helper*, who aids the hero and his or her quest;
- the *heroine*, who acts as a reward for the hero and is the object of the villain's schemes.

The importance of these characters is less to do with who they are or what they are like than with the part they play in the development of the narrative and our recognition of their general function. We recognise the hero and heroine and identify with the (usually male) hero – 'us' – and the resolution that should bring them together. We are encouraged to take sides and oppose the villain – 'them' – and occasionally even boo or hiss when they appear on the screen, the stage or wherever the narrative is being played out.

Propp's character functions allow for individual changes in attitudes and/or beliefs – for instance, the main character's coming to the view that war is useless or corrupting in *Born on the Fourth of July* or *Apocalypse Now;* for the undertaking of a mythic 'quest' or search, perhaps for some personal justice as in *The Searchers* or *Mona Lisa*; and for conflict between hierarchies or within subcultures, in films like *Rebel Without a Cause, My Beautiful Laundrette* or *The Godfather* series.

Different types of narrative may be identified by their gender characteristics. Clarke (1987) suggests that 'male' narratives tend to be clearly resolved at the end of each segment, with the 'hero' overcoming the problem, and the status quo being re-established. These fictional narratives are found particularly in police or adventure series and can be seen as integral to news bulletins, where order and equilibrium is restored at the end of every programme. Film narratives tend to have a more distinct closure whereas television often tries to create some sense of narrative continuity. 'Female' narratives, Geraghty (1991) suggests, tend to be more open-ended, ongoing and not so clearly resolved. These types of narrative can often be found in soap operas and are one possible reason why this genre tends to be popular with female audiences. (See the section on gender preferences in chapter 4.)

ACTIVITY 2.7

Consider the five character functions identified above and how they apply to various films that you are familiar with: for example the *Batman* films, or James Bond or Harrison Ford's *Indiana Jones* series. In what ways do these character types help 'advance' the narrative?

Genre

Familiarity through repetition is one of the key elements in the way audiences understand and relate to media texts:

> Repetition in the TV narrative occurs at the level of the series: formats are repeated, situations return week after week. Each time there is novelty. The characters of the situation comedy encounter a new dilemma; the documentary reveals a new problem; the news gives us a fresh strike, a new government, another earthquake, the first panda born in captivity ... The series is composed of segments. The recognition of the series format tends to hold segments together and to provide them with an element of continuity and narrative progression from one to the next.
>
> *Ellis (1992), p. 147*

The concept of genre, developed particularly in the study of film and literature, can be seen as a way of classifying particular styles or types of media texts by identifying common

Fig. 2.18
Crossfire, *1947*
Source: Kobal Collection/RKO

elements, that recur by being repeated again and again and act as a set of rules associated by both producers and audiences with certain types of text. These common elements may be related to the 'look' of particular films, for example the western or *film noir* from Hollywood in the 1930s and 1940s, through the use of particular costumes, settings and other styles of performance, lighting, action and narrative. See figures 2.18 and 2.19.

However, the notion of genre also allows us to categorise other conventions associated with particular types of films, including narrative structures, certain directors or actors, and character types. Hollywood westerns share a number of generic codes including narrative themes ('Indian' uprisings, people being cheated out of their land, prospecting for gold, family feuds), props (guns, horses, stagecoaches, cactus), and settings ('famous' towns like Tombstone or Dodge City, saloons, prairies, cavalry forts). There are also particular directors (John Ford), actors (John Wayne or Clint Eastwood), character types (the heroic loner or outsider, like Ethan in *The Searchers*), sets and locations (Monument Valley) and even theme music (*The Good, the Bad and the Ugly*).

The concept of genre can, however, be problematic when applied to all media texts because of the range, complexity and

Fig. 2.19
Stagecoach, *1939*
Source: Kobal Collection/United Artists

constant 'flux' of texts being produced at any one time. Many western films can be seen to encourage a strong ideological message about the triumph of law and order and the 'good guy' but this cannot be said of all westerns, as some, like the spaghetti westerns, appeared to be more ambiguous in their ideological message and perhaps represent a sub-genre of the western, coming to terms with changed social and cultural circumstances.

For a long time television situation comedy was considered to be a genre, but the generic term may now be too narrow to cover the wide and varied output of comedy that appears on television. It is now possible to identify a set of sub-genres of television comedy – alternative comedy, sitcom, American comedy, satire, stand-up comedy – and it becomes difficult to categorise successful programmes like *Absolutely Fabulous* into one particular generic pigeonhole (It may of course be argued that *Absolutely Fabulous* owed its success partially to defying classification and therefore offering something new.) Different production locations may also produce specific characteristics; for instance, British soap operas tend to be described as 'realistic' or 'gritty', whereas American soaps are more escapist, and Australian soaps may seem more idealistic.

Science fiction

Science fiction has been a popular film genre since Georges Méliès's 1902 film *Le Voyage dans la lune*. Science fiction films often have strong *ideological* messages and *representations* (see chapter 3) that reflect the concerns of the society at the time of their production and usually centre around some notion of 'conflict' between 'us' and 'them' and the positive or negative aspects of science and the future. Fritz Lang's *Metropolis* (1927) reflected concerns about 'new technology' and the dehumanising and exploitative potential of the new 'machine age' as well as introducing much of the genre's *iconography* (mad scientists and evil robots). Many of the science fiction films made in America during the 1950s – *It Came from Beneath the Sea* (1955), *The Invasion of the Body Snatchers* (1956) and *The Beast from 20,000 Fathoms* (1953) – featured invasion by aliens and reflected America's anxieties about communist spies, the Cold War with the USSR and the danger of nuclear annihilation. *Barbarella*, in contrast, made in 1967, offered a more positive reflection of the values and interests of the 'swinging sixties'.

One of the key films of the genre is *2001: A Space Odyssey* (1968), which combines optimism and spiritual development with exploration of new worlds. The film also set the standard

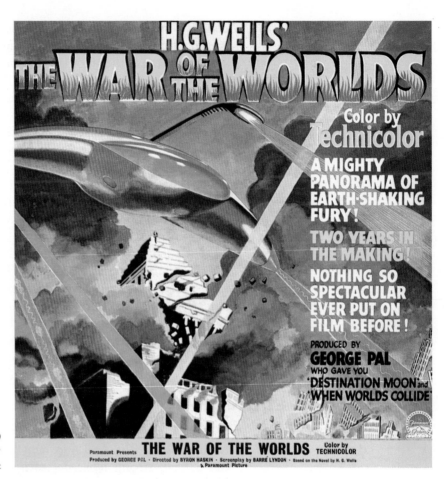

Fig. 2.20
War of the Worlds, *1953*
Source: Kobal Collection/Paramount

for the iconography of the 1980s and 1990s science fiction films with its emphasis on the new technology of spacecrafts, 'dangerous' computers with minds of their own and the use of music and image to create a sense of space and grandeur. Many of these conventions were used in the *Star Wars* films (1977 onwards), which were seen by many writers as the traditional western relocated to outer space with state-of-the-art special effects added (see Nelmes, 1996). In the 1980s, dystopias, the opposite of the utopian 'perfect' or idealised societies, were common, with *Bladerunner* (1982), *Brazil* (1985) and the various *Robocop/Terminator* films. In the late 1990s, the science fiction genre seems to have become popular again with 'we are not alone' type films like *Independence Day* (1996), or *Mars Attacks!* (1997) and the continued popularity of the *Star Trek* series that ironically refers back to an earlier, television, version of the

Fig. 2.21
Close Encounters of the Third Kind,
1977
Source: Kobal Collection/Columbia

ACTIVITY 2.8

The *Star Trek* films and television series are part of a large multimedia merchandising industry. Identify the range of *Star Trek* merchandising (products and services) that is available. This may include books, audio cassettes, clothing, conventions and a web site on the Internet as well as films and videos.

● What particular aspects of *Star Trek* are most commonly used?
● Are there any images that are significantly more dominant than others?
● Are there any images closely associated with *Star Trek* that do not appear at all (the Klingons)?
● To whom is most of this multimedia merchandising addressed?
● Does this activity significantly increase at any particular time of the year (e.g. around Christmas)?
● Can you identify any other recent examples of merchandising based on the success of film or television genres?

future as well as reinforcing a particular and pro-American ideological message.

When we try to define the genre of science fiction we can see the limitations of the concept. If it is to include all those films that have what one commentator has called 'the fictitious use of science' in them we should include films like *Frankenstein* which, it could be argued, should belong to the horror genre. If we limit the definition we may exclude films like *Westworld* or *The War Game*, both of which also employ 'the fictitious use of science'. Although a general definition of the science fiction genre is difficult, it is true to say that there are a number of films that contain a certain set of conventions – narrative structures, character types, gender roles, decor and setting, specific directors and possibly titles (consider *Star Wars*, *Starman*, *Star Trek*, *Stargate*, *Star Crash*, *The Last Starfighter*) – that we would recognise as belonging to a broad generic type of film.

It should be noted that genre is not just a way of categorising 'types' of film but that the notion of genre is important to both audiences and producers. Audiences are said to like the idea of genre (although they may not identify it by that term) because of its reassuring and familiar promise of patterns of repetition and variation. They know what to expect: if they enjoyed *Home Alone 1* they will most probably enjoy *Home Alone 2*. (See chapter 5 for discussion of sequels.) Producers are said to use genres

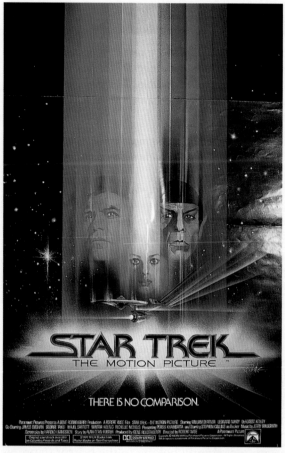

(a)

(b)

Fig. 2.22 *a and b*
Star Trek
Source: Kobal Collection/Paramount

ACTIVITY 2.9

In films some genres move in and out of fashion; for instance, until relatively recently, the western had been described as being dead; some years ago disaster movies were popular, and in the late 1980s and early 1990s there was a fad for 'baby' movies like *Three Men and a Baby*, *Look Who's Talking* and *Baby Boom*.

Look at some recent films and try to categorise them into genres by looking for their common, basic ingredients. What story types do these films have? What sorts of character do they have? What actors and actresses are particularly associated with them? Are there particularly distinctive sets, lighting or other 'production values' associated with them? How do they offer something new within the requirements of the genre?

Are there current films that replicate the features of the earlier western genre? Compare a recent western film with one made at an earlier point in the century.

ACTIVITY 2.10

Watch several quiz shows on television and decide whether you agree with the list of components. Are there other ingredients that should be included? How do quiz shows like *Mastermind* or *Bollywood or Bust* fit the genre? To what extent do radio quiz shows fit? You can also start to identify other genres of popular television and compare their common characteristics.

because they can exploit a winning formula and minimise risks. The concept of genre also helps institutions budget and plan their finances more accurately. It is important to note, however, that the formula approach does not always work; for example, *Crocodile Dundee 2* was not as successful as *Crocodile Dundee 1*.

The concept of genre is now widely used as a way both of categorising media production and output, whether it be from women's magazines or television quiz shows, and of explaining how we, the audience, make sense of the 'flow' of media output by identifying and 'organising' certain types of television programme within an evening's viewing, or certain features within a daily newspaper or weekly magazine. The concept allows us to name the process by which we identify certain landmarks on the map of the media's 'flow' in the same way as we go to different sections in a library or music shop.

Quiz or game shows are a particular genre of radio and television, and their common components are likely to include, to a greater or lesser degree, the following:

- a personality who hosts the show, often an ex-comedian;
- prizes;
- women as decoration and/or assistants;
- live audiences;
- 'real' people – members of the general public – as competitors;
- a sense of competition;
- excitement;
- glamour;
- catch phrases, questions and music.

It has been suggested that the dominance of genre, particularly in television, has several consequences, one of which is to marginalise those programmes that do not easily fit into generic conventions, because it is suggested that audiences will not recognise or accept them. Although this is true to some extent, there are instances where the notion of genre has been specifically challenged; for instance, in television series such as *Police Story* and *Twin Peaks* or the films *Pulp Fiction*, *Blazing Saddles* and *The Rocky Horror Picture Show*, where the genre conventions and characteristics have been deliberately subverted or parodied.

The other consequence relates to the power of the generic structure, which can be ideologically limiting and in which the form can dominate over content. In police series such as *The Bill* or *Inspector Morse* we are conventionally placed on the side of the police, who are the familiar characters that we are encouraged to identify with. In sitcom there is a need to maintain the status quo so that the original situation can be used again. This may mean that although an interesting problem might be set up, such as those of the mother's personal fulfilment and satisfaction in *2.4 Children* or of changing the way the old people's home is run in *Waiting for God*, it can never actually be resolved or allow for any real progression, because that would destroy the generic formula that has made the programmes successful.

Conclusion

This chapter has focused on introducing some of the *conventions*, the codes or grammars, of language and signs, which help us to construct the meanings of media texts. These provide the ways in which certain meanings can be shared and understood. They are often not written down but are hidden or unspoken rules that we learn to accept, apply and recognise. They are part of culture and are therefore culturally specific, but as television and the cinema particularly become more homogenised across the world, these conventions appear to be becoming more 'global' or linked to a television or film culture dominated by American and western ideologies. (See chapter 7.) They influence processes both of production and of reception and are in many cases so familiar that they appear to be the only, or 'natural', way of doing or understanding something.

The next chapter moves on to look at both the content and the connotations of media texts, focusing in particular on the ideological messages they represent to us about the world.

FURTHER ACTIVITIES

1 Using the McMahon and Quinn categories of codes outlined on page 36, analyse a selection of newspaper front pages chosen on the same day. It is useful to compare and contrast broadsheet and tabloid newspapers to highlight the conventions that are used to make tabloids more popular.
2 Select a television or film genre, such as *film noir*, and list its distinctive characteristics. Choose one particular film and analyse it in detail: how does it 'fit' into a particular genre; does it try to break the rules of the genre in any way?
3 Consider the extent to which the concept of 'genre' is useful in analysing and categorising media texts. Summarise the ways in which the idea of genre might be helpful for media producers and for media audiences.

Further reading

Berger, J. 1972: *Ways of Seeing*. Penguin.

Bignall, J. 1997: *Media Semiotics: An Introduction*. Manchester University Press.

Clute, J. and Nicholls, P. (eds). 1993: *The Encyclopedia of Science Fiction*. Orbit.

Ellis, J. 1992: *Visible Fictions: Cinema, Television, Radio*. Routledge.

Goodwin, A. and Whannel, G. (eds). 1990: *Understanding Television*. Routledge.

Grahame J., Jempson, M., Simons, M. 1995: *The News Pack*. English & Media Centre, London.

Izod, J. 1989: *Reading the Screen*. Longman.

James, E. 1994: *Science Fiction in the 20th Century*. Oxford University Press.

McMahon, B. and Quinn, R. 1986: *Real Images*. Macmillan.

Monaco, J. 1977: *How to Read a Film: The Art, Technology, Language, History and Theory of Film and Media*. Oxford University Press.

Morgan, J. and Welton, P. 1992: *See What I Mean*. Edward Arnold.

Nelmes, J. (ed.) 1996: *An Introduction to Film Studies*. Routledge.

Shippey, T. (ed.). 1991: *Fictional Space: Essays on Contemporary Science Fiction*. Oxford University Press.

Tolson, A. 1996: *Mediations: Text and Discourse in Media Studies*. Arnold.

Williamson, J. 1978: *Decoding Advertisements: Ideology and Meaning in Advertising*. Marion Boyars.

3

Representations and realism

The concept of representation embodies the theme that the media construct meanings about the world – they *re*present it, and in doing so, help audiences to make sense of it. For representation to be meaningful to audiences, there needs to be a shared recognition of people, situations, ideas, etc. What require closer examination are the ideas and meanings produced by those representations. There may be shared recognition of the world as represented through familiar or *dominant* images and ideas, but there is little social consensus about how to interpret those representations, and always the possibility of *alternative* representations.

What kinds of media representation are more typical, and what explanations might be made to account for such patterns? Given that society is increasingly pluralistic in terms of variety of social groups, interests and perspectives, emphasis will be given to key social identities such as gender and ethnicity, and also problems of achieving political unity.

Whose representations?

Before considering what kinds of representation appear in the media, it needs to be made clear that any examination cannot be entirely innocent. Academic approaches to the study of human culture either start or end with broad explanatory models, or theories, which are used to make sense of all the information gathered in the course of research. Media studies embraces a number of such theoretical frameworks which have been applied over the years, not least in the analysis of media content. Here we give a brief outline of two alternative models which have been influential in their analysis of media content. There is a fuller discussion of the key determinants of media output in chapter 5.

The hegemonic model

The underlying assumption of those subscribing to a hegemonic view of society is that there are fundamental inequalities in power between social groups. Those groups with most power are, in the main, able to exercise their influence culturally rather than by force. The concept has its origins in Marxist theory, where writers have attempted to explain how the ruling capitalist class has been able to protect their economic interests. According to this theory, hegemony refers to the winning of popular consent through everyday cultural life, including media representations of the world, as well as other social institutions, such as education and the family. To understand how hegemony may be achieved, it is necessary to consider the concept of ideology.

Ideology

Ideology is a complex concept but, broadly speaking, refers to a set of ideas which produces a partial and selective view of reality. This in turn serves the interests of those with power in society. It has its roots in the nineteenth-century writings of Karl Marx, who argued that the property-owning classes were able to rule by ideas which represented as natural the class relationships of production, therefore justifying their own wealth and privilege. These ideas could be found in all areas of social knowledge, such as religion: for example, the notion that it is 'God's will' that some are born rich and that the poor will be rewarded in the next life. Thus the notion of ideology entails widely held ideas or beliefs, which may often be seen as 'common sense', *legitimising* or making widely acceptable certain forms of social inequality. In so doing, ideologies are able to disguise or suppress the real structure of domination and exploitation which exists in society.

Modern writers (Marxist and others) have adapted and developed this idea so that all belief systems or world views are thought to be ideological. Although some ideas and beliefs seem more 'natural' or 'truthful', there is no absolute truth with which to measure the accuracy of representations. What interests those who analyse media representations is whose ideological perspective is privileged. This raises the issue of power inequalities. While Marxists have emphasised social class differences, others have increasingly pointed to gender and racial inequalities. What is agreed is that popular culture, especially media output, is the site of a constant struggle over the production of meaning. The media's role may be seen as:

- circulating and reinforcing dominant ideologies; or
- (less frequently), undermining and challenging such ideologies.

What is important to note is that the media and the audience are both part of the process of producing ideological meaning. (Where the balance of power lies is addressed in the next chapter.)

Myth

Ideologies 'work' through symbolic codes (see chapter 2), which represent and explain cultural phenomena. Barthes (1973) labels this symbolic representation as mythic, not in the traditional sense of being false (as in fairy tales), but in the sense of having the appearance of being 'natural' or 'commonsense', so that it is not questioned. Advertising draws heavily on myth, using cultural signifiers to represent qualities which can be realised through consumption of the advertised product. Williamson (1978) has identified some of the value systems which are represented in the language of advertising. Particularly prominent in her analysis are adverts which she claims invite us to reunite ourselves with nature (even more relevant in the 'green' 1990s), and those which attribute the power of science and technology to products. In nearly all adverts, she sees two processes at work: first, an appeal to our belief in the 'magical' powers of products to solve our problems; and second, the divorce of production from consumption. Hidden from our view are the capitalist conditions from which advertised products originate (conditions which Marxist writers see as alienating and exploitative of workers: figure 3.1).

The British nation: an ideological construction

What does it mean to be British? The extent to which the people of Britain can be considered a nation is problematic. A shared sense of belonging and identity is certainly a real sentiment for many people living in Britain. However, closer scrutiny raises questions concerning divisions between various groups comprising the British population, not least nationalism within Scotland and Wales. And where England is taken as a national 'core', further divisions can be identified along ethnic, religious, regional and class lines. If there are so many alterna-

Fig. 3.1
How does this Hovis advert work as a myth?
Source: Hovis, Collett, Dickenson, Pearce and Partners Ltd

tive sources of identity, how has the national sense of identity achieved such a strong hold? While there is not the space here to address this question adequately, we can examine how the media may contribute towards the symbolic representation of what it means to be British.

It is in the context of 'us' and 'them' that a sense of national identity may be articulated. International competition or conflict provides a good opportunity for 'British values' to be asserted in contrast to an enemy, real or imagined. The Second World War inspired countless stories celebrating the triumphant British spirit in the face of overwhelming odds, including many films like *Battle of Britain* (1969) and *The Dam Busters* (1954), which are still regularly recycled on television. Such transparent patriotism was invoked in 1982 by the popular press during the Falklands War (most notoriously with the *Sun*'s headline 'Gotcha!', in reference to the sinking of the

Fig. 3.2
Source: *Daily Express*

Argentinian ship, the *Belgrano*), and also in 1991 during the Gulf War. Perceived attempts to dilute our national identity or sovereignty, especially via the European Union, also provoke a patriotic response, particularly in the tabloid press. A recent example was the reaction to the decision by the EU to introduce a worldwide ban on British beef until BSE, so-called 'mad cow disease', was brought under control. Many newspapers portrayed the British government's stand against the EU as virtually a declaration of war (figure 3.2).

At the heart of the sense of being British is the idea of tradition, and this is most strongly personified by the monarchy. The Queen, as head of state, symbolises national unity as well as being a historical point of reference, reminding us of our 'great' history. Standing above day-to-day politics, she is often seen as epitomising what is good about Britain. Her ritualistic role is strongly supported by a largely deferential media. Within broadcasting she is exempt from the critical scrutiny normally applied to anyone with her power and status. The annual Christmas address to the nation, broadcast on all national television and radio channels, is supplemented by frequent documentary features which celebrate her role.

An alternative perspective is voiced by writers like Rosalind Brunt, who perceive the monarch to be a barrier to real democratic freedom and self-determination:

Fig. 3.3

How does this Radio Times *front cover represent the relationship between the royal family, history and the nation?*

Source: *Radio Times* and Cecil Beaton/Camera Press

Fig. 3.4a
Source: The *Sun*, 4 September 1997

Fig. 3.4b
Source: The *Express*, 4 September 1997

In so far as ideologies are never simply ideas in people's heads but are indeed the myths we live by and which contribute to our sense of self and self-worth, then I think it actually matters that the British have no real identity as 'we the people' but continue to consign ourselves to a subordinated position as 'subjects' of the Queen. Not that we see it that way; the commonsense view is that the British are freer than their monarch; we can go anywhere we please without a police escort and 'I wouldn't have her job for the world!' In this way we happily consent to the monarch's continuing to act on our behalf. But the very popularity of present day monarchy is also how we, the British, tell ourselves that we're not quite ready for self-government yet.

Brunt (1992)

How can the Queen be seen as an ideological force? As she is the country's richest landowner and a member of a privileged elite, the Queen's status as unifying the nation is seen as mythic.

The media, not least television, appear to have conspired in perpetuating this myth by acting as public relations agent on behalf of the royal family.

The pluralist model

Instead of seeing media content as narrowly ideological, pluralists argue that there is diversity and choice. Just as society comprises a range of interest groups and points of view, so do the media. If and when certain values and beliefs predominate in media output, then it is due to their being shared by most of society. This is because media production is essentially based on the need to please the audience. If audience needs are ignored then the likely outcome is commercial failure.

In the case of the monarchy, pluralists would argue that the media's endorsement of the Queen simply reflects genuine popular support. Furthermore, not all media coverage is necessarily sympathetic. The tabloid newspapers have been sharply critical of members of the royal family, exposing adultery and deceit within the royal marriages, as well as questioning the Queen's right to tax exemption and her response to the death of Princess Diana (figure 3.4). Even television has ridiculed the royal family in programmes like *Spitting Image* and *Pallas* (a spoof soap opera employing voice-overs dubbed on to news footage of the royals).

Political representations

It is when the media represent political issues that the hegemonic and pluralist perspectives can be clearly contrasted. The question of political bias has been the focus of much academic debate.

Propaganda

There is general consensus that some political content in the media qualifies as *propaganda*. In broad terms, propaganda is the conscious manipulation of information in order to gain political advantage. Historically, it has been most evident during times of war or national crisis, when the need for national unity has led governments to seek control over the media. In such situations, dissenting or alternative views are usually suppressed or marginalised.

Two fairly recent examples in Britain, which provoked much controversy, were the Falklands War of 1982 and the Gulf War of 1991. In both cases there was strict external control (mainly by the Ministry of Defence) of how the wars were reported. Ostensibly, this was for reasons of military security. However, it could also be argued that the aim was to ensure public support was not undermined by information (especially pictures) revealing the less attractive aspects of the wars, such as military and civilian casualties. (American support for the Vietnam War in the late 1960s had been eroded by the media's close scrutiny and questioning of American aims and methods, contributing towards the country's eventual withdrawal from Vietnam.)

External censorship was reinforced by media self-censorship and propagandistic reporting. Tabloid newspapers like the *Sun* were vociferous in support for 'our lads' against 'the Argies' in the Falklands War and 'the evil dictator' (Saddam Hussein) in the Gulf War (figure 3.5). The BBC even went to the extreme of banning certain records from being played on its radio stations during the Gulf War. The list included Abba's 'Waterloo', The Bangles' 'Walk Like an Egyptian', and Elton John's 'Saturday Night's Alright for Fighting!' Nevertheless, it was still possible to find some media coverage which allowed space for alternative or oppositional views to be expressed. Channel 4 broadcast 'The Gulf Between Us' just prior to the Gulf War, presenting an Arab perspective on the conflict. In the build-up to the Falklands War, the BBC's current affairs programme *Panorama*, contained criticism of the decision to send the task force. Consequently, the BBC was accused of treachery by both the government and newspapers promoting military action.

Other than during wartime, media propaganda is largely confined to either political advertising, such as party election broadcasts, or politically partisan newspapers and magazines seeking to persuade audiences to support a particular political party (figure 3.6a–c). However, there is no clear demarcation between propaganda and the ideological bias that could be said to characterise much political representation in the media. If a distinction can be made, it concerns the question of how conscious media professionals are of any bias in their coverage. While some newspaper journalists would admit to being selective in their political reporting (especially in the tabloid newspapers), many would claim to apply rigorous but fair standards of news journalism, especially in broadcasting.

We have	They have
Army, Navy and Air Force	A war machine
Reporting guidelines	Censorship
Press briefings	Propaganda
We	**They**
Take out	Destroy
Suppress	Destroy
Eliminate	Kill
Neutralise or decapitate	Kill
Decapitate	Kill
Dig in	Cower in their foxholes
We launch	**They launch**
First strikes	Sneak missile attacks
Pre-emptively	Without provocation
Our men are ...	**Their men are ...**
Boys	Troops
Lads	Hordes
Our boys are ...	**Theirs are ...**
Professional	Brainwashed
Lion-hearts	Paper tigers
Cautious	Cowardly
Confident	Desperate
Heroes	Cornered
Dare-devils	Cannon fodder
Young knights of the skies	Bastards of Baghdad
Loyal	Blindly obedient
Desert rats	Mad dogs
Resolute	Ruthless
Brave	Fanatical
Our boys are motivated by	**Their boys are motivated by**
An old-fashioned sense of duty	Fear of Saddam
Our boys	**Their boys**
Fly into the jaws of hell	Cower in concrete bunkers
Our ships are ...	**Iraqi ships are ...**
An armada	A navy
Israeli non-retaliation is	**Iraqi non-retaliation is**
An act of great statesmanship	Blundering/Cowardly
The Belgians are ...	**The Belgians are also ...**
Yellow	Two-faced
Our missiles are ...	**Their missiles are ...**
Like Luke Skywalker zapping Darth Vader	Ageing duds (*rhymes with Scuds*)
Our missiles cause ...	**Their missiles cause ...**
Collateral damage	Civilian casualties
We ...	**They ...**
Precision bomb	Fire wildly at anything in the skies
Our PoWs are ...	**Their PoWs are ...**
Gallant boys	Overgrown schoolchildren
George Bush is ...	**Saddam Hussein is ...**
At peace with himself	Demented
Resolute	Defiant
Statesmanlike	An evil tyrant
Assured	A crackpot monster
Our planes ...	**Their planes ...**
Suffer a high rate of attrition	Are shot out of the sky
Fail to return from missions	Are Zapped

Fig. 3.5

Source: *Guardian*, 25 January 1991

* All the expressions above have been used by the British press in the past week

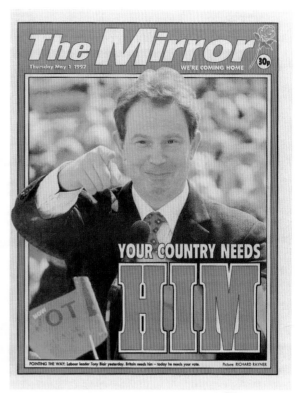

Fig. 3.6a

Front page from the Sun, *Election day 1992. Contrast this with the* Daily Mirror *front page on election day 1997 (figure 3.6b) as examples of political propaganda*
Source: Sun, *9 April 1992*

Fig. 3.6b

Front page of the Daily Mirror, *Election day 1997*
Source: Daily Mirror, *1 May 1997*

Broadcasting and political bias

Television and radio are required by law to be politically impartial. Audiences support the perception that they are so, as reflected in surveys which show that a large majority of the population regard television as their most trusted source of information. Furthermore, when it comes to accusing broadcasters of political bias, the attacks have come from all positions in the political spectrum.

Consider the following extracts:

Contrary to the claims, conventions, and culture of television journalism, the news is not a neutral product. For television news is a cultural artefact; it is a sequence of socially manufactured messages, which carry many of the culturally dominant assumptions of our society. From the accents of the newscasters to the vocabulary of camera angles; from who gets on and

Fig. 3.6c

Front page of the Sun, 18 March 1997. In 1997 the Sun switched its support to the Labour Party after having supported the Conservatives for the previous twenty years. The decision (taken by the proprietor, Rupert Murdoch) reflected the perception that the Tories had lost favour with many of the Sun's readers, but also that the Labour Party no longer posed a threat to News Corporation's commercial interests

Source: *Sun*, 18 March 1997

what questions they are asked, via selection of stories to presentation of bulletins, the news is a highly mediated product.

Glasgow University Media Group (1976)

The proposition that emerges is this: that the main television news channels have done their best to present a fair, balanced and accurate account; that there were occasional mistakes, misjudgements and inadequacies; but that, in the face of real difficulties, they offered their audiences a generally reliable and dispassionate news service.

Hetherington (1985)

In our third report, which covered the period April to December 1988, *World in Action* featured one-sided programmes on a whole range of issues, including the Neighbourhood Watch scheme, the 'discovery' that 'unemployment can damage your health', the Rowntree takeover, the so-called 'safer' cigarette, the dangers of roll-on-roll-off ferries, reform of the Official Secrets Act, and environmental pollution. Each programme shared a common theme: an overwhelming desire to embarrass the present Conservative Government and/or 'capitalist' multi-nationals whose desire for profit allegedly ignores the interests and safety of their customers.

Media Monitoring Unit (1990)

The Glasgow University Media Group have been the most consistent critics of what they see as the inbuilt bias in television news coverage. Beginning with *Bad News* in 1976, the research team have produced a series of case studies in which they have subjected television news to a form of content analysis (see chapter 9). In each case, hundreds of hours of news broadcasts are recorded and analysed for the explanations of certain events they offer. The group have particularly focused on industrial relations, and their main conclusion is that strike coverage is biased against workers and trades unions and in favour of management and the government. This is because, first, journalists share certain 'consensual assumptions' about the world which are rarely questioned. In relation to industrial relations, these include: strikes are harmful and disruptive, whereas uninterrupted production is a 'good thing'; management exercises control as of right, whereas workers' industrial actions are often illegitimate; etc.

The second main explanation for biased reporting is that those in power have privileged access when it comes to setting the agenda for reporting news stories. In the case of the 1984–85 miners' strike, this meant that the dominant framework for reporting strike developments centred on two issues: the 'return to work' of those giving up the strike, and the violence used by pickets in confrontations with both police and non-striking miners. Such an emphasis served to undermine the strikers' solidarity as well as public sympathy, according to the Glasgow Media Group, who largely attributed it to the skilful news management employed by the Coal Board and the government. Alternative frameworks for understanding the dynamics of the strike, such as the plan to close pits, and Coal Board and police provocation, were notable by their absence from the main news bulletins.

The findings of the Glasgow Media Group have been challenged, not least by the broadcasters themselves. Hetherington (1985), for example, did research into the coverage of the miners' strike that suggests both the BBC and ITN provided a fair account of events. Any inaccuracy, he feels, is due to the practical constraints under which journalists work, especially having to distinguish facts from opinion within a tight time schedule. Even the Glasgow Media Group acknowledges that current affairs programmes such as *World in Action*, or, in the case of the miners' strike, *Brass Tacks*, do supply the kinds of interpretation for controversial issues which may be absent in news bulletins.

Hetherington is not the only critic who has reached different conclusions to the Glasgow Media Group when studying the same event as covered on television. This could imply that content analysis as a method is not as scientific as it may appear. There are questions not only of how systematic or comprehensive the monitoring of television output is, but also of which criteria are applied to the recorded material. The many possible strategies for interrogating the recordings include investigating the following:

● Which sources are given priority (for example, who is interviewed and where)?
● Which explanations are given priority (e.g. made into headlines)?
● Does the story sequence produce certain meanings?
● What terms of reference (language) are used to describe or label the participants and their actions?
● What point of view is produced by the camera shots?

The dispute between those like the Glasgow Media Group, who assert that all news is constructed and by implication cannot be value-free, and those like Hetherington, who claim that some news is neutral and detached, is tied to how the term 'impartiality' is interpreted. As stated in law, it means broadcasters are not allowed to express a point of view on matters of public policy. This was reinforced by the 1990 Broadcasting Act, so that broadcasters can now be prosecuted if they do not preserve due impartiality on 'major matters' such as political and industrial controversies. In practice, this has come to mean that there should be balanced reporting. This does not necessarily mean equal coverage for all points of view, but those which are thought to reflect existing public opinion.

Hetherington concludes that news broadcasters are mostly fair because he sees them as 'socio-centralist', or positioned within the political and social middle ground, which is shared by a majority of the population. However, who decides on whether or which 'minority' points of view should be granted access to a debate? In the Gulf War, should President Bush's views have been balanced with those of Saddam Hussein? Should the government's views on the need for the poll tax have been balanced by those advocating (illegal) non-payment of the tax? Besides the issue of which views should be legitimately represented, there is the problem of adjudicating on

ACTIVITY 3.1

Record a television news broadcast and choose a news story which involves a degree of political controversy. Find a second treatment of the same story in either radio or the press and subject both to the criteria listed above (substituting photographic images or sound effects, if relevant, for television camera shots).

when broadcasts have been imbalanced in their coverage. Academic differences of opinion point to some of the difficulties involved; there is also the question of how audiences interpret such coverage.

Many of the issues raised in the debate about impartiality are pertinent to the discussion of how the conflict in Northern Ireland has been covered. One critic, Liz Curtis (1984), feels that broadcasters operate a policy of 'hidden censorship'. While stories are not often overtly censored, there is a system of 'checks and balances', which in effect means key positions and points of view, largely Republican, are not represented. One procedure in the BBC is for all Northern Ireland stories to be referred upwards for managerial approval. Consequently, according to Curtis, between 1970 and 1983 as many as forty-four programmes or items were 'banned, censored or delayed', including a video, 'Invisible Sun', being banned from *Top of the Pops*!

A prime source of information for stories in Northern Ireland is the army, who are accepted by most of the news media as pursuing a legitimate objective. The accepted 'enemy' is the 'terrorists'. This raises questions about how the political motivations of those using violence can be explained to audiences. Terrorism has connotations of being irrational, criminal and lacking any legitimacy whatsoever. Attempts made to investigate either the philosophy of members of terrorist organisations like the IRA (as in *Real Lives*, 1985) or whether the security forces have acted illegally (as in *Death on the Rock*, 1988) have met with strong official resistance. *Real Lives* was temporarily banned by the BBC governors, and only shown after re-editing; *Death on the Rock*, about the killing of three IRA members in Gibraltar by British agents, was subject to an enquiry (which subsequently cleared Thames TV, the programme makers).

In 1988, control of broadcasters' coverage of Northern Ireland was extended with a ban on interviews with members of terrorist groups to prevent them being given what Margaret Thatcher called 'the oxygen of publicity'. The interviews could be shown if the subjects' voices were removed and replaced by dubbing or subtitles. The ban had the desired effect in severely restricting appearances of the IRA on television and in other media news reports. Critics of the ban claimed that this meant denying a voice to those people whom the censored groups represented – often legitimately as in the case of Sinn Fein MPs elected by their constituencies. The ban was finally lifted late in 1994 following the IRA ceasefire of that year.

Stereotypes

A stereotype is a label which involves a process of categorisation and evaluation. Although it may refer to situations or places, it is most often used in conjunction with representations of social groups. In its simplest terms, an easily grasped characteristic (usually negative) is presumed to belong to a whole group, e.g. estate agents are insincere, devious and smooth-talking.

In ideological terms, stereotyping is a means by which support is provided for one group's differential (often discriminatory) treatment of another. If black Africans could be represented as uncivilised and savage in the nineteenth century, then slavery and exploitation of blacks by their white rulers could be justified. In contemporary society, old people are frequently portrayed as physically and mentally infirm, asexual and unable to adapt to social change. Such 'ageist' sentiments contribute to a lowering of the social status of the aged, including a lowering of their own self-esteem.

However, stereotyping is not a simple process. Tessa Perkins (1979) has identified many shortcomings in the way that stereotyping is normally assumed to operate:

- stereotypes are not always negative (e.g. 'The French are good cooks');
- they are not always about minority groups or the less powerful (e.g. 'upper-class twits');
- they can be held about one's own group;
- they are not rigid or unchanging (e.g. the 'cloth-cap worker' of the 1950s became the 1980s 'consumerist home-owner who holidays in Spain');
- they are not always false, but can be supported by empirical evidence (e.g. 'Media studies teachers tend to be liberal/left-wing in their politics').

Indeed, Perkins argues that stereotypes would not work culturally if they were so simple and erroneous.

Martin Barker (1989) goes further, to the extent of dismissing the concept of the stereotype as a 'useless tool for investigating media texts'. His first objection is that stereotypes are condemned both for misrepresenting the 'real world', e.g. for reinforcing the (false) stereotype that women are available for sex at any time, and for being too close to the 'real world', e.g. for showing women mainly in the home and servicing men – which many in fact do. However, this example bears out Perkins' point that for stereotypes to work they need audience

ACTIVITY 3.2

Compile a list of ten stereotypes from media material, identifying examples which might be considered to be stereotypical representations. Examine where each of the stereotypes fits the points made by Perkins.

Terrace trendies

A new breed of soccer hooligan — dressed in £800 suits and drinking bubbly at fifty quid a bottle — is replacing the traditional soccer thug.

And you won't catch them wearing scarves, hats or Doctor Marten boots. Instead the new yuppie yobs sport dapper suits by Giorgio Armani. Lager is out too. The new generation of louts quaff Dom Perignon champagne by the crate full. No expense is spared. Unlike their predecessors the terrace trouble makers of today hold down highly paid jobs in the City.

FLICK KNIVES

Flick knives are replaced by filofaxes. The new breed of thug is highly organised. And tattoos are frowned upon. A diamond encrusted Cartier wristwatch is more in keeping with the new image.

Football thugs who dress to kill

MACHETE

With their £250 hand stitched Jermyn Street silk shirts, you won't catch these thugs 'putting the boot in'. They wouldn't want to risk chaffing their made-to-order Italian pig skin brogues, at £300 a pair.

SAMURAI SWORD

And it isn't their style to look for trouble. Indeed with their £500 leather Gucci ties, they don't go to football matches at all. Instead they go out, in their solid gold Dunhill cufflinks and Chinchilla socks at £900 a pair, and eat nouvelle cuisine in fasionable restaurants, or just stay at home in their £2 million converted dockland warehouses, relaxing and listening to their £3000 top-of-the-range Nakamichi CD players, with quadraphonic sound.

Viz, edition 35

Fig. 3.7
Source: © John Brown Publishing Ltd/House of Viz

recognition, i.e. to appear 'natural' and everyday. The ideological process, though, reinforces this 'naturalness' by failing to reveal any contradictions or inequalities in the representation, e.g. that women may feel trapped, undervalued and lacking economic independence in their domestic role.

Barker's second main objection is that the concept of stereotyping implies that it is wrong to see people in categories. Yet within social psychology, it has long been recognised that categorisation is a fundamental cognitive process necessary to make sense of the world. Humans constantly impose structure on events, experiences and people, particularly when faced with only limited information. Thus stereotypical judgements are made by everyone as part of creating order out of everyday life, as well as providing a sense of group identity.

Media representation may serve to inform, reinforce or challenge such stereotypes. This is partly for reasons of economy. Constraints of time and space, plus the desire to achieve rapid audience recognition, mean that stereotypical representations are constructed rather than fully fledged characters with individual identities. This is articulated effectively by Trevor Griffiths in his play *Comedians*, which is about an evening class for budding comedians led by an experienced comedian, Eddie Waters, who rails against the easy laugh achieved at the expense of minority groups:

WATERS (*driving home*): If I've told you once I've told you a thousand times. We work through laughter, not for it. If all you're about is raising a laugh, OK, get on with it, good luck to you, but don't waste my time. There's plenty others as'll tek your money and do the necessary. Not Eddie Waters.

MCBRAIN (*conciliatory, apologetic*): So, a few crappy jokes, Mr Waters ...

WATERS: It's not the jokes. It's not the jokes. It's what lies behind 'em. It's the attitude. A real comedian – that's a daring man. He dares to see what his listeners shy away from, fear to express. And what he sees is a sort of truth, about people, about their situation, about what hurts or terrifies them, about what's hard, above all, about what they want. A joke releases the tension, says the unsayable, any joke pretty well. But a true joke, a comedian's joke, has to do more than release tension, it has to liberate the will and the desire, it has to change the situation. (*Pause.*) There's very little won't take a joke. But when a joke bases itself upon a distortion – (*at* PRICE, *deliberately*) – a 'stereotype' perhaps – and gives the lie to the truth so as to win a laugh and stay in favour, we've moved away from a comic art and into the world of 'entertainment' and slick success. (*Pause.*) You're better than that, damn you. And even if you're not, you should bloody well want to be.

Griffiths (1976)

The dumb blonde

Some of the complexities of utilising stereotyped labels in analysis of media representations can be seen through a consideration of one example: the dumb blonde. A list of the main ingredients for a dumb blonde stereotype might include: blondeness, seductive body language, strong make-up, innocence or naivety, childlike voice, humour and wit, illogical thinking, etc.

The first problem is that not all these ingredients are consistent: childlike *and* seductive; witty *and* simple and empty-headed. In terms of whether the label is descriptive or evaluative, much depends on social perceptions of what kind of female image and behaviour is desirable. To be blonde is often defined as more attractive ('blondes have more fun'), while to be 'dumb' may be seen as both (sexually) appealing (to many men) and undesirable – being considered of low intelligence.

DUMB BLONDE CHARACTERISTICS

Childlike
High or breathy voice, rounded face, wide eyes; deliberate, self-conscious or awkward movements; naive responses, lack of concentration, an emphasis on 'fun' and 'play'; irresponsibility and emotional indulgence.

Inappropriate
Behaviour or appearance showing 'inability' to grasp (or refusal to obey?) rules of conventional (particularly middle-class) social contact. Includes over-dressing, unrestrained voice (volume/pitch) or especially 'excessive' laughter.

Unconventional
Unusual forms of logic, exaggerated gestures, unexpected responses; characteristics, behaviour and desires which do not concur with feminine roles; emphasizing a unique individuality.

G. *Swanson (1991)*

What kinds of judgement may be made about women possessing the above characteristics, individually or in combination?

An examination of specific examples of dumb blonde types quickly reveals variations, which reflect both changes in the way the dumb blonde has been perceived over time and personal qualities brought to the role by individual performers. Marilyn Monroe is often considered to epitomise the dumb blonde, yet her own performances in the 1950s (both off and on screen) clearly accentuated sexuality and seduction (e.g. in the film *The Seven Year Itch*) (figure 3.8). In contrast, Goldie Hawn's film and television performances in the 1970s emphasised the giggly or kooky facets of her personality (figure 3.9). In the 1990s, the dumb blonde is as likely to be the source of parody (e.g. within adverts) as to be represented seriously (although Marilyn in *Home and Away*, the Australian television soap opera, could be said to maintain the essence of the type).

Gender and ideology

Before considering media representations of *gender*, it is necessary to establish what is meant by the term. To be male or

Fig. 3.8
The Seven Year Itch, *1955*
Source: Kobal Collection/Twentieth Century
Fox

Fig. 3.9
Private Benjamin, *1980*
Source: Kobal Collection/Warner Brothers

female can be defined biologically, but 'masculinity' and 'femininity' are socially constructed. This can be demonstrated by both cultural and historical comparison: ideas about what it means to be masculine or feminine vary between societies and change over time, even though there may be some aspects of gender difference which are found virtually universally, e.g. the mother–child bond, and hence are closely linked to biology.

Ideas about gender difference are produced and reflected within language. Both objects and abstract concepts can be seen as gendered. While this applies as part of the grammatical system in other languages like French, in English it is quite selective. Modes of transport – cars, ships, steam engines, etc. – are given feminine labels as if to signify something possessed and controlled by men. Likewise, countries, nations and nature itself are ascribed a female status as representing caring, home and a sense of belonging. In contrast, ultimate power rests with a masculine God, and the word 'man' has been used to represent all humans, as in 'mankind', 'man in the street' or 'man-made'.

'Feminism' is a label that refers to a broad range of views containing one shared assumption – that there are profound gender inequalities in society, and that historically masculine power (patriarchy) has been exercised at the expense of women's interests and rights. This power may be expressed physically, but is more generally reproduced ideologically. Language is seen to be a form of social control in so far as the terms 'masculine' and 'feminine' carry very strong connotations of what is 'natural' for each sex, whether that refers to personal traits (like rationality or emotionalism) or to social roles (like businessman or housewife).

Appearance

One of the strongest cultural values concerning gender difference is that women are judged by their looks more than men. In the world of popular culture this is especially noticeable. When comparing the social attributes of male and female Hollywood film stars between 1932 and 1984, Emanuel Levy (1990) concluded that physical looks and youth were far more important for the female stars (the list of stars being based on box-office appeal). For men, attractive looks were a weak basis for longevity of appeal – indeed, many of the most successful men – Humphrey Bogart, Jerry Lewis and Dustin Hoffman, for example – were anything but handsome.

Associated with appearance was age. The median age for female stars was 27, compared to 36 for men; and many men only achieved stardom after 40, e.g. John Wayne (at 42) and Charles Bronson (at 52). Given the ephemeral nature of youthful attractiveness, it is not surprising that few women stars have been able to sustain their box-office appeal over many years. Those who have lasted longer have tended to possess 'something else' beyond glamour and beauty, e.g. Barbra Streisand's singing voice plus her ability to play career women. The list below shows the number of years the listed actors appeared in the American Motion Picture Poll, a survey of which performers had drawn the largest audiences according to cinema owners and film distributors.

America's most durable film stars (over four years on the poll)

Men				Women	
John Wayne	25	James Cagney	6	Betty Grable	10
Gary Cooper	18	Mickey Rooney	6	Doris Day	10
Clint Eastwood	18	William Holden	6	Barbra Streisand	10
Clark Gable	16	Frank Sinatra	6	Elizabeth Taylor	9
Bing Crosby	14	Sylvester Stallone	6	Shirley Temple	6
Bob Hope	13	Wallace Beery	5	Joan Crawford	5
Paul Newman	13	Marlon Brando	5	Greer Garson	5
Jerry Lewis	12	Lee Marvin	5	Jane Fonda	5
Burt Reynolds	12	Woody Allen	5	Bette Davis	4
Cary Grant	12	Harrison Ford	5	Sandra Dee	4
Spencer Tracy	10	Will Rogers	4	Julie Andrews	4
James Stewart	10	Randolph Scott	4		
Steve McQueen	9	Richard Burton	4		
Dean Martin	8	Sean Connery	4		
Abbott and Costello	8	Charles Bronson	4		
Humphrey Bogart	8	Al Pacino	4		
Rock Hudson	8	John Travolta	4		
Jack Lemmon	8				
Elvis Presley	7				
Dustin Hoffman	7				
Robert Redford	7				

Levy (1990)

What is clearly apparent from Levy's research is the sheer inequality in number of male and female stars, a pattern that shows no sign of changing, and that also applies to other areas of the media like television, where it has been estimated that men outnumber women by two to one within programmes as a whole.

TELEVISION ADVERTISING AND SEX ROLE STEREOTYPING
1 Overview
Men outnumbered women by a ratio of nearly 2:1. The vast majority of adverts had a male voice-over (89 per cent).

ACTIVITY 3.3

Select two male and two female stars from the above list, and, with the help of background research, try and identify what individual qualities may have contributed to their box-office appeal. You will need to consider the kind of image and appeal produced by a combination of personal characteristics, on-screen performances and general publicity.

2 *Physical attributes*

Overall, one half of women were judged to be between 21 and 30 years old, compared with less than one third (30 per cent) of males. Among those judged over 30 years old, men outnumbered women by a ratio of 3:1 (men 75 per cent, women 25 per cent).

In terms of body type, most people were characterised as 'ordinary'. The slim, model or 'ideal' category was applied to only one in ten (11 per cent) men compared with more than one in three (35 per cent) women.

One third (34 per cent) of women were blonde compared with only one in ten (11 per cent) males.

Being 'attractive' (defined as the kind of person who might appear in a clothes magazine) fitted the description for nearly two thirds (64 per cent) of females but under one quarter (22 per cent) of males. One in five (21 per cent) females were judged 'beautiful' (for example, the Cadbury's Flake model) compared with only 4 per cent of males.

The conclusion is that women occupy a decorative role far more commonly than men. In the few examples of women characters predominating, they were almost all for 'personal maintenance' products.

3 *Activities and roles*

Occupation, when given or implied, revealed that men were almost twice as likely as women to be represented in some kind of paid employment (30 per cent of men, 16 per cent of women).

In only 7 per cent of cases was housework shown as the dominant activity for women. However, women were more than twice as likely to engage in household labour as were men (45 per cent of women, 21 per cent of men). Cooking was performed by a greater proportion of men (32 per cent) than women (24 per cent), but when men cook, it is portrayed as a special and skilled activity.

4 *Relationships*

In terms of marital status, most men could not be coded. Although women were more likely than men to be single (19 per cent female, 11 per cent male), they were much more likely to be married (27 per cent female, 18 per cent male). This would explain why their social integration was twice as likely to be with a partner (female 24 per cent, male 10 per cent) as with members of the same sex (11 per cent females, 26 per cent males). Same-sex adverts were most common in adverts for alcohol.

Women were twice as likely both to attract (25 per cent females, 13 per cent males) and to show they were attracted (26

ACTIVITY 3.4

Conduct a content analysis similar to this 1990 research by recording thirty television adverts from different times of the day and coding the content according to the same criteria. Compare your findings to those of Cumberbatch *et al.*

What do you think are the shortcomings of using this method to analyse gender representations in television adverts?

per cent females, 12 per cent males). Moreover, while only 9 per cent of men received some sort of sexual advance, nearly twice as many women (17 per cent) did so. In categorising the gain achieved by characters from the product being advertised, implied sexual success was almost twice as common for women (18 per cent) as for men (10 per cent).

Conclusion

The patterns that emerge lend strong support to the concern that women exist in what is essentially a man's world.

Adapted from research undertaken for the Broadcasting Standards Council by Cumberbatch, et al. (1990)

Looking at women

The objectification of women's bodies in the media has been a consistent theme in analyses of women's representation. Laura Mulvey (1975) argues that the dominant point of view within cinema is masculine, especially where a woman is concerned. The female body is displayed for the **male gaze** in order to provide erotic pleasure (**voyeurism**), and ultimately a sense of control over her. She is rendered a passive object. This tendency is carried to the extreme in pornography, where erotic pleasure from looking is the sole motivation for the production. This issue has spilled over into newspapers in recent years with the growth of the 'pin-up', most notably in the *Sun* on page three. Some feminists feel that these images reinforce a 'fantasy of willingness: the page three girl is waiting "to kiss the next man she sees"' (Joan Smith, 1990).

There is little doubt that sexual behaviour has considerable news value, especially stories involving sexual crime like rape. A survey by Channel 4's *Hard News* research team in the first six months of 1990 found more than six hundred articles on rape in the ten major national daily newspapers, an average of more than four a day. (The *Sun* topped the league, followed by the *Daily Telegraph*.) What concerned the researchers was the way in which rape tended to be misrepresented. Rape victims were stereotyped as either 'good' women who had been violated or 'bad' women who had led men on. Rapists were overwhelmingly portrayed as strangers in the guise of a 'sex fiend' or 'beast', despite the fact that in two out of three rapes the rapist is known intimately by the victim. Regarding the crime itself, many newspaper reports dwelt on the details provided by the

ACTIVITY 3.5

1 From a popular tabloid paper, analyse how women are represented in terms of:
   a the number of stories featuring women as the main subject;
   b the approximate proportion of the overall editorial content (excluding adverts).

2 Identify the main categories of story within which women appear in order of frequency, e.g. borrowed status, sportswomen, etc.

3 Are there any distinctive differences in the photographic images of female and male subjects?

4 Choose one story featuring a female subject and one story featuring a male subject, and examine whether there are any differences in the language used and details provided for each story.

victim under courtroom cross-examination to the exclusion of other details, such as forensic or medical evidence.

The difficulties of dealing effectively with rape in the context of fictional 'entertainment' are very well illustrated by the controversy surrounding *The Accused* (a 1988 film based on a real court case) in which the actual rape itself is left to the climax of the film. Some concern was expressed that the prelude to the rape and some of the camera shots included in the attack might offer some members of the male audience voyeuristic pleasure, even though the film was praised for its overall treatment of the case. (For a discussion of women's responses to *The Accused* see Schlesinger *et al.*, 1992.)

Physical attacks on women have also been the subject of numerous films, often containing a combination of voyeurism, female fear and extreme violence. Notable examples include *Psycho* (1980), *Dressed to Kill* (1980) and *Peeping Tom* (1980). In the last example, the voyeurism of the male killer is itself subject to scrutiny, and he is eventually challenged by a woman who refuses to be intimidated. Indeed, it is not clear that masculine control over women is always a product of the camera's gaze at women. Women playing lead roles in *film noir* in the 1940s often projected power and mystery as well as sexuality, and in the role of '*femme fatale*' were able to exercise control over men. In a pop video by Madonna for her song 'Open Your Heart', she performs in a 'peep show' for a variety of male voyeurs, but the gaze is reversed so that the men are seen through Madonna's eyes – as pathetic and frustrated. Madonna is an example of a growing self-consciousness among female performers who are able to exercise greater control over their look and image.

Looking at men

Conventional approaches to looking at male subjects within the media tend to be limited to acceptable contexts in which traditional masculinity is not threatened. Television sports coverage provides numerous moments of close-ups of male bodies, but this is not given any sexual legitimacy by the camerawork or commentary, despite the fact that there is evidence that female viewers may gain pleasure from such images. Dorothy Hobson (1985) suggests that the strong appeal of television snooker for women is that the players exude a masculinity stripped of unattractive aggression and competitiveness. Until recently, it was only in gay culture that an open display and objectification of

Fig. 3.10

Feature in the Sun. *How equivalent is this coverage of male sexual appeal to tabloid newspapers' representation of females as objects of sexual appeal?*
Source: *Sun*, 10 January 1991

the male body for sexual pleasure was able to flourish. This has become less true in recent years, particularly as more women assert their own sexual desires and men have become more sensitive to how they look (figure 3.10).

Pop music has had many male singers willing to submit themselves to the female gaze, whether in girls' magazines or, more recently, in pop videos. Some have consciously feminised their appearance so as to create considerable ambiguity about their sexual identity, for example David Bowie, Boy George and Michael Jackson. Growing consciousness of the masculine body has also been reflected in advertising, whether it be for aftershave or clothes, and in the rise of men's magazines such as *GQ* and *Arena*. The question also arises to what extent these images are for the male gaze or female gaze (figures 3.11 and 3.12). Audience identification and pleasure are discussed in the next chapter.

Gender roles

In so far as the classical narrative structure in cinema involves a drive towards resolving a problem or disruption posed early on in a story, it could be said that it is the male hero who usually makes things happen and moves the narrative along. More often than not, the female serves either as the reward for the hero's action or as the target of that action, e.g. 'the damsel in distress'. This masculine form of narrative is not confined to cinema, but has been a dominant feature of most areas of popular culture. Meanwhile, women's 'action' is more likely to be confined to the domestic domain, revolving around the search for a man or the care of the family. These have been prominent themes within women's magazines over the years.

> I have argued that women's magazines collectively comprise a social institution which serves to foster and maintain a cult of femininity. This cult is manifested both as a social group to which all those born female can belong, and as a set of practices and beliefs: rites and rituals, sacrifices and ceremonies, whose periodic performance re-affirms a common femininity. These journals are not merely reflecting the female role in society; they are also supplying one source of definitions of, and socialisation into, that role.
>
> *Ferguson (1983)*

Women's magazines could be seen as providing step-by-step instructions in how to achieve womanhood, with two roles being central to that status: 'wife' and 'mother'. Marjorie Ferguson (1983), surveying changes in women's magazines in postwar Britain, identifies two main changes. First, there has been a shift from 'getting and keeping your man' to 'self-help'. This involves 'achieving perfection' (being a better mother, lover, worker, cook, and staying slim) and 'overcoming misfortune' (such as physical or emotional crises). Second, the role of

Fig. 3.11

To what extent do this image and the image in figure 3.12 challenge traditional ideas of masculinity?

Source: Kouros, Yves Saint Laurent

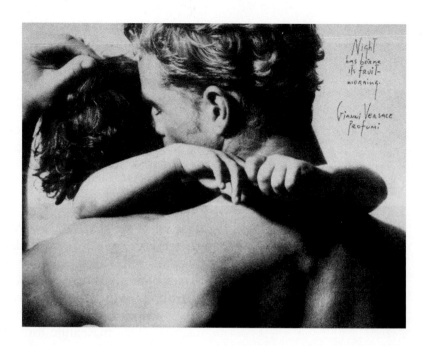

Fig. 3.12
Advert for Gianni Versace perfumes
Source: photograph by Gianpaolo Barbieri

paid worker or 'independent woman' has emerged from the
mid 1970s in magazines like *Cosmopolitan*. Despite these
changes, Ferguson feels the basic message has still prevailed –
that women should identify with a femininity which 'focuses
on Him, Home and Looking Good'. She considers only one
mainstream women's magazine as challenging this orthodoxy,
MS, an American production recently made available in Britain.

Not everyone accepts Ferguson's emphasis on the narrow
agenda constructed by women's magazines. Janice Winship
(1987) stresses the supporting role the magazines play, which is
important given women's exclusion from the masculine world
of work and leisure, and the lack of similar editorial content (in
any depth) in other areas of the media. Even in teenage magazines, readers are being supplied with a broader range of
options than before. For example, *Just Seventeen*, the market
leader at the beginning of the 1990s, tackles problems such as
domestic violence and sexual abuse, as well as offering advice
on how to pursue an independent lifestyle. This shift is
acknowledged by Angela McRobbie (1996), who in an earlier
study had argued that adolescent girls' magazines like *Jackie*
constructed an ideology of 'romantic individualism' in which a
girl's main quest in life was a loving relationship with a man, a
relationship in which she would acquiesce to his demands and
needs. In contrast to the *Jackie* of the 1970s and early 1980s,

Fig. 3.13
Source: More!/EMAP Elan Ltd

McRobbie sees the 1990s *More* as much less idealistic in its representation of relationships with males. Instead, *More* encourages female readers to explore and satisfy their own sexual needs. Alongside a more egalitarian treatment of relationships with males, there is an emphasis on humour and irony rather than romantic escapism (figure 3.13). Judging from the significant number of male readers of women's magazines, there seems to be a latent demand for information and advice on how to succeed in personal relationships and other subjects which are not given space anywhere else in the media.

Strong, independent women are not just a recent phenomenon in the media. In the 1930s, actresses like Bette Davis and Katharine Hepburn specialised in playing tough women who fought to gain acceptance in male-dominated worlds. What is new is the emergence of female lead characters in masculine-dominated genres, such as science fiction and police detective stories. The *Terminator* films, *Alien* (1979) and *The Abyss* (1989) are three examples of action-adventure films with a woman as the 'hero', yet surrounded by males in supporting roles (see figure 3.14: Linda Hamilton in *Terminator 2* (1991)). In television,

Fig. 3.14
Terminator 2: Judgment Day, *1991*
Source: Kobal Collection/Pacific Western/Le Studio
Canal Plus/Lightstorm

the last decade has seen numerous examples of women starring as detectives. *Cagney and Lacey* provided an alternative to the male 'buddy' police action series of the 1970s, such as *Starsky and Hutch*, and in Britain, Helen Mirren played a strong female detective succeeding in spite of male chauvinism in *Prime Suspect*. Moreover, for the last thirty years, there has been a series of independent and assertive female characters in television soap opera. *Coronation Street* has had a succession of such characters, from Elsie Tanner to Bet Lynch. In contrast, strong and sympathetic male characters are notable by their absence in British soaps. Rather the opposite is the case, with most men being exposed for their weaknesses, whether they be emotional instability, vanity or just plain incompetence. Advertising has begun to employ images of women which counter traditional stereotypes of female representation – see figures 3.15 and 3.16.

Masculine representations have also become more varied. The Gillette advertising campaign of the late 1980s/early 1990s

Fig. 3.15
Source: Rainey Kelly Campbell Roalfe

Fig. 3.16
Source: © Coty

displayed a full spectrum of masculine images: father, lover, companion, sportsman, businessman, etc. The role of fatherhood came to prominence in the 1979 Hollywood film, *Kramer vs Kramer*, which made the case for men being capable of taking responsibility for children. In this case, the man (Dustin Hoffman) is successful in breaking away from the traditional masculine role. In the 1980s, the label 'new man' came to be associated with a softening of traditional masculinity and the display of a more sensitive, caring image (see figure 3.12). However, the extent to which this media image reflected a genuine reform of masculine roles is questionable.

Meanwhile, for women it is less clear that seeking independence is the 'right' path. Women seen as turning their back on the family have long been represented as unfulfilled or even punished in Hollywood cinema. Examples of this in recent popular films include *Fatal Attraction* (1987) (a neurotically obsessed

single woman eventually suffers death), *The Hand that Rocks the Cradle* (1992) (a career woman nearly loses her husband and children to the nanny) and *A Stranger Among Us* (1992; a female detective realises motherhood is superior to having a career). Another trend has been the re-emergence of the 'femme fatale', a seductive but dangerous woman, who manipulates men for her own ends. The detective writer played by Sharon Stone in the 1992 thriller, *Basic Instinct* (figure 3.17), is just such a character, with the added twist that she is bisexual with psychopathic tendencies! Barbara Stanwyck represents an earlier example of a femme fatale who seduces Fred MacMurray into murdering her husband for insurance money in the 1944 film *Double Indemnity* (figure 3.18).

Basic Instinct also highlights the homophobic tendency to render homosexual characters as a 'problem' or 'maladjusted'. Lesbians, in the few cases where they appear on the screen, are inclined to be represented as neurotic or childlike, while gay men are invariably seen as camp or butch. There are notable exceptions, for example *Desert Hearts* (1985) and *Another Country* (1984) in the cinema, and increasingly both television and radio have been prepared to include gay and lesbian characters in leading roles, especially within soap opera. A notable contrast to the dominant butch stereotype of the lesbian is provided by the

Fig. 3.19
Loaded, *November 1996. An example of*
sexist stereotyping, or postmodern irony?
Source: Loaded/IPC Magazines

character of Beth Jordache, a young, pretty and feminine lesbian (played by Anna Friel) in Channel 4's soap opera, *Brookside*. She was quickly identified as belonging to a new stereotype, the 'lipstick lesbian'. However, even she followed the conventional fate of lesbians in film and television drama by suffering a tragic fate (committing suicide). Mainstream Hollywood has also found that gay and lesbian heroes/heroines can be good box office in the case of *Philadelphia* (1993) – a 'feel good' AIDS film, and *Bound* (1996), a thriller featuring lesbian lovers.

It is easy to overstate the extent of recent changes in media representations of gender. The 'new man' has been superseded by the 'new lad', a not-so-new masculine culture which celebrates sex, sport and alcohol, albeit with a 1990s inflection of irony and style. *Loaded* magazine (figure 3.19), whose circulation reached over 250 000 two years after its 1994 launch, has successfully managed to tap into this culture. Its popularity in

Fig. 3.20
Source: TBWA Ltd

turn has influenced other men's magazines to resort to employing sexually seductive images of contemporary sex icons such as Pamela Anderson and Ulrika Johnsson on their front cover in place of masculine role models. Within advertising, there has been the re-emergence of the sexually provocative female image as a selling strategy (figure 3.20) – to the consternation of many feminist critics.

In conclusion, it has to be said that much of the above discussion has dwelt on the more dominant patterns of gender representation in the media. These are only patterns, and the more closely media texts are analysed, the more evident the variety of gender representation becomes, particularly once it is recognised that many texts are capable of more than one audience reading. Outside the mainstream, production also flourishes at the margins, which may challenge the dominant ideologies, whether this production be Channel 4's 'Dyke Television' lesbian season or independent films like *My Own Private Idaho* (1991).

Race and ideology

Racial difference is based on biologically determined human variations which have long ceased to exist in the world. Colonisation and interracial mixing mean that there are no simple racially distinctive groups left. However, perceived physical and culture difference is the basis for social definitions of racial or, more specifically, ethnic difference (an ethnic group having a shared culture usually linked to national and religious identity). The belief that other racial/ethnic groups are inferior is at the root of racism/ethnocentrism, and such ideologies can usually be traced back to imperialism and colonialism as a means of justifying the colonial conquest and exploitation of other social groups.

Most western societies today are multicultural, largely as a result of immigration from ex-colonies linked to the demand for cheap labour. How far this multiculturalism is adequately reflected in the media is questionable. Since many of the ethnic minorities in countries like Britain and the USA are not white, the extent to which racism is prevalent in media representations needs to be examined.

Race and entertainment

Having dark skin has long been thought to signify difference not just of colour but also of 'nature' from a white perspective.

Fig. 3.22
Waiting to Exhale, *1995*
Source: Kobal Collection/Twentieth Century Fox

Fig. 3.21
Reservoir Dogs, *1992. Together with*
Waiting to Exhale *(figure 3.22), two*
contrasting representations of masculine and
feminine culture
Source: Kobal Collection/Dog Eat Dog
Productions

The idea that black people are more physically expressive than whites is deep-rooted in western culture. Blacks have been able to achieve most visibility in the media via music and sport, both of which reinforce the notion of 'natural rhythm'. The fact that their disproportionate achievements in such areas may be a product of poverty and the lack of alternative avenues to gain success is rarely considered. In such roles, black people remain unthreatening and only reinforce existing stereotypes. Indeed, early performances by blacks in Hollywood cinema consciously played up to white prejudices – e.g. the eyeball-rolling servant and 'mammy' stereotypes in films like *Gone with the Wind* (1939).

Within both pop and jazz music, much of the creative drive and inspiration has been provided by Afro-American musical culture. Yet most black musicians have been marginalised. More often than not, white versions of black music have predominated, frequently watering down the emotive and sexual power of the music in the process. For example, rock and roll, the new 'youth rebellion' music of the 1950s, was simply black rhythm and blues sung by white performers like Bill Haley and Elvis Presley. This was seen by many American whites as an unwelcome infiltration of their culture by the back door, as they tried (unsuccessfully) to suppress the 'nigger music'.

It is not only in pre-war Hollywood that patronising and demeaning images of blacks were produced. The tradition of 'blacking up' by white singers such as Al Jolson in *The Jazz Singer* was sustained on British television up to 1976 with *The Black and White Minstrel Show*. Likewise, the 'simple' and 'quaint' delivery of English by ethnic minorities has been a constant source or ridicule, as in *It Ain't Half Hot Mum* (Indians living under colonial rule), *Fawlty Towers* (Manuel, the half-witted Spanish waiter) and *Mind Your Language* (a foreign student class containing several crude stereotypes). All of these are 1970s British television sitcoms, frequently repeated over subsequent years.

Much racism in comedy is unconscious, and is rarely perceived as racism by the white audience – 'It's only a laugh.' Indeed, the pleasures of comedy are complex and the reasons for laughing not easily explained by either audiences or comedians. One function served would seem to be the sense of collective identity produced by laughing at 'others' – those who are perceived as different and possibly a threat. Too often, when blacks appear alongside whites in comedies, racial issues become a main focus for the humour, for example *Rising Damp* and *In Sickness and In Health*, rather than these being comic characters who just happen to be black or white. Furthermore, the audience may well end up laughing with, rather than at, the racial bigotry expressed by characters such as Alf Garnett.

Race and social problems

Portraying black people as problems
The main way in which black people are treated in newspapers is as a social problem. Black people are portrayed as constituting a threat to white British society, first through their immigration to this country and then, when settled here, as posing a law and order problem. This is done in a number of ways: through dramatic presentation of stories involving banner headlines and prominent positioning, provocative or damning quotations and statements from people portrayed as authoritative figures, popular stereotypes, repetition of unreliable stories, and the creation and manipulation of popular fears.

Gordon and Rosenberg (1989)

Given that 'bad news is good news' when it comes to choosing stories in the press and broadcasting, it is not surprising that incidents involving violence and crime and ethnic minorities are given prominence. What matters is the explanatory framework offered to enable the audience to understand such stories.

All journalists in the media are bound by a professional code of conduct which forbids racist reporting, and most would claim they simply report the facts without prejudice. However,

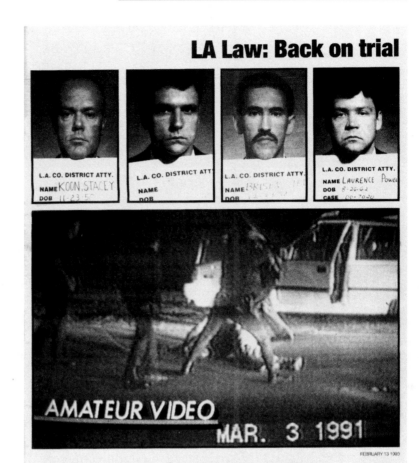

LA Law: Back on trial

L.A. CO. DISTRICT ATTY.
NAME KOON, STACEY
DOB 11-23-50

L.A. CO. DISTRICT ATT
NAME
DOB

L.A. CO. DISTRICT ATTY.
NAME BRISE
DOB

L.A. CO. DISTRICT ATTY.
NAME LAURENCE Powell
DOB 8-26-62
CASE 00-7020

AMATEUR VIDEO
MAR. 3 1991

FEBRUARY 13 1993

Fig. 3.23

In 1991, the police in Los Angeles were captured by an amateur video operator in the process of beating up Rodney King, a seemingly defenceless black man. On the basis of the video evidence, the police were brought to trial, but were (initially) found not guilty, a verdict which sparked widespread disturbances
Source: *Guardian Weekend*, 13 February 1993/Rex Features

unconscious or inferential racism may be detected in the language used to tell a story: 'riots' imply rampaging mobs who need to be controlled; 'uprisings' imply rebellion against injustice. The desire for simple stories with single causes and themes of 'good' and 'bad' often means that long-term causes and morally ambiguous actions may be overlooked or not understood by the journalists themselves (figure 3.23).

The Los Angeles riots of 1992 were widely seen as a rerun of previous examples in inner-city black 'ghettoes' (except this time the initial outcry was based on the broadcast of an amateur home video showing white police officers beating a defenceless black man). What was not revealed was the fact that blacks were now a minority in the inner city of Los Angeles (Hispanics and Latinos were by far the majority), and much of the violence and looting was directed against Korean immigrants who owned most of the stores in the 'ghetto'. Meanwhile, the amateur video images of the police beating have become an icon for racial inequality in the USA and elsewhere, being incorporated into Spike Lee's 1992 film, *Malcolm X*. The broadcast of the video on television helped to bring about a criminal trial of the officers involved and it was the not-guilty verdict which finally led to the riots.

Another example of television images provoking a strong public response can be found in the dramatic television news pictures of famine in Ethiopia during 1984, which stimulated the subsequent 'media event' Live Aid the following summer figure 3.24).

Third World images

Black and white inequalities within western societies are reproduced on a global scale when the inequalities between the affluent minority living in modern industrialised countries like the USA and the poor majority of the Third World are examined. As with the reporting of racial problems within western countries, the causes of problems like famine are grossly simplified for audience consumption, the one difference being that sympathy and pity are offered. Yet the emphasis on aid as a solution only serves to reinforce the sense that Third World countries (especially in Africa) are largely helpless, and depend for their survival on 'our' help; it also obscures the history of colonial exploitation and subsequent economic dependency which have played a significant role in the failure of Third World economies to become self-sufficient.

An alternative to the image of poverty or war is that of the 'exotic' and 'colourful'. Television holiday programmes are

Fig. 3.24
British media at work in a relief camp at Haiya in the Red Sea Hills, Eastern Sudan, in December 1984. People in the camp put the child on the ground for display, aware that publicity for their plight might eventually bring some help.
What are the problems in using images of starving children to highlight famine in Africa and other parts of the world?
What alternative images might be used to represent problems of poverty and exploitation in Third World countries?
Source: photograph by Wendy Wallace

inclined to dwell on these qualities when featuring long-distance tourist packages, complete with a backdrop of the locals' friendly smiling faces and atmospheric native music. An exception to this is BBC2's *Rough Guide* series, which attempted to provide a social and political context within which tourist attractions could be experienced. The 'Singapore Girl' of the airline advert is a reassuring and (sexually) seductive image promising the western male 'service with a smile', effectively effacing the widespread hardship and sometimes sexual

travel

High tea in Sri Lanka

Amid relics of the colonial past, MATTHEW GWYTHER is reminded of Sri Lanka's strife-torn present

What do Tigger Stack Ramsay-Brown MC, Bo Derek, Yuri Gagarin, Noël Coward and Emperor Hirohito of Japan have in common? Answer: they have all stayed at the Galle Face Hotel in Colombo, lucky people.

Sitting with a sundowner on the 128-year-old veranda bar, surrounded by colonnades of white-washed columns and acres of marble floor, watched over by attentive staff in spotless white sarongs and pressed linen tunics with gold epaulettes as the sun descends into the Indian Ocean – what better way to come to one's senses after being canned up for the 5,500 mile long haul from London?

Sri Lanka has a growing supply of modern beach hotels, particularly down the coast to the south of Colombo, but it is the older establishments dating from colonial times, such as the Galle Face, that offer something truly out of the ordinary. If you would rather have a fan and a mosquito net than an air-conditioner, birds flying around the lobby rather than piped music, mild eccentricity rather than smooth, five-star efficiency, then the Galle Face is your kind of place.

In fact the Galle Face does have air-conditioners, but they are of the old fashioned free-standing variety rather than the noisy through-the-window type. The chairman of the Galle Face, Cyril Gardiner, ensures that nothing disturbs the GFH's unique combination of 'Yesterday's charm and Tomorrow's Comfort'. The King Emperor Suite has a living room in which, once you had put the antique furniture to one side, a five-a-side football match could be conducted. The suite is thought to be one of the largest in the world but can be yours for the absurdly low price of £100 per night. (The rate is actually £200 but all the GFH's rooms are currently at a long-term 50 per cent discount.)

Dotted all over the GFH are maxims and polite entreaties on plaques: 'Please don't smoke in bed because the ashes we find may be yours' and next to the lift, 'Please walk down. It's good for you. Two flights only.' The Thoughts of Chairman Cyril are even carried over to the hotel's headed notepaper, which proclaims, 'Share wealth, grow food, conserve water, keep fit, don't gamble.' The effect is to envelop guests in a kindly paternalism which is highly seductive. The maître d' wears an oversized pair of Chaplinesque shoes without socks as he bounces over the teak floorboards to take your order – Scotch broth or brown Windsor soup to kick off. The GFH is one of the few establishments left in the world where you will find a menu section headed 'Farinaceous Dishes'. ▷

Main photograph: lotus carriers personify Sri Lanka's lush beauty. **Right:** ancient sites abound, such as Polonnaruwa's rock temple. **Centre:** K. C. Kuttan began working at the Galle Face Hotel (far right) in 1942

62

Fig. 3.25

A magazine feature on Sri Lanka. How does this travel feature represent Sri Lanka to the potential western tourist?

Source: *Observer Magazine*/Panos Pictures

exploitation faced by many young women in South East Asian countries like Thailand and the Philippines (figure 3.25).

As society changes, so do the media. The shift in how black people in the USA have been represented in Hollywood films reflects wider social changes in American society. In their own way, the films themselves will have contributed to the changing perceptions of black and white identities in the USA.

The pre-war period was characterised by the use of black characters as light relief – as song-and-dance acts or wide-eyed simpletons. These patronising images drew heavily from white perceptions of black life in the southern plantations. In the post-war period, a growing number of films reflected the growing consciousness of racial injustice, particularly the segregation policies of the south. In *The Defiant Ones* (1958), two convicts, one black and one white, are symbolically chained together and forced into cooperating in their bid to stay free. The film starred Sidney Poitier, who later appeared in numerous films in which he challenged, and usually overcame, white prejudices, for example *In the Heat of the Night* (1967) as a black detective working with a white police force in the southern states of the USA.

It was not until the 1970s that films began to feature predominantly black casts and thus move closer to capturing black American culture. However, the emphasis was on large doses of violence and sex, in a bid to be commercial. The cycle which began with *Shaft* (1971) (figure 3.26) came to be known as 'blaxploitation' films. While containing some ethnic authenticity (e.g. the argot), and often reflecting a sense of black pride, the films also could be said to reinforce white perceptions of the black man as aggressive gangster or drug dealer.

A few black actors, such as Eddie Murphy and Richard Pryor, became 'stars' in the 1980s. Nevertheless, most of their roles could be seen as 'safe' for white audiences in the sense that they could be said to be 'deracinated'. This means that they tended to play isolated black characters whose black culture is used only as an entertaining decoration, for example Eddie Murphy's street-talking, wisecracking detective in *Beverly Hills Cop, Beverly Hills Cop II, 48 Hours* and so on.

At the start of the 1990s there was a surge in American films made by and starring blacks. This was precipitated by the commercial success of *Do the Right Thing* (figure 3.27) and *House Party* in 1989 (both made over $26 million profit), and the growth in young (mostly male) black film-makers eager to represent the many facets of black culture largely ignored by

Fig. 3.26
Shaft, *1971*
Source: Kobal Collection/MGM

Fig. 3.27
Do The Right Thing, *1989*
Source: Kobal Collection/40 Acres and a Mule

white-dominated Hollywood. Some of the films contained a political agenda and ethnic assertiveness derived from hip-hop and rap music culture. However, the freedom for such film-makers as Spike Lee to pursue these themes is contingent, as always, on continued success at the box office.

Growth in visibility on television

In both American and British television, there has been a steady growth in the number and range of ethnic representations on the screen: news readers (Trevor McDonald), chat-show hosts (Oprah Winfrey) and police series (*Hill Street Blues*). One development has been the emergence of the ethnic minority sitcom.

In the 1970s, early examples were *The Jeffersons* (USA) and *The Fosters* (UK). Beginning in 1984, *The Cosby Show* has been the most successful, but not without some controversy. In many respects, it represents a recoding of some of the traditional black stereotypes shared by white Americans. The family is a strong and cohesive unit with the perfect father figure. Both parents are successful professional workers (doctor and lawyer) who, although affluent, are not frivolous in their consumption. There is a strong emphasis on the value of education (particularly in the spin-off series *A Different World*, set in a black college). From time to time, the theme of racial pride is foregrounded with references to black history and culture, and yet the family is clearly well integrated into a multiracial America.

Critics of *The Cosby Show* argue that it fails to address questions of racial or class conflict, and that its representation of black culture and lifestyle is very superficial and idealised. The series is seen as reassuring white American audiences that the American Dream is alive and well, and that black people can be successful through hard work and discipline. (See p. 147 for audience responses.) On British television, ethnic minority representation in soap opera has been a contentious issue. *Coronation Street*, Britain's most successful soap opera, has failed to feature a black character in a prominent role throughout its history (beginning in 1960), despite being set in an area which would in reality be multicultural. In contrast, *EastEnders* has included a range of ethnic minorities (Bengali, Turkish, West Indian, etc.) and has tackled the issue of racism, albeit as a transient 'story'.

Christine Geraghty (1991) proposes that there have been three strategies adopted by soaps in handling black characters. First, there is 'the exotic' – the one-off character who is used to add drama to a story, but whose blackness does not become an issue itself. For 'the singleton', Geraghty's second category, being black means being used as a vehicle for stories about racial issues, which tends to produce a separate and marginalised status for the character. Finally, there is 'incorporation', where blacks share similar problems to those of other members of the community, and clearly belong to that community as insiders. This allows the characters to be much more varied in their representation, and to be active in developing the narrative.

With the mainstream media failing to represent ethnic minorities adequately, such groups have found their interests more effectively served by independent media production. The growth of incremental and community radio stations has included ethnically based services such as Sunrise Radio (for Asians in

West London) and Choice (for the Afro-Caribbean community in South London). Newspapers for Britain's black population include *The Voice* (figure 3.28). Independent black media production in the USA has been gaining strength, particularly in response to a growing black middle class. An early success story was the Tamla Motown record label headed by Berry Gordy, which provided strong support for artists such as Stevie Wonder and Diana Ross. More recently, labels like Def Jam have helped

Fig. 3.28
Source: The Voice 27 August 1996

rap and hip-hop acts to flourish. This is in stark contrast to the British music industry, where record companies (almost exclusively controlled by whites) have been accused of failing to develop black talent (with the possible exception of Island Records, for whom Bob Marley recorded).

Independent television producers catering for ethnic minority audiences in Britain do have two channels (BBC2 and Channel 4) that are committed to creating space in their schedules for such groups. Consequently, there has been a variety of programmes targeting Afro-Caribbean and Asian audiences, including an Asian soap, *Family Pride*, a sitcom, *Desmond's*, and *Badass TV*, an entertainment show presented by Ice T!

Realism

Chapter 2 discussed how the media *mediate* reality via various recognised codes and conventions. Because of the intervening technology, it is impossible to gain first-hand direct experience of the world via the media, no matter how 'transparent' their representation of reality. Even live television coverage of events, such as a football match, involves continuous selection through the choice of camera perspective as well as interpretation via the accompanying commentary and discussion which anchor the meaning of the pictures.

Part of the process of creating meaning is the degree to which we, the audience, can recognise and identify with what is being portrayed – the media text's credibility or realism. We expect what we see, listen to or read to have some connection with our own lives and experiences and the world we inhabit, or to appear to be based upon some sort of recognisable reality of the world 'out there'. This then helps us to identify and understand the text and its meaning. We often judge how successful this illusion or story is by measuring the text against our own experiences, our own 'situated culture' and biography. What is 'real' therefore can become a subjective and controversial concept, where a text that one person perhaps considers to be realistic may not be considered so by someone else with another perspective. A programme that describes all football fans as 'hooligans' may appear convincing to someone who knows nothing about football fans except what they read or see in the media, but to someone who has been supporting a football club for many years this may seem to be a very unfair and one-sided portrayal.

ACTIVITY 3.6

Record a short segment (of 10–15 minutes) of a live television broadcast of a football match and list the range of camera shots used to represent the action. Say why you think these particular shots have been chosen. In what ways do you think the television viewing experience of the game contrasts with the experience of actually seeing the match from within the ground?

In assessing the realism of a media text there is no single measure which can be applied. Four distinctive criteria have been identified as contributing toward a sense of realism. Firstly, there is the *surface realism*. This means 'getting the details right'. For example, a period costume drama should have the characters wearing the clothes appropriate to that period, and the houses should not be adorned with modern accessories like television aerials or satellite dishes. Considerable expense is often incurred ensuring that such period drama precisely recreates the right environment, such as in the popular police series *Heartbeat* set in the 1960s complete with steam trains and British motorbikes (although the programme's signature tune is from the 1950s!).

The second criterion refers to the *'inner' or emotional realism* of the characters and their motivation. This allows the audience to identify with the situation and characters portrayed and in particular 'feel' or 'share' the emotions that are an essential part of the story-telling process; for instance, the sadness in tear-jerkers like *Love Story* or the fear and suspense in films like *Jaws* or *Jurassic Park*.

A third criterion of realism concerns the logic or *plausibility of the plot* or characters that appear appropriate to the text's particular terms of reference. Viewers often complain if well-established characters in soap operas suddenly shift their typical behaviour pattern and act 'out of character'. In their search for publicity and higher ratings, some British soaps like *Brookside* and *Emmerdale* have introduced a high quota of intensive dramatic incident such as a plane crash, murders, and drug-based crime, which have led to criticisms that these incidents undermine the sense of realism achieved by the soaps' claim to represent ordinary everyday lives and situations. Related to this is the notion that there is some degree of consensus as to the nature of 'reality' and 'truth'. Media texts which challenge certain 'commonsense' or taken-for-granted assumptions, such as the honesty and integrity of the legal and medical professions, may be rejected by audiences as implausible or 'far fetched'.

The fourth criterion of realism refers to the employment of technical and symbolic codes that correspond with those recognised and expected by the audience. We have learned to accept the use of music in the background as a 'mood enhancer', but only so long as it is discreet. Audience or 'canned' laughter is the norm for situation comedies. These codes and conventions change over time, especially as technical advances shift our perceptions of what seems 'real'. Originally, silent films were accompanied by a live piano player who musically 'signalled' the climax of a scene or speech, or the development of the narrative was indicated by captions. The actors wore heavy make-up and performed very theatrically. Contemporary cinema audiences now expect to experience a radically different form of realism made possible by sophisticated technological innovations such as the use of computer-generated special effects and 'surround sound' theatres. Indeed, the marketing hyperbole would lead us to believe we are on the verge of experiencing 'virtual reality'.

Therefore, it is important to recognise that audiences do not apply a unified set of standards to differing media texts in terms of their realism. Depending on the respective media form or genre, we apply varying *modality judgements* of the realism of a text. Although we know that science fiction and cartoons are not 'real', we suspend disbelief and adjust our perceptions in accordance with the accepted codes and conventions of such media categories. Consequently, an animated cartoon comedy like *The Simpsons* is able to achieve a level of realism equal, if not superior to, television situation comedies which employ 'real' human subjects. However, if the generic codes are not adhered to with some degree of consistency, then audiences may well reject the realism of the text. This is particularly apparent when genres are blended together and it is not clear which mode of realism is dominant. For example, *Coprock*, a 1980s American television police series, alienated audiences by incorporating song and dance numbers into the gritty police narrative. More successful in juxtaposing codes from several genres, such as soap opera, gothic horror and murder mystery, was *Twin Peaks* (figure 3.29) which became a cult television serial. Its constantly shifting modes of realism mean it could be defined as a surreal text.

This kind of generic playfulness is a feature of the postmodern tendency found in many contemporary media texts. It can also be detected in the ironic, parodic reworking of conventional genres such as the television chat show (*Mrs Merton, Dame Edna Everage*, etc). Audiences are increasingly invited to witness the processes of media construction such as in the regular shots of the production crew in the *Big Breakfast Show*, the effect of which is to seemingly expose the illusion of realism (although such 'exposure' is still carefully controlled). Nevertheless, the dominant aesthetic is still one in which media construction is disguised and the audience (usually very willingly) is drawn into an ensuing seamless reality.

Fig. 3.29
Twin Peaks, *1989*
Source: Kobal Collection/Lynch/Frost
Productions

News and documentary realism

Despite the differing modes of media realism, audiences generally accord most credibility to representations of reality produced in broadcast news and documentaries. This credibility is rooted in the perceived accuracy and reliability of the reporting (its factuality). As mentioned earlier, legally, broadcasters are required to be impartial in covering news and current affairs, which means refraining from favouring one particular point of view or exercising any editorial bias. Whether this impartiality is actually achieved is controversial and is discussed over the following pages. Nevertheless, British broadcasters clearly do wish to be seen as providing an authoritative and truthful news service, whose high status is emphasised through its occupation of key positions in the prime-time television and radio schedules.

In terms of representing the 'truth', documentaries are generally accorded the highest status. To 'document' a subject implies keeping a factual record for future reference. However, the founder of British documentary film-making, John Grierson, argued that documentaries should combine information with education and propaganda. He oversaw the production of over forty documentaries on aspects of British life in the 1930s and 1940s. The idea was to engineer social reform by highlighting some of the deprivation and hardship endured by working-class people – as in *Coalface* (1935), as well as providing a degree of poetic sensitivity to ordinary lives – as in *Night Mail* (1936).

It wasn't until the 1950s that the more detailed and naturalistic approach to documentary film-making developed, particularly in France where the style was labelled *cinéma vérité* – literally 'cinema truth'. The intention was to observe and record the reality of everyday life as it happened without the usual organisational planning and structured direction. The approach was made possible by new lightweight mobile cameras with synchronised sound recording.

Meanwhile, by the 1960s, television had become the principal medium for documentary production and the genre was typified by the use of an authoritative presenter and/or voice-over, recorded interviews with experts and ordinary people, and visual 'evidence' via location shots, archive film, photographs, etc. The seamless editing and smooth narrative flow of such documentaries, which are still prevalent in today's television, contribute to creating a sense of irrefutable truth and authenticity which disguises the editorial values and choices which shape the making of

ACTIVITY 3.7

Examine how television and radio create the impression that their news is factual/objective and authoritative by analysing:

(a) the title sequences – including the music, graphics, images, and voice-over announcement;

(b) the newsreader – status, appearance, accent, mode of delivery and camera framing;

(c) the studio set – the furniture, lighting, backdrop and props.

such documentaries (figure 3.30). On the basis of Robert Fisk's discussion, list what you think are the relative strengths and weaknesses of television documentary realism and the realism of newspaper/magazine feature reporting.

During the past twenty years the *cinéma vérité* style of documentary film-making has become increasingly popular in television. Known as **fly-on-the-wall**, this approach represents the subject apparently unmediated by a film crew, a presenter or reshooting. Those participating in this type of documentary tend to speak for themselves, and their words or actions are apparently merely recorded and observed, not reflected upon or mediated by a presenter. Examples include Paul Watson's *The Family* (1974), a six-week series focusing on a working-class family living on a council estate in Reading, and Roger Graef's *Police* (1982), also shot in Reading.

In helping to define the distinctive fly-on-the-wall approach, Roger Graef listed certain 'ground rules' to be applied in the production. These included:

- filming events exactly as they happen;
- agreeing in advance the specific subjects to be filmed;
- showing the edited version to the participants, but only to ensure any factual errors may be corrected.

However, in practice there is variation between documentary teams, and critics have argued that while seeming more 'natural' and unmediated, these documentaries are subject to considerable editorial control during post-production. With a shooting ratio of up to fifty hours of recorded video to one hour broadcast, the onus is on the editor to generate as much dramatic interest and entertainment as possible. For example, in Paul Watson's *Sylvania Waters* (1993), a series built around Noele Donaher, a *nouveau riche* Australian woman and her family, Ms Donaher complained that the producers had unduly focused on her domestic arguments and highlighted her casual racist remarks about black/Asian Australians. To many Australians it did seem as though the British production team had set out to reinforce certain negative stereotypes about them.

Sylvania Waters also employed a title sequence and incidental music which were similar to those used in Australian soap operas. Although this was meant to be ironic, it reflects the growing convergence and overlap of documentary and drama on television. As early as 1966, Ken Loach had applied *cinéma vérité*-style filming to a drama about homelessness, *Cathy Come*

Michael Duffield had worked for *Panorama* and made a host of prizewinning documentaries. And his heart was devoted to the theme of the films we found ourselves making: the despair and contempt and sometimes hatred felt by growing numbers of Muslims towards the West. It was he who had refused to stop filming when Israeli troops repeatedly tried to arrest us on the streets of Gaza. It was he who found the brave little Palestinian family of Mohamed Khatib outside Jerusalem – whose tiny home was to be bulldozed away so that the Jewish settlement surrounding it could be further enlarged.

But there was something about Michael's approach towards films – the approach of all directors – that troubled me. It was not the theatricality I identified in documentary film-making – cruelly and wrongly in Michael's eyes – but the refusal to acknowledge it. I was to learn a lot – "not enough" I hear Michael remark as he reads this – about film-making. And I learnt to admire what it can achieve. I also learnt to be deeply suspicious of it.

"If you try to tell that story to my 82-year-old Mum, she'll be so confused she'll fall off her chair," Michael would say each time a Palestinian or a Bosnian had finished a long and complicated political explanation on film. Michael's 82-year-old Mum – a lady whom I did not have the honour to meet – began to dominate my life. The moment a UN officer tried to outline the problems his soldiers experienced in Lebanon with the "de-facto forces" of Israel's "South Labanon Army allies", the second an Egyptian fundamentalist embarked on the history of his movement, I experienced a clear picture of Michael's 82-year-old Mum crashing to the floor. She wouldn't understand the detail, was what Michael was saying. Just as viewers would get the "wrong idea" if I wrote this article. I found this a strange argument.

If it was not shaped for television, reality had to be made digestible. It had to meet certain requirements, the first of them being simplicity. And it also had to show what the director regarded as the reality, even if the occasional item of furniture tended to contradict this. [...] We had, in effect, to move the furniture in order to accommodate the "reality" of the camera. Just as we had to shoot and re-shoot street scenes to accommodate the different camera angles needed to establish the verisimilitude of the film. [...] "Don't look at the camera" became a kind of law. Because, of course, the camera is not supposed to be there. In hospitals in Gaza and Sarajevo, in the Chatila camp, in the "ethnically cleansed" villages of northern Bosnia, we were always telling people not to look at the camera.

Michael returned to his maternal explanation "How do I explain to my 82-year-old Mum that you're driving through the streets of Beirut if I haven't got a clear shot of you driving there?" he asked. "If you're going to Baalbek, my 82-year-old Mum wants to see you going there. I can't afford eight film crews lining the road from Beirut to Baalbek in the hope that just one of them manages to get a good shot of Lord Fisk as he passes on his way. So we have to ask you to do it like this." [...]

But what really concerned Michael, I think, was the idea that by discussing the technical side of the film, we would be revealing the camera's drawbacks and limitations, the failure rather than the success of the technology in which we – making these films – expected the public to believe. How else can one explain the problems we had in choosing those who would or would not appear in the films? In Beirut and Gaza and Sarajevo, we would talk to crowds of Lebanese, Palestinians or Bosnian Muslims, seeking out not only those who had a story to tell and who were prepared to tell it – but who could tell it simply, and preferably in English. Given the fashion for dubbing, Michael's decision to allow men and women to speak in their original language with subtitles was honourable. But the process of seeking out those whom we wanted to appear in the film involved their ability to speak coherently in their own language, let alone in English. We judged them on their performance in private conversation. Or, as Michael would say on such occasions, we would "audition" them. [...] Men and women who looked and sounded convincing could appear in the film. Those who did not rarely got before the camera. In television terms, this made obvious sense. But not in journalistic terms. [...]

An equally important issue arose when we wanted to include Arab fighters in the Bosnian film. We found a young Algerian guerrilla who had been wounded in the battle for Sarajevo and who was happy to meet me and chat about his life. But he refused to appear on film. His story appeared at the top of a page in the *Independent* but is not even mentioned in the film. He would not appear on television; so it could not acknowledge his existence.

Even when I talked to Muslims who spoke both fluently and passionately, the sheer expense of filming – we were using real film-stock, not video – became a burden. In newspaper interviewing, you let people talk for as long as they like, make them feel relaxed and at last they'll answer all your questions. But at £20 a minute, we could not allow our television interviewees – whether they be Shia women, Palestinian doctors or Israeli families – to ramble on. I would have to interrupt, interject, cut into their monologue to bring them back to the point. [...]

But when it was used spontaneously, Steve's camera possessed an awesome power – an "authenticity", Michael called it – which I had to acknowledge. Here Michael came into his own. In Gaza City, Israeli troops were shooting down demonstrators and repeatedly ordering us to turn off the camera; which Michael refused to do. One of the Israelis walked right up to us with his hand outstretched towards the camera lens, saying in Arabic and English: "Yalla [Go] ... Finished for today. Take your things and go away. It's finished. It's over. It's a closed military area." The reason for his fear of the camera – which we did not know as we filmed him – was that he and his men were vandalising and then blowing up the homes of 17 Palestinian families.[...]

And that, of course, is the point. "The film is cut for the power and duration of the pictures," Michael wrote to me before I scripted my commentary for the series. "...the commentary should be written to fit – not the other way round." In writing journalism, we are in control. In film journalism, we can decide what we want to record, but the camera dictates the way in which we do it. We are, in a sense, prisoners of the technology.[...]

Michael took a more aggressive view. "Why should you claim that films are artificial? This is part of the myth of written journalism. When you send your report to the *Independent*, they put it into type, they put a box and lines round it, they choose a picture for it which you didn't take. And you have to 'clean' quotes because people don't speak in proper sentences. You have to put in full stops and commas and paragraphs. That's what we're doing when we have to use lights or film you in your car. Like your reports, film has to end up as a language. Film is a compromise between words and realism."[...]

Fig. 3.30

Source: *Independent on Sunday Review*, 5 December 1993 Robert Fisk

Home. The documentary feel of the film created a stronger sense of realism and contributed to its strong impact on audiences (which in turn contributed to the establishment of Shelter, the charity for the homeless). More contemporary drama employing a *vérité* naturalism includes *NYPD, This Life* and *ER*. *NYPD* and *This Life* use hand-held cameras, which seem to react 'spontaneously' to the characters and situations, natural atmospheric sound effects which sometimes make the dialogue difficult to follow, and jump-cut editing. The intention is to achieve a sense of voyeurism, of watching a slice of 'real life' policing on the streets of New York.

Reality television

A growing range of media texts have emphasised that they feature 'real life' and 'real people'. The term 'reality television' has been increasingly applied to all those programmes which seemingly allow people access to appear as themselves, utilising actual or sometimes reconstructed scenes, often made possible by the growth in availability and technical sophistication of the video camcorder. In practice, the label embraces a wide variety of programmes which feature people in a range of different roles:

- as professionals employed in the police and emergency services via either dramatised reconstructions of real events (*999* or *True Crimes*), or real video action recorded by video journalists and/or the police (*Police, Camera, Action!*);
- as subjects of entertainment or humour in spontaneous or contrived situations (*You've Been Framed* or *Candid Camera*);
- as subjects within a professionally produced fly-on-the-wall or *vérité* documentary (*Culloden: A Year in the Life of a Primary School*);
- as amateur directors offering a personalised documentary of an event or way of life (*Video Diaries* and *Video Nation*).

Despite the use of real people and authentic action, many critics have argued that much of this 'reality television' fails to be genuinely informative or revelatory. At its worst, video footage of ordinary people's personal experiences or emotions may be exploitative in pandering solely to audience voyeurism, helping to achieve high ratings at relatively low expense. Andrew Goodwin (1993b) is scathing of the claims of those programmes featuring the police and emergency services which he says cite their educational and investigative value as an excuse for depicting graphic details of real or reconstructed crimes and disasters. He also argues that the viewer is placed

ACTIVITY 3.8

Choose two distinct examples of 'reality television' and consider:

(a) How and why the people were chosen as subjects for the programmes.
(b) From whose point of view the subjects have been represented.

firmly on the side of the police and rescue workers, and that the optimistic, upbeat message reassures viewers of the good work performed by such workers.

In contrast, the *Video Diaries* format has been praised for genuinely facilitating the empowerment of ordinary people via the video camcorder. The main reason is the transfer of editorial control from the professional to the amateur (the video diarist). However, as pointed out by Peter Keighron (1993), professional mediation still plays a significant part in the production process. Firstly, in deciding who has the opportunity to make a video diary Keighron notes that the BBC's Community Programme Unit, the originators of *Video Diaries*, favours a left/liberal political perspective in choosing the diarists. Furthermore, in overseeing the editing of *Video Diaries*, the producers are prone to intervene to ensure the programmes are not too egocentric or self-indulgent.

Further reading

Baehr, H. and Dyer, G. (eds). 1987: *Boxed In: Women and Television*. Pandora.

Bignall, J. 1997: *Media Semiotics: An Introduction*. Manchester University Press.

Daniels, T. and Gerson, J. 1990: *The Colour Black*. BFI.

Geraghty, C. 1991: *Women and Soap Opera*. Polity Press.

Glasgow University Media Group. 1985: *War and Peace News*. Open University Press.

Goodwin, A. and Whannel, G. (eds). 1990: *Understanding Television*. Routledge.

McDonald, M. 1995: *Representing Women*. Arnold.

McNair, B. 1995: *An Introduction to Political Communication*. Routledge.

O'Sullivan, T. and Jewkes, Y. (eds). 1997: *The Media Studies Reader*. Arnold.

Pines, J. (ed.). 1992: *Black and White in Colour*. BFI.

Ross, K. 1996: *Black and White Media*. Polity Press.

Stead, P. 1989: *Film and the Working Class*. Routledge.

Strinati, D and Wagg, S. (eds). 1992: *Come On Down: Popular Media Culture in Post War Britain*. Routledge.

Tasker, Y. 1993: *Spectacular Bodies: Gender, Genre and the Action Cinema*. Routledge.

Winship, J. 1987: *Inside Women's Magazines*. Pandora.

4

Audiences and reception

In chapter 1, it was emphasised that the media play a prominent part in people's everyday lives. Given the time spent by audiences consuming the media, it is hardly surprising that much speculation and debate has focused on the exact nature of the relationship between audiences and media output. In reviewing the progress of this debate, it is possible to identify distinct phases of audience analysis. What makes these phases distinct is the degree to which the balance of power and influence is attributed to the media, in terms of production and content, or to the audience, as receiver of that production.

Phase 1: from mass manipulation to uses and gratification

Mass manipulation model

Concern about media 'effects' on audiences, especially harmful influences, has been expressed almost continuously since the turn of the century. The idea that the media are a powerful social and political force gathered momentum in the 1920s and 1930s, when the political propaganda of first Soviet Russia and then Nazi Germany seemed capable of seducing and persuading ordinary citizens in ways not thought possible prior to an age of mass media.

Audiences came to be seen as comprising a mass of isolated individuals vulnerable to the influence of the powerful new media such as cinema and radio – hence the label 'mass manipulation'. Propaganda of a different sort, advertising, was later perceived in the same way by writers such as Vance Packard.

Fig. 4.1
Source: © Steve Bell

His best-selling book, *The Hidden Persuaders* (1957), claimed to expose some of the ways advertisers were manipulating ordinary people to consume goods, unaware of the persuasive techniques in question.

Children and teenagers have consistently been considered susceptible to the harmful influence of popular entertainment. From time to time, moral panics have been generated, often orchestrated via the media, especially tabloid newspapers. Each medium in turn has been accused of corrupting young people, whether it be Hollywood crime films in the 1920s, pop music in the 1950s or 'video nasties' in the 1980s. The heightened social concern and anxiety associated with moral panics often stimulates more stringent controls over the media to protect 'the innocent' from any damage. In the case of video nasties, the 1983 Video Recordings Act was passed. This introduced strict regulation of videos via the British Board of Film Classification. However, concern over young people's access to violent videos rose again in the early 1990s. A number of highly publicised crimes of aggression in which a violent film was implicated (most notably the linking of the James Bulger murder with a video, *Child's Play 3*) resulted in further restrictions being enacted in 1994. The British Board of Film Classification (BBFC) now has to take into account:

> any harm that may be caused to potential viewers or, through their behaviour, to society by the manner in which the work (film) deals with: criminal behaviour, illegal drugs, violent

behaviour or incidents, horrific behaviour or incidents, or human sexual activity.

Soon after this tightening of the regulation there was considerable controversy surrounding the granting of a certificate to Oliver Stone's film *Natural Born Killers* (1994), which was accused of glamorising violence and precipitating copycat murders in America and France.

Television has also been singled out by many critics as being responsible for anti-social and psychologically injurious outcomes. Marie Winn's book *The Plug-in Drug* (1977) is typical in its claim that children watch television in a 'trance', their eyes having a 'glazed vacuous look'. Using the drug analogy, with its notions of addiction and passivity, is a familiar ploy, most recently employed in the context of video games. Consequently the mass manipulation model is sometimes referred to as the hypodermic-needle or magic-bullet theory because it implies such a direct and linear influence.

Despite these continuous alarms about the power of the media over audiences, much of the concern has been based on flimsy evidence. In the case of *Natural Born Killers*, the BBFC followed up the alleged ten cases of copycat killings and in only two cases had the accused seen the film in question, and these two involved one with a record of violent crime, and another who had repeatedly expressed his intention to commit the murders prior to seeing the film.

Effects research

The last sixty years have seen a mountain of academic research investigating the potential links between media content and audience thinking and behaviour. As early as the 1930s, the Payne studies in the USA assessed the effects of cinema on audiences, and concluded that films did in fact cause harm to children by disrupting sleep, encouraging delinquency and crime through imitation, and so on (Peterson and Thurstone, 1933).

One media production alone, Orson Welles' *War of the Worlds* broadcast on radio in 1938, seemed to demonstrate the potential power of the media. As many as one million Americans (who either failed to hear the intro or tuned in during the programme) believed their country was being invaded by Martians, as a result of the play being produced in the form of a spoof 'live' news report with eye witnesses, sound effects, etc. Their trust in radio 'news' caused considerable panic and hysteria. Although

Halloween spoof riles BBC viewers

THE BBC yesterday refused to disclose how many calls had been received from angry viewers after a spoof Halloween-night TV documentary proved too realistic.

But a spokesman conceded there had been a "substantial reaction", with many people convinced the gory scenes in Saturday night's Screen One special, Ghosts, were real.

Most callers simply rang to ask if the 90-minute show — starring Michael Parkinson, Sarah Greene and Mike Smith, all playing themselves — was a genuine documentary.

But BBC staff said many others were angry at realistic scenes including an interview with a young girl apparently possessed by spirits and with blood dripping down her face.

"People thought it was real," said one.

"We've had anything from being sworn at to people who say they are going to write to the director-general."

Last night the BBC insisted the programme had been clearly billed as a drama in the Radio Times and other listings magazines, and in an on-air announcement before the start.

In the show, Michael Parkinson played the anchorman of a Watchdog-style current affairs programme and Mike Smith hosted a spoof phone-in on ghostly manifestations. Meanwhile, a mock outside broadcast team investigated "Britain's most haunted house" — a council house in Northolt, west London — where the fictional Early family had complained of paranormal experiences.

These included objects flying around rooms, dark figures and mysterious puddles — all owing a great deal to the BBC's special effects department.

Fig. 4.2

Source: Guardian, 2 November 1992. © Guardian

contemporary audiences might be considered more sophisticated and sceptical, spoof productions continue to fool large numbers of people, a recent example being 'Ghostwatch', broadcast during Halloween night on BBC television in 1992 (figure 4.2).

To pursue the issue of media effects, let's discuss two areas of considerable debate: children and political persuasion.

Children

Most of the research claiming proof of direct effects, especially on young audiences, is rooted in behaviourist psychology or social learning theory. The assumption is that children learn through conditioning. 'Good' behaviour is rewarded, and this is reinforced by seeing positive adult role models. Supporting evidence cited frequently centres on experiments in which children are exposed to a media stimulus and their response is then measured. An example is Bandura and Walters' 'Bobo Doll' experiment of 1963, in which children were shown films of adults acting aggressively towards the doll, behaviour later imitated by the children when left alone with the dolls. Such experiments have been criticised for failing to reflect normal viewing conditions under which the media are consumed. Children do not usually encounter such a strictly controlled media diet, and the aggression shown may well result from a desire to please the experimenter. Furthermore, children can distinguish between real and simulated violence both in media content and in their own play.

Other psychologists, drawing on developmental psychology, have instead emphasised how the media, particularly television, affect cognitive development. While this is a complex and multifaceted subject, much of the work stresses the active learning which accompanies media consumption. Marie Messenger Davies' book, *Television is Good for Kids* (1989), describes many positive learning outcomes which have been identified in various academic studies. These include: the development of television literary skills, such as understanding visual narrative, editing conventions, etc.; improved memory of events due to visual aids, which also stimulate imagination; being able to differentiate different degrees of realism (so-called 'modality judgements') across narrative forms; the acquisition of knowledge, understanding and practical skills; and not least the play value, usually involving social games in which favourite television programmes are 'remade' or re-enacted.

These claims need to be qualified on the grounds that psychological frameworks of research, whether behaviourist or developmental, often lack an adequate account of the social context. Children's response to the media will vary according to social group membership such as family, class and gender. Television viewing needs to be seen as only one form of social learning within the immediate and broader cultural environment, including other forms of media. Little empirical work has been undertaken on the ideological 'effects' of media representation, such as gender or ethnic stereotypes, on children.

Political persuasion

One of the most influential studies of media effects on audiences was *The People's Choice* in 1944, which focused on political persuasion. Lazarsfeld, Berelson and Gaudet set out to discover what influence the media exerted over voters during the American presidential campaign. Using a panel sample over a period of six months, they concluded that voting intentions were very resistant to media influence. This was due to a combination of individual cognitive and wider social processes. A majority of the sample already had well-formed political attitudes, and this pre-disposition was reinforced through selective exposure, whereby people read newspapers which were likely to support existing views. Even when confronted with politically challenging ideas, these could be resisted via selective perception – filtering the message to fit existing attitudes, or interpersonal discussion. The research identified opinion leaders – people whose political views were trusted – and suggested that they were a much more signif-icant influence than the media, whose information the sample could mediate via a process the authors called the *two-step flow*. The overall conclusion was that the media's 'effect' on the audi-ence was one of reinforcement rather than change.

Although subsequent research in Britain supported these findings, the potential for media influence on political behav-iour seems to have increased in recent years as the strength of voters' loyalty to one party has declined. At the same time, the British tabloid newspapers have become more politically parti-san (especially in support of the Conservatives). W. Miller's research (1992) into the British general elections of 1987 and 1992 identifies a disproportionate swing towards the Conservatives during the campaigns among readers of the Conservative-supporting tabloids (see the *Sun*'s front cover at figure 3.6a on p. 81).

Nevertheless, it seems clear that as an agent of direct social and political influence, the media's power is quite modest (figure 4.3). Persuading consumers which brand of jeans or breakfast cereal to buy pays dividends for the advertiser, but advertising which attempts to alter more deep-rooted and com-plex forms of behaviour, such as drug-taking or forms of sexual practice, has been found to have minimal impact (figure 4.4).

In summary, instead of the media being seen as an all-powerful force working directly on the audience in isolation, during the 1960s there emerged the view that:

Fig. 4.3

Newspaper readership and voting intentions, UK 1996 (percentages). What does this table reveal about the influence of newspapers over their readers' political judgements?
Source: NOP, Jan–Dec 1996

	Con	Lab	Lib	Other	Don't know (or won't vote)
Daily Mirror	11	65	8	2	14
Daily Star	14	56	7	4	19
Sun	21	46	9	5	19
Daily Express	42	26	11	4	17
Daily Mail	37	28	13	3	19
Daily Telegraph	44	21	13	4	18
Financial Times	38	27	12	4	19
Independent	14	49	19	5	13
Guardian	6	66	14	4	10
The Times	34	33	14	4	15

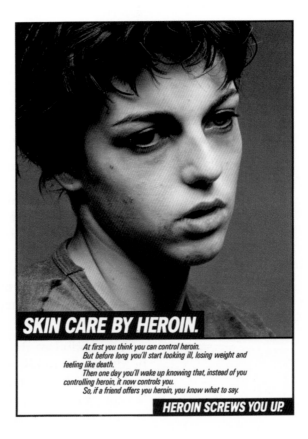

Fig. 4.4

This 1987 anti-heroin poster failed because the boy proved too appealing for some girls, who wrote in for the poster

Source: Central Office of Information

- audiences are active in interpreting media content;
- audiences comprise individuals whose membership of social groups should not be ignored.

Therefore, the concept of 'effect' has come to be seen as problematic within media studies because:

- it implies some degree of audience passivity;
- there can be confusion between short-term effects, such as during elections, and long-term ideological effects of a much more subtle but profound nature, e.g. on gender identities;
- it is virtually impossible to measure media effects – the media cannot be isolated from all the other potential influences at work within society.

Consequently, there was a shift in perspective within audience research, represented by James Halloran's (1970) much-repeated phrase: 'We must get away from the habit of thinking in terms of what the media do to people and substitute for it the idea of what people do with the media.'

Uses and gratifications

The basic tenet underlying this new approach to studying audiences was that individuals actively consume and use the media in order to meet certain needs. Blumler and Katz (1974) undertook group discussions in which subjects' statements were listed and categorised, and consequently listed four broad needs fulfilled by viewers' watching of television:

1 Diversion – a form of escape or emotional release from everyday pressures.
2 Personal relationships – companionship via television personalities and characters, and sociability through discussion about television with other people.
3 Personal identity – the ability to compare one's life with the characters and situations within programmes, and hence explore personal problems and perspectives.
4 Surveillance – a supply of information about 'what's going on' in the world.

The notion of the media providing resolutions to certain needs and pleasures continues to inform much contemporary audience research. Blumler and Katz's concept of 'diversion' or 'escape' was developed by Richard Dyer (1977) in relation to cinema and television entertainment. In trying to answer the question of how 'escapism' works, he offers three suggestions of how real life is suspended or temporarily erased. First, it may be obliterated in so far as the content completely ignores reality, as within dance, music, magic, slapstick comedy, etc. Secondly, it may work via contrast. Here, the reality provides a pleasing

---

ACTIVITY 4.1

Undertake a survey of uses and gratifications by:

1 recording informal conversations about specific programmes or genres with a sample of television viewers;
2 listing the most common motives mentioned for viewing such programmes;
3 clustering together similar statements under a collective heading (e.g. for quiz shows: excitement appeal, basis for social interaction, etc.);
4 presenting the list of headings to a further sample as a self-report survey allowing for a graduated response to each heading (e.g. from 'very much' to 'not at all' or 1 to 5).

positive alternative for the audience, e.g. within soap operas like *Coronation Street* which supplies a sense of close community. Finally, Dyer identifies incorporation, where reality is shown to be better than imagined, thus creating a sense of optimism. An example of this might be the television telethon promoting a sense of a caring and altruistic society. (For a further discussion of Dyer's scheme see p. 145)

Nevertheless, 'uses and gratifications' as an analytical model for understanding audiences does have its limitations. At its crudest, it implies that audiences comprise individuals whose conscious search for gratification elicits a media response which supplies their needs. This *laissez faire* market concept overlooks the extent to which audience needs are partly a product of media supply (learning to enjoy what is available), and the social context from which the audience originates, e.g. class and ethnic subcultures.

Another criticism is that of the tendency to concentrate solely on why audiences consume the media rather than extending the investigation to discover what meanings and interpretations are produced and in what circumstances, i.e. how the media are received. These issues form the focus of *reception theory*, discussed below.

Phase 2: textual determination to audience reception

Audience positioning

During the 1970s, a new theoretical framework emerged which could be applied to analysing the relationship between media content and audiences. Drawing heavily on semiology and structuralism, media texts were seen as structured according to well-defined codes and conventions (see chapter 2 for a fuller discussion). Rather than recognising the polysemic nature of such texts, some writers chose to emphasise how audiences (or subjects) were positioned by the text.

Much of this theory was applied to film, and in Britain was articulated most strongly in the academic journal *Screen*. The main thrust of the argument is that the structure of film language produces a perspective or point of view for the audience. The spectator is drawn into the flow of the narrative through various strategies of camera work. One example is the shot/reverse shot, where the perspectives of two characters are interchanged so we as an audience are able to 'stand in' for each subject and identify with their view. Another example is the glance/object shot. Here we are shown a close-up of a character as he or she looks off screen. A second shot reveals what the character can see and thus simultaneously situates us in his or her position. Through the editing of camera shots and perspectives the spectator is able to gain a privileged view of events, and yet unconsciously has been 'sewn in' to the narration, a process referred to as 'suture'. It is as if we are invisible onlookers, an effect most films never deny, in order to produce a sense of witnessing objective reality.

As noted on p. 94, it has been argued by writers such as Laura Mulvey that the spectator perspective achieved by dominant Hollywood cinema is masculine. The camera shots and editing conventionally reproduce a male gaze or subject position, with the woman as object. Given strong characterisation in association with this process of spectator suture, the sharing of the character's experiences and emotions will lead to effective audience identification. This works powerfully when identification and attraction are combined in a sexual or romantic context.

Mode of address

This refers to how a media text 'speaks to' its audience. It thus helps to establish a relationship between media producer and audience. It implies a less determinate outcome than audience positioning and identification. To quote Martin Barker (1989), ' "Identification" suggests that we are spoken for. "Dialogue" suggests we are spoken to.'

Cinema

Spectators are rarely acknowledged within Hollywood films. The dominant mode of address is impersonal. There is little sense of an author or identifiable source beyond the film credits. That does not mean there are no points of view supplied; indeed, some films contain a first-person voice-over to guide us through the story. Nevertheless, there is normally a sense of reality being pre-existent, 'out there', waiting to unfold before us.

A kind of variety of address may be achieved through differing narrative viewpoints: it is possible for the audience to know more than the characters, the dominant perspective of popular cinema; sometimes audiences know only as much as one or more of the characters, e.g. in many detective films; and finally, some films deny audiences as much knowledge as the characters.

Occasionally, the impersonal mode of address is broken when characters look into the camera to speak to the audience, thereby undermining the illusion of transparent 'reality'. This is most common in comedy, where the audience is invited to share a character's feelings towards events. An early example is that of Laurel and Hardy, where Hardy's looks of exasperation with Laurel are frequently directed to the camera. Recent examples from Hollywood include *Kuffs* (1991) and *Ferris Bueller's Day Off* (1986).

Television

Robert Allen (1987) has characterised television viewing as centrifugal, in contrast to cinema, where watching a film is centripetal. By this he means that whereas the cinema screen draws in the audience to witness another world, television's programmes are directed outwards to viewers:

> In those instances in which contestants are selected from the studio audience, they are plucked from among 'us'.
>
> By splitting off one or more characterized viewers from the rest of the studio audience, the game show sets up a circuit of viewer involvement. When Bob Barker asks the contestant to guess how much the travel trailer costs, we almost automatically slip into the role of contestant, guessing along with him or her. If we guess correctly along with the contestant, the bells and whistles go off for us as well as for him or her. But we can also distance ourselves from the contestants and take up the position of the studio audience as they encourage the contestants and, on *The Price Is Right*, at least, shout out what they believe to be the correct guess. As we watch a game show, we constantly shift from one viewer position to another, collapsing the distance between contestants and ourselves as we answer along with them, falling back into the role of studio audience as we assess contestant prowess and luck (or lack thereof), assuming a position superior to both when we know more than they. The viewer-positioning strategy of the game show encourages us to mimic the responses of the characterized viewer in the text.
>
> *Robert Allen (1987)*

Two factors help to explain this situation. First, television texts tend to refuse resolution – the news, soap opera, sitcoms, etc., are continuous, daily or weekly. In conjunction with this, viewing is intermittent or casual, and thus television needs to 'work' to attract our attention. Apart from obvious strategies like strong music, studio applause and laughter, etc., one prominent feature is the use of direct address. The viewer is openly acknowledged. Allen considers this to be a rhetorical mode of address in that television is 'pretending' to speak on behalf of the viewer. Presenters, reporters, comedians, and so on look directly into the camera as if in a face-to-face conversation, yet of course it is only one-way communication. Hence the use of phrases like 'we', 'you the viewer', 'what the viewer at home wants to know'.

It is usually assumed that the audience comprises members of a family situated within the living room as part of a wider community or nation of viewers. This is underlined by the family viewing policy which regulates against explicit language or controversial 'adult' material being represented before nine o'clock in the evening. The sense of a national audience tends to be inscribed within representations of certain annual rituals, such as the Queen's Christmas address to the nation or sporting occasions like the FA Cup Final. Moreover, in international competitions, like the World Cup or Olympic Games, British commentators and presenters shift from a detached and neutral form of address to a more partisan and emotional delivery when describing British participants. As television audiences become more fragmentary it seems likely that different types of viewer will be more specifically addressed. Already, there is clear variance in the modes of address contained in breakfast television, late-afternoon children's television and late-night weekend programmes. Furthermore, differing channels may adopt distinctive styles of delivery in accordance with both their perceived audience and the organisation's sense of its own identity: Channel 4's mode of address is frequently different from ITV's. This latter point is particularly pertinent when considering radio.

Radio

When the BBC maintained a monopolistic situation as Britain's only national radio service, it adopted a mode of address which was designed to reflect its public service ideals – to be authoritative and set high standards. This meant speaking a form of English which used correct standard grammar, had no regional accent and was delivered in a formal tone – what came to be called 'BBC English' or (more technically accurate) 'received pronunciation'. Only gradually in the post-war period did this verbal style decline and leave space for more varied forms of address, for example on Radio 1.

With the shift away from national to local and regional radio services, and the conscious targeting of distinctive audiences, there is a greater need for radio's mode of address to fit its perceived audience identity. The use of accent and vernacular language, the tone and pace of delivery and the structuring of a dialogue with the audience (e.g. via the phone-in programme) are all differing ways by which the listener is addressed. One telling clue to a station's sense of identity and consequent mode of address is its choice of signature jingle, which is repetitively broadcast between programmes or segments within programmes. These jingles are often given as much thought and attention as the rest of the station's schedule.

Newspapers and magazines

The front page or cover of newspapers and magazines is the key to creating both a sense of identity and a point of contact with the potential reader:

> On any magazine stand each women's magazine attempts to differentiate itself from others also vying for attention. Each does so by a variety of means: the title and its print type, size and texture of paper, design and lay-out of image and sell-lines (the term the magazine trade aptly uses for the cover captions), and the style of model image – but without paying much attention to how a regular reader will quickly be able to pick out her favourite from others nestling competitively by it. Cover images and sell-lines, however, also reveal a wealth of knowledge about the cultural place of women's magazines. The woman's face which is their hallmark is usually white, usually young, usually smoothly attractive and immaculately groomed, and usually smiling or seductive. The various magazines inflect the image to convey their respective styles – domestic or girl-about-town, cheeky or staid, upmarket or downmarket – by subtle changes of hairstyle, neckline and facial pose...
>
> There is one other important and defining characteristic of this cover image: the woman's gaze. It intimately holds the attention of 'you', the reader and viewer... The gaze is not simply a sexual look between woman and man, it is the steady, self-contained, calm look of unruffled temper. She is the woman who can manage her emotions and her life. She is the woman whom 'you' as reader can trust as friend; she looks as one woman to another speaking about what women share: the intimate knowledge of being a woman. Thus the focus on the

ACTIVITY 4.2

Compare the mode of address adopted in the following:

1 the different breakfast television services offered on BBC, ITV and Channel 4;
2 the different news programmes broadcast on BBC Radios 1 to 5 and your local ILR station(s);
3 quiz/game shows on radio and television.

ACTIVITY 4.3

With reference to Janice Winship's analysis of how women's magazine covers vie for readers' attention, compare the mode of address employed by three different women's magazine covers.

face and the eyes – aspects which most obviously characterise the person, the woman – suggests that inside the magazine is a world of personal life, of emotions and relationships, clearly involving men and heterosexuality, but a world largely shunned by men. This is all women's territory.

Janice Winship (1987)

Broadsheet newspapers can be distinguished from tabloids in Britain by their more impersonal, formal and detached mode of address. The tone is subdued and measured, in contrast to that of the emotive 'loudness' of papers like the *Sun* and the *Daily Mirror*. Even here there are important differences. As described by Peter Chippendale and Chris Horrie (1990), the *Sun* under Rupert Murdoch cultivated a sense of the 'cheeky cockney' who, while happy to stick two fingers up at the establishment, was keen to show it was speaking on behalf of its readers. It continues to hail its readers whenever possible through encouraging participatory action or gestures, including various xenophobic stances towards foreign 'enemies' like Argentina or the EU.

As with radio, the more specialised the target audience, the more distinctive will be the mode of address. Some magazines, like those representing computer interests, will incorporate a style and argot which exclude access to those without the necessary knowledge and expertise.

Encoding–decoding

Parallel to the work of those privileging the ways in which media texts position audiences was the contribution made by members of the Centre for Contemporary Cultural Studies in Birmingham under the leadership of Stuart Hall. His own encoding–decoding model, discussed below, was very influential in examining the relationship between text and audience (figure 4.5).

To some extent, the encoding process tends to contain a sense of textual power at work. Using a hegemonic theoretical framework, Hall argues that media texts such as television programmes contain dominant ideological discourses. This is due to the fact that media producers' own professional routines and practice contain certain assumptions and ideas about how programmes should be made (the 'relations of production'). They draw agendas and meanings – 'definitions of the situation' – from the wider society, which are ideological in nature (the 'framework of knowledge'). Finally, television's own codes and

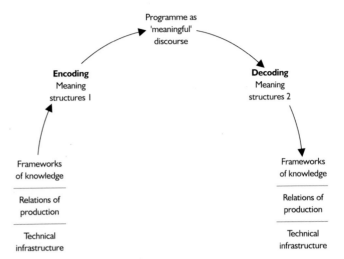

Fig. 4.5

Source: S. Hall (ed.), *Culture, Media, Languages*, Hutchinson, 1980

conventions are employed to complete the encoding process, whose effect is to naturalise or make transparent the meaning of the programme for the audience (to deny its own ideological construction).

However, because the communication is achieved in a coded form – i.e. it is polysemic – there is no guarantee that the audience's decoding (how they make sense of the programme) will 'fit' or be consistent with the encoded meaning. Despite this possibility, polysemy does not equate with there being a plurality of possible interpretations. Instead, Hall argues that texts are structured in such a way that they contain a dominant or preferred meaning which limits the scope for different audience interpretations. The more closed the text, the more obvious is the preferred meaning. Thus an advert whose images are heavily anchored by rhetorical language will be 'read' with considerable consistency by audiences, whereas the relative openness of a television soap opera may make the 'preferred meaning' more problematic.

The concept of '**preferred meaning**' has been subject to some criticism. The main objections raised are as follows:

- Preferred meanings are more applicable when analysing factually based texts like news reports or television documentaries. Fictional narrative is more likely to contain competing perspectives and values.
- It is not clear whether preferred meanings are a property of the text (they are there whether we see them or not), something identified by 'expert' analysis, or that which is agreed

by most members of the audience. Ultimately, who decides what is the preferred meaning?

● Are hegemonic values so dominant that professional practice within the media cannot undermine and challenge such ideologies through producing a 'progressive' or radical text?

Despite these problems in acknowledging that the audience plays a key role in producing the meaning of media texts, Hall's encoding–decoding model is a significant shift away from the overdetermined subject as represented in some of the theory found in *Screen* magazine, discussed above. Hall's model identifies three types of audience decoding:

1 A *dominant hegemonic* position is established when the audience takes the full preferred meaning offered by the text.
2 A *negotiated* position is established when there is a mixture of adaptation and opposition to the dominant codes.
3 An *oppositional* position is established when the preferred reading is understood but reconstructed drawing on alternative values and attitudes (figure 4.6).

It is possible to include a fourth audience response – that of *aberrant decoding*, where the text is read in a deviant and largely unanticipated manner, the preferred reading not being recognised.

Fig. 4.6
Jill Posener's book features the work of graffiti artists who specialise in producing political messages, especially on advertising billboards
Source: J. Posener, *Spray It Loud*, Pandora, 1982

Hall's encoding–decoding model is essentially a theoretical construction, but it helped in redirecting attention as to how audiences interpret media texts.

Reception theory

'The unity of a text lies in its destination not its origin' (Eco, 1981). Eco's famous quotation is a recognition of the fact that whatever an author may intend when writing a text, it is the reader's interpretation which really matters in terms of the end result. During the past ten to fifteen years, considerable research, largely of an ethnographic nature, has gone into uncovering what meanings audiences produce from media texts and under what conditions.

The active reader

The concept of audience identification has been reviewed as a result of some of these audience studies. Total audience identification rarely occurs while audiences are engaged with media narrative. Instead, there is likely to be a constant shift between *implication* – when the audience imagines how they would behave in the situation represented – and *extrication* – the release from that involvement. What helps to prevent over-involvement is a sense of critical distance brought to the proceedings, for example judgements made about how 'real' the story is, or the quality of acting.

In writing about children's responses to *EastEnders*, David Buckingham (1987) concluded that they were 'by turns deeply involved, amused, bored, mocking and irreverent', and regularly moved between these positions. This is expressed in another way by Ien Ang (1985), in writing about women's pleasure in watching *Dallas*: 'The "flight" into a fictional fantasy world is not so much a denial of reality as playing with it.' This 'playing' with reality in soap operas may include direct responses to the characters and episodes (e.g. sending letters) not because reality is confused with fiction, but because the audience has chosen to treat the serial as 'real' in order to gain more pleasure.

Cultural competence

In 1978, David Morley investigated how different audience groups (largely based on economic class) decoded (made sense of) a television current affairs magazine programme, *Nationwide* (Morley, 1980). While he found differences that in part fitted Hall's encoding–decoding model – of dominant, negotiated and oppositional readings – much of the response failed to fit.

This was, first, because additional social variables like gender and ethnicity were at work, and, second, because for many of the sample the programme either was irrelevant or failed to make much sense. Morley later reflected that it is more appropriate for audience research to recognise the knowledge, experiences and taste which different people bring to their media usage: what has been called **cultural competence** or **cultural capital**. It is a key concept, as it helps to explain varying audience preferences and pleasures. As Richard Dyer (1977) has argued, this means that the decoding model based on agreement or opposition to encoded ideologies needs to be replaced by one that recognises audience enjoyment or boredom. This in turn opens up space for audience readings of texts which are unanticipated or alternative to any presumed preferred reading, as will be seen in some of the research reported below.

However, before considering differential readings of media texts it is important to recognise that audiences' consumption of the media is often markedly patterned according to social factors such as gender, age, class and ethnicity (figure 4.7).

Gender preferences

Various studies have confirmed that males generally prefer factual programmes (news, current affairs and documentaries), sport, action-based narrative where there is a minimum of dialogue and emotion (for a discussion of 'masculine' versus 'feminine' narrative see p. 97–101) and realist fiction. David Morley (1986) found that men often disapproved of watching fiction on the grounds it was not 'real life' or sufficiently serious. They were consequently inclined to define their own preferences as more important. It is clear that large numbers of males do watch 'feminine' programmes such as soap opera, but to admit as much seems to present a threat to their sense of masculinity.

These observations were also echoed in Gray's research of women's use of video, based on interviews with thirty women she contacted via a video library in Yorkshire. All the women took pleasure in texts which focused on personal relationships, believable characters and a strong story. Men were perceived as disliking texts in which emotions were openly displayed.

'Love Story ... I've seen that about half a dozen times, I think it's just as good, no matter how many times you watch it – it can still make you cry. Men find them soppy, don't they? I think probably because they're frightened that they might

	Total attendances (millions)	Age (%)						Sex (%)		Social class (%)	
		7–11	12–14	15–17	18–24	25–34	35+	Male	Female	ABC1	C2DE
1991											
Robin Hood: Prince of Thieves (PG)	6.026	14	— 19 —		23	18	26	53	47	58	42
Home Alone (PG)	5.099	14	— 23 —		29	15	19	49	51	51	49
Terminator 2 (15)	4.536	–	–	–	36	31	16	60	40	52	48
Silence of the Lambs (18)	4.453	–	–	–	37	31	32	53	47	59	41
1992											
Hook (U)	5.344	20	9	6	21	24	20	45	55	52	48
Peter Pan (U)	2.273	29	6	5	15	29	16	41	59	50	50
Howards End (PG)	0.979	4	5	4	12	27	48	49	51	74	26
Batman Returns (12)	4.212	–	12	11	35	23	19	58	42	53	47
JFK (15)	2.784	–	–	6	35	28	31	60	40	56	44
Cape Fear (18)	2.860	–	–	–	46	26	28	57	43	48	52
1993											
Beauty and the Beast (U)	4.532	22	7	5	15	23	28	37	63	51	49
Jurassic Park (PG)	14.223	15	9	7	19	20	30	50	50	52	48
The Fugitive (12)	3.876	–	7	8	34	26	25	50	50	52	48
The Bodyguard (15)	7.230	–	–	9	32	31	28	46	54	48	52
Bram Stoker's Dracula (18)	3.337	–	–	–	44	34	22	50	50	56	44
1994											
Aladdin (U)	7.233	20	9	6	16	23	26	41	59	55	45
The Flinstones (U)	7.783	22	11	6	14	24	23	49	51	50	50
Mrs Doubtfire (U)	7.848	5	9	8	21	25	32	45	55	55	45
Philadelphia (12)	4.046	–	4	12	31	27	27	54	46	69	31
Four Weddings and a Funeral (15)	7.957	–	–	7	24	26	43	43	57	70	30
Carlito's Way (18)	1.054	–	–	–	38	38	24	65	35	68	32
1995											
The Lion King (U)	9.775	20	10	6	15	17	32	41	59	54	46
Little Women (U)	1.601	11	7	6	15	15	46	24	76	67	33
Casper (PG)	6.110	27	12	6	12	19	24	46	54	48	52
Batman Forever (PG)	8.095	10	10	11	23	23	23	61	39	55	45
The Madness of King George (PG)	2.292	–	1	2	13	27	57	53	47	81	19
Dumb & Dumber (12)	3.937	–	14	15	36	19	16	63	37	52	48
Die Hard: With a Vengeance (15)	4.311	–	–	12	28	32	28	62	38	63	37
Muriel's Wedding (15)	2.253	–	–	9	22	25	44	35	65	66	34
Braveheart (15)	3.918	–	–	6	27	30	37	55	45	58	42
Pulp Fiction (18)	4.330	–	–	–	43	34	23	65	35	60	40

Fig. 4.7

Profiles of cinema audiences for selected mainstream releases: by age, sex and social class, 1991–95. What factors may account for the different social profiles of audiences for these films?

Source: Cinema and Video Industry Audience Research (CAVIAR)

actually feel some little bit of sympathy or feeling … men don't like to show their emotions very much, do they? (Barbara)

Gray (1992)

A further distinction Gray made was that of education. She found that women with a minimum experience of education (i.e. leaving school between ages 14 and 16) were much more likely to be critical of their own tastes, using phrases like 'soppy' or 'silly', whereas those women with experience of higher education were more inclined to retain a critical distance from what were perceived as more 'trashy' or 'trivial' media texts.

In terms of narrative themes, Gray summarised the contrast in responses between male and female preferences (as reported by the women) as follows:

Male	**Female**
heroic	romantic
public	domestic
societal	familial
physical	emotional

These divisions cut across traditional 'masculine' and 'feminine' genres, so that women could enjoy a war film which

Programme type	Female percentage of mentions	Male percentage of mentions
Drama	67	31
Drama series/specials	32	14
Chinese opera	26	8
Foreign drama	2	4
Movies	3	2
War dramas	1	3
Foreign movies	1	0
Historical drama	1	0
Sports	4	35
Sports (all)	2	27
Kung-fu	2	8
Information	10	25
News	5	16
Educational/TVU	3	3
Travel	1	3
Documentaries	1	1
Language	1	1
Political	0	0
Light entertainment	19	9
Variety	11	5
Children/cartoon	2	1
Animal shows	2	1
Crosstalk	1	1
Game shows	1	0
Music shows	1	1
Comedy	1	0
Totals	100	100

Note: * excludes children 11 years old and younger

Fig. 4.8

*China: family members' favourite TV programme types**

Source: J. Lull (ed.), *World Families Watch Television*, Sage, 1988

Fig. 4.9a

Our Price video promotion. What criteria have Our Price employed in their selection of videos for female and male audiences? (See also p. 144)

Source: Our Price Video

strongly featured a character's emotions (rather than actions). Nevertheless, it is fair to say that gender thematic preferences are closely linked to particular film and television genres – even on a global scale (figure 4.8).

Christine Geraghty (1991) argues that there are four elements which explain the appeal of so-called 'women's fiction' – a label embracing soap opera, romance and melodrama:

Fig. 4.9b

Our Price video promotion. What criteria have Our Price employed in their selection of videos for female and male audiences? (see also p. 143)

Source: Our Price Video

1. Black Robe

Bruce Beresford's stunning film about one man's mission to help save a tribe living in the hostile wilderness of seventeenth century North America.
Cert 15

2. Annie Hall

Woody Allen's autobiographical "nervous romance", which has won four Oscars, including Best Picture. An intelligent adult comedy which incisively comments on contemporary social issues. Starring Woody Allen and Diane Keaton.
Cert 15

3. The Accidental Tourist

Based on Anne Tyler's novel, with a challenging script. Stars William Hurt, Kathleen Turner and an Oscar-Winning performance by Geena Davis.
Cert PG

4. The Darling Buds Of May

Comedy from the series adapted from H.E. Bates' popular stories, featuring television's favourite family, the Larkins. Stars David Jason and Catherine Zeta Jones.
Cert PG

5. The Shape Challenge

A unique programme, containing both a diet and exercise plan, to help you shape up and lose inches. Devised by RSA qualified Libby Roberts.
Cert E

6. The Man Who Cried

Catherine Cookson's romance set against the background of the Depression. Abel Mason conducts a desperate search for love and happiness in relationships with four women.
Cert PG

7. Jennie Garth's Body In Progress

The star of "Beverly Hills 90210" introduces her personal fitness plan, using low-impact body toning, and a careful diet.
Cert E

8. French And Saunders 3

The first three episodes from the comedy duo's third series, with over twenty-five sketches, including the terrific "Star Test" sketches with Sonia and Bros.
Cert PG

9. Egypt - Land Of Ancient Wonder

Visit Cairo, travel along Egypt's lifeblood the Nile, and see the monumental pyramids of Giza and the mighty Sphinx. All this and more in the comfort of your own home.
Cert E

10. Sting - Ten Summoner's Tales

The eleven songs in this new video, performed at Sting's home in Wiltshire, make up his new album. The video includes the latest single, "It's Probably Me".
Cert E

11. So You Want To Be A Model?

A step by step guide to modelling, made in association with Elite Premier, one of the world's top model agencies. This will show you what it takes, but more importantly how you can get started.
Cert E

12. Ballroom Dancing For Absolute Beginners

Learn the basics of ballroom dancing in your own home with acknowledged expert Peggy Spencer. Dances include the Tango and the Waltz.
Cert E

1 an emphasis on a central woman whom the audience is invited to support;
2 a division between the public and private sphere, with women understanding and controlling the private sphere;
3 an emphasis on building and maintaining relationships;
4 an element of fantasy in which values linked to the personal private sphere are privileged.

ACTIVITY 4.4

1 Choose an example of British and American soap opera, and examine the extent to which it seems to reflect the patterns described by Geraghty.
2 Where would an Australian soap opera like *Neighbours* fit in the table?

As a case study in a television genre with strong female appeal, soap opera research illustrates much of Geraghty's case. Dorothy Hobson's (1982) pioneering study into the unfashionable *Crossroads* revealed how many women saw it as 'their' programme – a kind of cultural space or even resistance to masculine control. Hobson describes how outraged the women were when the lead character, Noele Gordon, was written out of the serial, as if a close relative or friend had been murdered (by male producers). In seeking to explain the pleasures of soap opera for women, Christine Geraghty has applied Richard Dyer's categories of 'utopian solutions'. These refer to compensations offered by popular entertainment in relation to specific inadequacies in society which people experience. Energy contrasts with the exhaustion of daily life; abundance with scarcity and deprivation; intensity with dreariness and monotony; transparency with manipulation and dishonesty; and community with isolation and transience.

Much of the above discussion on gender preferences assumes a heterosexual audience. Given the paucity of explicit gay and lesbian media representation, it is not surprising that such groups have tended to find pleasures in those texts perceived as providing an alternative gay or lesbian reading to the dominant heterosexual discourse. An example of this is *Dynasty*, which in the 1980s became a cult serial among gays in America. They took pleasure in its camp discourse as personified by the

	Energy	Abundance	Intensity	Transparency	Community
British soaps	strong women, characters quick repartee, pace of plot		emotions strongly expressed at key moments, Angie/Den Sheila/Bobby	sincerity of key characters; Deirdre Barlow, Kathy Beale, Sheila Grant, *True Love:* Deirdre/Ken Chris/Frank	characters offer support, friendship, gossip outside programme
US soaps	strong male characters, business activity, pace of plot	glamorous settings clothes, luxurious objects food etc.	emotions strongly expressed at key moments, Sue Ellen's madness	sincerity of key characters: Bobby, Pamela, Miss Ellie, Krystle *True Love:* Blake/Krystle Bobby/Pamela	asserted within family, rarely achieved, relationship with audience

Fig. 4.10

Utopian possibilities in women's fiction
Source: C. Geraghty, *Women and Soap Opera*, Polity Press, 1991

'masculine' Joan Collins character, Alexis, and the programme's emphasis on high fashion and personal rivalry. *Prisoner Cell Block H*, an Australian drama serial based on a women's prison, has a lesbian following in Britain, while in Australia research by Hodge and Tripp (1986) discovered a strong empathy among children with the situation of the prisoners. They compared the prison to their school, and the warders to their own teachers. Particularly appealing were the prisoners' attempts to oppose and subvert official authority. For girls, the relatively rare sight of strong, active women fighting the system was a source of support for their own identity and self-esteem.

A similar kind of subversive reading has been identified by Martin Barker (1989) in his analysis of how comics in Britain give pleasure to children. Characters like Dennis the Menace and the Bash Street Kids in the *Beano* guarantee adult power will be constantly challenged in a way which is likely to under-mine adults' image as sensible figures of respect for children. Barker argues that adult 'policing' of many comics and their general denigration by parents and teachers serves to enhance their appeal to children. It might be argued that computer video games have begun to take over this role in the 1990s.

The most popular forms of media text seem to succeed because they contain a degree of openness and ambiguity which allows very different groups in society to decode them in a plea-surable way. In the pop world during the late 1980s the two most successful artists, Michael Jackson and Madonna, not only created music with 'crossover' appeal, focusing on dance, but also contrived images of gender and race which were polysemic to say the least! Madonna's performances provided sufficient support either for a view of her as a strong, liberated woman or as a sexual plaything:

> 'She's sexy and she doesn't need men... she's kind of there all by herself.'
>   or
> 'She gives us ideas. It's really women's lib, not being afraid of what guys think.'
>   (quoted in *Time*, 27 May 1985)
> 'Best of all, her onstage contortions and Boy Toy voice have put sopping sex where it belongs – front and centre in the limelight.' (quoted in *Playboy*, September 1985)
>
> *Fiske (1987)*

Michael Jackson's physical appearance has generated consid-erable controversy – has he attempted to dilute or deracinate his blackness? Like Madonna, he has consciously played with his image, not least in his video, *Thriller* (1983), where he calls his own identity into question via a blend of generic codes – horror, musical, pop video and 'teen pic movie'. *Thriller* is a classic example of intertextuality at work.

Ethnic preferences

The only black performers in America to rival Michael Jackson in black/white crossover appeal in the late 1980s were Bill Cosby and Eddie Murphy. *The Cosby Show* regularly topped the television ratings and attracted much academic speculation as to its racial message (see p. 112). In an attempt to discover how black and white audiences in America responded to it as a black situation comedy, Justin Lewis (1991) conducted interviews with fifty black and white viewers of the show of mixed social-class origins. Most of the subjects' reading of the specific episode watched were consistent with that of the programme's 'preferred reading' (a gently progressive feminist narrative in which women proved they could outperform men in the mechanics of fixing a car). However, Lewis found significant racial differences in their perceptions of the Huxtables as a black family. The dominant white perspective was one of colour blindness. Cliff Huxtable (Cosby) was seen as 'typical' or 'everyday', an observation reinforced by his upper-middle-class status and home (like those of many white families on American sitcoms). The show was thought to be different from other black television sitcoms in its absence of 'black humour' and style – defined as being loud and slapstick in nature. Lewis concluded that for most of the white audience *The Cosby Show* served to sustain the ideal of the 'American Dream', i.e. that colour is not a barrier to upward mobility.

In contrast, black interviewees were very sensitive to the show's reference to black culture, for example anti-apartheid posters on the wall. Lewis comments that this is indicative of how the show treads a thin racial dividing line: 'The symbols of black culture are strong enough to incorporate a black audience and weak enough to entice a white audience.' Moreover, blacks approved of the show because of their awareness of how few positive black representations appear on American television. That is not to say they were not also conscious of absences in the form of social realism. The lack of struggle and racism was regretted by many blacks, but this reservation was largely suppressed by the desire to have positive black representations made available.

A further example demonstrating racially differentiated audience readings for a massively popular American television 'event' was that of the trial of O. J. Simpson during 1995. Surveys of viewers' responses showed clear racial division concerning perceptions of whether O. J. Simpson was guilty of murdering his (white) wife and whether the law enforcement system was racially biased against blacks.

As an example of an internationally consumed media text, *Dallas* has been subjected to considerable academic analysis involving a number of audience studies in different countries. Far from *Dallas* being a case of 'cultural imperialism' (see p. 292), whereby American capitalist values are spread throughout the world, the audience research makes clear that *Dallas* is made sense of via the local cultural framework of interpretation that people bring to the programme. In Israel, Katz and Liebes (1986) discussed a *Dallas* episode with several ethnic groups including Israeli Arabs, Moroccans and Russian Jews. The more traditional ethnic groups, e.g. Israeli Arabs, tended to see the 'message' of *Dallas* as being that wealth cannot bring happiness and that rich Americans are immoral. Meanwhile, in Holland, Ien Ang (1985) found some female viewers enjoyed the programme through adopting an ironic attitude, treating it as 'trashy' and inferior. Some even applied a Marxist/feminist perspective and enjoyed it for its excess of sexism and capitalism, which could be viewed as evidence to support their own criticisms of American cultural values.

Clearly, much of the audience research summarised above has provided important insights into the limits of power that media texts may exert over their audiences. Furthermore, it is now accepted that the meanings audiences produce will to some extent be shaped by their own cultural competences and social origins. However, there is a danger that the pendulum swings too far the other way and audience power over the text is exaggerated. As with uses and gratifications, there may be a tendency to attribute consumer sovereignty to the audience and hence ignore the wider constraints which determined the production, circulation and reception of media texts. In the context of the hegemony–pluralism debate, this is a case of veering towards a pluralistic position.

Likewise, in celebrating the ability of the audience to resist dominant ideologies, there is frequently a conflation of *alternative* with *oppositional* readings. The fact that the polysemy or ambiguity of texts allows a variety of meanings to be produced is not the same thing as the text being actively challenged for its ideological content. As Justin Lewis points out with *The Cosby Show*, its hegemonic or ideological power actually depends upon its ability to strike a chord with different audiences in different ways.

The context of reception

Much of the academic controversy surrounding the encoding and decoding of media texts has had to be significantly qualified in the light of recent research into how audiences receive the media. The assumption that full attention is given when listening to the radio, reading magazines, etc., has been discarded in favour of schemes which differentiate between levels of attention. One example is Jeremy Tunstall's (1983) definitions of levels as *primary* (close attention), *secondary* (the medium in question is relegated to the background) and *tertiary* (although the medium is present, no conscious monitoring of it is taking place). These varying levels of attention are in turn influenced by the specific nature of the medium in terms of technology, audiovisual codes, and so on, and the social context in which it is received.

Andrew Crisell (1986) argues that the defining characteristic of radio as a medium of communication is '**flow**' (a term borrowed from Raymond Williams, 1974 – see below), analogous to water pouring from a tap when switched on. There is a lack of clear programme boundaries, because listeners tend to dip in and out as it suits them. More often than not this sporadic listening is accompanied by other activities such as driving the car, or making the breakfast, and so radio seems to be clearly a secondary medium. It is used in conjunction with the routines of daily life in a way which no other media can achieve. This is because it does not require visual concentration and is extremely portable. This quality of mobility has led some people to claim that radio is capable of considerable intimacy, since it can function as a 'personal companion' accompanying us into very private situations, not least in bed! The Walkman, or 'personal stereo', delivering radio and music, has been criticised on the grounds that its wearers retreat behind the headphones into their personal space, which excludes everybody else.

In contrast to radio, cinema requires an audience commitment in every sense of the word. A deliberate decision to visit a cinema, and the cinematic environment itself, contribute to the sense of this activity as a special occasion. The viewing conditions deny almost all alternative activities apart from watching

Fig. 4.11
Source: Paul Hickinbotham

ACTIVITY 4.5

Ask a sample of radio listeners to keep a diary of their daily listening, including details of:

1 what radio programmes are listened to;
2 for how long (on average);
3 under what conditions, e.g. alone, in the car, at work, etc.

the screen: the large screen size, the powerful sound system, the darkness and collective audience concentration, etc., all of which make cinema a primary medium. What is to some extent ambiguous is the degree to which the conditions privilege a private/personal or collective response to the film. The audience usually comprises a large public gathering, but the opportunities for social interaction are minimal.

Print media by their nature require some degree of close attention, if only to read the words! Nevertheless, reading newspapers and magazines is qualitatively different to reading a book. Selectivity, skimming and scanning all reflect the sense of leisurely engagement which characterises much newspaper and magazine reading. Having said that, there is little in the way of contemporary research into this area.

It was Raymond Williams (1974) who first described television programming as a 'flow'. Unlike the singular text foregrounded at the cinema, television emits a constant fragmentary stream, including adverts, trailers, continuity announcements, etc. An excellent example of this pattern can be found on MTV, where the core form of the pop video informs the style of the accompanying adverts, title sequences and features. As mentioned in chapter 2, John Ellis (1982) has refined the notion of flow to one of *segments*: relatively self-contained scenes conveying an incident, mood or particular meaning. He argues that these segments, which rarely last more than five minutes and usually contain a kind of climax, link closely to the context of television viewing.

Television is above all a domestic medium. It is watched in the home and consequently is part of the domestic atmosphere, providing mood and comfort. The flickering set in the corner is almost equivalent to the 'warmth' of a fire, and, from the 1950s, replaced the radio as the focus of the living room. Given that a large variety of social activity takes place in the home it is not surprising that much television viewing is intermittent in nature.

This is borne out by the results of Peter Collett's research (1986), which involved installing a specially designed television cabinet that contained a video camera directed at those watching television. From the resulting 350 hours of videotape Collett concluded that people have their eyes on the screen for only about 65 per cent of the time they are in the room. For the rest of the time, they are engaged in eating, sleeping, talking, ironing, and so on. It also confirmed the social nature of much viewing: 'Even the more popular programmes like soap operas and the news are punctuated with conversation and idle chatter. People exchange views on the plot, complain about the mismanagement of the weather, or comment on the newscaster's hairdo.'

Family viewing

One trend that television has contributed towards is that of families staying at home for their evening entertainment – part of the privatisation of family life. The specific dynamics of how television interacts with family relationships and domestic life is a subject of much recent research. Using cross-cultural evidence, the following extract indicates how domestic time usage is affected both by general cultural values and the nature of television itself as a structuring social activity:

> Cultures also have their own general sense of time, and there are tendencies to regulate social activity accordingly. Let me illustrate how cultural orientations toward time can influence family television viewing: time means something very different in Denmark compared to Pakistan. In Denmark, nearly all families eat the evening meal at almost precisely the same time – 6:00 p.m. The evening television news is broadcast at 7:30, so that it won't interfere with dinner. The systematic, predictable pattern of the Danish orientation toward time, including the scheduling and viewing of television shows, is an extension of this very orderly culture. In Pakistan, on the other hand, television programs often appear on the state system at times that differ from the published schedules, or fail to appear at all. Audiences generally are not surprised or angered by these irregularities…
>
> But in the long run television also influences perceptions and uses of time within cultures that are very different. Mealtimes, bedtimes, chore-times, periods for doing school homework, and patterns of verbal interaction, among other activities, are influenced by the scheduling of television shows. Television is transforming the lives of some rural Indian families by changing their routines away from regulation by nature to regulation by the clock and by television. As Behl reported in her article, Sunday has become a 'TV holiday' and 'TV time' in the evening has replaced time that was previously used for transacting business and 'integrating thought' in rural Indian culture. The reports from India and China demonstrate another phenomenon that has occurred in all cultures with television – the speeding up of home activity, especially the preparation and consumption of the evening meal. Parts of the day become redefined and struc-

Fig. 4.12
Source: Tim O'Sullivan

ACTIVITY 4.6

Investigate how family routines are related to television by asking each member of the family sampled to keep a daily diary for a week, with all television viewing recorded along with accompanying activities (if any) and other members of the sample with whom the viewing is shared.

tured around the scheduling of TV shows, and certain behaviors (such as differing meal times for men and women in rural India) are consolidated in the interest of preserving time for viewing.

Lull (1988)

As to whether television integrates or divides families, there is no single pattern. In some families, television acts as a point of common reference and discussion, whereas in other families, it offers a means of avoiding social contact or even potential conflict. A growing pattern which seems likely to mean a decline in family viewing of television is that of the multiset home. It is not unusual for homes to contain three or four television sets, and, with the growth in choice of channels, it seems inevitable that individual viewing will increase. The only countervailing influence to this trend is the fact that video rental has a special status which often makes the event more social.

Gender and television viewing

In what David Morley (1986) calls the 'politics of the living room', the question of who exercises the most power and control over programme choice is firmly linked to gender. His own research, based on eighteen families in South London, confirmed that where men are in paid employment, they have the most control over what is watched. This was symbolised by their domination over the use of the remote control handset. (Peter Collett [1986] recorded one instance where the man carried the remote control with him even when he left the room to make coffee!)

Another difference Morley discovered was that men preferred to watch television attentively, in silence and without interruption, whereas women were more inclined to engage in conversation or perform other domestic activities while viewing. Men's approach to viewing was generally more deliberately planned, closely scrutinising the evening's schedule. These differences reflect more general distinctions in gender roles and identities, particularly in relation to work and leisure. Men make quite a sharp demarcation between work outside the home and leisure within it. Women, however, are more inclined to define home as a site of labour, and therefore watch television more distractedly and with a sense of guilt (hence their greater enjoyment of viewing when the rest of the family is absent). Finally, as the main 'breadwinners' in most families,

Fig. 4.13
Source: Paul Hickinbotham

men see it as their 'right' to exercise first choice, and in the event of any dispute may invoke this as a justification for prevailing over what is watched.

Such patriarchal patterns are not necessarily universal. James Lull (1988) reports that in China there is no dominance of night-time viewing by males, and that in Venezuela it is women who control viewing (especially with respect to the viewing of the *telenovelas* – soap operas) as a reflection of their greater control of domestic space. Finally, in India, television viewing has actually helped to increase democracy in the household at the expense of traditional patriarchy.

Gender and media technology

The main theme of Ann Gray's (1992) research into women's response to video in the household is that gender is a key determinant in the use of, and expertise in, specific domestic technologies. In the case of the video cassette recorder (VCR), men's influence prevailed in a number of ways, ranging across the initial decision to purchase or rent a VCR, the mastery and control of the timer programming and the ownership of videotapes (men being more inclined to develop their own personal archive). When it came to time shifting, many of the women failed to operate the timer with any confidence. This was partly due to lack of motivation and a sense that it was masculine terrain.

The gendering of video technology as masculine is a key issue emphasised by Gray and others and recognisable in some of the commercial advertising stressing the 'hi-tech' nature of VCRs. This is in contrast to 'feminine' technology like microwave ovens, dishwashers and washing machines, which are no less technically demanding. Apart from VCRs, other new technology defined as masculine includes computers and video games.

Sherry Turkle (1984) has argued that computer culture appeals to masculine pleasures because of its abstract formal systems and its ability to offer a safe and protective retreat from personal relationships. 'Hackers' are preoccupied with winning and take risks, qualities traditionally perceived by women as 'non-feminine'. Meanwhile, video-games software seems to emphasise masculinised images of action–adventure scenarios in which a single male hero tackles overwhelming odds. The games focus on a quest which is attained via technological intervention.

ACTIVITY 4.7

Compare two households, as in the case study in figure 4.14, in terms of information and communications technology (ICT) in the home.

1 Profile each household in terms of occupation, housing, age and education where possible.
2 List the ICT owned and its physical distribution in the house (see list below).
3 How is ICT regarded in general by each member of the household?
4 Identify which member(s) of the household 'own' and control which items of ICT (e.g. use of remote control). Include the number of each item possessed or rented.

ICT: Television (Teletext?)
      Video recorder
      Satellite/cable receiver
      Camcorder
      Video-game console
      Computer/CD ROM/Internet
      Radio (Walkman?)
      Music centre/hi-fi/CD

For the national figures for some of these see figure 1.10.

James Family: Mother (36) manager of accountants, father (43) gas service engineer, son (18) trainee apprentice, daughter (17) student.
All share a three-bedroomed bungalow. Daughter is currently studying for A-levels and mother has a degree in business management. Social class: lower middle class.

ICT [information and communications technology] owned:

Father: television and double-decker video situated in the front room as well as separates including multiplay CD, tuner, tape deck and amplifier. Clock/TV/radio alarm situated in bedroom as well as radio in the en suite bathroom and Walkman for personal use.

Mother: washing machine, tumble dryer (gas).

Son: TV, video, CD player, amplifier, radio alarm, car radio.

Daughter: TV, video, CD player, amplifier, radio alarm, radio (portable), Walkman.

General (shared by everyone): dishwasher, oven, microwave, sandwich toaster, chip-fryer.

The television, although bought by the father, is situated in the living room, a place where the family congregate. It is the meeting place of the family. Therefore the television is watched by all members, yet only the father and daughter know how to fully operate the video recorder. This also applies to the stereo equipment situated in this room. All things technical are usually used and operated by the father and daughter. The son has too many other outside interests and a car which he is more interested in than the father's latest addition to the stereo system. The mother will only watch *Coronation Street* and has no idea how to work the video. 'It fazes me'. The remote control passes to and from father to daughter with the father's position as head of family taking precedence should he want to watch *Top Gear* whilst the daughter would prefer a new sitcom.

The stereo is used by the father but more often by the daughter, as it is she who buys the CDs and she who prefers the loudness of her father's stereo to her own.

General ICTs which include the dishwasher and oven are not referred to as 'mum's' because mum works full-time and all house-work and cooking is shared equally. The washing machine, however, belongs to the mother, as it is she who knows when it is about to fill up too much on certain pro-grammes.

Both son and daughter's ICTs are similar and are mostly used in the morning (radio alarm) and in the evening, when they escape to their own private domain to relax, do homework or have friends round.

Most items owned by the father tend to be situated in the front room and are considered as being for use by the whole family, yet the son and daughter's stereos and televisions are their own personal property and any using of the other's equipment without permission is seen as an 'invasion of privacy'.

The mother's lack of items draws attention to the fact that she rarely watches television and is too busy studying, besides the fact that she would prefer to read a book than listen to loud music.

Pacey Family: Mother (42), father (42), elder son (20) works as a bank clerk, son (10) at school, daughter (19) currently at university, younger daughter (17) A-level student. Father is a painter/decorator who is currently out of work. Mother works part-time as a sales assistant in a department store.

ICT owned:

Father: television (situated in front room), record player.

Mother: fridge/freezer, washing machine, dryer, cooker, toaster.

Elder son: Walkman, car stereo, cassette deck.

Son: Sega games console, Walkman.

Elder daughter: CD stack system.

Daughter: cassette deck, Walkman.

General: a TV and video which is rotated: one month in the girls' room and the next in the boys'. A share scheme.

The television in this household is on for many hours in the day due to the fact that it is one of only two in a six-person household. It is the focus of the living room and even more so for the younger son, who spends at least three hours a day using it in conjunction with his Sega games console.

The mother has full dominance over the kitchen. She may work part-time but the kitchen is regarded as her territory; it is she who cooks the meals and washes the clothes and cleans the house. The technology involved in working the cooker is virtually unknown to the father and each child (yes, even the girls). This is in stark contrast to the James family, who share the chores and are all quite capable of distinguishing between the oven and the kettle.

What the father says, in regard to the remote control and choice of channels, goes. He has dominance over this as do most men over the television. Yet when the father is out the remote is held by the elder son, standing in for the father: the girls do not get a look in.

The stereo is the least used equipment in the house, because of the fact that it only plays records while the majority of the children prefer the latest technology of their CDs and non-scratch cassettes. The record player, however, is not replaced as it belongs to the father, and it plays all his old 78s and is handy for those family parties.

The sharing of the TV is biased as well as that of the video, male dominance being shown in the fact that the 'boys' month share usually turns into six weeks. The daughter much prefers to listen to her music and often lets the extra two weeks pass; after all, the 'family' TV downstairs is available and she has no idea how to work the video properly anyway.

Summary

The major difference between the two households is the male dominance over all things 'technical' (but not involved in cooking) in the Pacey household. The James family tend to share all technical items, with the daughter interested in the latest technology as much as the next man.

Fig. 4.14

Comparison of two households: a student case study

Source: Selected from a sixth-form college sample of students' descriptions of media technology in their households, conducted in 1994 (unpublished)

Further reading

Barker, M. and Petley, J. (eds). 1997: *Ill-Effects: The Media/Violence Debate*. Routledge.

Buckingham, D. 1987: *Public Secrets:* EastEnders *and its Audience*. BFI.

Geraghty, C. 1991: *Women and Soap Opera*. Polity Press.

Gray, A. 1992: *Video Playtime*. Routledge.

Lewis, J. 1991: *The Ideological Octopus*. Routledge.

Lull, J. (ed.). 1988: *World Families Watch Television*. Sage.

Morley, D. 1992: *Television Audiences and Cultural Studies*. Routledge.

Nightingale, V. 1996: *Studying Audiences: The Shock of the Real*. Routledge.

Peterson, R.C. and Thurstone, L. 1933: *Motion Pictures and Social Attitudes*. Macmillan.

Schlesinger, P., Dobash, R.E., Dobash, R.P. and Weaver, C. 1992: *Women Viewing Violence*. BFI.

5

Media institutions and production

This chapter examines the media as a contemporary social institution with specific determinants and processes of production (whose historical antecedents are discussed in chapter 6). After providing an overview of institutional determinants, the analysis will focus on three case studies of media production: pop music, local newspapers and community radio.

The media as institution

One of the key themes of this book is that the media form a significant part of the everyday cultural life of modern industrial societies. As audiences, our routines are often structured around viewing, reading and listening to media output, and we regularly refer to specific media texts in social encounters. There is a sense in which the media are part of the social fabric. When certain social practices take on a regularity and structure which are apparent to ordinary people, then they may be called an institution. This is not to be confused with the more common usage of the term as referring to a specific organisation or building (e.g. a prison).

There is a helpful framework for examining the constituent elements of institutions.

It may be useful to think of all social institutions in terms of the varying degrees to which they represent historical and continuing social responses to conflicts at the level of:

1 *Economy*, concerned with the production and distribution of raw materials, manufactured goods and wealth.
2 *Politics*, concerned with the exercise of power and processes of social regulation.

3 *Culture*, concerned with the production, exchange and reproduction of meaning.

O'Sullivan et al. *(1994)*

The emphasis in previous chapters, especially chapters 3 and 4, has been on the third element in the list, the making of cultural meaning. While this is a critical ingredient in the analysis of institutional processes, the intention here is to focus on the economic and political dimensions and how these shape media production, distribution and consumption.

Institutional determinants: economic

Despite the fact that media texts are an important source of cultural meaning, they also share many of the characteristics of industrial commodities like motor cars or washing powder. Assembly-line production, marketing, research and development, etc., can all be found in media industries. The capital investment for a typical Hollywood feature film in the 1990s is likely to be over $25 million, and that does not include the marketing cost which could be in some cases as much as the production budget. Up to 1996, the most expensive Hollywood production was *Waterworld*, which cost $155 million to produce and market (and did not recoup its costs at the box office). For Hollywood studios, such costs can only be justified by success at the box office, manifested as profit in the form of revenue from admissions, video rights, etc.

With such high financial stakes, it is not surprising that companies make every effort to minimise their risks in what is at times a very uncertain and risky market. For Hollywood, this has meant the increasing tendency to produce sequels for successful films like *Batman* (1989), *Alien* (1979), and *Nightmare on Elm Street* (1984) until public interest declines. A further strategy is to rely more on research-based marketing from the initial packaging of a film (title, synopsis, stars, etc.) to the selection of the final cut on the basis of test screenings of alternative climaxes. For example, the ending to *Fatal Attraction* was eventually chosen (against the director's wishes) by a vote of preview audiences. The simplest way of maximising your chances of profit in media production is by extending your control of the market.

Concentration of ownership

In all industrial markets there is a tendency for the bigger, more successful companies to take over smaller companies in a search

	% market share		Top 5 commercial % share
Television			
BBC	43.6		
Channel 4	11.1		
Carlton (Carlton TV, Central TV, Westcountry TV)	11.0		
Granada (Granada TV, LWT)	8.9		
Yorks/Tyne Tees TV	5.5		33.9
BSkyB	4.5		
United News and Media (Meridian, Anglia)	4.1		
			Source: Broadcasters' Audience Research Bureau (BARB)
Radio			
BBC	49.0		
Capital (9 licences)	9.0		
CLT (Talk Radio, Atlantic)	4.5		
EMAP (9 licences)	4.8		28.1
GWR (20 licences including Classic FM)	6.7		
Virgin	3.1		
			Source: BARB
National newspapers			
News International (4 titles)	35.0		
Mirror Group (6 titles)	26.0		
United News and Media (3 titles)	13.0		93
Daily Mail and General Trust (2 titles)	12.0		
The Telegraph (2 titles)	7.0		
Guardian Media Group (2 titles)	3.0		
			Source: Audit Bureau of Circulation (ABC)
Magazines			
IPC	25.0		
BBC	7.6		
Bauer	7.5		
National Magazine	4.6		44.5
EMAP	4.4		
DC Thompson	3.0		
			Source: ABC
Music	*Albums*		*Singles*
PolyGram	20.3		20.6
CBS – Sony	15.5		12.0
WEA – Warners	13.6	71.9	9.9 64
RCA – BMG	13.0		8.1
EMI	9.5		13.4
			Source: British Phonographic Industries (BPI)

Fig. 5.1
Concentration of media ownership, Jan 1996

for even greater growth. When the takeover involves a direct competitor in the same sector then the process is referred to as *horizontal integration*, for example a newspaper publisher buying out a rival publisher. *Vertical integration* is when a company takes over another company which is responsible for other stages of the production cycle, for example a newspaper company buying out a newsagents' chain or a paper manufacturer. Such processes of integration are occurring almost daily in the media, as can be detected by a quick survey of the industry's trade magazines. What they mean in practice is that mainstream media production is characterised by a growing concentration of ownership. In all the media industries, a few (between five and six) large companies control a sizeable share of the market (figure 5.1). When these companies own shares in several media sectors and on an international scale, they are referred to as multimedia conglomerates (see Figure 5.2).

Often these companies are seeking to achieve vertical integration in order to guarantee a means of distributing the media product to the audience. This has long been a feature of the film industry where production companies have controlled the means of distribution and exhibition of films, but has become even more significant with the development of new media technologies of distribution, e.g. high band cable. Thus there have been deals forged such as that between Rupert Murdoch's

TELE-COMMUNICATION INC.
Key assets: Cable systems serving about 14 million subscribers, including pending deal; stakes in cable channels including the Discovery Channel, Home Shopping Network and QVC (another home shopping cable channel). Allied with Sprint, a long-distance phone company, and two other cable operators to offer wireless phone services; part owner of an online service run by Microsoft.

NEWS CORPORATION
Key assets: Fox Broadcasting (*Melrose Place, The Simpsons*); Star TV; BSkyB; Twentieth Century Fox studio (*Speed, Die Hard*); TV Guide magazine; newspapers in the UK (*The Times, Sunday Times,* the *Sun, News of the World, Today*), Australia (*The Australian, Sunday Telegraph*) and the US (*New York Post*); HarperCollins Publishers; Delphi Internet.

WALT DISNEY
Key assets: ABC television network; Walt Disney Pictures (*Pocahontas, The Lion King*); Touchstone Pictures; Hollywood Pictures; Miramax; The Disney cable channel; controlling or partial interest in ESPN2, A&E and Lifetime cable channels; Disneyland; Disney World; interests in Tokyo Disneyland and Euro Disney; Fairchild Publications; newspapers and magazines.

SEAGRAM
Key assets: Seagram brands include Chivas Regal, Martell Cognac, Glenlivet and Tropicana fruit juices. MCA assets: Universal Pictures (*Schindler's List, Waterworld*); MCA Home Entertainment Group (videos of *Jurassic Park, The Flintstones*); MCA Music Entertainment Group (Meatloaf, Patti LaBelle); MCA Television Group (*Rockford Files, New York Undercover*); MCA Publishing Group.

TIME WARNER
Key assets: CNN Time Inc., which includes magazines such as *Time, People, Sports Illustrated*; Warner Books, publisher of *Bridges of Madison County*; Warner Music Group (Simply Red, Nine Inch Nails); Warner Bros. (*Batman Forever, Bridges of Madison County*); Warner Bros. Television; Time Warner Cable; Home Box Office.

VIACOM
Key assets: Paramount Motion Picture Group (*Braveheart, Congo*); United Paramount Network – a fledgling TV network; MTV Networks; Showtime pay TV channel; Simon & Schuster publishing; Blockbuster Video stores; North American Paramount theme parks.

Fig. 5.2
Major media conglomerates
Source: *Guardian*, 7 August 1995

News International and telecom companies BT in Britain and MCI in the USA.

These media conglomerates are in a much stronger position to take advantage of the growing international media markets (see chapter 7 for a discussion of globalisation) as well as exploiting opportunities to sell their own products across the various sectors of the corporation. Such multimarketing is a growing media phenomenon. The profits made from a film's release may be multiplied through sales of accompanying music soundtrack, video sell-through, paperback novel, television spin-off rights, etc.

Perhaps the greatest profits are to be made in licensed merchandising, whereby the media brand is attached to various consumer products such as toys, clothes or food and drink. For example, it is estimated that in the past twenty years the *Star Wars* films have earned more than $3 billion in merchandising. The Disney Corporation is probably the most adroit in capitalising on merchandise related to its films. Such merchandise is usually made available in the shops *prior* to the release of a film thus building anticipation and interest in the film. British media companies have also begun to exploit their popular characters, a good example being DC Thompson, publisher of the *Beano* comic which includes the long-running Dennis the Menace stories. There are now a whole range of Dennis the Menace foods, clothing, bicycles, and so on, not to mention the television cartoon series and accompanying videos.

A similar example of media secondary marketing is integral to the concept of **synergy** – the selling of two or more compatible products simultaneously. In the late 1980s, a series of 'classic' pop songs from the past were used to create the desired atmosphere and mood for the advertising of Levi 501 jeans on television. Apart from the massive boost to sales of 501 jeans, the revived songs invariably recharted, often reaching number one. This pattern has been repeated with recent films such as *Robin Hood, Prince of Thieves* (1990; Bryan Adams, 'Everything I Do', topping the singles chart for nine weeks) and *The Bodyguard* (1992; Whitney Houston's 'I Will Always Love You' also reaching number one – see p. 198).

Finally, media conglomerates are also able to take advantage of their cross-media ownership to promote products within the company. For example, Rupert Murdoch's British newspapers have been consistent supporters of his satellite station, BSkyB, and its services. Indeed, at one time the chief executive of BSkyB, Andrew Neil, was also editor of the *Sunday Times*.

ACTIVITY 5.1

Undertake your own research into the multi-marketing of a well-publicised (or hyped) new media product. Try in particular to identify the various media spin-offs such as supporting books, music and videos.

Ownership and power

What has concerned many people about the trend towards concentration of ownership and the rise of international conglomerates is the potential for using media outlets to exercise potential power and influence. Marxist writers have particularly emphasised how, under capitalism, the property-owning class promote and defend their own interests at the expense of the rest of society – the thesis of political economy. The search for profit is seen as the key arbiter of what is produced in the media, first in the economic sense of achieving surplus revenue and secondly in the ideological sense of promoting those values and beliefs which support capitalism. (This echoes the hegemonic model outlined in chapter 3.)

There is little doubt that the major companies do exercise their economic muscles in squeezing, or taking over, new competition. This might involve, for example, undercutting the competitors' prices and advertising rates, or increasing the marketing budget. When the *Daily Star* was launched in 1978, the *Sun* implemented all these strategies and almost managed to deliver its new rival a fatal blow. In 1993, Rupert Murdoch initiated a newspaper 'price war' by slashing the price of *The Times* (by 50 per cent) and the *Sun* (20 per cent) which although it cost him millions of pounds in the short term he managed to squeeze his rivals, in particular the *Independent* whose future is in doubt. Ironically, the first casualty of the circulation battle was Murdoch's own paper *Today*, which closed in November 1995. From the consumer's point of view, the net result is less choice and diversity.

As to the ideological effect of concentrated ownership, it is difficult to arrive at a conclusive judgement. Curran and Seaton (1997) argue that with respect to the press, owners have sought to promote business interests in general, usually by ensuring their newspaper supported the Conservative Party. In return, newspaper editors and proprietors have been given honorary titles (e.g. Sir Larry Lamb, ex-editor of the *Sun*, and Sir David English, ex-editor of the *Daily Mail*).

The proprietor most notorious in recent times for his interventionism is Rupert Murdoch. His admiration for Margaret Thatcher was strongly echoed in the *Sun* despite the fact that the majority of its readers were not Conservative voters. On his acquiring *The Times* and the *Sunday Times* in 1981, the editors of both titles came under strong pressure to endorse Thatcherite policies, and duly obliged or resigned (Harold Evans resigned from *The Times* in 1983). Such is the perceived political power of Rupert Murdoch in Britain, Australia and even America emanating from his ownership of the media, that his critics have argued that politicians have refrained from threatening his business interests in these countries. This is despite the fact that Murdoch has often flouted the rules in extending his media empire. For example, in Britain BSkyB is virtually a monopoly provider of satellite television via its control of the satellite decoder technology. In Australia, the rules were actually changed to permit him to own newspaper titles despite being a foreign citizen (previously only national citizens could own Australian newspapers, and Murdoch, originally from Australia, had become an American citizen – in order to acquire American newspapers!).

Even so-called 'independent' newspapers do not seem to be immune from proprietorial pressures. While the *Observer* was owned by Lonrho, its editor, Donald Trelford, often allowed the paper to carry stories favourable to the activities of Tiny Rowland, Lonrho's chairman (e.g. Rowland's attempt to take over the Fraser Group, owner of Harrods department store). Figure 5.3 shows the front page of the *Daily Mirror* the day after its proprietor's death was announced. Within days the *Daily Mirror* was savagely criticising its former 'saviour' owner in the light of revelations about his corrupt misuse of *Daily Mirror* pension funds (the paper had suppressed all criticism of Maxwell whilst he was its owner).

The limits of ownership power

The profit drive in media industries is not always consistent with upholding dominant ideologies. Rupert Murdoch, famous for shifting his publications towards the political right, has allowed some of his titles to advocate minority or ideologically ambiguous views. In 1991, the Scottish edition of the *Sun*, anxious to boost its relatively poor sales north of the border, switched its political support to the Scottish Nationalists. In 1993, *Today* newspaper, still in search of a clear identity, moved leftwards towards the Labour Party. Furthermore, *The Simpsons*, the hugely popular cartoon series produced by Murdoch's Fox Television, has been attacked in America for having as its 'hero' a streetwise educational underachiever who belongs to a dysfunctional family.

In the music industry, few companies have hesitated to release and promote songs containing politically radical or

Fig. 5.3
Source: *Daily Mirror*, 6 November 1991

unorthodox ideas if there was a reasonable chance of such songs being commercially successful. In the late 1960s, CBS records in the USA had a large roster of 'countercultural' artists, many of whose music expressed anti-Vietnam war sentiments, and yet CBS itself was part of a corporation with investments in military expenditure.

Unlike the other consumer commodities, media products can never be uniformly standardised. This makes control of the market virtually impossible to attain. Nowhere is this more apparent than in the film industry, where the size of the budget, the casting of stars and the intensity of publicity cannot guarantee a profitable outcome, such is the unpredictability of the audience response. Contrast the fate of *Ishtar*, a comedy film starring Dustin Hoffman and Warren Beatty which lost $37 million in 1987, with *Rocky*, which starred the then unknown Sylvester Stallone in 1976 and made $56 million, having cost only $1.5 million to make. There are numerous similar instances from across the media of audiences supporting or rejecting media products in a seemingly capricious manner. Prominent recent examples include *Viz* (comic), *The Darling Buds of May* (television) and Classic FM (radio), all of whose popular appeal took most media people by surprise.

It is far easier for major companies to dominate the market when the capital costs of investment (especially in technology) are high. The potential for would-be rivals to BSkyB is modest, given the hundreds of millions of pounds necessary for starting up a satellite service. In contrast, making a pop record or launching a fanzine is within the means of most people who might wish to take a small step into such media markets. Given the size and complexity of much media production today, the actual *control* of such production usually lies with the professional who has the requisite technical expertise. Such professional autonomy is discussed in the next main section.

Market freedoms are not unfettered. Not only are there monopoly controls to prevent a single company exercising complete control in the market, but all the media are also subject to regulatory frameworks often backed up by legal sanctions. (See *The limits of freedom*, below.)

While acknowledging the variety of institutional determinants of media production, most commentators would probably stress the *economic* forces as being of greatest significance. However, the phenomenon can be interpreted in different ways. As we have seen, hegemonic theorists would relate it to the structure of economic inequality in society and the perpetuation of powerful group interests, particularly via the direct or indirect influence of owners; pluralist thinkers would rather wish to emphasise the sovereignty of the audience, with media production acting as a barometer of changing tastes and preferences. Diverse audience interests are reflected in a diversity of media choice.

But how effective are the media in fulfilling the 'demands of the market' (if these can ever be known)? As stated above, the larger media conglomerates have the power to squeeze the new competition and thus keep control of the market. Furthermore, audiences are not of equal commercial interest to media producers.

Advertising revenue

Apart from revenue gained from sales of newspapers, magazines, videos, etc., the other main source of revenue for the media is advertising. For commercial television and radio, advertising is the lifeblood of the industry. What concerns advertisers using the media is reaching the target audience, i.e. those people most likely to buy the product in question. Consequently, there is little point advertising Armani clothes in the *Sun* or MFI furniture in the *Financial Times*. The size of audience is obviously of interest, especially on television, where advertising rates are in direct proportion to numbers of viewers as revealed in the ratings. As a consequence, the profitability of ITV and Channel 4, as well as independent local radio (ILR), is dependent on the ability to achieve good viewing and listening figures. This in turn has implications for the type of programming scheduled. Those programmes which have a broad popular appeal – soap opera, films, sitcoms – invariably predominate over programmes which are seen as attracting minority audiences.

The second criterion for advertisers is the social profile (or demographics) of the audience in terms of social class, gender and age. Of least interest to most advertisers are older working-class people, who have the lowest disposable income. This is particularly significant for those media productions with a well-defined audience profile. The more 'upmarket' the audience, the easier it is to attract advertisers and hence achieve profitability. Consequently, there is a greater choice for younger, more middle-class audiences (figure 5.4).

This distribution of revenue from advertising also has implications for the political bias of national newspapers. Because newspapers like the *Daily Mirror* need a large circulation to flourish, they tend to ignore hard political news and focus on entertainment values. More in-depth political coverage is left to the more upmarket tabloids (like the *Daily Mail*) or the broadsheets, whose more affluent middle-class readership prefers conservative political values. In the past, this has meant the closure of a Labour-supporting paper like the *Daily Herald* (which folded in 1964 with a circulation five times that of *The Times*) and the Liberal *News Chronicle* (whose circulation equalled that

ACTIVITY 5.2

From listing the adverts which appear within different television programmes (at varying times of day) on ITV and Channel 4, see if there is any pattern which indicates a target audience for that programme (age, gender, class, etc.).

A similar exercise can be undertaken with newspapers and magazines, whose readership is usually better defined in terms of social profile.

	Sex			Social grade		Age		Readership	Circulation
	Total	Men	Women	ABC1	C2DE	15–44	45+	(millions)	(millions)
	(% of adults)								
Daily newspapers									
Sun	22	26	19	14	30	26	18	10.3	4.0
Daily Mirror	14	16	13	9	19	14	15	6.6	2.4
Daily Record	4	4	4	3	5	4	4	1.9	0.7
Daily Mail	10	11	10	14	7	8	13	4.8	2.0
Daily Express	7	7	6	8	5	8	8	3.0	1.2
Daily Telegraph	5	8	6	10	1	4	7	2.5	1.1
Daily Star	5	6	3	2	7	6	3	2.1	0.8
The Times	4	4	3	6	1	2	3	1.7	0.7
Guardian	3	3	2	5	1	3	2	1.2	0.4
Independent	2	2	1	3	1	2	1	0.8	0.3
Financial Times	2	2	1	3	–	2	1	0.7	0.3
Any daily newspaper	58	62	54	57	59	55	61	26.7	13.9

Fig. 5.4

Readership of national daily newspapers: by sex, social class and age, 1996

Source: National Readership Survey, Jan–June 1996, Audit Bureau of Circulation, June 1996

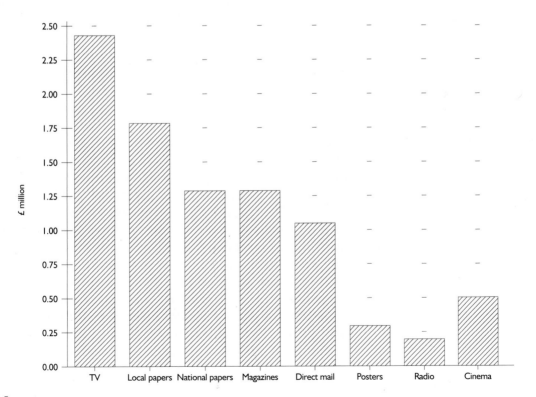

Fig. 5.5

Advertising expenditure by medium

Source: Advertising Association, 1995

of the *Daily Telegraph* when it closed in 1960). Even the *Daily Mirror's* commitment to the Labour Party seems threatened following the death of Robert Maxwell in 1991 and the attempt to make the paper an attractive commercial proposition to new owners in the face of intense competition from the *Sun*.

There is every danger that, in the future, the more advertisers are keen to pinpoint their target audiences via the media, the more those audiences unattractive to advertisers will tend to be ignored. This is because the trend is towards *narrowcasting* (or niche targeting) in the media – i.e. supplying customised services to specialist audience groups: as with other market-based services, those with most disposable income exercise greatest choice.

Institutional determinants: professional autonomy

Although ownership of media companies makes possible power over production from the point of view of allocating resources (capital investment, budgets, etc.), the day-to-day management of media organisations in the operational sense lies with media professionals. Of course, in small-scale enterprises the owners and controllers of production may well be the same people, but most organisations require a division of labour based on specialised areas of skill and technical expertise.

Such skills and expertise are often elevated to an occupational ideal, making it possible to lay claim to professionalism. Most media organisations require new recruits to undertake considerable in-house training on top of any formal qualifications already obtained. The ethos of the organisation – what it stands for and how it goes about things, together with the 'house style' of production – are central to the process of occupational socialisation. The ensuing collective thinking and practice provide a degree of solidarity from which external threats (owners, the government, the public, etc.) can be resisted. This also has implications for the boundaries of creative freedom within media production. The 'correct' or conventional way of doing something becomes enshrined in professional practice until, and if, someone is bold or strong enough to break or question the 'rules'.

The freedom to deviate from the accepted codes and conventions will very much depend on a previous hierarchical position. In cinema and television, producers and directors exercise the greatest control over the content and style of films and programmes. Some film directors have been seen as *'auteurs'* or artistic authors, able to imbue their films with a personal vision or look: e.g. Orson Welles, Alfred Hitchcock, David Lynch. However, media production, not least film, is essentially a cooperative venture, necessitating considerable mutual assistance and interdependence (figure 5.6).

In newspapers and magazines, editors are in the strongest position to influence the shape and direction of the publication. Some individual editors have made a recognisable impression on their newspaper or magazine's identity: the *Sun* under the editorship of Kelvin MacKenzie is one example:

> But it was in the afternoon, as the paper built up to its creative climax of going to press, that the real performance would begin. MacKenzie would burst through the door after lunch with his cry of 'Whaddya got for me?' and the heat would be on. He had total control – not just over the front page, but over every page lead going right through the paper. Shrimsley was remembered as a fast and furious corrector of proofs, but MacKenzie was even faster, drawing up layouts, plucking headline after headline out of the air, and all the time driving towards the motto he hammered into them all: 'Shock and amaze on every page.'[...]
>
> True to the code of sarff London MacKenzie also wanted to be surrounded by 'made men', who had proved themselves by pulling off some outrageous stunt at the expense of the opposition. One way of becoming a made man was to phone the *Mirror* and ask for the 'stone' where the final versions of pages were assembled for the presses. The trick was to imitate another member of the *Mirror* staff to fool the stone sub into revealing the front-page splash. One features exec became a made man by walking across Fleet Street into the *Express* and stealing some crucial pictures from the library. Hacks refusing to get involved in this sort of behaviour were suspect – falling into the category of those who were not fully with him, and could therefore be presumed to be against him.
>
> *Chippendale and Horrie (1990)*

The limits of freedom

The ability of media professionals to achieve autonomy is subject to two key constraints:

1 *Profitability*. Few owners of the media are content to maintain a 'hands-off' policy if there is not a healthy flow of profit or

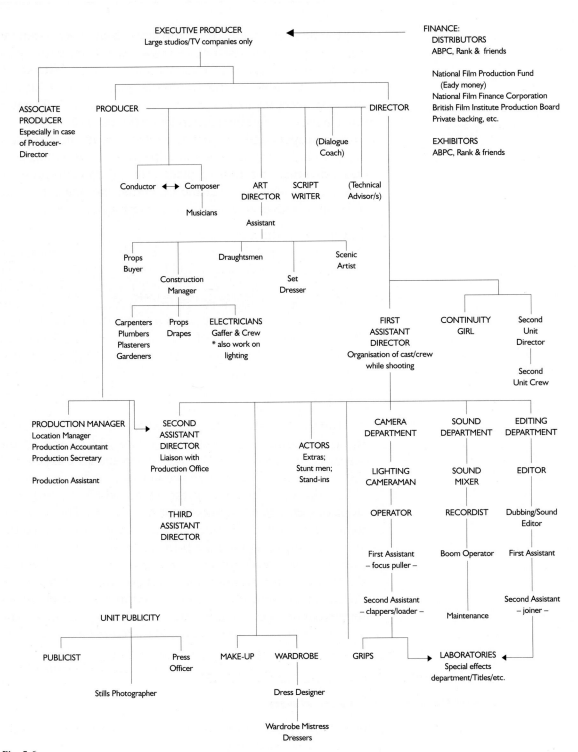

Fig. 5.6

Film unit structure

Source: J. Hartley, H. Goulden, T. O'Sullivan, *Making Sense of the Media*, Comedia, 1985

at least the prospect of one. 'Creative' film directors are only indulged by Hollywood studios if their last film was a blockbuster. Virtually no part of the media is now immune from economic pressures. The BBC's decision to axe *Eldorado*, their expensive soap opera, in 1993, was largely due to a need to bolster their falling share of the ratings (and thus strengthen their case for the continuation of the licence fee).

Equally, media professionals may be trapped by success. Productions with popular appeal become formularised, with writers, editors, actors, etc. working in assembly-line 'factory' conditions, allowing little scope for experimentation or risk-taking (e.g. television soap operas).

When it comes to a showdown between proprietor and professional, the former nearly always prevails. Even the ebullient Kelvin MacKenzie of the *Sun* was known for his subservience to Rupert Murdoch, and prior to his death Robert Maxwell was intolerant of any dissidence within his corporation. Curran and Seaton (1997) can find only one occasion when journalists actually succeeded in decisively defeating their proprietor (when the *Observer*'s staff resisted Lonrho's boss, Tiny Rowland, who tried to change the newspaper's liberal stance towards South African politics).

2 *Regulation*. On the one hand, professional independence is actually bolstered by self-regulation. Like doctors and lawyers, media professionals operate within codes of practice designed to prevent unacceptable standards of production or irresponsible behaviour. If members adhere to such codes, then there are less likely to be attempts made to impose conditions from outside the industry (e.g. by the government).

However, not surprisingly, there is limited state or public faith in any organisation's or industry's attempts to police itself, and all the media are subject to a variety of external controls either enshrined in the law and/or administered by external, independent bodies (figure 5.7).

Institutional determinants: external regulations

The media operate relatively freely in countries like Britain, compared to those under more repressive regimes such as China. Nevertheless, there are a plethora of laws and regulations which act as constraints on media production. Most of these emanate from the state, and are kept in reserve for when

The Press Complaints Commission are charged with enforcing the following Code of Practice which was framed by the newspaper and periodical industry and ratified by the Press Complaints Commission on 30 June 1993.

All members of the press have a duty to maintain the highest professional and ethical standards. In doing so, they should have regard to the provisions of this Code of Practice and to safeguarding the public's right to know.

Editors are responsible for the actions of journalists employed by their publications. They should also satisfy themselves as far as possible that material accepted from non-staff members was obtained in accordance with this Code.

While recognising that this involves a substantial element of self-restraint by editors and journalists, it is designed to be acceptable in the context of a system of self-regulation. The Code applies in the spirit as well as in the letter.

It is the responsibility of editors to co-operate as swiftly as possible in PCC enquiries.

Any publication which is criticised by the PCC under one of the following clauses is duty bound to print the adjudication which follows in full and with due prominence.

1 Accuracy

i) Newspapers and periodicals should take care not to publish inaccurate, misleading or distorted material.

ii) Whenever it is recognised that a significant inaccuracy, misleading statement or distorted report has been published, it should be corrected promptly and with due prominence.

iii) An apology should be published whenever appropriate.

iv) A newspaper or periodical should always report fairly and accurately the outcome of an action for defamation to which it has been a party.

2 Opportunities to reply

A fair opportunity for reply to inaccuracies should be given to individuals or organisations when reasonably called for.

3 Comment, conjecture and fact

Newspapers, whilst free to be partisan, should distinguish clearly between comment, conjecture and fact.

4 Privacy

Intrusions and enquiries into an individual's private life without his or her consent including the use of long-lens photography to take pictures of people on private property without their consent are not generally acceptable and publication can only be justified when in the public interest.

Note: Private property is defined as any private residence, together with its garden and outbuildings, but excluding any adjacent fields or parkland. In addition, hotel bedrooms (but not other areas in a hotel) and those parts of a hospital or nursing home where patients are treated or accommodated.

5 Listening devices

Unless justified by public interest, journalists should not obtain or publish material obtained by using clandestine listening devices or by intercepting private telephone conversations.

6 Hospitals

i) Journalists or photographers making enquiries at hospitals or similar institutions should identify themselves to a responsible official and obtain permission before entering non-public areas.

ii) The restriction on intruding into privacy are particularly relevant to enquiries about individuals in hospitals or similar institutions.

7 Misrepresentation

i) Journalists should not generally obtain or seek to obtain information or pictures through misrepresentation or subterfuge.

ii) Unless in the public interest, documents or photographs should be removed only with the express consent of the owner.

iii) Subterfuge can be justified only in the public interest and only when material cannot be obtained by any other means.

8 Harassment

i) Journalists should neither obtain nor seek to obtain information or pictures through intimidation or harassment.

ii) Unless their enquiries are in the public interest, journalists should not photograph individuals on private property without their consent; should not persist in telephoning or questioning individuals after having been asked to desist; should not remain on their property after having been asked to leave and should not follow them.

iii) It is the responsibility of editors to ensure that these requirements are carried out.

9 Payments for articles

Payment or offers of payment for stories, pictures or information, should not be made directly or through agents to witnesses or potential witnesses in current or criminal proceedings or to people engaged in crime or to their associate – which includes family, friends, neighbours and colleagues – except where the material concerned ought to be published in the public interest and the payment is necessary for this to be done.

10 Intrusion into grief or shock

In cases involving personal grief or shock, enquiries should be carried out and approaches made with sympathy and discretion.

11 Innocent relatives and friends

Unless it is contrary to the public's right to know, the press should generally avoid identifying relatives or friends of persons convicted or accused of crime.

12 Interviewing or photographing children

i) Journalists should not normally interview or photograph children under the age of 16 on subjects involving the personal welfare of the child, in the absence of or without the consent of a parent or other adult who is responsible for the children.

ii) Children should not be approached or photographed while at school without the permission of the school authorities.

13 Children in sex cases

1) The press should not, even where the law does not prohibit it, identify children under the age of 16 who are involved in cases concerning sexual offences, whether as victims, or as witnesses or defendants.

2) In any press report of a case involving a sexual offence against a child –

i) The adult should be identified.
ii) The term "incest" where applicable should not be used.
iii) The offence should be described as "serious offences against young children" or similar appropriate wording.
iv) The child should not be identified.
v) Care should be taken that nothing in the report implies the relationship between the accused and the child.

14 Victims of crime
The press should not identify victims of sexual assault or publish material likely to contribute to such identification unless, by law, they are free to do so.

15 Discrimination
i) The press should avoid prejudicial or pejorative reference to a person's race, colour, religion, sex or sexual orientation or to any physical or mental illness or handicap.
ii) It should avoid publishing details of a person's race, colour, religion, sex or sexual orientation, unless these are directly relevant to the story.

16 Financial journalism
i) Even where the law does not prohibit it, journalists should not use for their own profit, financial information they receive in advance of its general publication, nor should they pass such information to others.
ii) They should not write about shares or securities in whose performance they know that they or their close families have a significant financial interest, without disclosing the interest to the editor or financial editor.
iii) They should no buy or sell, either directly or through nominees or agents, shares or securities about which they have written recently or about which they intend to write in the near future.

17 Confidential sources
Journalists have a moral obligation to protect confidential sources of information.

18 The public interest
Clauses 4,5,7,8 and 9 create exceptions which may be covered by invoking the public interest. For the purposes of this code that is most easily defined as:
i) Detecting or exposing crime or a serious misdemeanour.
ii) Protecting public health and safety.
iii) Preventing the public from being misled by some statement or action of an individual or organisation.

In any cases raising issues beyond these three definitions the Press Complaints Commission will require a full explanation by the editor of the publication involved, seeking to demonstrate how the public interest was served.

Note: Following the death of Princess Diana, the PCC proposed in September 1997 to introduce additional clauses including: the prohibition of pictures obtained through 'persistent pursuit' or as a result of unlawful behaviour: and the expansion of definition of private places where individuals might expect to be free of media attention

Fig. 5.7
Press Code of Practice. Which of these clauses seems to have been most ignored by newspapers (especially tabloids) in recent years? Why should clause 18, 'The public interest', be the subject of so much controversy?
Source: Press Complaints Commission

MoD guidelines for the Gulf War

Fourteen categories (covering 32 subjects) of information cannot be published or broadcast without talking to the Ministry of Defence. These include:

- Numbers of troops, ships, aircraft and other equipment: specific locations of British or Allied military units; future military plans.
- Photographs showing locations of military forces. Photographs of wounded soldiers.
- Information about casualties should not be broadcast until next of kin contacted.
- Specific information on British ships and planes which have been hit.
- Information on how intelligence is collected.

Not the full story ...

First World War (1914–18)

Strict censorship began in August 1914. A government-appointed officer, Colonel Sir Ernest Swinton, wrote 'eye-witness' reports for the press, but they gave few details.
Newspaper proprietors Lord Northcliffe and Lord Beaverbrook were among those working closely with the government.

Second World War (1939–45)

The Ministry of Information employed, at one stage, 999 people to turn 'news' into an anti-German crusade. No British soldier could be named. The true extent of Japan's attack on Pearl Harbor was hidden until after 1945.

Vietnam War (1954–75)

The first television war: American journalists reported for the first time without direct censorship from the army. The US military issued general guidelines which journalists were expected to follow, but media criticism, especially of the 1968 Tet Offensive, helped turn American public opinion against the war.

Falklands War (1982)

Twenty-nine carefully selected British reporters were kept under strict Ministry of Defence control. Reporters, who had to agree to censorship, were told what was happening after the event. Some reports had to pass through three stages of vetting before they could be released.

Fig. 5.8
Government reporting guidelines in wartime
Source: *Guardian*, 29 January 1991. © *Guardian*

the media step out of line. We need to distinguish between general laws which apply to all the media, and more specific regulations relevant to individual media institutions.

Political controls

The government rarely intervenes directly to censor the media, as this would be perceived as anti-democratic. It reserves that right for national emergencies or crises such as wartime. For example, in 1939 Winston Churchill banned the *Daily Worker*, a communist newspaper, as it was seen as a threat to a united war effort. More recently, during the Falklands and Gulf Wars, the Ministry of Defence (MoD) vetted all news reports. This frequently led to censorship in the case of reporting the Falklands War, whereas in the Gulf War the MoD guidelines generally produced self-censorship in reports (figure 5.8).

The Official Secrets Act, passed originally in 1911 and updated in 1988, allows the media to be prosecuted for disclosing information about the security services, defence and the conduct of international relations. It is no defence to claim any leak of information is in the public interest. In the 1980s, a number of famous prosecutions occurred under the Act, including that of the journalist Duncan Campbell, whose *Secret Society* television series for the BBC contained an episode, on Britain's satellite spy system (called Zircon), which was banned. The affair included MI5 visiting a BBC office in Glasgow in a dawn raid. The Official Secrets Act is criticised by many as being a means by which the state hides its actions from proper public accountability. Equally controversial is the Prevention of Terrorism Act. Journalists who make contact with 'terrorist' or illegal organisations risk prosecution. In 1988, it was extended in the form of a specific ban on the broadcasting of the voices of any representative of proscribed Northern Ireland organisations and their political offshoots. It was still possible to report the words of such representatives but only if dubbed or with subtitles. Broadcasters largely adhered to the spirit of the law, thus seriously curtailing opportunities for organisations like the IRA to put their point of view on television and radio until late 1995 when the ban was lifted following the IRA ceasefire of that year.

Anti-monopoly controls

Fears of excessive concentration of media ownership should be allayed by the existence of legislation designed to maintain fair competition in the market place. Broadcasters, in particular, have been subject to strict control, preventing any one company owning more than one ITV franchise or owning both a national newspaper and television station. However, these controls are continually being eroded. Rupert Murdoch's takeover of national newspapers (he owned five national titles in 1993) and his monopolisation of British satellite television have been allowed to proceed without resistance from the Monopolies Commission. From November 1996, the rules on cross-media ownership were relaxed, allowing the growth of larger British media groups owning television and radio licences as well as newspapers, providing that their market share of television does not exceed 15 per cent, and that diversity of provision is maintained in any one region or locality.

Moral standards

In 1990, the Obscene Publications Act was extended to include all the media. It is designed to uphold standards of taste and decency and any material thought liable to 'deprave and corrupt' audiences is subject to prosecution. In the case of pornographic videos and magazines, this may be relatively straightforward, but it is frequently difficult to achieve any consensus on what is likely to 'deprave and corrupt'. This raises issues concerning not only what qualifies as obscene, but also how it can be demonstrated that audiences will be corrupted.

Libel

There have been numerous well-publicised cases of individuals being awarded damages against media organisations found guilty of issuing unjustified or harmful statements about the individual in question. The satirical magazine *Private Eye* is perhaps the most frequent offender as a result of its willingness to criticise and make fun of the rich and powerful. The problem is that it is the rich and powerful who are most able to take advantage of the protection offered by the libel law, through their ability to pay the huge court costs which such cases often incur. Robert Maxwell's success in not being exposed before his death as a corrupt businessman was certainly aided by the frequency with which he threatened his accusers with legal proceedings.

Each area of the media is also subject to more specific forms of control, either by separate legislation or by regulatory bodies.

Cinema/video

The British Board of Film Classification issues certificates for all cinema and video releases, applying the categories U (Universal), PG (Parental Guidance), 12, 15 and 18, plus UC for video, meaning it is particularly suitable for children. Controls are stricter for video because of the possibility of young children viewing films rented by adults or older children.

Newspapers

The Press Complaints Commission (see figure 5.7) exists primarily to consider complaints made by the public about the accuracy and standards of reporting in newspapers. It also issues guidelines for responsible behaviour and monitors how well the press adheres to these guidelines. There has been criticism of the ineffectiveness of the Commission and regular calls for stronger legal provision to prevent what is seen by some as excessive behaviour by some newspapers (especially following the death of Princess Diana for which some of the blame was attributed to harassment from newspaper photographers).

Broadcasting

Television and radio are subject to the strongest controls of any media, for technological and political reasons (see chapter 6). The BBC's licence is renewed every ten years, and the licence fee set by the government, which also appoints the board of governors. Their role is to ensure that the BBC fulfils its obligations as laid down by law, and if necessary to intervene if individual programmes are deemed to exceed the BBC's remit, e.g. the banning of *Real Lives* (see p. 85).

Non-BBC television services, including ITV, Channel 4, cable and satellite, are licensed and regulated by the Independent Television Commission (ITC). A similar role for radio is played by the Radio Authority. Both the ITC and the Radio Authority publish codes to which licensees must adhere, covering programmes, advertising and sponsorship. Viewers or listeners may complain to either body, which, if deciding the complaint is justified, may take action, such as requesting a broadcast apology.

The public can also complain to the Broadcasting Standards Commission, whose role is to consider complaints about violence, sex, taste and decency, as well as accusations of unfair treatment or invasion of privacy. The Commission can insist on a public apology if the broadcasters are found guilty.

Advertising

The Advertising Standards Authority (ASA) tries to ensure that advertisers live up to their much-quoted ideal of producing adverts that are 'honest, decent, legal and true'. They issue codes covering matters like cigarette advertising, monitor the flow of adverts being produced and respond to public complaints – sometimes by demanding the change or removal of an advert. Such requests are normally heeded, but this was not the case in 1992, when Benetton ignored the ASA. In a campaign which had depended on images of an increasingly provocative nature, Benetton caused most offence when they used a picture of a man suffering from AIDS at the moment of his death. Many people complained that it was immoral to use such an image within a commercial context, in this case promoting a brand name of clothing.

Independent production

What is independent production?

To be independent implies autonomy and freedom from external constraints. In the context of media production, it is most often seen as meaning not under the direct control of a larger organisation, be that commercial or governmental. As such, independence carries a positive status, and may even be invoked in order to lay claim to being more trustworthy or authentic. The *Independent* newspaper's advertising campaign used the phrase 'It is ... Are you?' when the paper was launched in 1986. This was designed to draw attention to both the absence of a corporate owner, such as Murdoch's News International Corporation which owns the *The Times*, and its editorial policy of political neutrality.

However, complete independence in media production is virtually impossible, as the support or cooperation of other organisations in the cycle of productions and distribution is necessary if any kind of 'mass' audience is to be reached. What is more, there are no agreed criteria by which any media organisation can be labelled 'independent'. 'Independent television' most often refers to the ITV companies holding the regional franchises, many of which are large media corporations, whereas 'independent video' is normally associated with small-scale, grassroots production, often involving voluntary labour.

Nevertheless, there are some principles to which most independent media production conforms, to varying degrees:

- A democratic/collectivist process of production. This may take the form of a workers' cooperative, an absence of hierarchy, participative decision-making, etc. Often audiences may be actively involved at both a consultative and productive level, e.g. fanzines.
- A targeting of minority audiences. Audiences perceived as being ignored by mainstream media include local, ethnic, political and subcultural groups. Such groups tend to be marginalised in terms of power and influence in society and may lack economic clout (and hence media profitability).
- A commitment to innovation or experimentation in form and/or content – so-called alternative media. This 'radicalism' can be manifested in experimental design and rule breaking within media conventions, as well as in a campaigning, political mode of address, which challenges the status quo, e.g. environmental action.

All three elements can be seen as being in contrast to mainstream or dominant media production practice, i.e. that which is widely accepted and recognised as 'the norm', and which is most available for audiences to consume. Only when independent production 'takes off' in popularity does it come to the attention of the wider public, as happened with the adult comic *Viz*. Most of the time, it is produced and distributed haphazardly or within a narrow social channel, access to which must be actively sought by audiences, for example through mail order or specialist group meetings.

From the radical press of the nineteenth century, through workers' film societies of the 1930s, to the 'underground' hippie press of the 1960s and up to the 1980s/1990s pirate radio stations, there has been a thriving tradition of independent production. The dynamics of such movements can be examined more closely by considering specific examples.

Football fanzines

Fanzines can be traced back to the 1940s when, in the USA, specialist magazines were distributed to fans of various cults like science fiction. The contemporary essence of fanzines is that they are produced by and for fans. Prior to the recent boom in football fanzines, music fanzines flourished in the late 1970s and early 1980s in the wake of the punk/new wave movement. It was estimated that in the 1988-89 season, approximately one million copies of football fanzines were sold, although most individual magazines averaged between 200 and 1 000 circulation (Leicester University research). A few of the less parochial titles, such as *When Saturday Comes*, have gained access to high-street newsagents. What, then, is their appeal?

A key factor is that they provide a forum for the views of fans hitherto ignored, especially by those running the game, who are often perceived as being 'out of touch' and bent on ruining the traditional experience of supporters standing on the terraces. The official view of the club is usually expressed via the club programme, which voices very different sentiments to those expressed in fanzines (figures 5.9 – 5.11).

Another attractive ingredient for the fans is the 'inside' humour, which draws on folklore, gossip and affectionate lampooning of players and rival fans. Fanzines for unfashionable and poorly supported clubs generate a participative *camaraderie* and sense of collective identity despite, or because of, the employment of basic, sometimes primitive, production techniques.

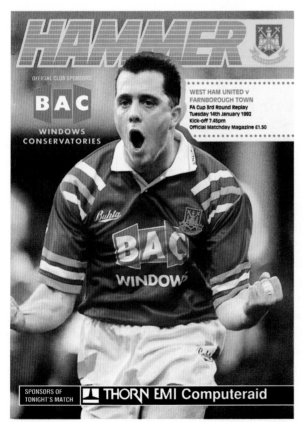

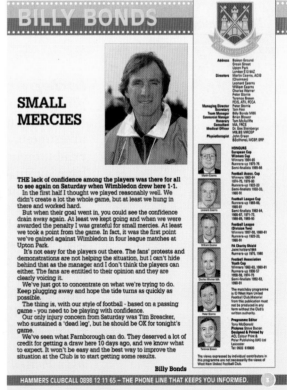

Fig. 5.9

Source: West Ham United Football Club

Fig. 5.10

Source: *Over Land and Sea*, January 1992

Independent film and video

Whereas fanzines can be produced at minimal cost with low-tech facilities, film production requires considerable capital investment. Added to that are problems of distribution and exhibition not faced by the major production companies, which have automatic access to cinema chains (particularly when there is vertical integration).

The fact that independent film and video production exists at all is largely due to some kind of subsidy or patronage. In the past, this has been from state-supported bodies like the Arts Council or the British Film Institute, but increasingly it has been television which has provided the key investment for independent British films. Channel 4's backing was vital for the stream of 1980s productions such as *My Beautiful Laundrette* (1985) and *A Letter to Brezhnev* (1985) which was followed by the even greater commercial success in the 1990s of *Four Weddings and a Funeral* (1994) (cost £2 million, earnings £72 million), *The Crying Game* (1992) and *Trainspotting* (1995). The latter example shows the possibility of reflecting aspects of British culture not found in the Hollywood-dominated contemporary cinema.

Fig. 5.11
Source: *The Water in Majorca*, October 1996

However, most of these films employed a narrative form and cinematic style which were very conventional, albeit on a modest scale compared to Hollywood. This is not surprising, since the primary motivation in making these films was commercial, i.e. to avoid excessive costs and, if possible, make a profit.

More radical independent cinema has emerged from film and video workshops, often rooted in local communities or interest groups eager to provide an alternative voice to that of mainstream cinema and television. Sometimes it has been possible for such productions to gain exposure via a loose-knit network of independent film distributors and exhibitors. With the increasing use of video as a means of communication, this has become less of a problem. For example, The *Miners Campaign Tapes*, produced during the coal strike of 1984-85 and representing the miners' perspective, were viewed nationally and internationally due to the flexibility of the video format.

Workshops have tended to focus on documentary forms of film-making as a means of projecting their own social and

the Wars' in the Oral History Journal.

HOW WE MADE THE FILM

The core of the film rests on the interviews we did with women in the Valleys. We met many of them through the screening groups we had set up in the Valleys. Out of these groups there also emerged a core of women who were interested in working with us on the film and acting as consultants. They formed a production group which saw the film through to its final stages. As well as the contacts made from the screening groups we also visited Old People's homes in the Valleys.

We then found a lot of our archive material from the BFI, the BBC film library, St Fagans, the Miner's library, Swansea and local libraries and museums. We also spoke to women historians like Dee Beddoe and Angela John and spent a lot of time talking to as many women as we could find, as well as employing a Welsh speaking feminist historian who found a lot of interesting material in the Welsh language.

'Mam' was very much a Red Flannel joint effort, all members of Red Flannel worked on its research and we had regular meetings where all our information was brought together and knocked into shape.

By the end of the research period we had a pretty thorough understanding of womens role in the developing history of the Valleys, but we wanted women themselves to tell the story, through their own memories and experiences.

From the very many women we spoke to during the research period we finally chose our film interviewees. We chose on the basis of firstly personality, women who could speak articulately and engagingly about

the past, secondly we needed a good age range so that the film could cover a long period in time. Lastly, it was important that their personal stories reflected what was the common experience.

The script was developed through the following process:

- Screening and discussions on questions raised under 'background'

- Formation of production group

- Sound interviews

- Archive research: feature films, documentary, stills

- Background reading: historical, sociological, economic, literature

- Choosing material for dramatisation and documentary development

- Creating basic structure of film

- Drama improvisations

- Shaping of documentary material into cohesive sequences

- Final scripting

The production group carried on working with us during the editing of the film, so that our decisions could be informed by their opinions.

Red Flannel feel that because of the long term involvement of Valleys women during the making of 'Mam', via screenings, discussions and within the production group, that the final result is a truer representation of their lifes, than a film made under normal mainstream constraints would allow.

Fig. 5.12
Mam, 1988
Source: Red Flannel Films Publicity

political concerns. Furthermore, it is relatively cheap compared to fictional film-making. A good example of a workshop incorporating many elements found in such organisations is that of Red Flannel, a women's film and video workshop based in South Wales and funded by Channel 4, the Welsh Arts Council and the South East Arts Association. They see themselves giving a voice to the women of the Welsh Valleys, hitherto largely neglected. An example of their work was *Mam* (1988), a historical documentary about working-class women and their role in the valley communities (figure 5.12).

Further examples of independent media production – in the music industry, local newspapers and community radio – are discussed in the three case studies which follow.

The life-cycle of independents

Given the precariousness of most independents in terms of insecure funding, small audiences and fragile staffing, it is not surprising that longevity is not easily achieved. More often than not, an independent will wither or collapse once a key supportive component is removed, such as a local authority grant or an inspirational and creative member of the organisation. However, there are occasions when independents flourish and 'break through' into the mainstream market. A spectacular case is that of *Viz*, a comic originally distributed in a few local Newcastle pubs, but eventually achieving a circulation of one million. With growth and commercial success frequently come takeover bids by major organisations, or else the independent itself becomes a company with diversifying interests to sustain its growth. For example, the *Viz* publishers John Brown have begun to launch new magazine titles on leisure topics, including gardening. Finally, some independents manage to maintain economic viability while retaining the core principles which stimulated their original conception, an outstanding example being *Private Eye*, the satirical magazine which has survived three decades of litigation.

CASE STUDY: THE MUSIC INDUSTRY

Majors versus indies: a historical overview

'To be totally ruthless about it, our job is to see the trends coming on the street, steal them, and sell them back to them'. This comment, made by a record company executive in the mid 1980s and quoted by Garfield (1986), might be said to epitomise the dynamic tension that exists between popular music as a culturally creative activity and as a form of cultural commodity marketed by industrial corporations. This tension has been mirrored to some extent in the contrasting roles of major and independent record companies (majors and indies) ever since pop music, or rock and roll, first became big business in the 1950s.

As an emergent musical style (based fundamentally on black rhythm-and-blues), rock and roll was launched on independent record labels in the USA. Small companies like Sun Records (whose roster included Elvis Presley) were willing and able to support new music for which there was initially a local, then a national, and finally an international market. The major record companies, after first ignoring what was perceived as a 'passing fad', eventually responded by signing up many of the new stars, like Presley (who switched from Sun to RCA in 1956), as well as supplying their own much less authentic versions in a bid to halt their declining market share, based mainly on older-established musical styles. Whereas prior to rock and roll in the early 1950s the top eight major companies enjoyed an average 95 per cent share of the singles market, by the early 1960s this had fallen to less than 50 per cent. Having stabilised during the 1960s era of pop and rock, the majors eventually regained a dominant market share of over 80 per cent by 1973. Peterson and Berger (1975) have indentified this pattern as a cyclic phenomenon; whereby the 'degree of diversity in musical forms is inversely related to the degree of market concentration'. In other words, when the major companies are in a dominant market situation it is because there is little variety of musical choice, but this is only temporary, as new musical styles burst on to the scene to be taken up by the indies and, much later on, by the majors. This could be seen as a process of generational renewal, whereby each new wave of teenagers rebels against the perceived conformity of the existing musical styles.

Soon after Peterson and Berger published their thesis, the cycle they described seemed to be back in full swing, when punk and new wave made a significant impact during the years 1976–79. Once again, independent labels, like Rough Trade and Chrysalis in Britain, played a key role. However, the cyclic model, although containing some legitimacy as a historical description, provides an over-simplistic view of the relationship between majors and indies, which is much less valid today. Even in the 1960s, for Britain many of the new beat and rhythm-and-blues groups, such as the Beatles and the Rolling Stones, were signed to majors from the start of their careers, while in the USA, some of the major labels like CBS were quite willing to 'experiment' with new acts during the hippie or counterculture period of the late 1960s. In actuality, there has always been an element of cooperation as well as competition between majors and indies in the music industry. Few indies have the resources to manufacture and distribute records, tapes, etc., other than on a localised scale, and so they have usually depended on the majors to gain access to a national or international market. Meanwhile, the majors have frequently relied on the indies as a source of new talent, a sort of 'research and development' role.

In previous decades the music market tended to be dominated by relatively few musical forms (e.g. the early 1970s was characterised by 'teenybop' singles and 'progressive' rock albums), but in recent years there has been a growing fragmentation. This is reflected in the diversity of charts published which monitor sales. Apart from the traditional Top 40, there are charts for dance, indy, reggae, metal and other forms of music. Consequently, it is much more difficult to control the market, as many of these musical styles are quite specialised, thus allowing independent labels with the requisite knowledge and reputation to carve out a niche in the market. This is not entirely new, as illustrated by the case of Atlantic (soul music) in the 1960s and Island (reggae music) in the 1970s. Some indies may even become a showcase for a local area's new talent, as Factory Records was for Manchester in the late 1980s.

Keith Negus (1992) argues that instead of seeing majors and indies as separate and oppositional organisations, it is more appropriate to distinguish between major and minor companies:

> Majors increasingly split into semi-autonomous working groups and label divisions, and minor companies connected to these by complex patterns of ownership, investment, licensing, formal and informal and sometimes deliberately obscured relationships. This has resulted in complex and confusing, continually shifting corporate constellations which are difficult to plot, as deals expire, new relationships are negotiated, new acquisitions made and joint ventures embarked upon. At the end of 1990 the trade magazine *Music Week* reported that 82 different labels were operating 'under the banner' of the PolyGram group in the UK alone. Which companies are owned, part owned or licensed becomes difficult to ascertain. If it can be done, what it means in terms of working practices becomes equally harder to infer, as the distinctions between an inside and outside, and between centre and margins, has given way to a web of mutually dependent work groupings radiating out from multiple centres.
>
> These organisational webs, of units within a company and connections to smaller companies, enable entertainment corporations to gain access to material and artists, and to operate a coordinating, monitoring and surveillance, operation rather than just centralised control. The corporation can still shape the nature of these webs through the use and distribution of investment. But it is a tight–loose approach, rather than a rigidly hierarchical form of organisation; tight enough to ensure a degree of predictability and stability in dealing with collaborators, but loose enough to manoeuvre, redirect or even reverse company activity.
>
> *Negus (1992)*

Music Week comes to similar conclusions:

> When the PJ Harvey album *Rid Of Me*, their first release on Island Records, entered the national chart at number three in May its success consolidated the group's position as one of the best new acts in Britain.

The chart position marked a vital breakthrough for Polly Harvey and her band. But it also had a wider significance for it was a prime example of just how much independent and major labels are now working together to develop new artists.

Nevertheless it still raised questions about the relationship between the two sectors. Like how much do the majors need independent acumen to help them develop new acts? And how much do independent labels need major muscle to secure commercial success both at home and abroad? And furthermore, what can the smaller labels do to protect their interest in the bands they discover and nurture?

In the case of PJ Harvey, of course, Island was involved almost from the beginning. An Island scout had seen the group's sixth gig and preliminary talks with the band had already taken place before the release of their debut Too Pure single, 'Dress'. And, when they ultimately signed to Island early in 1992, it was agreed that their first album, *Dry*, should appear on Too Pure, with whom the band had a longstanding verbal agreement.

The advantages of such an arrangement were immediately obvious. Secure in the knowledge that they had a longterm future with one of the country's most respected major labels, Harvey and her band were still able to grow their music organically, free of many of the commercial pressures that might have applied had they signed immediately to a major.

Island Records stood to benefit too. Too Pure's fully independent status meant that Harvey's profile could be developed modestly and inexpensively through the independent charts and a music press that is perceived to be biased in favour of the independent artist.

Music Week, 24 July 1993

The most successful British music act in 1996, Oasis, record for Creation Records which is defined as an indie record label for the purpose of the independent music charts. However, Creation is 51 per cent owned by Sony Music, one of the world's largest music companies.

One issue which does reflect a divergence of musical policy and investment strategy between majors and the minors, or indies, is the attitude towards the *format* for recorded music (figure 5.13). There is no doubt that the rise of the CD has been to the benefit of the major companies. It has several advantages. First, as music companies have increasingly been prone to vertical integration (e.g. Sony–CBS), the sales of CD hardware (the player) and software (the disc) have been mutually stimulating. Having purchased a CD player, new owners need to acquire a CD collection in order to justify the investment. Secondly, purchasers of CDs tend to be older and more affluent. Such an audience has a more conservative musical taste and is thus attracted to the artists who are well established (invariably tied to major companies). Indeed, reissuing 'old' music on CDs has been a prominent commercial ploy, resulting in up to 40 per cent of weekly album sales being based on back catalogues. Finally, profit margins on CDs are appreciably

---

ACTIVITY 5.3

Compare the Top 40 singles/album charts with the independent charts (e.g. in *New Musical Express* or *Music Week*), and identify the musical acts and styles with which the independent labels are achieving chart success.

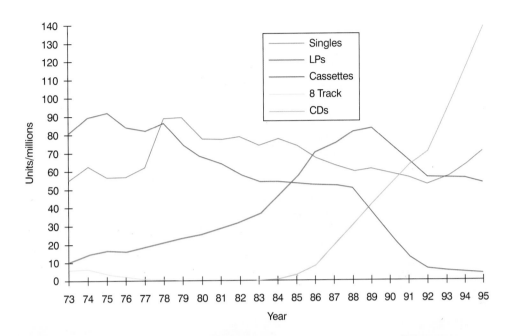

* Trade deliveries are defined as sales of records, cassettes and CDs invoiced to dealers, distributors and mail order houses

Fig. 5.13
UK sales of records, cassettes and CDs, 1973–95
Source: British Phonographic Industries Surveys

Fig. 5.14
Source: Paul Hickinbotham

higher than on cassette tape or vinyl, a fact which has generated considerable criticism, not least from hard-up music lovers (figure 5.15).

As the album and the CD have grown in strength, so has the power of the major companies. The 'big five' (CBS, WEA, EMI, PolyGram and BMG) share an estimated 65–70 per cent of the European recorded music market and well over a third of the world market. All five companies are part of entertainment conglomerates embracing electronics, music, film, video, etc., and so their music acts are often marketed in many forms, including CD, audio and video cassette, and various merchandising deals. In terms of global impact, it could be argued that contemporary pop stars such as Madonna and Michael Jackson have superseded Hollywood film stars (notwithstanding the fact that such artists often have a parallel film career).

Meanwhile, the single is in decline and vinyl has been effectively reduced to a marginalised role as either a cheap and flexible option for independent (especially dance) music or else a collector's item. The major companies argue that this is a consequence of consumer preference. Others see it as an outcome largely dictated by corporate power and self-interest. While the majors may have prevailed over the format of recorded music, the control of audience taste has been, and continues to be, less certain.

Mediating the market

Approximately 80 per cent of all recorded music released on to the market fails to make a profit. For example, of the 10 800 new albums issued in Britain in 1990, only 317 made it into the Top 40. Given this poor rate of success, together with the considerable fixed costs in terms of pressing plant, recording studios, etc., it is not surprising that much effort is directed towards stimulating consumer demand for the music in the search for the best-selling album or smash single which will offset the majority of failures.

Between those making the music and those purchasing the end product there exists a range of **gatekeepers** – filters sifting out the likely hits from the flow of excess production. Keith Negus (1992) prefers the concept of

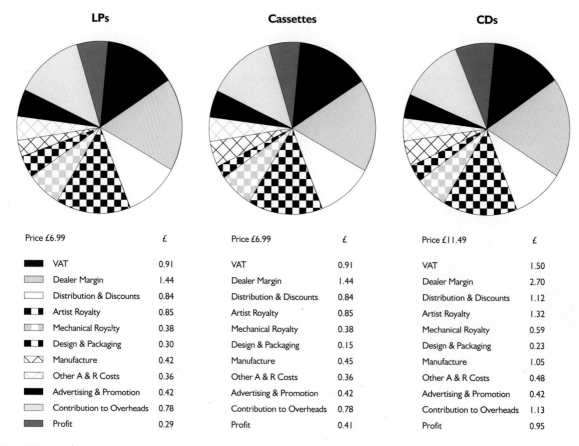

LPs		
Price £6.99		£
■■ VAT	0.91
▨ Dealer Margin	1.44
□ Distribution & Discounts	0.84
■□■ Artist Royalty	0.85
▨ Mechanical Royalty	0.38
■□■ Design & Packaging	0.30
▨ Manufacture	0.42
▨ Other A & R Costs	0.36
■■ Advertising & Promotion	0.42
▨ Contribution to Overheads	0.78
■■ Profit	0.29

Cassettes		
Price £6.99		£
VAT	0.91
Dealer Margin	1.44
Distribution & Discounts	0.84
Artist Royalty	0.85
Mechanical Royalty	0.38
Design & Packaging	0.15
Manufacture	0.45
Other A & R Costs	0.36
Advertising & Promotion	0.42
Contribution to Overheads	0.78
Profit	0.41

CDs		
Price £11.49		£
VAT	1.50
Dealer Margin	2.70
Distribution & Discounts	1.12
Artist Royalty	1.32
Mechanical Royalty	0.59
Design & Packaging	0.23
Manufacture	1.05
Other A & R Costs	0.48
Advertising & Promotion	0.42
Contribution to Overheads	1.13
Profit	0.95

Fig. 5.15

Price breakdown: LPs, cassettes and CDs

Source: British Phonographic Industries Yearbook, 1993

cultural intermediary, since it engages with the fact that music, unlike conventional industrial manufacturing, is a product with symbolic cultural value which affects how it is perceived by producers, distributors and consumers alike. The 'intermediaries' are those who help to shape the three key decisions identified by Simon Frith (1983) – 'who records, what is recorded, and which records reach the public'.

Of course, the music itself is not the whole 'product'. Performers add cultural meaning and value depending on their perceived image. For those with 'star' appeal, the actual music may be of secondary significance to the audience. Furthermore, music is often embedded within distinct subcultures which facilitate processes of identification and group solidarity among participants, especially in adolescent and teenage groups. Therefore, the analysis of music mediators which follows is necessarily contingent on the kinds of artist involved and their potential market niche.

A & R (artists and repertoire)

In the record company, at the front line of discovering and developing musical talent is the A & R *(artists and repertoire)* representative, whose responsibilities include: signing artists (perhaps 'poaching' them from other companies); examining the company catalogues for potential hits; and developing the musical policy and direction of a company's record labels. Negus (1992) describes A & R culture as predominantly white, male and college-educated (dating from the late 1960s/early 1970s). Consequently, there tends to be a conservative ethos in musical policy among the well-established, mainstream record labels – the rock-music aesthetic still being preferred at the expense of new styles, which are often viewed with suspicion or hostility.

When a band or performer has been signed to a record company, the producer plays a key role in organising and coordinating the actual recording of the music. Achieving 'the right sound' often involves skilful engineering during the mixing or post-production stage. Some producers' reputations have exceeded the artists' in being able to create a recognisable sound, e.g. Phil Spector in the 1960s ('the wall of sound'), Georgio Moroder in the 1970s (disco) and Paul Oakenfeld in the 1980s (remixing tracks to enhance the dance element). New technology, in the form of synthesisers, samplers, drum machines, etc., linked to a computer, has made possible DIY music production for a modest outlay, undermining the necessity of employing expensive studios owned by the major companies. The success of KLF in the early 1990s is testimony to the possibilities of using such new technology creatively in music production.

Marketing

Working in conjunction with the A & R team is the *marketing department*, which usually has a 'product manager' overseeing the packaging of an artist. This requires giving close attention to the appropriate image of the artist in relation to their target audience. In extreme cases, it may be possible to contrive totally an identity or image for a musical act that has been synthetically created by the company. Perhaps the best-known example is the Monkees, a group created and marketed as an attempt to imitate the success of the Beatles in the 1960s. The group were brought together by the company, Calpix, and provided with a television series along with the requisite songs and session musicians. More recent examples include a number of 'boy groups', such as Boyzone who were recruited through a newspaper advert, brought together and packaged primarily for a young female audience, and the hugely successful girl group the Spice Girls.

Pop music is as much image as music, and given the competitive nature of the business, the vital elements much sought after are 'uniqueness' and 'authenticity'. These qualities are frequently cited by fans to justify their support for particular artists. To claim that audiences are manipulated or duped by skilful marketing alone is to underestimate the critical scrutiny applied by the majority of such audiences to the music, performances, interviews, lifestyle and so on, of the artists. That is not to deny the existence of some degree of artifice and fantasy, especially within the traditional core of adolescent and pre-adolescent female fans, whose loyalty and identification is notoriously fickle. One of the greatest challenges, both in terms of music and image management, is making the transition from the teenage to the adult market. George Michael achieved this very successfully following the break-up of Wham! Less successful was Kylie Minogue, who attempted to replace the wholesome image sustained by her role in *Neighbours* with a more voluptuous and knowing performance in her post-*Neighbours* music career. Marketing images is further explored below in the discussion of the press, television and video.

Distribution

Apart from producing and marketing, the other key function for a record company is to ensure effective *distribution* of the music. Larger record companies employ a strike force whose aim is to ensure good visibility for the company's output in the high-street retailers, the shops from which the charts are compiled. Various strategies may be applied to persuade shops to cooperate, such as issuing glossy packages and point-of-sale displays, and joint advertising. The most influential ploy is to supply shops with cut-price or free copies of an artist's new single which are then sold to the consumer at a discount during the first week or fortnight of the single's release. This has contributed to a high rate of volatility in the singles chart with many singles entering the charts at number one only to disappear almost as quickly.

As with record companies, the trend for *music retailer*s is horizontal integration, so that in Britain the multiple stores like WH Smith, Our Price and HMV have emerged as the dominant outlets for music distribution and consumption. In some cases, record companies are able to guarantee outlets for their music via vertical integration, two examples in Britain being EMI–HMV and Virgin–Virgin. In contrast to the multiples and their flagship megastores are the specialist independent record shops, which focus on specific musical styles as well as catering for the beleaguered lovers of vinyl. Such shops often

Fig. 5.16
Source: Paul Hickinbotham

generate the initial sales for new music ignored by the conservative multiples until, and if, such music gains a chart entry (figure 5.17).

There is little doubt that the record company plays a significant role in determining the outcome to the questions of who records and what is recorded. Most companies negotiate contracts with artists that cede rights over the end product – what is released, when it is released, how it is promoted, etc. – to the company on their terms. Even artists with massive international appeal may find their artistic freedom curtailed by their music company, as George Michael found to his cost. He failed in his attempt to sue Sony for neglecting to promote his album, *Listen Without Prejudice* (1990), and was unable to release any music for over five years until he was able to transfer to a new company, EMI.

The music press

The answer to the third question as to what music reaches the public is more at the mercy of other mediators. The relationship between the *music press* and the music business is, on the whole, symbiotic. Most music journalists are dependent on the rest of the industry for news, interviews, access, etc., while the companies and artists are keen to gain as much favourable publicity as possible. Indeed, it is not unusual for careers to cross over in both directions: Neil Tennant of Pet Shop Boys began as a writer for *Smash Hits*. It is generally acknowledged that unfavourable reviews are not particularly influential in damaging sales, but that very positive reviews are helpful in the drive to 'break' new acts – in helping to stimulate a 'buzz' around an act.

	1991	1992	1993	1994	1995
Specialist chains					
HMV	80	84	91	88	95
Our Price	336	335	306	299	274
Virgin	11	13	23	27	46
MVC	–	–	–	n/a	29
Now	–	–	–	n/a	31
Multiples					
WH Smith	313	336	358	372	328
Woolworths	811	781	784	788	774
Menzies	178	170	171	163	156
Boots	255	251	239	235	207
Asda	n/a	n/a	n/a	n/a	203
Other multiples	347	319	350	193	750
Independent specialists					
Large	152	126	94	282	265
Medium	366	347	351	397	390
Small	666	648	848	601	605
Others (estimate)	800	800	800	800	400
Total	4 315	4 210	4 415	4 245	4 553

Fig. 5.17
Number of shops selling records, tapes and CDs
Source: Gallup/Millward Brown

In recent years, the range of music press has broadened to encompass the growth in musical diversity and audience taste. The long-standing teenage 'pop' magazines like *Smash Hits* act as quasi-consumer guides for a mainly female teen audience (although this role has become subsumed by the more general magazines like *Just Seventeen*). The attitude is unashamedly one of being a fan, unlike that of the weekly music 'newspapers' targeting an older, more musically knowledgeable (and usually male) readership, such as *New Musical Express*. Like its main rival, *Melody Maker*, *NME*'s identity and musical policy have undergone various shifts over the decades, but of late have focused on the independent or college-based music scene with only a limited interest in dance, hip-hop, metal, etc. To cater for these more specialised audiences there are contemporary titles such as *Kerrang!* and *Hip Hop Connection*, readership of which implies a commitment and knowledge well beyond the casual consumer. An even more partisan and dedicated audience can be found in the purchasers of the numerous music fanzines whose original inspiration can be traced back to the punk movement of the late 1970s. The cut-and-paste style and irreverence of such titles as *Sniffin Glue* can still be found in current examples, but others have taken advantage of desktop publishing to achieve a professional finish indistinguishable from that found in titles in the high-street newsagents. Finally, there is the new wave of glossy, more adult-oriented music magazines which are as much about past as present music. The brand leader is *Q* magazine, whose rise mirrors that of the CD at whose owners it is targeted. Much space is devoted to re-releases and charting the career of artists who rose to fame in the 1960s and 1970s (e.g. Eric Clapton, Dire Straits).

The agenda set by *Q* magazine is also paralleled in the broadsheet daily newspapers, each of which has at least one (usually male) pop music critic whose taste and selection reflects the age, education and class of the readers. Very different in approach is the tabloid press, whose rising interest in pop music (the *Sun* having established its first pop column, 'Bizarre', in 1982) ties in with the growth in entertainment news values of such papers. Journalists on the tabloids are more interested in the private lives of the artists than the music, and so their publicity value is certainly double-edged, as many, like Boy George, have found to their cost. Whatever the attitude of newspapers and magazines, the target for record companies and artists is maximum public exposure to coincide with the release of an album or single, and, via the company's own press officer and marketing department, considerable resources are directed to that goal.

Radio airplay

Given the fact that pop music is essentially aural in nature, and that most consumers like to hear a sample of music before buying it, it is not unreasonable to identify *radio* as the key form of mediation between artist and audience. Following scandals of bribery (or 'payola') in the American music industry in the early years of rock-and-roll, mainstream radio has been at pains to demonstrate its independence in the selection of what is played over the airwaves. Most radio stations in Britain use the playlist as a means of choosing which music is played most frequently. For Britain's most popular radio station, Radio 1, there are three playlists:

- an A list of 10–15 tracks guaranteed 20–25 plays per week
- a B list of 10–15 tracks guaranteed 15–19 plays per week
- a C list of 8–9 tracks guaranteed 10–14 plays per week.

In recognition of the much greater volume of albums sold than of singles, there is also an album list where six new album tracks receive a minimum of four plays per week. Records on the playlist account for approximately two thirds of Radio 1's mainstream shows.

In choosing tracks for playlists, the perceived needs of the station's audience are uppermost in the radio producers' minds. The Radio 1 playlist panel of disc jockeys and producers is anticipating the taste of those aged between 11 and 15, who account for the biggest proportion of singles buyers. On independent local radio (ILR), a similar, but more cautious, policy exists in compiling playlists. It is rare for an unknown artist to be selected for a playlist until the release enters the charts. Gallup, the company that compiles the charts, suggests (1993) that the majority of top 75 singles arrive in the charts without being originally playlisted. The purpose of the playlist is to help sustain sales of music once a chart position has been obtained.

For ILR, playlisted music is increasingly the only means of airplay for new releases. Its desire to maximise the audience for advertisers' benefit has led to the widespread practice of adhering to a musical format based on a mix of past and present hits selected by computer so that each song differs from the last in terms of tempo, mood and origin, but that none of the music is likely to alienate the target audience. Many stations split their frequencies in order to differentiate between music by generation – the AM service usually providing a more easy-listening format (often called 'gold') for older listeners. The formatting of radio services is a trend emanating from the USA, which has developed the system to a fine art, as documented by Simon Frith in 1988.

USA radio formatting

There are over 10 000 radio stations in the US, and in a bid to achieve a distinctive audience profile which might be attractive to advertisers, stations have increasingly adopted specialised formats, the most prominent of which are listed below.

Adult Contemporary (AC) is America's most popular radio format and aims for the 25- to 54-year-old group, advertisers' most desired group, by playing less abrasive contemporary hits. This means no hard rock, no raucous upbeat dance tunes, no pre-rock, no supper club singers. There are at least five main subspecies: full service stations are descendents of the huge MOR mainstays of the past and play soft hits with emphasis on news, talk and personalities; gold intensive stations play 80 to 90 per cent oldies with tiny current playlists of the safest hits; life encompasses everything from love songs to easy listening and aims for the upper end of the AC age bracket; music intensive have playlists of 20 or 30 records and are the most aggressive about playing new artists and crossovers; adult alternative stations feature an AC base with emphasis on other types of music such as jazz or soft rock.

Album Oriented Rock (AOR) grew out of progressive rock radio in the late Sixties and had a broader musical scope in the past. Nowadays it seldom strays from white rock, rarely playing more than one track from an LP during a two-month period. Presentations still try to preserve the 'rock and roll outlaw' attitude of the format's early years, though the music is now safe and predictable. The last remnants of AOR's free-form roots are the dozens of college stations which are increasingly important in exposing new music.

Contemporary Hit Radio (CHR) is the descendent of Top 40, which by the Eighties had a shopworn image. CHR made a comeback in 1983–85, bucking the narrowcast trend by picking up hits from Urban and AOR stations.

Classical has a long and lucrative history, with sufficient population to support its minority appeal. Listeners are few, but their economic standing is an ad agency's dream.

Comedy formats have been attempted at various junctures, most recently in Washington DC and suburban Los Angeles. They've never prospered. A constant comedy diet doesn't seem to have the appeal of comedy extracts interspersed with other elements.

Contemporary Christian Radio is a relatively recent development arising from a growing Christian music industry. Some stations are like other Adult Contemporary stations ('Christians need traffic reports too'); others maintain a more religious atmosphere.

Country is one of the oldest formats and, in total number of stations, the largest. Loyalty is to artists rather than the latest record. Country remains a heavily oldies-based format, but rarely reaches back before 1970.

Easy Listening Radio is an umbrella term encompassing nostalgia, big band, and other non-rock material. Though easy listening ratings are excellent, it means an older (45 plus), less-profitable audience to ad agencies.

Gold is a blanket term for a format playing exclusively post-1955 oldies, pioneered by WCBS in New York 20 years ago. In the last couple of years a second gold rush has materialised (the first came in the wake of 'American Graffiti' in the mid-Seventies). The biggest oldies phenomenon remains 'classic rock', concentrating on the 1967–75 heydey of progressive rock; loads of Cream, Doors and so on.

Gospel is divided into black and white stations, both concentrated in the South and serving constituencies too small to register in the ratings.

Hispanic stations specialising in modern and traditional Latin forms of music are bound to increase in importance as the nation's Hispanic population rises.

Jazz is rarely found as a full-time format. Similar to classical in attracting upscale, loyal listeners, but doesn't have the same prestigious image.

New Age music – instrumental atmospheric records largely popularised by the Windham Hill label and characterised by unbelievers as 'aural wallpaper' – has been a quiet industry phenomenon. Most stations also include jazz, AC or soft AOR programming.

News stations have found a successful AM-only niche. It's cheaper to play records than maintain a big news staff, so news stations aren't feasible outside big markets.

Quiet Storm is named after the Quiet Storm programme on WHUR in Washington in the mid-Seventies which played softer R and B ballads and mellow jazz. Increasingly popular.

Religious refers to religious talk programming, often 'dollar a holler' air time purchased from stations by exposure-seeking evangelists.

Sports radio received its first exclusive station last year – WFAN in New York, broadcasting sports talk shows and play-by-play events.

Talk stations consist mostly of call-in shows, with instructional programmes as ballast. Expensive to produce and therefore limited to major markets.

Urban Contemporary is a synonym for black radio but, with more and more white artists in traditionally black musical domains, it is a more accurate term. Urban stations have made great strides in the ratings.

Economic prosperity has not kept pace, however, as ad agencies persist in viewing Urban Listeners as denizens of the underclass.

From *Facing the Music* by Simon Frith. © 1988 by Simon Frith.
Reprinted by permission of Pantheon Books,
a division of Random House, Inc.

- To what extent are Simon Frith's formats reproduced on British radio?
- Are there any notable formats which have been overlooked?
- What do you consider to be the advantages and disadvantages of such a system in comparison with contemporary British radio?

It seems likely Britain will follow this pattern as more stations are granted licences. Already, many local incremental stations are dedicated to specific musical styles, such as Kiss (dance), Jazz, and WNK (various forms of black music). Minority music tastes ignored by ILR and daytime Radio 1 are only likely to be acknowledged by those disc jockeys still allowed freedom to make a personal choice of music for broadcasting, for example on evening Radio 1 or on pirate radio. Programmes or services containing a diverse range of musical styles in their output will be increasingly rare; examples are offered by Radio 1 under the BBC's public service remit. The more specialist music channels appear on radio (like Virgin, which targets the older, 25- to 45-year-old, Q-reading audience), the more Radio 1's audience share and future survival will be under threat.

Television and video

Television exposure is much sought after by companies and artists as a means of enhancing audience awareness and hence sales. Until Channel 4 pioneered youth programmes based on music, from *The Tube* to *The Word*, BBC's *Top of the Pops* (TOTP) was the main television showcase for pop music. While being consistently criticised for its musical conservatism and exclusive concern with the singles chart, its impact on sales is undeniable. A 1988 Gallup survey estimated that a single's sales were likely to be boosted by between 50 and 100 per cent overnight as a result of a TOTP performance. The only television opportunities to exceed this are those supplied by the annual BRIT awards (which have a similar effect to that of the Oscars on film audiences) and occasional live charity concerts, the most famous being Live Aid in 1985. Such events can significantly stimulate an artist's international sales.

At the heart of many television music performances is the *pop video*. Its potential as a promotional tool was first fully realised when Queen's 1975 video for their song 'Bohemian Rhapsody', broadcast on TOTP, played a vital role in sustaining the song for nine weeks at number one in the singles chart. The 1980s saw a huge expansion of pop videos, with some television programmes like *The Chart Show* relying almost exclusively on video clips. The rising costs of making the videos, plus a desire to gain international penetration, has meant that the pop video has favoured the established, better-known artists for whom making the video is more likely to be a safe investment. Furthermore, there has been a recent decline in the use of pop videos by mainstream television, due partly to the effect of transmission charges of between £500 and £800 per minute being levied on television companies from 1985 in a bid to recoup some of the high production costs, which can vary between a few thousand pounds and $2 million (for Michael Jackson's 1983 video *Thriller*).

Aside from terrestrial television, the main outlet for pop videos has been MTV. Launched in 1981 on American cable television, its rapid global growth has meant its impact on young audiences cannot be ignored (though this is less true in Britain, where satellite/cable access is still limited). In some respects, it resembles Top 40 commercial music radio, with its emphasis on a conservative playlist of singles and albums, mixing past and present hits but on a worldwide basis.

Likewise, videos that do not fit the normal parameters of style (e.g. fast editing) and content (e.g. avoidance of overt sex and violence) are unlikely to be playlisted. The extent to which the pop video has foregrounded image at the expense of music is debatable. It seems apparent that artists able to produce more imaginative or compelling videos, such as Madonna, do gain an advantage, not least in boosting sales of the videos themselves (especially when they have been subject to censorship on television, like Madonna's 'Justify My Love'). However, it is questionable how much close attention they receive. It has been suggested that, for most of the audience, pop videos (especially on MTV) are used as background entertainment, rather like radio. Nonetheless, it seems likely that in future audiovisual CDs will become a prominent format for consuming music (figure 5.18).

The pop video as a generic form overlaps with television advertising through the use of fast edits, special effects, unusual camera angles, etc. Indeed, it is a form of advertising in itself. Meanwhile, television adverts have been increasingly prone to apply music soundtracks drawn from the past. The Levi 501 jeans campaign is a notable example. Its resurrection of 'golden oldies' has led to a succession of chart successes for songs like 'I Heard It Through the Grapevine', 'When a Man Loves a Woman', etc. This has led to accusations of commercial values corrupting the original meaning and power of the songs themselves. (An extreme example is the use of Bob Dylan's 1960s protest anthem, 'The Times They Are a-Changin' to promote a Canadian bank.) Indeed, the ties between advertising and pop music have become ever more interwoven. Most major tours involve corporate sponsorship, star performers regularly endorse commercial products, and most recently, album and single releases have been sponsored, for example Häagen-Dazs ice cream launched a successful double CD of love songs via EMI and the Spice Girls' single 'Step to Me' was available only through a Pepsi promotion.

Another form of **synergy** is the use of music soundtracks to accompany films. Although this is not a recent phenomenon – Bill Haley's 'Rock Around The Clock' hit single featured in the 1955 film *Blackboard Jungle*, it was not until the spectacular success of the Bee Gees' disco-based music score for *Saturday Night Fever* in 1977 (figure 5.19) that the commercial potential of such soundtracks was fully realised. (This is discounting pop 'musicals', films designed to showcase pop stars performing their songs,

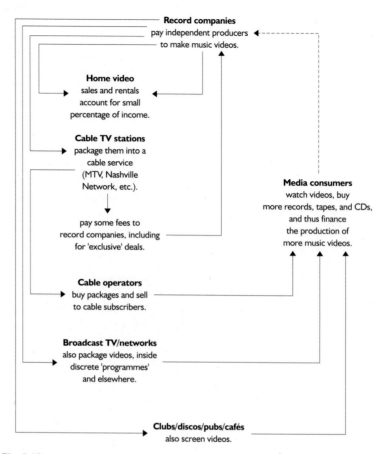

Fig. 5.18

This cycle illustrates the role of music videos in generating consumption of records, CDs and tapes, which in turn supply revenue for more videos

Source: A. Goodwin, *Dancing in the Distraction Factory*, Routledge, 1993

such as the Beatles' *A Hard Day's Night* and *Help!*). During the 1980s and '90s there have been dozens of films released which contain a sufficient sampling of music to justify an album release, or whose opening/closing credits feature a song targeted at the singles chart, e.g. Whitney Houston's 'I Will Always Love You' from *The Bodyguard* (1992).

The above discussion has focused on the most salient and trusted means by which music is chosen for audience consumption. All the mediators are subject to the normal commercial and regulatory constraints which work in favour of the major companies. However, there is an alternative 'system' by which music can flourish from the grassroots through to mainstream recognition.

Pop music has always had an undercurrent of subcultures or cults which have surfaced to gain more widespread recognition from time to time. In the 1960s it was folk 'protest' and hippie psychedelic music; in the 1970s, Northern Soul and gay disco; in the 1980s, hip-hop and rap, etc. The struc-

Try and identify a current example of music culture which is based wholly or partly on an 'alternative' system of support, as described in figure 5.20. You should consider the role of the following: independent record labels, clubs, fanzines and specialist music papers, pirate or incremental radio, DIY record and tape production, and independent record shops.

Fig. 5.19
Saturday Night Fever, *1977*
Source: Kobal Collection/Paramount

tural support for such music subcultures, particularly in recent years, revolves around the interplay between a few key ingredients, namely a thriving club scene, pirate radio, DIY or bootleg record production, fanzines and independent record shops. The case study in figure 5.20 includes examples of all these elements.

Thriving by night

A combination of black DJs, illicit bootleggers and pirate radio entrepreneurs have established an alternative entertainment sphere. Cynthia Rose traces the emergence of an unofficial enterprise culture.
"Recently," Jazzie B is saying, "I've been following this Jesse Jackson business in America. I was shocked that he's gettin' votes from white states – and I was thinkin' to myself, Oh *damn!* Maybe the time has come! It's kinda wound me up. And now, in what I do, I'm really adoptin' a more professional attitude."

What does Jazzie do? He's the DJ head of Funki Dredd Productions, and the founder of north London's 16-strong Soul II Soul crew. Started five years ago by Jazzie and an old school friend Philip 'Daddae' Harvey, Soul II Soul run a sound system, a weekly club (Centre of the World, every Sunday night in Old Street), and a shop: the Soul II Soul Basement Store at 162 Camden High Street. Soul II Soul is also the name on a Ten Records' release entitled "Fair Play", which entered May's pop charts at number 65. Jazzie B is a Renaissance dude – but the Renaissance of which he's a part has changed London itself.

During the past half-decade, Jazzie's milieu – DJs, nightclub aficionados, hustlers of vinyl and the men behind pirate radio – have made social history of a singular sort. They have established a completely alternative entertainment sphere; one which is powered by black aesthetics.

Jazzie's part of this new environment started to shape itself early in 1986, via the magnet of illicit warehouse parties. These were the result of young white entrepreneurs (like the Family Funktion team) working in tandem with black crews like Soul II Soul or Shake & Fingerpop, under black DJs such as Jazzie and Norman Jay.

"Family Funktion were middle-class white guys," notes DJ Trevor Nelson, a staffer at pirate radio Kiss-FM, and known as "Madhatter" for his affiliation to Madhatters sound system. "They were trendies: who knew a lot of people, all at college, all with a lot of money. With them and Soul II Soul, it was two complete opposites coming together – and pulling 3,000 people illegally."

"White guys invented the warehouse," says Nelson. "They had the know-how regarding the legalities. And they made sure it was never busted, which black kids could never have done. Put a white guy on the door and everything could be cool. You could make a couple of grand off an illegal affair – and half the police force's sons would be there."

Warehouse parties made big money and set bigger precedents. But more than this, they succeeded in integrating young London in a fashion which made the GLC or Rock Against Racism seem quaint. "Warehouses brought the cultures together, black kids and white kids," says Madhatter Trevor. "There were always soul boys and soul girls, who always came together. But their cultures were worlds apart. Now they're still together, though. Which is absolutely brilliant."

What warehouses initiated, pirate radio helps maintain. On London's 30-odd illegal stations, black musics provide the majority format (soul, hip-hop, jazz, reggae, house, and the 1970s soul called "rare groove"). And some of the stations have ambitious set-ups: like LWR ("once "London Weekend Radio", now "London-Wide Radio"), a five-year-old, single-proprietor enterprise which broadcasts 24 hours a day, seven days a week. Or KISS-FM, the two-year-old weekender which trades on a roster of "name" DJs from a burgeoning nightclub scene.

Drawing on personal knowledge and on family record collections which can span three generations, such DJs easily one-up the playlist-crippled commercial broadcasters. And their clear connections to and love for black music have generated a whole new market for soul in Greater London. The clearest symbol of this may be seen in Soho. There, where six record retailers have flourished for some years (Tower Records, Groove Records, Daddy Kool, Hitman Records, Virgin's Megastore and HMV Records), three more have chosen this moment to move in. They are Beak Street's Red Records (where Madhatter and KISS-FM's Lloyd Brown can be found), Black Market Records (the brainchild of two more DJs, Steve Jervier and Rene Gelston), and Bluebird Records.

Black Londoners who work for the pirates take pride in exercising an expertise excluded from the capital's entertainment mainstream. LWR jock Steve Edwards: "British legal radio is too controlled, too conservative. And its DJs are so complacent! We're not afraid to play *our* music. You know, you've got a collection – you blow the dust off a few things. You *think* about it It takes me two hours to put together a show. I don't just throw things on the turntable. I've always wondered why the legal stations don't utilise the skills of pirate DJs – because, at the end of the day – it *works*."

Indeed it does. The pirates use street news and gossip as well as music to provide a complement to the club scene. They've also discovered how to support themselves – with advertising for venues, gigs, shops and new record releases. (Several also run clubs and record fairs themselves.) Through plugs and airplay for each other's every project, the pirate DJs control the entire marketplace they inhabit.

Within those precincts, Lloyd "Daddy Bug" Brown of Red Records is known as the "cut-out king", a former independent wholesaler who has recycled many a "rare groove". "The pirates have created a whole thing for themselves," says Daddy Bug. "It goes like this: it's cheap to advertise on a pirate. But you get whatever it is plugged every hour, 24 hours a day. If you got something to offer, you know, that is gonna *work*."

Thus far, what talent mainstream entertainment has poached from the pirates has been white (radio's Gilles Peterson, *Night Network's* Tim Westwood). But, from Radio London's *Nite FM* through BBC's *Def II,* they have forced alterations in attitudes and responses. And airplay over establishment waves is often contingent on pirate success. Jazzie B's "Fair Play", for instance, was heard in clubs and on the pirates almost two months before it "appeared". (It was then "silenced" for a fortnight, to starve the marketplace.) "It can be an absolute pain," grins Madhatter Trevor Nelson. "Now the kids will come into your store asking for things before they've even been *pressed* – because some pirate has had a cassette. And they won't believe you when you say it's not out yet. After all – they've heard it!"

"The national radio boys," he adds, "now wait for us to make these records safe. Face it, they wouldn't know a good house track from a bad one." In financial terms, the "safe" record – this week's "boom cut" or certified hit – has never been more desirable. Sometimes it's a rare groove: a soul cut whose physical scarcity enhances its marketplace value. Other times, the pirates hype rap music, hip-hop hits or the neo-disco known as house. Each of these genres has played its part in London's recent deluge of DIY record production, aka bootlegging. Many pirate DJs also lend their knowledgeable ears to sampling, a digital collage which spikes new records with audible references from other hits.

Almost everyone dabbles, at least, in bootlegs. And more than curiosity drives them – "booties" can bring up to £30,000 per pressing. "It's all to do with information," explains Daddy Bug. "Knowing what tune will sell. Once you get the information, anybody can do it." ("If you don't put something on vinyl," argues another pirate DJ, "You ain't got no CV – you got no proof of what you do.")

Like hustling "rare grooves" or throwing a warehouse jam, this unofficial industry provides a foot in the door for black British business talent. "As black people in Britain," says Trevor Nelson wryly, "there's not a lot we are responsible for – apart from controlling our own hair products. All we've got in the general mind is we're good athletes, we can sing and dance, and so on. What upsets most of us is, if that's all we get, why can't we *control* it? That's why most guys are into blatantly bootleggin' records – they just feel blatantly left out."

And that is where a figure like Jazzie B comes in. Jazzie is determined that Soul II Soul should, in the words of one pirate ad, stand firm for the culture. "Black people in this city can't hide from the political thing," he contends. "Our living, our existence in this society, is really political. And I've made the assumption that I've got to anchor something here. To produce something from Britain that will be looked on as positive."

Touring as the Soul II Soul sound system has taught Jazzie B the kind of clout Anglo style is able to command abroad. But he considers respect at home a more important priority. "I want to see more young business people, more people doing what we're doing here in the shop. I want to see more of us in the charts, more of us in the media's eye.

"I know I'm black, right? I know I'm from the ghetto. I don't want to be reading that anymore. I want my nephews and my nieces, my friend's children and my godchildren to be readin' in the papers about this person doing *good*. And have it give them something to really think about."

It's unsurprising Jazzie B should feel ambivalence about the media. Truly interracial and composed of the young and the officially marginal, London's entertainment underground is rarely represented in the media. It supports its own cottage industries – booties, clubs, mixes, pirate radio and boutiques. From fanzines through to semi-slick mags such as *Soul Underground* or *Straight No Chaser,* it has started to foster a leisure press of its own. But the single mainstream commentator to comprehend its size and importance has been comic Lenny Henry. His pirate DJ character "Delbert Wilkins" benefits from primary-source smarts: Henry is the Chairman of pirate KISS-FM, which claims an audience of 200,000.

Home with CDs and VCRs (or languishing in the Groucho Club) by one am, other establishment pundits remain ignorant of that new London which thrives by night. Regardless of them, however, it operates seven days a week. "People who aren't a part of it," smiles Madhatter Trevor, "can't imagine the size this whole scene has grown to. Maybe they should just stand round Cambridge Circus between one and three am. They'd see hundreds of people go by, all eating dodgy takeaways, hustling to get the night bus. They're all under 20, all dressed the same. And they're black and white, and Chinese and Greek and Indian."

Its movers and shakers know this cosmopolitan scene faces stiff challenges. For one thing, among the competitive pirates, violence has increased. A faster-growing hazard, perhaps, is drug use on the circuit. And blind self-interest can rear its head in any sphere. Even so, men like Jazzie B feel it brings a specific hope. "There's definitely a generation out there now," says Jazzie, "which knows what 'multiracial' means. You're talking about youth of all kinds. All we need now is to stick together."

Fig. 5.20
Source: © *New Statesman & Society*, 17 June 1988

CASE STUDY: LOCAL NEWSPAPERS

Studies of the media have tended to focus on national or mutinational institutions and their output, but for many people one of the most immediate and 'close-to-life' examples of media consumption is the local newspaper that provides the news, events and values of their particular community. Research by Gunter *et al.* (1994) showed that 70 per cent of the public get their information about world news through television and about 20 per cent through newspapers, whilst 40 per cent of the public said that they get their local news through newspapers compared to about 35 per cent through television. If we consider the size of the geographical area served by local newspapers in comparison to local radio and television it is clear that local newspapers have a much tighter 'local' focus than most BBC or Independent radio or television stations. Local newspapers serve a function that neither commercially run local radio, usually based upon national music charts or golden oldies, nor local television, with its limited local slots sandwiched between the network output, can easily provide.

Ownership and control

In 1988, *Benn's Directory* registered 797 weekly paid-for local newspapers, 931 free local newspapers, 70 daily local newspapers (including 11 daily morning provincial newspapers) and 3 Sunday local newspapers in England alone. Many of these newspapers had circulations in excess of 100 000 and had over 80 per cent penetration in their local areas. By 1993 there were 722 paid-for titles and 826 freesheets registered with the Newspaper Society. The number of local weekly newspapers declined by 40 per cent between 1921 and 1983 and the circulation of those that continue to exist has dropped by 25 per cent since 1975.

One of the main growth areas for local newspapers during the 1980s was the freesheet, rising from 169 titles in 1978 to over 1000 by 1988. These local newspapers were distributed free, often directly into people's homes, and were partly the result of advances in new printing technology and low staffing overheads as well as the expansion in advertising revenue. One of the earliest and best-known of the freesheet groups was Eddie Shah's Messenger group, based in Stockport. Although primarily vehicles for advertising with little editorial or journalistic content, these freesheets did present serious competition for many established weekly 'paid-for' newspapers (Goodhart and Wintour, 1986, and McNair, 1996).

Many of the freesheet companies were bought up by existing local newspaper groups, or else the latter launched their own freesheet in direct competition, having the advantage of an established editorial and printing network. Some of the larger local newspaper groups, like Westminster Press and Reed Regional Newspapers, often published both 'paid-fors' and freesheets in the same area. However, during the economic recession of

ACTIVITY 5.6

Choose a period of time, say one week, and try to monitor across the range of different media that serve your locality the quality and frequency of 'local' news about your neighbourhood or community. List all press, radio and television sources. Where else does the local news come from?

the early 1990s, many of these freesheets closed down due to a decline in advertising revenue.

Franklin and Murphy (1991) and McNair (1996) have examined some recent developments in the local newspaper market, and their research suggests that there is a change taking place in the nature of local newspapers, most significantly in the structure of ownership and economic organisation of the local press. They identify an increasing concentration of ownership of local press into a small number of large media groups, intent on expanding their horizontal integration (see p. 160) by taking over competitors and creating regional monopolies.

These regional newspaper groups are now being bought up by other, larger cross-media groups who are keen to develop their cross-media interests, and see a 'synergy' between owning both local newspapers and television services in particular areas. The relaxation of ownership controls in the 1996 Broadcasting Bill has increased this move, with Channel 3 companies increasingly looking to merge their 'regional' infrastuctures with local newspapers to share newsgathering and advertising resources and to cut overheads.

One of the first television companies to move into local newspapers was Scottish TV who purchased Caledonian Newspapers, publishers of the daily *Glasgow Herald*. Correspondingly, as television companies seem to be moving into the local newspaper market, so many of the newspaper companies that have dominated the market for many years seem to be selling out.

Until recently one of the largest publishers of weekly newspapers was Reed Regional Newspapers with over 100 weekly titles and sales of over 5.5 million copies. This was bought out by its management and now operates as an independent company under the name of Newsquest Media Group. Newsquest is currently one of the largest local newspaper groups, with 118 weekly titles. Other top companies include Trinity International Holdings, Northcliffe Newspapers Group (part of the *Daily Mail* group), and United Provincial Newspapers (part of United News and Media group formed by the merger of MAI and United Newspapers).

As part of this concentration of ownership of the local press, Franklin and Murphy identify an increasing homogenisation, or 'sameness', in local newspapers, where small independent companies have been bought out by larger groups that want to eliminate competition, reduce costs and streamline production. For many newspapers this has resulted in a loss of 'local' identity, and many 'local' newspapers, like those of the Portsmouth and Sunderland Newspaper group, are now printed at regional centres away from their communities, and are often only one in a series of 'local' newspapers whose only difference is their front and back pages, while the articles and features on the inside may often be identical.

The consequences of this homogenisation can easily be seen by looking at the 'alternative' or independent local press that has tried over the years to establish various titles as voices for alternative views in society, often youthful and/or left-wing, such as the *Manchester Free Press*, *Leeds Other Paper*, *East End News*, *Northern Star* or *New Manchester Review*. Only a few

Fig. 5.21
Source: Paul Hickinbotham

of these titles have survived, usually by focusing on listings and 'lifestyle' rather than maintaining a radical alternative editorial line. Their success, as various commentators have noted (Franklin and Murphy, 1991; Whitaker, 1984), has been generally at the expense of any radicalism, and rather than extending choice and variety the 'alternative' newspapers that have survived have been absorbed into the mainstream values, attitudes and styles of big-business newspaper production and ownership. One of the few successful 'alternative' newspapers that has managed to retain some radical idealism is the *Big Issue*, which through its network of unemployed street vendors is now increasingly available throughout England and Wales.

Local newspapers traditionally used to be the entry point into the industry, where young cub reporters served their apprenticeship, their ambition being to move on to the national press of Fleet Street, or into local radio and/or television and then perhaps on to national news. This traditional route was overseen by the National Council for the Training of Journalists, originally set up in 1952. Today, however, learning to become a journalist is less about the acquisition of knowledge and more about gaining competencies. Beharrell (1993) points to this change in the training of journalists as one of the reasons for the change in style and content of local news reporting: 'For how a person has been equipped to deal with media situations, and how a media industry prepares its practitioners, will determine individual and group reactions to media situations both common-

Source	Total	Percentage
Courts	105	12.0
Coroner	10	1.0
Police	98	11.5
Other emergency services (fire, ambulance)	11	1.5
Council (and regional authorities)	199	23.0
Business	73	8.5
Government	32	3.5
MPs	11	1.5
Schools/colleges	33	4.0
Clubs/voluntary sector	107	12.5
Charitable appeals	36	4.0
Political parties/pressure groups	13	1.5
Churches	25	3.0
Public protest	14	1.5
Investigations	9	1.0
Other	89	10.5
Total	865	100.5

Fig. 5.22

Local Press: sources of news

Sources: Glossop Chronicle, Bury Times, Westmorland Gazette, Cumberland and Westmorland Herald, Burnley Express, Rochdale Observer, Rossendale Free Press, North Wales Weekly News, Wigan Observer, Lochaber News, Oban Times, Warrington Star, Stockport Express Advertiser, Lothian Courier

ACTIVITY 5.7

Look through a copy of your local newspaper and identify the main sources of news. How many of the stories will have been sent in and how many are the result of investigation or research by a journalist from the newspaper? How does your newspaper compare with figure 5.22?

place (and therefore predictable) and out of the ordinary.' Beharrell suggests that the modern reporter, trained in a climate of 'commercial reality', will rely upon previous success in the types of story that appeal to both the editor and readers. Stories become shorter in length, less detailed or informed, and instead simpler and more emotional. Local newspapers have tended to become more populist in character, relying on a 'house (or group) style' that consists of a diet of human-interest stories and moral panics, a style that is no longer the result of a professional ideology of balance and impartiality but rather a campaigning sensationalism that is aimed at increasing sales.

For many people the local newspaper is likely to be the single most important source of news and information within their area, especially as the local newspaper may reach over 80 per cent of households and be kept around the house for several days, rather than being thrown away the next day as often happens to daily newspapers. Local newspapers have an important relationship with the communities they serve, recording the 'organized output of symbolic events, decisions and official accounts produced by a local establishment in sectors of the state, business and the formal voluntary sector' (Franklin and Murphy, 1991). Advertising is vital for the industry and through the newspapers it also provides information about local services and products available in the community.

A report on the sources of 865 stories in fourteen British local newspapers, accounting for over 67 per cent of all news stories, revealed five main sources of news: local and regional government, voluntary organisations, the courts, the police and business (figure 5.22). Franklin and Murphy suggest that this reliance upon these limited sources means that the local press tends to reinforce the status quo and celebrate the values of a stable, well-ordered and, as much as possible, conflict-free community.

The Newbury Weekly News

A local 'paid-for' weekly newspaper that has served its local community since 1867 is the *Newbury Weekly News*. This is a broadsheet that was started during the explosion of small newspapers that resulted from the abolition of the various taxes (stamp duty, paper tax and advertising duty) on newspapers in the 1850s and 1860s (see chapter 6, p. 234–237). This meant that both the cost of production and the cover price of newspapers fell. For the first time, a legal, mass readership was possible, and legitimate newspapers like the *Newbury Weekly News* became an economic possibility and profitable reality. Originally, it contained only a small amount of local news and syndicated material from London-based newspapers. As the size and prosperity of Newbury grew, so the demand for local news and information on trade and agriculture developed. Today, very little of the newspaper's content is from sources outside the newspaper itself.

Ownership of the *Newbury Weekly News* is in the hands of a private company, whose shareholders include members of families who have controlled the newspaper since it started. The company also produces a weekly freesheet, the *Advertiser*, and monthly and quarterly supplements

Fig. 5.23

Source: *Newbury Weekly News*, 22 August 1996

aimed at the local business and leisure sectors. The *Newbury Weekly News* is unusual in owning its own presses, which give the paper increased flexibility for deadlines as well as providing additional income through commercial printing for outside organisations.

One of the advantages of being independent is the 'organic' nature of the realtionship between the newspaper and the community. The company claims that any decisions concerning the running of the *Newbury Weekly News* are made by a management team consisting of local people, living within the community the newspaper serves, who should therefore be able to keep in touch with the conditions and feelings of the community. Editorial decisions are internal, and unlike the editors of local newspapers that are members of large groups, the editor of the *Newbury Weekly News* does not have to worry about outside or group interests, although there are still commercial, and circulation, pressures to consider.

The *Newbury Weekly News* regards its readership as 'everyone who lives locally'. A survey it commissioned in 1989 suggested the paper reached over 70 per cent of adults in the area and up to 80 per cent in Newbury itself. In 1996 the circulation was 27 000, a reduction from its 1987 peak of about 32 000.

As there is no direct competition the *Newbury Weekly News* states that there is no overt 'segmentation' of readership, and that specific groups are not targeted in terms of age, socio-economic grouping or gender but are simply defined by locality; if you live in the Newbury area you are seen as a potential reader of the newspaper.

Competition for the *Newbury Weekly News* is limited, and one of the clues to its apparent success is its unique role as the only truly local medium for a fairly specific geographical area. Newbury and its surrounding villages exist on the edge of various other regions – southern, western, London or south Midlands – but none seems to offer the specific local service of the *Newbury Weekly News*. Other local newspapers, daily and weekly, that are available in the area come from towns several miles away, such as Reading, Swindon or Basingstoke, and are part of larger newspaper groups and therefore very different in character. These papers reflect the news and needs of their larger, more urban, communities.

Although freesheets from other newspaper groups are delivered in the area it is unlikely that any new newspaper will appear to challenge the hegemony of the *Newbury Weekly News*; the last competitor was seen off in the late 1890s. In 1977 the Royal Commission on the Press found that out of a sample of 24 local weekly newspapers launched since 1961, only one was established in direct competition with an existing local weekly (Curran and Seaton, 1991). There is no alternative or community press borne on the back of supposedly cheaper technology to challenge the *Newbury Weekly News*, and the local council does not produce its own PR-minded municipal free papers, as Franklin and Murphy suggest may occur in some urban areas.

An ILR station, 2TEN FM, is available in Newbury. Based in Reading, it is part of the GWR regional network and has some local programming, but generally offers chart or 'golden oldie' music. Its 'footprint' includes an

ACTIVITY 5.8

Try to establish a reader profile for your local newspaper. What categories of news and features are used and what does this tell you about:

1 the local community?
2 the newspaper that serves it?
3 how the newspaper defines its sense of community?

area that is served, in local newspaper terms, by at least four different weekly local newspapers and two daily local newspapers. In 1992 the BBC opened a local radio station, Radio Berkshire, which offered a limited local service and aimed to cover the whole county, a potential audience of nearly 70 000. In 1996, owing to financial pressures, it merged with the local BBC station based in nearby Oxford to form Thames Valley FM, thereby diluting further its local focus for the Newbury area.

The most recent challenge to the *Newbury Weekly News* came when the commercial television franchise changed in January 1993. Meridian took over from TVS and set up a local TV studio in Newbury, which, since January 1993, has had its own local news programme on ITV at 6.30 every evening. This has presented some competition to the *Newbury Weekly News*, mainly because it has the immediacy of a daily programme and the attraction of pictures over print.

The distinct geographical nature of the *Newbury Weekly News*'s catchment area makes it suitable for a community or 'incremental' radio station, although any group interested in offering such a service will probably need to include the paper and its news-gathering network as part of any bid to the Radio Authority. (See the following case study on community radio.)

The traditional nature of the paper and its readers is perhaps reflected in the debate about its page size. When most newspapers are moving to tabloid, letters to the *Newbury Weekly News* indicate a strong support among its readers for it to retain its traditional broadsheet format. The *Advertiser*, its freesheet sister, is tabloid and has a higher distribution. It is particularly popular in the neighbouring town of Thatcham with its higher concentration of new housing and 'non-professional' households (see figure 5.24).

Advertising provides the *Newbury Weekly News* with about 80 per cent of its revenue. Without this source of income the cover price would be around £1.50 per copy, rather than the 36p charged in 1996. Most of the advertising comes from local businesses and so the economic health of the paper is bound up with that of the town's businesses. During the late 1980s when Newbury was a 'boom' town, there would be up to a dozen pages advertising job vacancies; in 1996 the Situations Vacant adverts covered about four pages. There has been a similar decline in advertising for house and car sales, as well as in the amount of advertising taken out by local shops and businesses. It is therefore important that the *Newbury Weekly News* retains a good relationship with its advertisers, and to this end the newspaper and its management try to play a leading role in the local business community.

Like all newspapers, the *Newbury Weekly News* has a department responsible for attracting advertising to the paper. Although the advertising and editorial departments are separate (a fact that the editor emphasises), there has to be some cooperation, particularly for advertisement feature pages or supplements that may contain a combination of advertising and specially written supporting editorial copy.

Advertising is part of the service a local newspaper offers. The balance between adverts and editorial needs to be finely judged: if the newspaper contains too much advertising, readers become dissatisfied; too little, and

Fig. 5.24
Source: *Newbury Weekly News*

the newspaper loses money or has to raise its cover price. The *Newbury Weekly News* tried to keep that balance at about 65 per cent advertising to 35 per cent editorial. As the advertising pays for the editorial, the amount of advertising revenue available will affect the size of the paper. At its height in the late 1980s, editions of the paper could have up to 72 pages, but in the mid 1990s they fell to around 44 pages. There is a risk in becoming too thin, as the newspaper may start to lose readers if it is not considered good value.

Editorially the *Newbury Weekly News* tries to reflect the community that it serves – a conservative one, despite in 1993 electing a local Liberal Democrat MP after seventy years of Conservative control. Contrary to some local perceptions, Newbury is still a prosperous, middle-class town, rated one of the four wealthiest districts in the country in a survey carried out in 1993 by the School of Advanced Urban Studies at Bristol University. Although claiming to be impartial, the *Newbury Weekly News* echoes these local values and ambiguities, and its pages frequently reflect the issues that concern the more established or prosperous members of the community.

Letters to the editor can take up two or three pages and usually include contributions from local councillors, political activists and other local 'notables'. Beharrell (1993) notes that although the letters pages tend to reflect the concerns of the more vociferous members of the community, these are often local variations of national issues such as the health service or public spending, although in recent years high-profile stories like the peace camps at Greenham Common, possible nuclear accidents at the airbase and the Newbury bypass have all featured. The other significant feature of the letters pages are public expressions of gratitude for help or information, or congratulations for successes, public or private.

Franklin and Murphy note that one of the functions of the local press is to respond to national news events in a local way, reflecting the local dimension. After the massacre in nearby Hungerford in 1987, the *Newbury Weekly News* tried to deal with the incident as a local matter with personal dimensions, rather than in the more lurid and sensational way the national tabloids approached it. The *Newbury Weekly News* claims to have received only one complaint about its treatment of the story, whereas reporters from the national newspapers supposedly alienated many of the local population in their hunt for 'good' copy.

Beharrell contrasts the *Newbury Weekly News*'s treatment of the Greenham peace camps with the treatment given to New Age travellers in Birmingham, where the local newspaper, the *Birmingham Evening Mail* (part of the Ingersoll group), launched a campaign to 'Keep this scum out', and called on the police to 'hound 'em'. In contrast, the tone of the *Newbury Weekly News* seems aimed at the more 'educated' middle-class reader. The paragraphs are up to three times the length of those of other tabloid local newspapers, the language is generally more restrained, and sentences are longer than in most popular newspapers.

News stories at the *Newbury Weekly News* come mainly from its own reporters, but up to 40 per cent of the editorial can originate from other sources, such as the network of local correspondents in surrounding villages, members of the public, or more PR-minded businesses and organisations. The paper's pages reflect the concerns of its mainly middle-class readership, what Franklin and Murphy call the 'rituals of the community': weddings, Christmas concerts in local schools and churches, exam and degree results, and, of course, births, deaths and engagements. A regular feature on the letters pages is 'Old memories revived', with newspaper cuttings going back 125 years, helping to reinforce a sense of history for both the newspaper and the community. There is also a junior weekly news section and a monthly woman's page.

The *Newbury Weekly News* is apparently a successful newspaper because it reflects a large proportion of the community that it serves and that provides it with its market. It is a traditional newspaper, with perhaps

ACTIVITY 5.10

1   Draw up a profile of your own local newspaper, looking at such issues as: who owns it; what type of reader it is aimed at; what other local media are in competition with it; what proportion of its revenue comes from advertising and how that might affect the content of the newspaper and the types of story it contains. How successful is your local newspaper and what are its criteria for success?

2   Compare your local newspaper with another contrasting example, e.g. rural with urban, or independent with one that is part of a large group. Look at such aspects as news values, style, political bias and content.

slightly old-fashioned values, that assumes its readers are well informed and want to know both sides of a story. Like the town it serves, it has an air of 'quiet respectability' (Beharrell). The *Newbury Weekly News* is the type of newspaper that Franklin and Murphy see as becoming increasingly rare in England, although remaining still strong in America, where the locally owned newspaper offers a focus for the community's particular sense of itself, defined in terms of the local economy, the local political system and local social relationships. The *Newbury Weekly News* is the type of newspaper that tries to combine high moral and journalistic standards with a vested interest in maintaining the status quo and the comfortable 'middle-England' background of many of its readers and the community itself.

The lack of a real rival to the *Newbury Weekly News* means, at the moment, that it is unlikely to be bought out by a larger group trying to eliminate competition, and so as long as the community stays the same, or as long as the paper can change as the community changes, it should survive as a local, independent weekly newspaper.

CASE STUDY: COMMUNITY RADIO

Just as local newspapers provide a specialist service to their readers, so local radio appears to offer a similar opportunity to provide something that is different to the national media organisations. However, the reality appears to be that true local radio is in difficulty. Local BBC radio still espouses a Reithian philosophy that tries to balance its various claims to inform, educate and entertain and this is reflected in the airtime many local BBC stations give to ethnic minorities. However, much of local BBC radio's output can seem rather worthy, reflecting the limited budgets that BBC local radio operates under. Financial constraints frequently result in 'local' services combining with other local BBC stations to provide a service across a wide geographical area that is at best regional. Perhaps as a consequence of this, audiences for BBC local radio are generally small and reflect the interests of older listeners not targeted by the commercial stations and their advertisers.

ILR stations are driven by their need for advertising income and will specifically target those groups that the advertisers demand of them. The ILR sector is also affected by the dominance of a small number of large 'regional' groups such as GWR, Emap and Capital. Stations within the GWR group offer a similar format and conform to a group-wide music policy irrespective of where their broadcasts originate from. It is possible to travel the length of the M4 and listen to different GWR stations offering the same 'Better Music Mix' whether it is GWR based in Bristol or 2TEN FM based in Reading. After a survey of listeners' needs they decided to exclude 'rap' or 'dance' from their playlists as the majority of the target audience did not like this type of music. In 1996 GWR bought the INR (Independent National Radio) station Classic FM.

Emap Radio, owners of Kiss FM in London, has a concentration of stations in the North of England. It owns, amongst others, Piccadilly Radio, Radio City, Aire FM, Red Rose Radio and the Metro radio group. Through Kiss TV, it is moving into local television and plans to offer a dedicated dance music channel.

During the 1980s there was a proliferation of 'pirate' radio stations, like the original Kiss FM, operating without licences. This was caused by several factors: access to cheaper equipment; an increasingly fragmented youth culture which wanted radio stations that catered for particular musical tastes; and an increasing interest in creating 'independent' and 'alternative' radio production. Partly as a response to these pressures, the 1990 Broadcasting Act set out to encourage a third, more independent, tier between national and regional radio with the aim of providing community or incremental radio licences for specific groups such as ethnic minorities, special interest groups and other communities identified through specific culture, location or language. Community radio groups aim to offer opportunities for local people to become involved in producing programmes for their local communities and presenting a local focus. These community stations are also generally seen as 'non-profit-making', operating for the social and cultural benefit of a community and promoting what the Community Radio Association calls 'local media pluralism and diversity of information'. The Community Radio Association defines a community radio station as one that offers 'a service to the community in which it is located, or to which it broadcasts, while promoting the participation of this community in the radio.'

Community radio groups aim to produce an alternative to the ILR stations which, many claim, have dropped their local programming for the sake of commercial income. Many ILR stations claim that it is not financially viable to offer the diversity of speech-based programmes that people want and so have to concentrate on supplying their advertisers with large audience shares of particular 'attractive' groups, predominantly B, C1, and C2 listeners in the 20–35 age range.

This third tier of radio has, however, been slow to develop, partly for financial reasons and partly through listener resistance. Research by the Broadcasting Research Unit (Barnett, 1988) found only a very small interest among audiences for the idea of neighbourhood stations, although there is a suggestion that listeners are becoming increasingly disenchanted with the non-stop playlist of the majority of ILR stations.

One of the more successful aspects of the community radio legislation has been the introduction of RSLs (Restricted Service Licences) that allow individuals or groups to operate a licence for up to 28 days, usually based around specific events such as the festivals in Edinburgh, Brighton and Glastonbury or county shows or even Badminton Horse Trials. According to the Community Radio Association, RSLs provide a useful legal outlet for members of the public to gain live broadcast experience and help publicise and raise awareness of their group's intentions, abilities, etc. The Radio Authority increasingly regards RSLs as a very useful indicator of the potential a new group has to sustain a full local radio service and reserves the 105–108 MHz band primarily for such small-scale radio stations. In 1995 it issued over 300 RSL licences.

KICK FM

KICK FM was an RSL broadcast in the Berkshire town of Newbury during May 1996. Newbury has no hospital radio and so the group that originally had the idea were not so much radio enthusiasts as people who felt that Newbury was an area for which a community radio station was needed. Newbury is served by 2TEN FM, an ILR station that is part of the GWR group and whose 'footprint' includes other local towns such as Reading, Basingstoke, Hungerford and Andover. The local newspaper in Newbury, the *Newbury Weekly News*, has a much smaller circulation area, focused purely on the town of Newbury and its surrounding villages, and it was this truly local feel that KICK FM wanted to develop. In Newbury during 1996 there was also a 'pirate' radio station broadcasting, TREE FM based around the bypass protests.

It was decided early on that in a town like Newbury it would be impossible to challenge the power and dominance of the local newspaper and ILR station and so it was decided to ask them to work with KICK FM. A representative from each was asked to join a steering committee, along with representatives from the local council and the local college. It was originally decided to focus the RSL around the annual classical music festival which also coincided that year with the 400th anniversary of the town's Royal Charter, but changes to the Radio Authority's regulations allowed the RSL to run as a 'trial licence' to ascertain the demand and support for a possible full-time community radio licence in the local area. Adverts in the local paper asked for volunteers and a series of public meetings produced a group of over a hundred local people who expressed interest in the idea of offering a radio version of the local newspaper with its local news and views.

ACTIVITY 5.11

Conduct a survey of those who listen to your local radio stations. What stations are available? Who do they target as their listeners? How is this reflected in the programme content and the style of presenters? If you have a local ILR station, try to find out if it is part of a larger group and what, if anything, your particular station has in common with others in the same group.

Programme content

It was decided to offer a 24-hour service with a 'sustaining' service from 2TEN FM from 1am to 7am. This meant that anyone tuning into the station during the night would hear something and, hopefully, remain interested. For 2TEN FM it meant that they were helping to provide quality radio ser-

community radio in the kennet valley

Fig. 5.25
Source: KICK FM Ltd

vices and showing a local commitment that would look good when they next came to reapply for the renewal of their franchise.

It was also agreed that KICK FM should have an overall target of 30 per cent speech to 70 per cent music, although these percentages would vary throughout the day with late-night music shows and daytime talk shows. IRN news was broadcast every hour via a satellite feed from another, full-time, community radio station, Sunrise Radio, and local news was provided in association with the local newspaper. KICK FM tried to create an identity where the closest links were with the 'local' rather than the 'national' and in contrast to other local radio and television stations KICK FM put its local news before the IRN news. This meant that 'national' stories concerning Newbury and its bypass were first heard on KICK FM as 'local' stories.

KICK FM had to produce over 500 hours of original programming and, to be an effective contrast to the ILR station, had to produce a substantial amount of speech-based programming. Speech-based programmes are cheap to produce as no copyright is paid but they can be time-consuming and difficult to organise technically. Although for music-based programmes stations have to pay for licences from the Performing Right Society and Phonographic Performance Ltd, the studio requirements are limited to CD players and a mixing desk and only a minimum of introductions and jingles. Speech-based programming, although 'free', requires interviews either live in the studio or pre-recorded and edited, sometimes recorded in outside locations like schools, arts venues and churches (or in the case of KICK FM in a glider in the air!) – and this is a much more time-consuming activity than selecting a playlist.

Professional autonomy?

Because they want to involve local people and because of limited funding, community radio groups are generally very dependent upon volunteers. It is estimated that approximately 91 per cent of those working in community radio are volunteers. For some of these volunteers it may be an opportunity to gain more experience and perhaps eventually move into mainstream radio, especially in areas where the more traditional route of hospital radio is not available. Peter Lewis (1994) points out that as training provision in the mainstream radio sector is declining, partly through the BBC's reduction of many of its recruitment and training schemes and partly because ILR stations do not appear to have the interest or financial imperative for the longer-term investment that training requires, community radio is becoming increasingly significant as a source of training for the radio industry as a whole. A Skillset survey (Woolf and Holly, 1994) of those in paid employment in the radio industry in 1993 found that 19 per cent of all those working in the industry had started as volunteers, and of these 6 per cent had started in hospital radio and 1 per cent in community radio, although this doubled to 2 per cent for those who had joined the industry in the previous three years.

Community radio's dependence upon volunteers can mean a great variety, and different levels of expertise, that probably reflects the communities they are trying to serve. However, for a working station, either an RSL or a full-time station, this dependence upon volunteers, who generally come to work at different times of the day and the week and who work on a variety of programmes and tasks, can create additional problems of organisation and coordination. This means that for the most effective running of a small community station a small, dedicated work-force is preferable to a large 'army' of volunteers. However, if this small, dedicated workforce are to devote themselves entirely to the station they most probably need a wage and the station therefore will have an additional financial commitment to meet.

KICK FM had 45 presenters on air during its RSL, aged from 12 to 77. Of these only ten had had any previous 'on air' experience. As the Radio Authority requires any organisation broadcasting to comply with its Codes of Practice, each presenter had to be aware of their content as well as agree to conform to other legal constraints such as slander, avoidance of racism, etc. Each presenter was asked to sign an agreement that if they broke the regulations (by swearing, for example, or promoting brand names on air or showing political bias) it would be their own responsibility and the station itself would not be held liable.

This meant that all the on-air presenters were given a crash course in the 'professional' standards and codes and conventions that both the Radio Authority and listeners expect, in effect trying to produce a style that was similar to the occupational ideal and professionalism discussed on pp. 168–171. This could be seen to be in contrast to the aim of community radio to give members of the community, volunteers and generally inexperienced presenters a degree of freedom and to offer listeners an alternative. KICK FM, like other community radio stations, was trying to balance an 'alternative' output and content focus with a 'professional' and conventional delivery style. Unlike ILR stations dominated by their playlists, KICK FM presenters were given the freedom to choose their own music as long as the lyrics were not 'too strong' or offensive. It was agreed that stronger language could be used on the late-night music slots but some tracks were deemed still to be off-limits and others had to be vetted before they were broadcast.

Restrictions: regulatory

The Radio Authority monitors the output of all radio stations and KICK FM was required to log all their output and keep this log for 42 days. The Radio Authority has considerable power to 'punish' those stations that do not confirm to its rules. It has the right to instant, 24-hour access to the main transmitter and can switch a station off at any time. It can impose fines on those stations which fail to meet their requirements or who have complaints upheld against them. These faults would remain on file and could severely prejudice the chances of that group ever being successful in any future licence application.

The risk of complaints to the Radio Authority, prejudicing any future licence applications, made the organisers of KICK FM cautious and they imposed an 'in-house' censorship. Competitions were tightly regulated to

ACTIVITY 5.12

Try to find out what the music policy is for your local stations. Do they have a 'playlist'? How is it compiled? What is the range of music offered by the station? What controls does the station have to ensure that its output is not offensive, libellous, etc.?

make sure that there was no cause for complaints by the public or abuse by members of the station. Phone-ins were closely monitored and because the station could not afford a delay switch, all callers were closely checked before being allowed on air. Trying to reflect the local community at a time when the local community was divided among itself over the proposed bypass, and the desire not to antagonise any sectors of the community, or appear politically biased, meant that the station, whenever possible, tried to avoid discussion of the bypass – ironically, since this was one of the major issues in the community.

Restrictions: economic

It was estimated that KICK FM needed approximately £15 000 to meet all its expenses, such as licence applications, hire of equipment and materials. Accommodation was provided free of charge in a shop unit in the local shopping centre. KICK FM decided that it did not have the resources or infrastructure to sell spot advertising and so tried to raise its funds through grants and sponsorship. One of the difficulties facing an RSL is that as it is only on air for a short period, advertisers are not keen to make a financial commitment and if, as in the case of KICK FM, this is its first attempt, there is no guarantee or past evidence of success in getting the potential audience to listen. While there can be an enthusiasm for RSLs in the community that releases resources for that one particular occasion, if the community group is hoping to offer a permanent service then some degree of commercial viability becomes necessary to guarantee regular income, pay bills and support a nucleus of full-time staff. This can put pressure on the organisation to move to a more 'professional' attitude and perhaps to consider working with an existing ILR station.

Another difficulty caused by lack of money is the ability to tell the public that you exist. The Radio Authority announces what frequency a station has been given only a few weeks before it is due to start transmitting and so all the pre-publicity for KICK FM, press releases, etc., could not include the frequency. KICK FM did not have sufficient funds to buy space in the local newspaper to publicise either its frequency or its schedules and so was limited to trying to generate 'news stories' that would give it publicity, 'on-air' announcements of programmes coming up, handing out printed schedules to anyone who came into contact with the station and hoping for a build-up of 'word-of-mouth' familiarity.

Audience response

It is notoriously difficult to get the radio audience to alter their habits or retune their radios. If someone has woken up to Radio 2's breakfast show for several years they are likely to continue and need a lot of persuasion to change their habits, reset their radio and learn a new morning 'format'. In a small community most people will, hopefully, know someone who is involved in the new station and curiosity may make them give the station a try. Some listeners complained that they could not 'find' KICK FM on their radios and although this may have been true, some listeners may in fact have been listening to KICK FM but not recognised it.

The wider availability of RDS (Radio Data Systems) will make station search and identification much easier in the future.

As community radio stations like KICK FM are trying to offer a broad range of programming, it is quite possible that many people who tune in for the first time may not hear something they like. Some new listeners may try again and eventually find something that interests them but this requires a degree of commitment and other listeners may simply return to their 'old' station that will probably offer, non-stop, the type of radio that they like. As Crisell (1994) points out, the radio listener is 'undeniably active in the sense that she has no need to adjust to the daily schedules that radio provides; on the contrary, she imports it into her own daily schedule and often in a casual, fitful way'.

Partly to meet the expectations of the listening public, the KICK FM schedules largely replicated those of the mainstream media, 'drive-time' in the morning and early evening, and easy-listening and women-orientated programmes during the day, arts and specialist music during the evening, and 'youth' music late at night. Saturdays included sports results and there was a Sunday morning religious programme.

KICK FM claims to have been successful in achieving its aims of being 'Fun, Local and Caring'. However, like many other RSLs, this success reflects the problems community radio groups have in building upon their success. KICK FM built up a large local listener base after 28 days but, according to Radio Authority regulations, cannot broadcast more than twice a year and will perhaps be allocated a different frequency each time.

In 1997 KICK FM formed a consortium with other local media companies, including the local newspaper (the *Newbury Weekly News*), ran another RSL and planned to apply for the franchise to run a full-time local station when the Radio Authority eventually decides to advertise one.

The future of community radio

To describe stations like BBC's Thames Valley FM or ILR's 2TEN FM as 'local' stations is rather a misnomer as they serve quite large geographical areas. 'Local' in the sense that the word is understood by local newspapers means much closer involvement with smaller and more distinct communities.

Much of the idealism behind Community Radio is in its goal of producing 'independent' radio programmes aimed at minority audiences, through democratic and participatory organisations. This is often limited, however, by external constraints such as the Radio Authority, listener perception of what a radio station should sound like, and the need for some degree of commercial viability. Despite this, the notion of new local, community-based radio stations does potentially offer an alternative to the 'format-driven' ILR stations.

BBC Radio can be seen as trying to maintain its Reithian values 'to inform, to educate and to entertain', whilst ILR stations can be seen to provide a lot of entertainment, some information and very little education. Rather than offer a radical and possibly controversial alternative,

Fig. 5.26
KICK FM Internet home page
Source: KICK FM Ltd

Consider what a community radio station could offer your neighbourhood. In what ways would it offer an 'alternative' to the existing media available locally? Try to define specific community groups based on

- location and neighbour-hood, or
- language and culture, or
- a specific interest or cause.

Draw up an outline for a possible RSL proposal for your area. What event would it focus on? What are the possible sources of funding? What types of programmes and presenters would the RSL have? Write to the Radio Authority and ask for a licence application form, and try to supply answers to the questions they ask (Address at the end of this chapter.)

community stations like KICK FM are trying to develop a 'hybrid' that takes the best of the BBC and ILR formats and offers instead a financially viable and balanced mixture of entertainment and information.

Radio services are predicted to expand dramatically in the near future as a result of the advent of digital audio broadcasting (DAB), the growth of cable television services that can also deliver local community radio (as with MAX FM in Southampton), and through the Internet. This expansion of radio provides opportunities for greater 'segmentation' and a wider range of programming shaped to meet the needs of specific groups as well as providing opportunities for more people to be involved in producing programmes. However, it also provides opportunities for

ACTIVITY 5.14

Carry out a survey of what media are available in your local area. How do the different media define and represent your locality or region? Try to assess the extent to which they represent the views and issues of your locality. What participation do the local media offer to the members of the communities they are are addressing?

the existing radio companies, like GWR, to increase their control of the industry either through direct competition or by buying into, and providing necessary 'expertise' and hardware to, successful but under-funded community radio groups.

The Radio Authority is using RSLs as an opportunity for groups to show that there is a demand for a local radio station, other than that offered by ILR stations. This can lead to the paradox of companies like GWR's Amber Radio applying for the incremental radio licence in Cambridge that has been advertised by the Radio Authority precisely because of the success of the RSLs run by Cambridge Community Radio in proving the demand for the licence. GWR also operates Cambridge's other station, Q103, and was only allowed to bid for the second licence through the easing of the ownership controls in the 1996 Broadcasting Act. The Radio Authority awarded the licence to the local group, Cambridge Community Radio.

Increasingly the bigger, mainstream radio companies are looking at the markets being created by community-based stations and, as in the case of Cambridge, either directly challenging them, or, as in the case of south-east London's First Love Radio, buying into the community station. First Love Radio has run a series of successful RSLs and satisified the Radio Authority that there is the demand for a permanent licence in the area. Now that they look like winning the new full-time licence, UK Radio Developments, who have interests in other local stations in Manchester, Slough and Cornwall, have bought a 25 per cent stake in First Love Radio.

Peter Lewis calculates that the numbers working in the community radio sector now account for around a quarter of those working in the radio industry as a whole. This enthusiasm and commitment, coupled with the governement's drive to deregulate and offer choice in broadcasting, means that eventually Britain could, like America, have a radio station for every 25 000 people, targeting different segments of the local communities.

Further reading

Music industry

Frith, S. 1983: *Sound Effects.* Constable

Frith, S. and Goodwin, A. (eds). 1990: *On Record.* Routledge.

Garfield, S. 1986: *Expensive Habits: The Dark Side of the Music Industry.* Faber and Faber.

Gillett, C. 1983: *The Sound of the City.* Souvenir Press.

Longhurst, B. 1995: *Popular Music and Society.* Polity Press.

Negus, K. 1992: *Producing Pop.* Edward Arnold.

Negus, K. 1996: *Popular Music in Theory.* Polity Press.

Local newspapers

Fountain, N. 1988: *Underground: The London Alternative Press 1966-1974.* Comedia.

Goodhart, D. and Wintour, C. 1986: *Eddy Shah and the Newspaper Revolution.* Coronet.

Harcup, T. 1995: *A Northern Star – Leeds Other Paper and the Alternative Press 1974-1994.* Campaign for Press and Broadcasting Freedom.

Keeble, R. 1994: *The Newspapers Handbook.* Routledge.

McNair, B. 1996: *News and Journalism in the UK.* Routledge.

Schlesinger, P. 1987: *Putting 'Reality' Together – BBC News.* Methuen.

Tunstall, J. 1996: *Newspaper Power: The New National Press in Britain.* Clarendon Press.

Community radio

Crisell, A. 1994: *Understanding Radio.* Routledge.

Gunter, B., Sancho-Aldridge, J. and Winstone, P. 1994: *Television: The Public's View 1993.* Libbey.

Kaye, M. and Popperwell, A. 1992: *Making Radio.* Broadside Books.

Lewis, P. 1994: *Community Radio – A Gateway to Employment.* Community Radio Association.

Lewis, P. and Booth, J. 1989: *The Invisible Medium: Public, Commercial and Community Radio.* Macmillan.

Useful addresses

The Radio Authority, Holbrook House, 14 Great Queen Street, London WC2 5DG
(tel: 0171 430 2724).
The Community Radio Association, 15 Paternoster Row, Sheffield S1 2BX
(tel: 0114 279 5219)
KICK FM Ltd has a website at: http://www.kickfm.co.uk

6

The last chapter focused on the theme of media institutions, their regulation and their everyday relationships with the present tense – in the here and now. This chapter aims to develop a range of issues about the *historical* development of the modern media and the conditions which have shaped their respective development. These themes should not, however, be confined to this chapter. Attention to the historical development of media institutions and organisations is an essential component of media studies. In short, studying the historical formation and evolution of the various media – how they have emerged and under what conditions – makes possible a more informed understanding of their present forms of operation, regulation, use, and likely patterns of development and change.

History, or rather the study of history, is often associated with lists of dates, successions of undeniable, historic events and 'facts'. For example:

1476 William Caxton prints the first printed English book.

1702 The *Daily Courant*, the first English daily newspaper, is published.

1785 The first issue of *The Times* is published (as the *Daily Universal Register*).

1896 The first moving picture show, to a paying audience in London.

1922 The British Broadcasting Company (radio) is formed.

1927 The first full-length talking film is released.

1936 BBC Television starts broadcasting.

1946 Cinema attendance in Britain peaks at 1 635 million visits a year.

1962 The first communications satellite, Telstar, goes into orbit.

1969 Colour transmissions are introduced on BBC and ITV.

1973 The first independent local radio station opens (LBC).

1982 Channel 4 is launched.
1989 Sky Satellite Broadcasting launched.
1997 Channel 5 launched.

As Carr (1961) and others have argued, however, historians are involved in more than just the 'cult of facts', the uncritical compilation of lists of self-evidently important dates. Historical study always entails a sense of how and why certain events and processes, and their dates, are *selected* as significant, and how their significance should be *interpreted*. Popular ideas of history, for example, tend to be bound up with notions of 'progress' and 'development' and taken-for-granted ideas of 'industrialisation' or 'modernisation'.

A sense of history

The development of organised systems of mass communication has had important consequences for both personal and public perceptions of history. Our own biographies are connected to 'media generations', bound up with remembered media events and shared experience of particular media at certain phases of their development. The pre-television era and experience, for instance, when viewed from the late 1990s, seems a strange and rather alien, bygone time. The ages before film or pre-photographic records appear even more 'historical' and 'out of sight':

> The modern world almost seems to have begun with the birth of film, at any rate in retrospect. Because we're used to seeing film images of the First World War, the First World War seems to be part of the modern period. But anything more than twenty years earlier than that belongs to an era which we easily feel to be lost.
>
> *Chanan (1980), p. 16*

The Battle of Trafalgar

When the Battle of Trafalgar reached its conclusion in favour of the British fleet on 21 October 1805, it was more than a fortnight before the news of the victory, and of the death of Admiral Lord Nelson, was published in Britain. The first account of the events reached the pages of *The Times* on 6

ACTIVITY 6.1

The quotation from Chanan suggests that film and visual media have had an important impact on our sense of history.

List some of the most memorable media images associated with your own life. Conduct interviews or surveys among other members of your household or family, particularly from different generations, about their memories of earlier media and media coverage of significant events.

Think of other research you might do to explore this theme. You may find it useful to consider the impact of print media and the photograph as well, as extensions of this activity. Radio and television will also provide important topics for study.

As you work through the chapter you may find it useful to return to this activity.

November (figure 6.1). Admiral Collingwood's full despatch was published there on the morning of 7 November 1805.

> The news, having travelled variously via the British Consul in Lisbon and overland by coach, did not reach London until early November ... The story of Trafalgar was read in the newspapers of the day by at most a few thousand people.
>
> *Carter (1971), p. 9*

Needless to say, such events would not be covered in quite the same way in the late twentieth century. From the Falklands, the Gulf War and Bosnia, and in coverage of numerous other international conflicts and events, developments in the media have greatly increased the speed of transmission, the size of audiences and the amounts and types of information made available to them.

ACTIVITY 6.2

Compare the reporting of Trafalgar with that of any more contemporary international conflicts. What major differences would you identify in the patterns and forms of media coverage? How would the Battle of Trafalgar be covered by today's media?

For useful references see: Knightley (1978), Harris (1983), Taylor, J. (1991) and Taylor, P. (1992).

GLORIOUS AND DECISIVE
VICTORY
OVER THE
COMBINED FLEET,
AND
DEATH of LORD NELSON.

We know not whether we should mourn or rejoice. The country has gained the most splendid and decisive Victory that has ever graced the naval annals of England; but it has been dearly purchased. *The great and gallant* NELSON *is no more*: he was killed by almost the last shot that was fired by the enemy. The action took place off Cadiz, on the 21st ult.; the enemy were thirty-three sail of the line, Lord NELSON had only twenty-seven.

The following account we have received by express; we can pledge ourselves for its truth:

TIMES OFFICE, 11 o'Clock, A. M.

A Lieutenant of a man of war arrived this morning, with an account of a most glorious victory achieved by the British fleet, under the command of Lord NELSON.

The enemy's fleet consisted of THIRTY-THREE sail of the line, with frigates, &c. They came out of Cadiz on the 19th of October, and two days afterwards were encountered by the British fleet, consisting of only TWENTY-SEVEN sail of the line, (several having been detached under Rear-Admiral LOUIS) with some smaller ships. The battle continued during four hours, and ended in the capture of NINETEEN of the enemy's ships of the line, besides one which blew up in the action.

The *Victory* being closely engaged with several of the Enemy's Ships, a Musket-shot wounded Lord NELSON in the Shoulder, and thus terminated a Life of Glory.

A number of Prizes drifted on a lee-shore, in a gale of wind, a day or two afterwards, and probably many have been wrecked. Admiral COLLINGWOOD had ordered that every ship which could not be brought away should be destroyed. Two, however, effected their escape into Cadiz.

Admiral VILLENEUVE is a prisoner. On our side two Captains, we believe DUFF and COOKE, and three or four hundred men were killed. We have not lost a single ship.

Fig. 6.1

Source: *The Times*, 6 November 1805. Reproduced by permission

The conditions of media development: demand and supply

> The growth of mass communications is a dual process. On the one hand it describes the development of an industry, on the other the evolution of an audience. The relationship between the two is one of supply and demand for two basic social commodities: leisure facilities and information.
>
> *Golding (1974), p. 14*

Before proceeding to examine some detailed case studies of the historical development of particular media, it is useful to consider some general factors which have shaped and historically structured this relationship of supply and demand. In essence, this entails an analysis of certain general conditions which have had implications for media producers and processes of production (supply) and for media consumers and their access to reception of media output (demand).

Demand

The *demand* for information and entertainment has been influenced by a number of factors, three of which are of particular concern: the amounts of time available, the affluence or spending power of social groups, and a variety of other cultural factors.

Legal and technical changes in many forms of employment from the late nineteenth century onwards have resulted in decreased working hours, the widespread availability of statutory holidays, and more *time* being generally available for leisure or non-work activities. As we noted earlier in this book, media consumption has grown as a significant component of this 'discretionary' time. As we approach the end of the twentieth century, there are important differences in the leisure time available to men and women, and between many other groupings. Historically, the time available for media consumption has helped determine the meaning of leisure and hence the formation of various media markets. One study of the press in the first half of the nineteenth century, for example, notes that:

> To say that conditions were against the growth of a working class reading public would be to put it mildly. In the towns, a fourteen-hour working day was commonplace: those in even the most favoured trades did not get home until 6 or 7 pm; not until the 1860s was the Saturday half-holiday introduced. Another major problem was the absence of light: the

> window tax was not abolished until 1851 ... and in most houses tallow dips or candles were the only source of illumination apart from the fireplace. So the worker confined reading to Sundays – hence, of course, the popularity of Sunday newspapers.
>
> *Cranfield (1978), pp. 120–1*

The *amounts of money* that different groups have been able to spend on media products has also been a key variable in determining the demand side of media markets. In short, if people are not able to afford to invest in magazines, newspapers, films, videos, CDs or the licence or subscription fees for broadcast and other media, for example, this will have obvious consequences for the media organisations involved and their ability to operate viably or profitably. Consumer spending on entertainment and the media in Britain continues to represent a significant part of the UK economy overall.

There have been, and continue to be, important differences in media expenditure patterns – 'media spending power' – between low-income and high-income groups in British society. Actual expenditure on magazines and books, newspapers, cinema, video and computer-based software and hardware varies sharply with income. Different levels of income and resources are basic factors in wider social class differences and have had important consequences for the kinds of cultural demand that different audiences have been able to make on media markets and media institutions historically.

Cultural factors are perhaps a final set of issues to be considered as historical determinants of the demand for various kinds of entertainment and information. These are often the product of larger divisions of social class, gender, age or occupation, and are examined in more depth in chapter 4. For the purposes of this discussion, however, it is important to note that these factors are to do with *differential* styles and patterns of media consumption and media use. Part of the history of the media in Britain from the late nineteenth century onwards concerns the emergence of more distinct and differentiated groups of consumers, increasingly privatised and mobile. The post-1950s period, for example, saw rapid growth in media forms and industries – music, fashion, films, etc. – aimed at and responding to a range of youth audiences and subcultures. More recently, accelerating segmentation of demand has been claimed across gender ('new' men and women) and generation ('grey power'). Another important historical factor is literacy –

the educated ability to read and write. While Britain is assumed to have high literacy rates at this time, this has not always been the case. For the development of print and publishing industries and the press, particularly popular newspapers and magazines, literacy and the ability to read was an important cultural precondition, especially in the nineteenth century.

Supply

The historical growth and regulation of media industries and institutions have determined how the various demands for forms of mediated information, knowledge and entertainment have been met. The ability to *supply* forms of media output has at a general level been subject to three principal forms of constraint: commercial, legal and technological conditions. These forces are explored in contemporary detail in chapter 5.

Commercial markets and their operations have been significant in a number of ways. First, some of the principal historical dynamics of media development have resulted from the motives associated with commercial investment for profit. This broad aim has structured the operations of media producers and the contours of media markets in important ways. Since the late nineteenth century, investment in media industries has often been a high-risk business, and commercial success has been popularly characterised as 'giving the public what it wants', supplying the 'mainstream' or popular, profitable forms of demand. In practice this is an oversimplistic view, which neglects the ways in which demands are structured by what is supplied, and how, at any given moment, there are a range of dynamics in play. Although in the late twentieth century there are ways in which these blunt distinctions are held to be increasingly outmoded by the sophistication of 'deregulated' hi-tech, digital media, commercial logic remains an important and central historical determinant or condition of media production. An important, related issue here concerns commercial ownership and control. The history of media industries in Britain since the turn of the century involves studying the power of those who have owned them; from the press barons – Northcliffe or Beaverbrook – to modern-day media proprietors and owners, such as Rupert Murdoch. Media industries tend to have developed highly concentrated patterns of ownership, and questions of ownership and control have great significance for the historical analysis of the rise of commercial forms of broadcasting and other media (see chapter 5 and the case study on *Broadcasting in Britain* in this chapter).

ACTIVITY 6.3

Start to map the growth of local media histories for press, cinema, radio and TV, cable and so on, in your own locality or region. Research the ways in which time, affluence and other cultural factors have shaped the local historical demands for media consumption. What additional factors and issues need to be considered?

Statutory and legal controls have also played an important part in determining how media institutions and industries have been able to develop and operate. Alongside commercial considerations, a significant dimension in the history of the media in Britain is that of their regulation by law, by government and by the state. Given the ability of the media to deal in information, opinion and images, it is no surprise that, from their earliest days, media producers have attracted the attentions of established authority and governments, which have sought to control, repress or regulate their output and operation. Early print systems, for example, in the sixteenth and seventeenth centuries were subject to very strict regimes of licensing and pre-publication censorship – everything that was to be published was required to be vetted or censored first. As the last case study in this chapter will outline, the growth and development of broadcasting in Britain, first in radio and then in television, has been powerfully structured by the requirements of government policies and legal codes, which have conditioned and constrained broadcasters in a number of significant ways.

Technologies and inventions, whether in the form of the development of the rotary, steam-powered printing press in the 1820s, the 'wireless' of the 1920s or the communications satellite in the 1960s, have rightly been regarded as key factors in the historical growth of media industries.

> Technological changes further complicate the pattern of media supply, based often in underlying industrial and economic developments. Necessity, in the form of wars, imperial expansion, and commerce, has mothered a large proportion of the inventions which punctuate the history of the mass media. The steam printing press, wireless telegraphy, the cathode ray tube, satellites have all in turn recast the supply of media material and thus the range of options within which audiences exert their demands.
>
> *Golding (1974), p. 18*

While the development of new media technologies has undoubtedly had important consequences for the overall historical growth of media industries and forms, it is important to recognise that the history of the media entails more than a linear account of 'great inventions'. As Williams (1990) has noted, accounts of the impact of modern technologies are often characterised by an over-emphasis upon the technologies and inventions themselves. This belief in the inevitable power of technologies to cause widespread social change and effects is known as *technological determinism*:

> It is an immensely powerful and now largely orthodox view of the nature of social change. New technologies are discovered, by an essentially internal process of research and development, which then sets the conditions for social change and progress. Progress, in particular, is the history of these inventions, which 'created the modern world'. The effects of these technologies, whether direct or indirect, foreseen or unforeseen, are as it were the rest of history.
>
> *Williams (1990), p. 13*

To counter this view it is important to note several points. First, processes of invention are complex and interwoven and have been shaped in a number of ways by commercial or military factors (as in the case of wireless transmission or the cathode ray tube, for example). Secondly, once inventions have been made, there is a process whereby their social applications and uses are discovered. The potentials of inventions are realised in actual historical periods where social, economic and other forces operate to make them actual and regulate them in particular ways. The principal failing of accounts which adopt a technologically determinist view of media history is the tendency to cut the technology off from the many other forces and conditions which shape its invention and deployment. Some new technologies have not been taken up and have failed (such as the eight track sound system), while others have taken off in unanticipated ways (such as the personal stereo). (See chapter 7 for further discussion.)

The remainder of this chapter is devoted to three case studies. These are chronologically organised and begin with a study of aspects of the press and press development in the nineteenth century. This is followed by a study of the emergence of cinema in Britain from the 1890s to the 1920s. Both these case studies are brief outlines which should provide opportunity for further research. Finally, there is a more fully developed account of the development of broadcasting in Britain, from the 1920s to the present day.

ACTIVITY 6.4

Look back at the research on forms of local media production that you started in the last activity and consider the ways in which commercial, legal and technical factors have shaped their history.

Research the technological history of a selected medium. Compile a map of the key inventions which have been influential. How have these inventions subsequently been institutionalised and regulated by other historical forces?

CASE STUDY: RADICAL AND POPULAR PRESS IN THE NINETEENTH CENTURY

In the nineteenth century the press was the most important single medium for the communication of ideas, opinion and knowledge, and the newspaper was the first recognisable modern mass medium. Newspapers were not a nineteenth-century invention, although their production, forms and readerships changed considerably during that period as they became industrialised. The first daily newspaper, the *Daily Courant*, was published early in the eighteenth century (1702), and before that there were pamphlets, '*Mercuries*' and '*Intelligencers*', which carried reports of international events, limited forms of opinion and propagandist argument. By the end of the eighteenth century, the press had been granted the right to report parliamentary proceedings, and in spite of the fact that newspapers were controlled by means of the stamp taxes – duties paid per copy which kept the prices high – the foundations for a national, commercial press had been established.

The Times, published first as the *Daily Universal Register* in 1785, epitomised the new, respectable middle-class commercial press. By 1803 it had turned away from direct government subsidy, developing a stance which was independent of the government but generally supportive of establishment interests. This idea of 'independence', partly based on the view that newspapers should play an important intermediary role between governments and the governed, represented a significant historical shift, congruent with the formation of the new industrial and professional middle classes and their authority. In 1800 some 2000 copies of *The Times* were being produced daily. By 1817, with the installation of new technologies – the steam-driven press – production increased to over 7000.

Between the late 1790s and about the middle of the nineteenth century, the ascendancy and authority of this new model for the newspaper was powerfully challenged by another kind of press which served to articulate the demands of a very different culture and class. In this period, the radical press, also referred to as the 'pauper' or 'unstamped' press, emerged to play a part in voicing popular, oppositional opinion. As many social historians have noted, these papers played an important role in radicalising working-class ideas and politics, acting as agents or catalysts in the broader context of the development and experience of an industrialising, capitalist system. The period between the 1790s and the 1830s was marked by considerable political turbulence and instability. This was accompanied by rapid population growth centralised on cities, the growth of the factory system, economic depressions, poverty and disease. 'Revolutionary' ideas from the Continent, calls for political agitation or industrial unrest, demands for voting rights, reform and the fundamental necessity for a free press were all given voice and communicated by the radical press and its producers. For those in power, these publications were a subversive threat, often referred to as 'incendiary' or 'poisonous' elements requiring suppression.

The first wave of these papers broke the law by their existence and circulation. They were 'unstamped' – that is, they had not paid the required duties or taxes – and were the products of unlicensed presses. Important writers of this period include Tom Paine and William Cobbett. Their works were usually in the form of a pamphlet, often the script of a speech. Paine's *Rights of Man* sold 50 000 copies within a few weeks in 1791; Cobbett's *Address to Journeymen and Labourers* sold 200 000 in 1826. Other radical publications, from the many titles in the period, include the *Black Dwarf* (1817), which specialised in sarcasm and attacks on government and royal personalities; *the Gorgon* (1818), which advocated practical reform of voting rights; and the *Penny Politician* (1818), which was published under the masthead 'Let's Die Like Men and Not Like Slaves' and attacked the whole system of industrial production and corrupt politics.

The high point of this early period was reached with the Peterloo Massacre (1819), when armed troops forcibly broke up a mass meeting about parliamentary reform held at St Peter's Fields, Manchester. Eleven people were killed as a result. During this period, the radical press faced the Gagging Bills (1819–20), laws which extended and increased the stamp taxes and strengthened the legal offence of seditious libel. Many of the writers and publishers of radical papers were arrested and served lengthy periods in jail, in some cases continuing to write from prison. Against these odds, the papers had succeeded in establishing a radical reading public and providing a rallying point for oppositional politics. The attempts at their suppression were a sign of this success, as were the many counter-propaganda publications they gave rise to (the *White Dwarf*, for example).

By the 1830s, the early reformist types of argument became overlaid with a more radical critique of capitalism as a whole. The focus of attack for many radical publications switched from political oppression to the inequalities produced by the emergent economic and industrial order and the law. Increasingly, the papers called for mass agitation and the power of united action of the working and labouring classes. Some of the most famous radical titles are associated with this period (figures 6.2 and 6.3). The *Poor Man's Guardian* (1831), *Working Man's Friend* (1832), *Destructive* (1832), *Porcupine* (1833) and the *Gauntlet* (1833) all enjoyed high circulations by the standards of the day. In order to evade prosecution for not paying the stamp tax, some publications were printed either on cloth, like the *Political Handkerchief* (1831), or on a thin wooden veneer, like the *Political Touchwood* (1830).

Circulations for radical papers such as the *Poor Man's Guardian* are estimated to exceed 16 000 copies for some editions. This figure, high by comparison with other publications of the age, must be multiplied by the actual readership of each copy:

> even if a cautious estimate of ten readers per copy is taken as the norm for radical papers such as the 'Northern Star' and its successor, 'Reynolds News', each reached at their peak, before the repeal of the stamp duty, half a million readers when the population of England and Wales over the age of 14 was little over 10 million.
>
> *Curran and Seaton (1991), p.14*

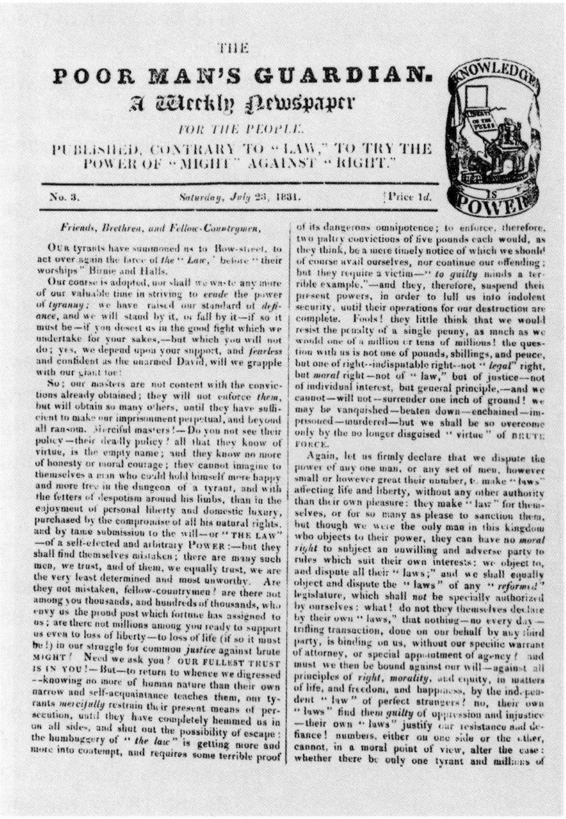

THE

POOR MAN'S GUARDIAN.

A Weekly Newspaper

FOR THE PEOPLE.

PUBLISHED, CONTRARY TO "LAW," TO TRY THE POWER OF "MIGHT" AGAINST "RIGHT."

KNOWLEDGE IS POWER

No. 3. *Saturday, July* 23, 1831. [Price 1*d*.

Friends, Brethren, and Fellow-Countrymen,

OUR tyrants have summoned us to Bow-street, to act over again the farce of *the* "*Law*," before "their worships" Birnie and Halls.

Our course is adopted, nor shall we waste any more of our valuable time in striving to *evade* the power of *tyranny*; we have raised our standard of *defiance*, and we will stand by it, or fall by it—if so it must be—if you desert us in the good fight which we undertake for your sakes,—but which you will not do; yes, we depend upon your support, and *fearless* and confident as the unarmed David, will we grapple with our giant foe!

So; our masters are not content with the convictions already obtained; they will not enforce *them*, but will obtain so many others, until they have sufficient to make our imprisonment perpetual, and beyond all ransom. Merciful masters!—Do you not see their policy—their deadly policy? all that they know of virtue, is the empty name; and they know no more of honesty or moral courage; they cannot imagine to themselves a man who could hold himself more happy and more free in the dungeon of a tyrant, and with the fetters of despotism around his limbs, than in the enjoyment of personal liberty and domestic luxury, purchased by the compromise of all his natural rights, and by tame submission to the will—or "THE LAW"—of a self-elected and arbitrary POWER:—but they shall find themselves mistaken; there are many such men, we trust, and of them, we equally trust, we are the very least determined and most unworthy. Are they not mistaken, fellow-countrymen? are there not among you thousands, and hundreds of thousands, who envy us the proud post which fortune has assigned to us; are there not millions among you ready to support us even to loss of liberty—to loss of life (if so it must be!) in our struggle for common *justice* against brute MIGHT? Need we ask you? OUR FULLEST TRUST IS IN YOU!—But—to return to whence we digressed—knowing no more of human nature than their own narrow and self-acquaintance teaches them, our tyrants *mercifully* restrain their present means of persecution, until they have completely hemmed us in on all sides, and shut out the possibility of escape: the humbuggery of "*the law*" is getting more and more into contempt, and requires some terrible proof of its dangerous omnipotence; to enforce, therefore, two paltry convictions of five pounds each would, as they think, be a mere timely notice of which we should of course avail ourselves, nor continue our offending; but they require a victim—"*to guilty* minds a terrible example."—and they, therefore, suspend their present powers, in order to lull us into indolent security, until their operations for our destruction are complete. Fools! they little think that we would resist the penalty of a single penny, as much as we would one of a million or tens of millions! the question with us is not one of pounds, shillings, and pence, but one of right—indisputable right—not "*legal*" right, but *moral* right—not of "law," but of justice—not of individual interest, but general principle,—and we cannot—will not—surrender one inch of ground! we may be vanquished—beaten down—enchained—imprisoned—murdered—but we shall be so overcome only by the no longer disguised "virtue" of BRUTE FORCE.

Again, let us firmly declare that we dispute the power of any one man, or any set of men, however small or however great their number, to make "laws" affecting life and liberty, without any other authority than their own pleasure: they make "law" for themselves, or for so many as please to sanction them, but though we were the only man in this kingdom who objects to their power, they can have no *moral right* to subject an unwilling and adverse party to rules which suit their own interests; we object to, and dispute all their "laws;" and we shall equally object and dispute the "laws" of any "*reformed*" legislature, which shall *not* be specially authorized by ourselves: what! do not they themselves declare by their own "laws," that nothing—no every day—trifling transaction, done on our behalf by any third party, is binding on us, without our specific warrant of attorney, or special appointment of agency? and must we then be bound against our will—against all principles of *right, morality*, and equity, in matters of life, and freedom, and happiness, by the independent "law" of perfect strangers? no, their own "laws" find them *guilty* of oppression and injustice—their own "laws" justify our resistance and defiance! numbers, either on one side or the other, cannot, in a moral point of view, alter the case: whether there be only one tyrant and millions of

***Fig.* 6.2**
Source: Bodleian Library, Johnson, d. 383(3)

From the late 1840s onwards, however, the power of this type of newspaper began to decline. Some titles became affiliated to organised labour and union movements and, rather than advocating total change in society, they argued instead for practical reform. The decline in radical publications is also explained in a number of other ways.

From the 1830s onwards, the radical press had to compete for sales with new publications which were stamped and legal and aimed at a more popular, educational or entertainment market. These appeared as weekly, instructive periodicals or as popular Sunday newspapers: *Lloyd's Weekly News*, the *Illustrated London News* and the *News of the World* all developed large, popular circulations during this period (figures 6.4 and 6.5). The opposition to the stamp tax, or the 'tax on knowledge' as it became known, increased, and it became recognised that, contrary to its intended

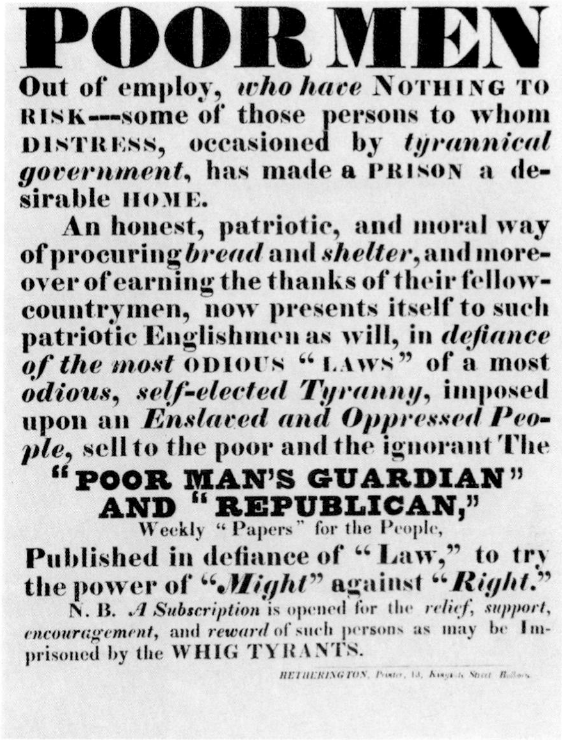

POOR MEN

Out of employ, *who have* NOTHING TO RISK---some of those persons to whom DISTRESS, occasioned by *tyrannical government*, has made a PRISON a desirable HOME.

An honest, patriotic, and moral way of procuring *bread* and *shelter*, and moreover of earning the thanks of their fellow-countrymen, now presents itself to such patriotic Englishmen as will, in *defiance of the most* ODIOUS " LAWS" of a most *odious, self-elected Tyranny*, imposed upon an *Enslaved and Oppressed People*, sell to the poor and the ignorant The

" POOR MAN'S GUARDIAN " AND " REPUBLICAN,"

Weekly " Papers" for the People, Published in defiance of " Law," to try the power of "*Might*" against "*Right.*"

N. B. *A Subscription* is opened for the *relief, support, encouragement,* and *reward* of such persons as may be Imprisoned by the WHIG TYRANTS.

HETHERINGTON, Printer, 13, Kingsgate Street, Holborn.

Fig. 6.3
Source: Bodleian Library, John Johnson Collection

functions, it depressed the sales of the legal and respectable papers rather than those which continued unstamped. The solution to this paradox, for those in authority, lay in the reduction and then removal of the tax, which was finally repealed in 1855. As prices dropped and new technologies of production made possible cheaper, faster, more efficient processes, advertising came to play a central role in determining profitability, establishing what Curran and Seaton (1991) have called a 'new licensing system'. Newspapers like the *Daily Telegraph* (1855) championed new forms of popular daily journalism developed first in the Sunday press, often illustrated, and featuring crime, sports stories and fashion reports, for instance. Newspapers came to depend upon large-scale investment, and became businesses. The latter half of the nineteenth century saw the continued expansion of this popular market, in part assisted by growing levels of literacy.

THE PENNY MAGAZINE

OF THE

Society for the Diffusion of Useful Knowledge.

36.]   PUBLISHED EVERY SATURDAY.   [OCTOBER 27, 1832.

THE BOA CONSTRICTOR.

[The Boa Constrictor about to strike a Rabbit.]

ONE of the most interesting objects in the fine collection of animals at the Surrey Zoological Gardens, is the Boa Constrictor. Curled up in a large box, through the upper grating of which it may be conveniently examined, this enormous reptile lies for weeks in a quiet and almost torpid state. The capacity which this class of animals possess of requiring food only at very long intervals, accounts for the inactive condition in which they principally live; but when the feeling of hunger becomes strong they rouse themselves from their long repose, and the voracity of their appetite is then as remarkable as their previous indifference. In a state of confinement the boa takes food at intervals of a month or six weeks; but he then swallows an entire rabbit or fowl, which is put in his cage. The artist who made the drawing for the above wood-cut, saw the box at the Surrey Zoological Gardens precisely in the attitude which he has represented. The time having arrived when he was expected to require food, a live rabbit was put into his box. The poor little quadruped remained uninjured for several days, till he became familiar with his terrible enemy. On a sudden, while the artist was observing the ill-sorted pair, the reptile suddenly rose up, and, opening his fearful jaws, made a stroke at the rabbit, who was climbing up the end of the box; but, as if his appetite was not sufficiently eager, he suddenly drew back, when within an inch of his prey, and sunk into his wonted lethargy. The rabbit, unconscious of the danger which was passed for a short season, began to play about the scaly folds of his companion; but the keeper said that his respite would be brief, and that he would be swallowed the next day without any qualms.

All the tribe of serpents are sustained by animal food. The smaller species devour insects, lizards, frogs, and snails; but the larger species, and especially the boa, not unfrequently attack very large quadrupeds. In seizing upon so small a victim as a rabbit, the boa constrictor would swallow it without much difficulty; because the peculiar construction of the mouth and throat of this species enables them to expand, so as to receive within

VOL. I.

2 P

JOHN  BULL.

"FOR GOD, THE KING, AND THE PEOPLE!"

Vol. VIII.—No. 403.   **SUNDAY, AUGUST 31, 1828.**   **Price 7d.**

UNDER THE ESPECIAL PATRONAGE OF HIS MAJESTY.
ROYAL GARDENS, VAUXHALL.—OPEN A FEW NIGHTS LONGER.—The Proprietors respectfully acquaint the public, that in consequence of the decidedly favourable change in the weather, the Gardens will be open next MONDAY, WEDNESDAY, and FRIDAY, when the UNION GALA

Will be Repeated, with, if possible, increased splendour and effect. The whole of the ILLUMINATIONS, DECORATIONS, MOTTOS, &c. Which afforded so much delight last week, will be again exhibited, and a continual succession of Entertainments take place from the time the doors open, including the amusing LOTTERY PRESENTS.

Doors open at Seven.—Admission, 4s.

THEATRE ROYAL HAYMARKET.—To-morrow Evening, the Opera of CLARI, with The GREEN EYED MONSTER, and The TWO FRIENDS.—Tuesday, Love in a Village, with The Green Eyed Monster, and Love, Law, and Physic.—Wednesday, The Way to Keep Him, with The Green Eyed Monster, and The Sleeping Draught.—Thursday, The Lord of the Manor, with The Green Eyed Monster, and The Two Friends.—Friday, She Would and She Would Not, with Twixt the Cup and the Lip, and The Green Eyed Monster.—Saturday, The Green Eyed Monster, with The Two Friends, and other Entertainments.

SURREY THEATRE.—Under the Direction of Mr. Elliston.—To-morrow Evening, JANE SHORE, with POLICINEL VAMPIRE, and The IRRESISTIBLES.—On Tuesday, a New Opera, entitled SYLVANA! (the first production of the late C. M. Von Weber), the principal characters by Miss Graddon, Mr. Philipps, Mr. Vardey, Mrs. Fitzwilliam, Mrs. Vale, Miss Helme, &c. &c. After which, The Irresistibles.—On Wednesday, Thursday, Friday, and Saturday Evenings, A Favourite Opera, with The Irresistibles.—The Public will please to notice, that the doors of this Theatre will not in future be opened before Six o'clock—the performance will commence as usual at half-past Six.

SADLER'S WELLS.—Under the Patronage of the Duke of Clarence.—To-morrow, and following Evenings, The FALSE MARRIAGE; or, Brother and Sister. After which, the new admired Ballet, by Mrs. Searle and Thirty of her Pupils, called the BRIDE and BRIDEGROOM. To which will be added the Melo-drama of The SWISS BOY; or, the Wanderers. The whole to conclude with, for this week only, the popular Comic Sketch, called JACK SHEPPARD, the Housebreaker.—In addition to the above performances, on Wednesday, Thursday, Friday, and Saturday, will be exhibited a Grand Display of FIRE WORKS.

ROYAL AMPHITHEATRE (ASTLEY'S).—Mr. WEST has the pleasure of announcing to the Public, that Mr. Price, Manager of the Theatre Royal, Drury-lane, having kindly granted permission to him to perform the magnificent Spectacle of BLUE BEARD; or, Female Curiosity, it will be produced (for the first time at this Theatre) TO MORROW EVENING, Monday, Sept. 1, for the BENEFIT of Mrs. WEST; to commence at half-past six precisely. In the procession over the mountains, Blue Beard will appear on a real Elephant. After Blue Beard, the Elephant will go through his ingenious tricks in the Circle. First night of the Double Tight Rope, by Miss Woolford and Miss Cooke—Mr. Ducrow will appear three times in the Circle, and introduce his new acts, and amuse his beautiful Persian Horse—The Flying Indian on the Slack Rope. To conclude with "Cest l'Amour, l'Amour, l'Amour;" or, Who can Help it?—The whole of the Company will appear in the different performances of this evening, for particulars of which, see the bills of the day.

NOT FOR ME, OR, THE APPLE OF DISCORD.—Evening, composed by L. Maurer, and arranged by W. Hawes, as performed at the Theatre Royal, English Opera House, is now published and to be had at No. 2, Adelphi Terrace, Strand, and at the principal Music-shops. Also, Mozart's Opera "Tit for Tat, or the Table Turned," and Paer's Opera of "The Freebooters."

MUSICAL COMPOSITION.
Recently published, in folio, half-bound, price 31s.
A TREATISE on the ART of MUSIC; in which the Elements of Harmony and Air are practically considered, and illustrated by an Hundred and Fifty Examples, in Notes, many of them taken from the best Authors; the whole being intended as a course of Lectures preparatory to the Practice of THOROUGH-BASS and MUSICAL COMPOSITION. By the Rev. W. JONES, M.A., F.R.S., late of Nayland, Suffolk; Author of "Lectures on the Figurative Language of Scripture;" "The Catholic Doctrine of the Trinity Proved," &c. &c.

THE MESSIAH; a Sacred Oratorio, composed by G. F. Handel, with an additional Accompaniments by Mozart, Part One. The full Score, with a compressed Accompaniment for the Organ or Piano-forte; by J. Addison.

SAMSON, and JUDAS MACCABEUS; in full Score, with a compressed Accompaniment, by J. Addison.

THE HARMONICON, a Popular Journal of Music. In each Monthly Number of this elegant publication are given seven Pieces of Vocal and Instrumental music, arranged for the Piano forte and Harp, and occasionally with Accompaniments for the Flute and Violin.

THE THIRD YORKSHIRE MUSICAL FESTIVAL for the BENEFIT of the York County Hospital, and the Infirmaries of Leeds, Hull, and Sheffield, by Permission, and with the Sanction, of the Very Rev. the Dean, and of the Venerable the Chapter of York, is appointed to be held in YORK MINSTER, on TUESDAY, SEPTEMBER 23, 1828, and the Three following Days.

PRESIDENT—His Grace the Lord Archbishop of York.
And under the Patronage of the principal Nobility and Gentry of the County.

Chairman of the Committee of Management—Mr. W. H. Dixon.

On TUESDAY and WEDNESDAY, September 23 and 24, will be performed in the Minster, SELECTIONS of SACRED MUSIC.

On THURSDAY, September 25, The MESSIAH.
And on FRIDAY, Sept. 26, a THIRD SELECTION of SACRED MUSIC.

On TUESDAY EVENING, Sept. 23, and the Two following Evenings, will be GRAND CONCERTS, in the FESTIVAL CONCERT ROOM.

The following Performers are already engaged:—
VOCAL.
Madame CATALANI, Madame CARADORI ALLAN, Miss STEPHENS, Mrs. W. KNYVETT, and Mrs. P. ATKINSON.
Mr. BRAHAM, Mr. VAUGHAN, Mr. PHILLIPS, Mr. W. KNYVETT, Mr. TERRAIL, Mr. E. TAYLOR, and Signor DE BEGNIS.

INSTRUMENTAL.
Leaders of the Band—Morning, Mr. Cramer........ Evening, Mr. Mori.
Other Principal Performers: Messrs. R. Ashley, Daniels, R. Lindley, W. Lindley, Mortell, Dragonetti, Anfossi, Nicholson, Card, Willman, Ling, Powell, Sharp, Wilton, Tully, Addison, Gledhill, Lyon, J. Mackintosh, Harper, Walls, A. Griesbach, Mariott, Smithies, Schoengen, Chip, Wilson, Fleischer, Blew, Brooks, Watkins, Bannister, Binfield, Ella, Reeve, Anfossi, Dance, Taylor, Gatlie, Jolly, Guynemer, Anderson, R. Mackintosh, Cole, Thomas, Pigott, Nicks, S. Collet, J. Calkin, Platt, Rae, Cummins, Penson, &c. &c.
Conductor, Mr. Greatorex—Assistant Conductors, Mr. Camidge, and Dr. Camidge, Organists of the Cathedral; Mr. White, and Mr. F. Knapton.

In addition to the names which have been particularised, the Orchestra will contain many other eminent Performers. The Chorus will be complete and effective; and the entire Band will consist of SIX HUNDRED PERFORMERS.

On the EVENING of MONDAY, Sept. 22, there will be a BALL in the ASSEMBLY ROOMS; and on the EVENING of FRIDAY, Sept. 26, a GRAND FANCY DRESS BALL, in the Festival Concert Room and Assembly Rooms, for which Catani's celebrated Quadrille band is engaged.

PIANO-FORTES TUNED, by KIRKMAN, late Tuner at Broadwood's, (Son of Kirkman, Maker to his Majesty), N.B. Instruments within 10 miles of town attended on moderate terms. Address, (post paid), at 15, Mortimer street, Cavendish-square.

TO THE CLERGY.—A Beneficed Clergyman, having fluence of non-residence, is anxious to obtain a CURACY or CHAPEL to a desirable sphere of usefulness. Full punctuation being his principal object, stipend would not be particularly regarded. He would be willing to EXCHANGE his Village Living under value and with light duty, or the CURACY thereof, which might be accepted as a Title; for a more active scene of labour.—Letters with full particulars only, and real address, to be directed, post paid, to F. G., at Walsh and Son's, No. 7, Inner Temple-lane.

A LIVING.—WANTED to PURCHASE, the PERPETUAL ADVOWSON of a LIVING, within 120 miles of London, with prospect of very early possession.—Apply, if by letter, post paid, to A. B., Mr. James Bazley's, Bookseller, 12, Little Queen-street, Lincoln's Inn-fields.

PRIVATE PUPIL.—a Married CLERGYMAN, four years Tutor to a Nobleman, and subsequently receiving Six Pupils into his house, a moderate distance from London, would be glad to fill a VACANCY with a GENTLEMAN'S SON, whose education or health may require more than common attention.—Letters addressed to Rev. J. S., Messrs. Harding and Lepard's, Booksellers, 4, Pall-mall East, London, will be duly forwarded to him in the country.

ETON or HARROW SCHOOL.—A Private Tutor, whose wishes to add to his number of Pupils. Parents who are under the necessity of keeping their children from school through illness, can engage the Advertiser for an indefinite period. References highly respectable will be adduced.—Direct, post paid, to R. A. at Mr. Cresswell's, 131, Cheapside-street, Portman-square.

ALL Persons having any Demands on the Estate of JOHN FOX, Esq. formerly of Kingston, Jamaica, and late of Loose Hill, near Maidstone, Kent, deceased, are requested to forward the particulars thereof forthwith to Messrs. Gee, and Park Nelson, Solicitors to the Executors, No. 11, Essex-street, Strand, London.

ONE HUNDRED POUND NOTE.—FIVE POUNDS REWARD—LOST a £100 NOTE, No. 1709, and dated the 29th day of July, 1825; whoever has found the same, or will give information to Messrs. Bromley, Solicitors, 3, Gray's Inn-square, whereby the same may be recovered, shall receive the sum of 5l.—The note has been stopped at the Bank of England.

THEATRE of ANATOMY, Great Windmill-street.—The following COURSES of LECTURES will be delivered during the ensuing Season:—
ANATOMY, PHYSIOLOGY, PATHOLOGY, and SURGERY, by Mr. Charles Bell, Mr. Herbert Mayo, and Mr. Caesar Hawkins.
ANATOMICAL DEMONSTRATIONS, by Mr. Caesar Hawkins.
THEORY and PRACTICE of PHYSIC, by Dr. Chambers and Dr. Macleod.
THEORY and PRACTICE of MIDWIFERY, by Mr. Brodie.
PRINCIPLES and PRACTICE of MIDWIFERY, by Mr. Stone.
MATERIA MEDICA, by Dr. Macleod.
BOTANY, by Mr. Bagrett.
For further particulars enquire at the Theatre; at the Hospital; or of the Demonstrator at the West End of London; or at the Residences of the different Lecturers.

TO BE LET.—BOARDING and DAY SCHOOL, which has been established more than 50 years, to be disposed of; the present owner and occupier is induced to relinquish it through the state of his health only. The situation and adaptation of the premises are most eligible; the inhabitants of the place about forty thousand, for neighbourhood respectable and wealthy. Apply to A. T., at Combe and Son's, Booksellers, Leicester, if by letter, paid.

COLE WINE, free from Spirit, possessing a very agreeable flavour.—Mr. de Jerze, 28, per Hogshead, of 13. per quarter pipe. A native of Spain has devised a considerable time to the cultivation of the Sherry Grape, at the Cane of Good Hope, with such success, that the Governor and Inhabitants have declared his productions equal to the best Spanish Wine; which a simple trial will prove, and remove the prejudices that exist against the wines of that Colony. Orders addressed to Signor Darroy, No. 3, Pall-Mall-place, Pall Mall, will meet due attention.

NATIONAL MEDAL.—To His Royal Highness PRINCE WILLIAM HENRY, DUKE of CLARENCE, Lord High Admiral of Great Britain and Ireland.—THIS MEDAL, IN COMMEMORATION OF HIS ROYAL HIGHNESS'S ACCESSION TO THE ANCIENT AND IMPORTANT OFFICE OF LORD HIGH ADMIRAL, is, with permission, dedicated by the Subscribers.—The Portrait of His Royal Highness, expressly for this Medal, is modelled from the life, and executed in Steel by Mr. Henning. The Reverse, selected from the Drawings of eminent Artists, to represent the Prowess of Messrs. Rundell, Bridge, and Rundell. The MEDALS are of Silver Gilt, in purple cases, price Five Guineas; and of Copper, from His Majesty's Ships most distinguished in the late War, price One Guinea; STRUCK on the ANNIVERSARY of His Royal Highness the LORD HIGH ADMIRAL'S APPOINTMENT.

THEATRE of ANATOMY and MEDICINE, Webb-street, Snow Pond, Borough.—The WINTER COURSE OF LECTURES delivered at this Theatre, will commence on WEDNESDAY, October 1st.
ANATOMY and PHYSIOLOGY, by Mr. Grainger and Mr. Pilcher.
DISSECTIONS as usual.
PRINCIPLES and PRACTICE of PHYSIC, by Dr. Armstrong.
MATERIA MEDICA, and BOTANY, by Dr. Hooth.
PRINCIPLES and PRACTICE of MIDWIFERY, and the Diseases of Women and Children, by Dr. Hopkins.
CHEMISTRY, by Mr. Cooper.
For particulars apply to Mr. Highley, Medical Bookseller, at the Theatre, or 174, Fleet-street.
Mr. Highley is authorised to enter Gentlemen to the above Lectures.

GUY'S HOSPITAL.—The Autumnal COURSE of LECTURES will commence on WEDNESDAY, the 1st of October.
THEORY and PRACTICE of MEDICINE—Dr. Bright and Dr. Addison.
MATERIA MEDICA and THERAPEUTICS—Dr. Addison.
ANATOMY and OPERATIONS of SURGERY—Mr. Bransby Cooper.
PRINCIPLES and PRACTICE of SURGERY, (including Operations)—Mr. Key and Mr. Morgan.
MIDWIFERY, and Diseases of Women and Children—Dr. Blundell.
PHYSIOLOGY, or Laws of the Animal Economy—Dr. Blundell.
CHEMISTRY—Mr. A. Aikin and Mr. Barry.
STRUCTURE and DISEASES of the TEETH—Mr. Bell.
EXPERIMENTAL PHILOSOPHY—Professor Millington and Mr. Barry.
Clinical Lectures and Instructions, with Demonstrations in Morbid Anatomy, will be given during the Session.
For particulars apply to Mr. Stocker, Apothecary to the Hospital.

SCHOOL of ANATOMY, MEDICINE, SURGERY, and MIDWIFERY, Little Dean-street, Dean-street, Soho-square, London, (within a short distance of St. George's, St. Bartholomew's, the Middlesex, and Westminster Hospitals.)
The WINTER COURSES of LECTURES will be commenced on 2d of October.
ANATOMY and PHYSIOLOGY, with Demonstrations, Dissections and Examinations. By J. Smith, M.D., M.R.C.S.
PRINCIPLES and PRACTICE of MEDICINE, with Practical Instructions and Examinations. By Dr. Copland.
MATERIA MEDICA, PHARMACY, and MEDICAL BOTANY. By Dr. Wilmot.
PRINCIPLES and PRACTICE of SURGERY, with Practical Instructions and Examinations. By Mr. Alcock.
PRINCIPLES and PRACTICE of MIDWIFERY, with Cases and Clinical Instructions. By Dr. Hopkins.
MEDICAL JURISPRUDENCE, by Dr. Wilmot, (during the Summer.)

UNIVERSITY of LONDON.
THE MEDICAL CLASSES will OPEN on WEDNESDAY, the 1st of October.
ANATOMY and OPERATIVE SURGERY—Granville S. Pattison, Esq.
PHYSIOLOGY—Charles Bell, Esq., F.R.S. three times a week, 11 to 12.
NATURE and TREATMENT of DISEASES—John Conolly, M.D., daily (except Saturday), nine to Ten a.m.
MIDWIFERY and DISEASES of WOMEN and CHILDREN—David D. Davis, M.D., four times a week, 10 to 11 a.m.
CLINICAL MEDICINE—Thomas Watson, M.D. Physician to the Middlesex Hospital, twice a week, six to seven p.m.
SURGERY and CLINICAL SURGERY—Charles Bell, Esq. Surgeon to the Middlesex Hospital, three times a week, six to seven p.m.
MATERIA MEDICA and PHARMACY—Anthony Todd Thomson, M.D. daily (except Saturday), eight to nine a.m.
CHEMISTRY—Edward Turner, M.D., daily, 10 to 11, commencing on the 3d November.
COMPARATIVE ANATOMY—Robert Grant, M.D., three times a week, from three to four p.m.
MEDICAL JURISPRUDENCE—John Gordon Smith, M.D.
DISSECTIONS and DEMONSTRATIONS—James Bennett, Esq., daily.
HOSPITAL PRACTICE—Middlesex Hospital, daily, half-past twelve to half-past one.
DISPENSARY PRACTICE—University Dispensary, daily, from half-past twelve to half past one.
The MEDICAL CLASSES will close in May, but each Professor will give a Winter and Spring Course.

GUINEAS REWARD.—The following Persons having been indicted for ESCAPES out of the RULES of the KING'S BENCH PRISON, the above Reward will be paid by the Marshal, to any person or persons that will apprehend them, or any of them, or furnish the Marshal with such information as will enable him to apprehend them, or any of them, in this kingdom, viz.:—

TWENTY SIXTH LIST.
King's Bench, 30th August, 1828.

CASE STUDY: THE DEVELOPMENT OF BRITISH CINEMA FROM THE 1890s TO THE 1920s

An historical survey needs to begin with the problem of how the cinema came into existence and to consider the reasons why certain potentials were realised and others ignored.

Armes (1978), p. 7

There is considerable debate over the first cinematic performance in Britain. The first projected moving photographic picture show to a paying audience in Britain is generally recognised to have taken place at the London Polytechnic, Regent Street, in February 1896. This was a screening organised by the British representative of the French Lumière brothers, Louis and Auguste, who had staged what is generally regarded as the very first cinematic showing in the world, involving projection and audience payment, in Paris, December 1895. While this event is regarded as the forerunner of cinema, it is important to note that many other inventors and entrepreneurs across Europe and in the USA were on the brink of claiming to be the first to exhibit moving pictures. In 1894, the first English Kinetoscope Parlour had opened. This offered customers the chance to try Thomas Edison's patent kinetoscope, which was a coin-in-the-slot machine for viewing animated photographs.

The cinema is generally regarded as a means of modern mass communication which was invented. The technical development of *film* and the apparatus to project moving images were the result of processes of invention; however, the *cinema*, as a social institution, was discovered and evolved to realise the potentials of the technologies in particular ways. It did not emerge 'naturally' from the technologies. The principles underlying visual projection had been known and operated for centuries before the 1890s. The camera obscura, for example – a darkened room into which light passed through a small hole or lens, producing a projected picture on the wall opposite – had been used in Italy in the sixteenth century. Many inventions, including those central to the early development of cinematography, are best viewed as parts of complex and interwoven relationships:

cinematography was unusually the by-product of such various developments as the search for new types of explosives, the industrialisation of agriculture, and the invention of a new material for printers' rollers.

Chanan (1980), p. 10

The formative influences on the emergence of moving picture technologies prior to this period include:

1 *Developments in photography* from the 1820s onwards. These include not only technical innovations but also consideration of the impact of photography on the visual arts and systems of representation.

2 *Developments in the 'science of perception'.* From the early nineteenth century some scientists had experimented with optical devices in the

search for a more adequate understanding of how people 'saw' their environment. Several experiments were conducted which examined optical illusions, and the machines produced to test scientific hypotheses were later exploited in the Victorian, middle-class fascination for parlour spectacles and games. The bioscope and early animation machines were developed partly with this scientific impetus.

3 *Developments in the 'scientific study of motion'.* These were greatly assisted by, and in turn perfected, cameras and other photographic technologies. The work of some physiologists and photographers in Europe and the United States became concerned with capturing motion on **film** as realistically as possible.

4 *Pre-existing forms of exhibition and spectacle*, which included a diverse number of influences. Puppet shows and peep shows were popular much earlier than the nineteenth century. Theatrical traditions and devices, often using sophisticated lighting techniques, were also an important consideration. Of these precursors of the modern cinematic experience, one of the most important was the Magic Lantern, with which the principle of projection, albeit of still images, was firmly established. Throughout the nineteenth century Magic Lanterns were developed to produce more and more sophisticated effects, some involving simple types of movement. The lantern developed, as Chanan has noted, somewhere 'between science and magic'. It was employed as a means of entertainment in music halls and fairgrounds, as a means of instruction, typically in the lecture hall, and as a domestic toy. Of these settings, the music hall and the travelling fairground became major exhibition centres for magic lantern shows, introducing the idea of frequent and reproducible visual performances: spectacles, often introduced by showmen, for which audiences paid money.

In the few years immediately before and after the Lumière brothers' invention in 1895, critics, journalists, and the pioneer cinematographers disagreed considerably among themselves as to the *social function* that they attributed to, or predicted, for the new machine; whether it was a means of preservation or of making archives, whether it was an auxiliary technology for research and teaching in sciences like botany or surgery; whether it was a new form of journalism, or an instrument of sentimental devotion, either private or public, which could perpetuate the living image of the dear departed one, and so on. That, over all these possibilities, the cinema could evolve into a machine for telling stories had never been considered.

Metz (1974), p. 93

It was, however, the ability to tell stories, recognised and developed by the traditions and expanding industry of popular entertainment, motivated principally by commercial gain and opportunity, which accounted for the very rapid take-off of cinema as a mass medium. By the end of 1896, only eight months after the initial public performance of film in Britain, moving pictures were part of many music hall shows up and down the country (figures 6.6 and 6.7). The spectacle of moving pictures was augmented by

Fig. 6.6
Source: D.J. Wendon, *The Birth of the Movies*, E.P. Dutton & Co., 1974

music and often by live, spoken commentary or narrative to accompany the visual performance.

This expansion in exhibition continued with accelerating speed and profitability into the 1900s. Renting and hiring circuits developed to supply and distribute films. Specialised premises and commercial interests pulled the exhibition of films out of music halls, first into vacant shops, known as 'shop shows' or 'penny gaffs', and after 1906 into custom-built premises – 'picture palaces', 'bijoux palaces' and 'majestics' (figure 6.8). By 1909, largely to regulate the size of auditoria, but also to introduce safety regulations concerning cinema assemblies, the First Cinematographic Act was passed in Parliament. In this year, estimates suggest that British production amounted to only about 20 per cent of films shown in British cinemas, and that 40 per cent were French, 30 per cent American and 10 per cent Italian.

By 1910, some 1600 cinemas were in existence, and, by the outbreak of the First World War in 1914, this figure had jumped to 4000. The Cinema Commission of 1917 estimates annual weekly attendances at cinemas as 7–8 million pre-1914. It reported attendances of 20 million per week in 1917. By the end of the war, British cinema exhibition had developed into a major industry, based on a cinematic form inconceivable in the 1890s – the extended fictional feature film. This was reliant upon an increasingly complex product: melodramas, comedies, westerns, travelogues and superspectaculars were some of the early genres of popular 'silent' film (figure 6.9). By the outbreak of war in 1914, however, Hollywood-produced American films accounted for over half of the domestic market: 'Ever since 1913 British audiences have seen more American than British films. Hollywood imagery, values and myths have for over sixty years been part of the imaginative and fantasy furniture of British minds' (Tunstall, 1983,

To-Night! To-Night!

CALDER'S FAMOUS

CINEMATOGRAPH

AND

Popular Concert.

Don't miss seeing the Grand **NEW PICTURES** of

THE DREYFUS COURT MARTIAL.

The Prince of Wales in Edinburgh.

Sir Redvers Buller Embarking for Transvaal.

Scenes at the Highland Brigade Camp.

The Invercharron Gathering.

The Grand Fire Dance.

Barnum & Bailey's Procession.

The Mysterious Astrologer's Dream.

Spendid Train Scenes.

Grand Coloured Dances.

Comicalities and Burlesque Scenes, &c., &c.

Pictures of absorbing interest and Astounding Transformations.

SPLENDID • CONCERT

By First=Class Artistes.

DOORS OPEN AT 7.30.   CONCERT AT 8 P.M.

Popular Prices See Bills.

A BRIGHT UP TO DATE SPARKLING ENTERTAINMENT

Fig. 6.7

A poster advertising a cinematographic show. The trial and imprisonment of Alfred Dreyfus was a cause célèbre in France in the 1890s

Source: D.J. Wendon, *The Birth of the Movies*, E.P. Dutton & Co., 1974

ACTIVITY 6.6

Conduct some independent research on the early history of cinema in Britain. Oral history and local library and historical archives can be useful sources.

Research and build up a history of cinema from the earliest years onwards in your own local town or area. Supplement this where possible with interviews and local newspaper archive research.

Investigate the reasons why the American Hollywood industry, and its films, have dominated British exhibition and production from the 1920s onwards.

---

p. 55). This trend – a domestic market dominated by overseas, mainly American productions – continued into the 1920s and, arguably, to the present day. Government legislation in 1927, the year of the first 'talkie', attempted to guarantee and preserve a quota of the home market for domestic production. Cinema attendances grew rapidly in the 1920s and throughout the inter-war period, becoming 'the essential social habit of the age' (Taylor, 1965).

Fig. 6.9
Source: D.J. Wendon, *The Birth of the Movies*, E.P. Dutton & Co., 1974

Fig. 6.8
Source: D.J. Wendon, *The Birth of the Movies*, E.P. Dutton & Co., 1974

CASE STUDY: BROADCASTING IN BRITAIN 1920–1998

The development of broadcasting from the 1920s to the present day covers a period of significant technological and cultural change, particularly in the areas of domestic affluence and lifestyle. The development of broadcasting can be seen as part of a relationship that also includes the state as regulator and the public as consumers. The dynamic nature of this relationship has meant that the means, structures and functions of broadcasting have had to evolve to meet the needs of new audiences and changing government legislation.

In the early stages of its history, broadcasting was shaped by government policy directed at establishing a national monopoly that was inseparable from notions of providing a *public service*. This was an attempt to control both broadcasters, by limiting who had access to the airwaves, and, through the licence fee, audiences. However, more recently, government legislation has been aimed at loosening many of these controls and 'deregulating' the duopoly of the BBC and the Independent Broadcasting Authority (IBA, replaced in 1990 by the Independent Television Commission, ITC), in order to open up broadcasting and allow free-market commercialism to determine what is available to whom on what channels and at what cost.

1920–1945: The BBC – the voice of the nation

From the beginning of broadcasting, various governments have tried to control its production. As early as 1904 the Postmaster General took responsibility for the allocation of broadcasting frequencies to avoid the 'chaos of the airwaves' that the introduction of commercial radio had created in America. In 1922 a group of radio equipment manufacturers, called the British Broadcasting Company, were given a licence to run a monopoly broadcasting service in London, Manchester and Birmingham.

The general manager of this new company was John Reith. All radio or 'wireless' set owners were supposed to pay a fee of ten shillings (50p) which was collected by the Post Office, who then passed on half to the company. As Scannell and Cardiff (1991) note, without any real discussion or ideological rationale two key ideas that were to shape broadcasting for the next seventy years had been established: the annual licence fee and the notion of a monopoly.

In 1923, when the *Radio Times* was first published, 80 000 licences had been issued. In 1924, King George V's opening of the Wembley Exhibition was broadcast live and heard by 10 million people; by 1925, the company's transmission covered 85 per cent of the United Kingdom. By 1927, the number of licences issued had increased to 2 million and there was concern from newspaper owners and producers that this new source of news and information might affect their profits from sales. As a result of their pressure the BBC was severely restricted, with a ban on news programmes before 7pm each day and a clause that stipulated that the company could not broadcast any news or information unless it had been obtained and paid for from the news agencies, which were controlled by the newspaper industry. Only in 1927, when the BBC became the state corporation, was it allowed to broadcast news bulletins earlier in the day but these were still severely limited and contained very little 'hard' news.

In 1925 the government concluded that, although radio was too important to be left in the hands of a commercial company and that it was inappropriate in a democracy for broadcasting to be under direct state control, there was a need to maintain some kind of regulation on who provided what types of radio service. As a compromise, by Royal

THE FIRST ISSUE OF 'THE RADIO TIMES', 28 SEPTEMBER 1923
What was inside? Find out on page 24 and turn the page for 100 more covers

Fig. 6.10
First issue of the Radio Times, *28 September 1923*

Charter, the British Broadcasting Company was changed from a public commercial company into an independent national organisation, the British Broadcasting Corporation, which would act as a monopoly and 'as a trustee for the national interest' (HMSO, 1966).

The Royal Charter laid out the BBC's constitution: there would be twelve governors (the 'great and the good') appointed by the Privy Council for a five-year period and headed by a chairman. The governors would in turn appoint a Director-General who would be responsible for the day-to-day management of the BBC. This structure has continued into the 1990s with John Birt as the current Director-General.

Reith's legacy

According to many commentators, including Garnham (1973), Hood (1980), Curran and Seaton (1991) and Scannell and Cardiff (1991), one of the strongest criticisms that has been made of Reith was his apparent political naivety. Although he had a clear idea of what broadcasting should offer in cultural and moral terms, he never questioned its political role, perhaps assuming that 'independence' guaranteed impartiality. Partly because of the limits the charter placed upon the BBC's ability to deal with issues of 'controversy' and partly because of Reith's identification of a national culture that included the state, the church, the monarchy and his own 'elite' upper-middle-class Calvinist values, the BBC always seemed firmly to support the state, the establishment, and what was often identified as the 'national interest'. Reith believed that the BBC should be above political fighting and he defended the use of the BBC by the government during the General Strike of 1926 as an attempt to 'draw together the contending parties by creating an atmosphere of goodwill' (Curran and Seaton, 1991). However, at this time Reith also stated that, 'Since the BBC was a national institution and since the Government in this crisis was acting for the people ... the BBC was for the Government in the crisis too' (quoted in Garnham, 1980, p.19).

Reith's philosophy is often summed up as simply being 'to educate, to inform and to entertain'. He believed that the BBC, through the new medium of radio, presented a great opportunity for helping the less educated (schools' broadcasts had been available since 1924) and the less informed, and for both 'bringing culture to the masses' and 'bringing the nation together'. Reith's vision was that the BBC had a responsibility to unify the whole nation with a public service where everyone had access to a wide range of high-quality programmes and reliable and objective news (figure 6.11).

One of the main legacies of Reith's time as Director-General is the acceptance of the system of financing the BBC through the licence fee. As Garnham points out, the BBC has never been financed independently by the licence fee but rather by the government deciding how much that licence fee should be. The BBC is therefore dependent upon the 'goodwill' of the government when its charter comes up for renewal and sometimes this goodwill is absent. The BBC is also dependent upon the ideological imperatives of whatever political party is currently in power, and during the 1980s and 1990s, when the philosophy of 'deregulation' and 'market forces' have been paramount, the licence fee's increases have been severely limited and the BBC has been put under considerable financial pressure and pressure to increase its income from commercial activities (figure 6.12).

By the time John Reith retired from the BBC in 1938, nearly 9 million radio licences were being issued annually (representing nearly three-quarters of all households in Britain). The radio had become the 'wireless', often combined with a record player to become a radiogram and given pride of place in the living room. The BBC was established as 'the voice of the nation' and was providing a service for people throughout Britain.

PROGRAMMES for TUESDAY, January 10

2LO LONDON and ₅XX DAVENTRY

10.30 a.m.	Time Signal; Weather forecast.
11.00	The Daventry Quartet with Frederick Allen (Daventry only).
12.00 p.m.	The Carlton Mason Sextet.
2.00	Interlude
3.00	The Daventry Quartet and Gerald Crofts, Anne Ballantyne.
4.00	William Hodgson's Marble Arch Pavilion Orchestra.
5.00	Miss Barbara Cartland: 'Settling into a House'.
5.15	The Children's Hour.
6.00	Gramophone Recital.
6.30	Time Signal; Weather Forecast; First General News Bulletin.
6.45	Gramophone Recital (continued).
7.00	Mr. J.W. Robertson Scott: 'The Month's Reviews'.
7.15	The Foundations of Music: Mozart's Violin Sonatas.
7.25	Topical talk.
7.45	A Light Operatic Programme.
9.00	Weather Forecast; Second General News Bulletin.
9.15	Prof. J. Arthur Thompson: 'Wonders of Deep Sea Life'.
9.30	Local Announcements (Daventry only).
9.35	Vaudeville.
10.30	Dance Music: Jay Whidden's Band.
12.00	Close Down.

Fig. 6.11

Schedule from the Radio Times, *6 January 1928*
Source: Radio Times

Second World War

With the crisis brought about by the outbreak of war in 1939, and particularly after Dunkirk in 1940, the BBC's role had to change. The audience could no longer be seen as the comfortable middle classes, actual or aspiring, but instead had to include workers in munitions factories, soldiers, sailors and airmen, as well as their wives, sisters and girlfriends, who were now being encouraged to move out of their domestic world and work in the factories or on the land. Instead of individual middle-class families sitting around the fireside, the audience had to be conceived of as a national, communal one in factory canteens or military camps. In an attempt to address this 'new' audience, the BBC's newly formed Listener Research Unit actually asked people what they wanted and reported back on the popularity or otherwise of particular programmes.

Income: £1.5 billion Expenditure:	£
TV	
BBC1	£ 648m
BBC2	£ 328m
Regional	£ 154m
	£ 1130m
Radio	
R.1	£ 37m
R.2	£ 39m
R.3	£ 57m
R.4	£ 80m
R.5	£ 46m
Regional	£ 47m
Local	£ 76m
	£ 382m
Total	£ 1512m

Fig. 6.12
The BBC's finances, 1995/96
Sources: various

Fig. 6.13
People in a London pub listening to a broadcast by Winston Churchill in August 1941
Source: Hulton Getty Picture Collection Ltd

The idea of 'segmenting' the BBC's provision to meet different audience requirements meant that its National Service was split into two: the Home Service, which continued to follow the style of the old National Service closely with its talks, plays and classical music, and the new, lighter, more popular Forces Programme, which was aimed specifically at this new working-class audience. The Forces Programme took on many of the populist styles and personalities of Radios Luxemburg and Normandy, including American shows by Bob Hope and Jack Benny, in an attempt to please listeners as well as boosting their morale.

The style and content of the language became more popular and down-to-earth, with slang, humour, innuendo and occasionally some irreverence or vulgarity. Shows were often broadcast from factory canteens or barracks, and the 'live' audience was heard either through their laughter and applause or when 'ordinary' members of the public spoke directly into the microphone to make requests or to send messages. New programmes like *We Speak for Ourselves* allowed working-class people to be heard for the first time on radio, and fictional drama series like *The Plums* were based on a supposedly 'typical' working-class family and tried to reflect the realities of urban wartime life: bombings, rationing, shift work and members of the family fighting away from home.

The need for news and information during the war resulted in the rapid growth of the BBC's own news-gathering service. Topicality became an important news value: 'on-the-spot' reports from journalists accompanying troops in France and Germany towards the end of the war had a freshness and immediacy that would have been impossible pre-1938.

Fig. 6.14
A wartime OB (Outside Broadcast)
Source: BBC Picture Archives

1945–1990: Expansion and commercialism

After the war this new 'popularist' philosophy remained: the Forces Programme was renamed the Light Programme and many of its shows carried on. The Home Service also continued and the Third Programme was introduced in 1946, most closely reflecting Reith's original aim of offering 'high cultural quality'. These three stations – the Light Programme, the Home Service and the Third Programme – continued the BBC's monopoly of national radio and remained unchanged until 1967.

Independent television

The BBC had been broadcasting television regularly since 1936, although the broadcasts were stopped in 1939 for the duration of the Second World War. After 1945 the BBC resumed its transmissions and until 1956 maintained a monopoly.

One of the events that brought people into contact with television for the first time was the live coverage of the Coronation of Elizabeth II in 1953 (see chapter 3, figure 3.3). It was watched by 50 per cent of the population, about 25 million people – twice the radio audience. The transmission lasted all day and used 21 cameras spread around the centre of London and including, after some resistance, cameras in Westminster Abbey. The commentary

ACTIVITY 6.7

Research what BBC
Television was like before
the introduction of com-
mercial television. Look in
libraries to see what information is available: there
may be old copies of the
Radio Times, or old newspapers may have details of
daily broadcasts. Interview
someone who used to
watch television in its early
days.

Try to find out the
types of programme being
broadcast, the time slots
or scheduling of these programmes (look particularly
at Sundays), how people
'consumed' television in
those days and how that is
different to the way we
use television today.

was by Richard Dimbleby, who from that point on became a household name and the 'voice of the BBC'.

In 1954 the Conservative government introduced a Television Act which proposed the setting up of an Independent Television Authority (ITA) which would oversee 'television broadcasting services additional to those of the BBC and of high quality ... which may include advertisements' (HMSO, 1966). The Television Act, partly in recognition of the role that the BBC was playing in the daily cultural lives of British people, included the remit that commercial television, too, should offer a 'public service' and strive to 'inform, educate and entertain' the national audience.

The ITA, like the BBC, was licensed by the Home Office. Like the BBC, it had a governing body of twelve members (again the great and the good) who oversaw the setting up of the regional 'networks' – the awarding of the franchises – that would provide a mixture of local and national televi-sion, and the leasing of the transmitters. The ITA would also oversee the content of the programmes and advertising. The new television companies were to be 'independent', that, is, free of the licence fee. They received their income from the selling of advertising space and in return had to pay the ITA rental for the transmitters, plus a levy to the government based on each company's advertising revenue. Any money left over would be profit paid to the company's shareholders.

One of ITV's most important early contributions to the development of television was its current affairs and news broadcasts, presented by Independent Television News (ITN) (see, for example, Curran and Seaton, 1991). They introduced probing interviews and on-the-spot reports, which were very different from the BBC's deferential attitude to politicians and the practice of allowing them to give their viewpoints unchallenged. Commentators like ITN's Robin Day were not so deferential in their ques-tioning of politicians and the reporting of 'great' events like the state open-ing of Parliament. Through ITN, commercial television offered an alternative to the reverence of Richard Dimbleby's BBC commentaries.

Television's 'Golden Age'

Many writers have referred to the 1960s as the 'Golden Age' of television. BBC television in particular, under the Director-General Sir Hugh Greene, can be seen to have played a major role in confronting viewers with the social changes that had taken place during the previous decades. Just as radio in 1930s had brought its version of the realities of unemployment in the north of England or slum conditions in the cities to Home Counties audiences, so the television drama *Cathy Come Home* exposed the plight of the homeless in what prime minister Harold Macmillan had called, in 1959, a society where people had 'never had it so good'. It was a version of Reith's 'public service' *par excellence*. As a result of *Cathy Come Home*, the Labour government introduced new policies, and organisations such as Shelter were set up to help the homeless.

Television genres that are familiar today were becoming established. Satirical programmes like *That Was The Week That Was*, soap operas like

Fig. 6.15
Cathy Come Home, *1966*
Source: BFI

Coronation Street, police series like *Z Cars* and situation comedies like *Steptoe and Son* all provided entertainment but at the same time allowed 'ordinary domestic life' to be shown – what Richard Hoggart (1957) and Raymond Williams (1965) called the 'lived experience', the 'popular' culture, the everyday life of everyday people. Television could be seen to be discovering and disclosing information and images about segments of society that had either been ignored or else only portrayed in the cosy images of *Dixon of Dock Green* or Ealing comedies, or as second-best imitations of 'high culture'. This 'domestication' of television, Scannell (1987b) suggests, reflects both the daily experiences of the majority of people and the method of their consumption of television. Sitting at home in their living rooms, watching other people, real or fictitious, sitting in their homes, keeping each other company, helping to cope with life, and the next day sharing the experience with others, talking about what they had watched the night before. Television and domestic life became indistinguishable, television also became part of national and personal identity and memory (e.g. the way in which many people were able to remember how they first heard the news of the assassination of President Kennedy in 1963, or in 1997, watched the funeral of Diana, Princess of Wales).

Although television appeared to be operating under two different systems, BBC and ITA, many analysts have noted that the people who managed these systems still appeared to be from the same social background:

public-school educated, university-trained, and with similar ideas about 'public service' and 'public interest' (see Kumar, 1977). Both systems had similar boards of management drawn from the same small and restricted social elite. The programme makers often moved between the two organisations and having been trained by the BBC, shared a common professional 'ethos'. Both organisations were dependent upon the goodwill of the government for their finances, the BBC through the increases of the licence fee and the ITA through the advertising levy that the broadcasting companies had to pay to the government.

From pirates to independent radio

During the 1950s and 1960s, a new, profitable, teenage audience had grown up, which wanted radio that reflected their interests in pop music and 'youth' culture. The BBC's Light Programme had offered programmes like *Saturday Club, Easy Beat* and *Pick of the Pops* as a concession to the new generation of bands like the Beatles and their fans, but still maintained its *Music While You Work, Uncle Mac* and other programmes developed during the Second World War.

In 1964 an alternative became available, as pirate radio stations started broadcasting from ships moored outside territorial waters. Stations like Radio Caroline and Radio London were based on the American format and broadcast, 24 hours a day, a continual flow of pop music interspersed with advertising, station identity jingles and the words of disc jockeys. These stations offered new, popular ways of using radio, based, like commercial television, on entertainment appealing to a mass local market and financed by advertising. At their peak in 1967 about 20 million people listened to the pirate stations.

Eventually, in August 1967, in an attempt to outlaw the pirates, the Labour government passed the Marine Broadcasting Offences Bill, which made it illegal for any British subject to supply or work on the pirate stations. In September 1967 the BBC, belatedly acknowledging the demands of this new audience, changed the Light Programme into Radio 2, the Home Service into Radio 4, and the Third Programme into Radio 3, and created a new pop music service called Radio 1, which took many of the features – and disc jockeys – from the pirate stations.

In 1967 the BBC started to develop a network of local radio stations, starting with Radio Leicester. In 1971 the Conservative government gave the go-ahead for privately owned local radio stations funded by advertising, although there was still a requirement to offer a 'truly public service' but at a local level. This new service was called Independent Local Radio (ILR). At the same time the ITA changed its name to the IBA (Independent Broadcasting Authority) to encompass radio as well as television.

Minority broadcasting: BBC2 and Channel 4

When, in 1962, the Pilkington Committee investigated the service offered by the ITV companies, it concluded that they equated 'quality with box-office success' and 'failed to live up to [their] responsibilities as a public

		1977 Q2	1988 Q2	1994 Q4	1995 Q1	1995 Q2	1995 Q3	1995 Q4*	1996 Q1*	1996 Q2
All radio	Reach	92	86	86	86	87	86	86	86	86
	Hours	22.9	21.4	20.8	21.0	20.9	20.7	21.5	21.6	20.3
BBC Radio One	Reach	48	37	23	22	23	24	24	24	23
	Hours	11.2	11.9	8.7	8.7	9.0	8.9	9.3	9.9	9.6
	Share	25.9	23.9	11.3	10.8	11.7	11.8	12.0	12.7	12.8
Two	Reach	41	28	19	19	18	18	18	18	18
	Hours	10.2	11.7	12.2	13.1	12.2	11.5	12.1	12.7	11.9
	Share	19.8	17.8	12.8	13.4	12.0	11.8	11.6	12.2	12.2
Three	Reach	10	8	5	5	5	6	5	5	5
	Hours	4.2	4.7	3.4	3.2	3.7	3.5	3.7	3.5	3.4
	Share	1.9	2.1	1.0	0.9	1.0	1.1	1.0	0.9	1.0
Four	Reach	30	21	18	18	18	18	18	18	17
	Hours	10.5	11.9	10.6	10.1	10.6	10.0	10.1	10.6	10.3
	Share	14.7	13.3	10.6	9.8	10.4	10.3	9.7	10.5	10.1
Five Live	Reach			10	11	11	10	10	11	10
	Hours			4.7	5.0	5.0	5.2	5.1	5.3	5.2
	Share			2.7	3.1	2.9	3.0	2.8	3.1	3.1
Local/ Regional	Reach	19	19	21	21	20	19	20	20	18
	Hours	7.2	8.0	8.9	9.3	8.8	9.0	9.3	10.0	8.9
	Share	6.5	8.2	10.2	10.7	9.8	9.7	10.1	10.9	9.4
Local commercial	Reach	49	42	49	49	49	49	52	49	49
	Hours	12.4	13.5	14.0	14.3	14.3	14.0	13.9	14.0	13.7
	Share	28.3	30.8	38.0	38.5	38.8	38.7	39.1	36.7	38.5
Classic FM	Reach			10	10	10	10	10	10	10
	Hours			5.7	5.8	5.2	5.3	5.7	5.8	5.6
	Share			3.2	3.1	2.9	2.9	3.0	3.3	3.1
Virgin	Reach			9	8	7	8	7	7	7
	Hours			8.3	7.9	7.7	7.6	7.4	8.2	7.6
	Share			3.9	3.5	3.2	3.3	2.9	3.1	3.0
Atlantic 252	Reach			10	9	10	10	10	8	8
	Hours			7.2	6.4	6.9	6.2	6.3	6.6	6.3
	Share			3.9	3.3	3.8	3.5	3.3	2.9	2.9
Talk Radio†	Reach				3	4	5	4	4	5
	Hours				5.1	5.9	6.3	6.5	6.6	6.6
	Share				0.9	1.4	1.7	1.5	1.6	1.8
Luxembourg	Reach	7	2							
	Hours	3.2	2.8							
	Share	1.1	0.3							
Others	Reach	NR	10	7	8	6	7	7	6	6
	Hours	NR	7.0	6.5	6.3	6.0	5.8	7.9	6.4	6.1
	Share		3.2	4.0	2.4	2.9	2.1	2.1	3.1	2..0	2.1

Notes:

1. Q: calendar quarter (Q2 = April–June).

2. Figures are weekly averages. Data are for adults.

3. Reach: percentage of national adult population (measures audience awareness and use of station).

4. Share: percentage of total listening time (measures a station's competitiveness).

5. NR: not reported.

6. * Includes 'ascribed' data.

7. † First survey shown was for less than full fieldwork period.

Fig. 6.16

Networks' key ratings
Source: JICAR (1977–92); RAJAR/RSL

Look at the data contained in figure 6.16. What do they tell us about the overall trends in radio listening? Consider the reasons for any trends that you may have identified.

Draw up a 'profile' of a local radio station that you have access to. Find out who owns it and what competition (if any) it has. Establish what types of programming it offers, what type of audience it appeals to, and how that audience is 'targeted'. If you have access to both BBC and ILR stations, compare and contrast their outputs.

service' (Garnham, 1973). Because of this, according to Goodwin and Whannell (1990), ITV was not allowed to extend its services and the next allocated television channel was given to the BBC. BBC2 started transmission in 1964 and pioneered colour transmission in 1967. ITV had to wait until the Annan Report on Broadcasting before it was allowed a second commercial channel. The 1981 Broadcasting Act granted the new franchise to the ITV companies and Channel 4 in England and Scotland (S4C in Wales) started broadcasting in 1982.

Both BBC2 and Channel 4 were set up to provide an alternative to mainstream stations. Channel 4 is specifically required to 'cater for tastes, interests and audiences not served by ITV (or other television channels), to innovate in the form and content of programmes and to devote a proportion of its airtime to educational programming' (Channel 4, 1991). In Wales, S4C has a remit to produce Welsh-language programmes. Channel 4 is a 'publisher broadcaster': the only programme it makes is *Right to Reply*, and all others are commissioned and produced by independent programme makers, or other television companies including those imported from abroad.

Channel 4 was originally funded by a levy on all the ITV companies, who in return sold the advertising space on the new channel. This guaranteed Channel 4 an income and released it from direct commercial

Fig. 6.17
Channel 4's opening programmes
Source: T.V. Times, 30 October –
5 November 1982

pressures. However, under the 1990 Broadcasting Act, the channel became responsible for its own funding by selling its own airtime. Many commentators feel that this has resulted in Channel 4 being less adventurous and point to the high price the channel was prepared to pay to keep the popular American sitcom *Friends*, as well as the increasing numbers of early-evening American sitcoms, *My Two Dads*, *The Wonder Years*, *The Cosby Show*, and talk shows, as evidence of Channel 4's more cautious and popularist scheduling. As Channel 4 has become increasingly commercially successful there were suggestions that John Major's Conservative government planned to privatise the channel.

Satellite television

British Satellite Broadcasting (BSB) was awarded the British satellite franchise in 1986. BSB became famous for its 'squarial' (a square aerial), and produced its own programmes aimed at a 'broadsheet', ABC1 audience. At the same time Rupert Murdoch's News International bought an ailing satellite transmission station based in Luxembourg, called SKY. In 1989 Murdoch launched the first satellite service in Britain, a few months before BSB came on stream. SKY offered a bought-in diet of American and Australian soaps and quizzes, with some of its own programmes aimed at a 'tabloid' C2DE market.

The two systems were in competition and both losing large amounts of money – at one point News International was reputed to be losing £2 million per week – and in 1990 the two systems combined to form BSkyB. The new service was run from the old SKY headquarters and was run by the SKY personnel; most traces of BSB disappeared including the squarial and the ABC1 target audience. By the end of 1997 BSkyB claim that they will have over 500 channels available to subscribers on both satellite and cable.

1990 Onwards: deregulation – competition, choice and quality

ACTIVITY 6.9

Both BBC2 and Channel 4 were introduced to cater for minority interests and special needs groups. Look through past and present schedules for both BBC2 and Channel 4 and try to assess to what extent these channels have fulfilled their remits.

The period since the 1990 Broadcasting Act has seen both a substantial increase in broadcasting services available to consumers in Britain and a merging and concentration of media companies. Broadcasting in the 1990s is going through a radical change of emphasis that seems to mark the end of the 'Reithian' philosophy of public service that has underpinned British broadcasting since the 1920s. The ideal of 'free' quality broadcasting available to all is being replaced by a free-market philosophy that expects the audience to pay for what it wants.

In 1988 the Conservative government published a White Paper 'Broadcasting in the 1990s', which highlighted three key Conservative concepts for broadcasting: competition, choice and quality. The free-market philosophy behind the White Paper suggested that if competition among broadcasters was increased then listeners and viewers would have more choice; this would in turn mean that only the successful stations would attract high enough ratings to survive and bring in the required advertising revenue. To attract the higher ratings broadcasters would have to raise standards, and so viewers would benefit from improved quality.

1990 Broadcasting Act: television

The Conservative government's argument was incorporated in the 1990 Broadcasting Act which aimed to fundamentally change the way broadcasting operated and to 'deregulate' the airwaves.

One of the central pieces of legislation was the 'auctioning' of the new ten-year franchises for Channel Three (C3) as from 1 January 1993. The new franchises were to be 'auctioned' and be awarded to the highest bidder after passing a 'quality' threshold. Only in 'exceptional circumstances' would the franchise not go to the highest bidder. New franchise holders could be 'publisher broadcasters' on the Channel 4 model and some public service responsibilities were included.

Although C3 companies like Anglia and London Weekend were commercial organisations, some people saw the old public service 'ethos' as still being strong within these companies. There was also pressure from Rupert Murdoch, a close ally of the Conservative government and, through the *Sunday Times*, a strong critic of Thames TV's documentary *Death on the Rock* (see chapter 3, p. 85) as well as, through News International, 40 per cent owner of BSkyB. At the 1989 Edinburgh International Television Festival, Murdoch described British television as 'no more than a reflection of the values of the narrow elite which controls it and has always thought that its tastes are synonymous with quality'. He went on to describe the 'old' Reithian notion of public service broadcasting as 'obsessed by an anachronistic fear of commercial interests'.

As a result of the auction process, four new franchise holders became part of the C3 network: Carlton, which replaced Thames in weekday London; Meridian, which replaced TVS in the south of England (although TVS bid more, the ITC decided that TVS's bid was financially 'unrealistic' and threatened the quality of programming they could offer); Westcountry Television, which replaced TSW in Devon and Cornwall; and GMTV, which replaced TV-AM. The auction system was based on the 'value' of the potential advertising revenue in the different regions. Central Television, however, with one of the most lucrative areas, retained its franchise with a bid of only £2000, as no other company bid against them. (Figure 6.18.)

The Act also set out plans for a fifth, sixth or even seventh terrestrial television channel as well as promoting the expansion of cable and local, small-scale microwave television. However, by the original deadline of June 1992 the ITC had received only one application to run the Channel Five franchise and the ITC had to readvertise the franchise in 1995 when it was won by Channel 5 Broadcasting – a consortium of well-established media companies, MAI, Pearsons and CLT, and an American investment company. A rival bid by UKTV, although the highest, was rejected by the

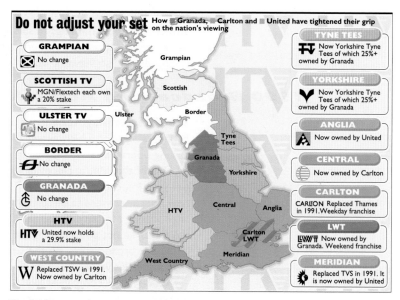

Fig. 6.18
The UK television franchise areas from 1 January 1993
Source: *Observer*, 1 December 1996

ITC on the grounds that its programming featured too many repeats. (Figure 6.19.)

Channel 5, launched by the Spice Girls on Sunday 30 March 1997, describes itself as 'modern and mainstream'. It aims to produce about 60 per cent of its own programming although its budget for making programmes is considerably smaller than those of the other terrestial channels (£110 million compared to C3's £800 million). Channel 5 hopes to achieve 8 per cent of the television audience by the year 2001 when it plans to have recouped its starting up costs including the estimated £150 million for retuning video recorders. The channel is hoping to attract a younger audience through its programming of a daily film shown at 9pm and uninterrupted by a break for the news, by its reliance on imports from the USA such as *The Bold and the Beautiful, Beverly Hills 90210* and *Sunset Beach* (its daily soap) and what it claims is a new-style, innovative and informal, daily evening news programme.

The 1990 Broadcasting Act also put a limit on 'cross-media' ownership. It originally specified that British newspaper companies could not own more than 20 per cent of any British television or radio service and that one television company could not own more than 20 per cent of another. Later this was amended to allow two television franchise companies to merge and as a result Meridian merged with Anglia, Yorkshire with Tyne Tees, Granada with LWT and Central with Carlton.

The 1990 Broadcasting Act also altered the regulatory bodies for commercial radio and television. The IBA and the Cable Authority were

FIg. 6.19
Source: *Guardian*, 28 October 1995

replaced by the Independent Television Commission (ITC), which now has responsibility for terrestrial television (C3, Channel 4 and Channel 5) as well as cable and satellite.

1990 Broadcasting Act: radio

Radio is now controlled by the Radio Authority, which is responsible for independent radio, both local and national, and community radio.

The 1990 Act attempted to 'open up' radio, too, by introducing three new independent national radio (INR) stations and encourage the expansion of a new 'tier' of community radio. The first INR franchise offered was for a 'non-pop' station on the FM wavelength. Initially the franchise was offered to Showtime Radio, but as they could not secure funding the franchise then went to the runner-up, Classic FM, who offered a service of light classical music, a popularist commercial alternative to BBC's Radio 3. The second franchise, on medium wave, went to Virgin 1215 (originally jointly owned by Virgin and TV-AM although eventually Virgin bought out TV-AM). Virgin then won a local London franchise and so offers the same service nationally on medium wave and on FM in the London area. In 1997 Virgin 1215 was taken over by Chris Evans who plans to use Virgin 1215's national frequency to challenge the BBC Radio 1 market. The Radio Authority delayed advertising the third franchise, also on medium wave, and 'speech-based', because of the difficulty of starting up a new station in a period of economic recession, and eventually in 1995 it was awarded to Talk Radio UK.

The Broadcasting Act of 1990 also set out to encourage community, or 'incremental', radio. This is intended to offer specific groups, such as ethnic minorities, special-interest groups, and communities based on location or language, their own services, produced by members of those communities. (See the case study on *Community radio* in chapter 5.)

1996 Broadcasting Act

The 1996 Broadcasting Act, in part as a response to pressure from leading press and other UK media groups who want to compete more successfully in the larger global multinational media market dominated by companies such as Time Warner, Bertelsmann, Sony and Matsushita, modified the ownership rules to allow newspaper groups with less than 20 per cent of the national market to own television companies outright and C3 companies with less than 15 per cent of the total television audience to buy national newspapers. Other cross-media companies like News International and the Mirror Group, who already each control more than 20 per cent of the total newspaper circulation, are not to be allowed to expand into terrestial television but as with Mirror Group's L!VE TV and Daily Mail's Channel One they can expand into cable, satellite and digital television services. One of the first of the new cross-media companies was United News and Media, created by the merger of MAI (owners of Meridian/Anglia and part owners of HTV and Channel 5) and United Newspapers (owners of the *Daily Express* and *Sunday Express* and the *Star*, and over 100 regional newspapers and 300 magazines including *Exchange and Mart*). Carlton, already owners of Central, took over Westcountry Television to control nearly 11 per cent of the total C3 television market. (See chapter 5, p. 159)

The 1996 Broadcasting Act tried to 'protect' certain big sports events on terrestial television that were being bought up by the expansionist BSkyB. The Act highlighted a series of 'listed events' (such as the Olympics, the Grand National, the Wimbledon tennis finals and the FA Cup Final) that were deemed to be too nationally important to be excluded from non-subscription terrestrial television.

Expansion of satellite and cable

ACTIVITY 6.10

Try to assess the success or otherwise of the government's aim to increase competition, choice and quality. Look specifically at either television or radio and consider the following questions:

- In what ways can competition between services be considered to have increased? Is there any way in which competition could be considered to have decreased?

- In what ways may viewers or listeners feel that they now have more choice? Has there been any reduction in choice?

- Are viewers and listeners aware of an increase in quality on new or existing services? Is there any evidence to suggest that there may have been a decrease in quality in some services?

- Is there a difference between the ways the Broadcasting Acts have affected radio and the ways they have affected television?

BSkyB, based in Luxembourg, is not a British company, and so does not contravene the cross-media ownership limitations of the Broadcasting Acts. (See chapter 5 for further discussion of News International.) Both Granada and Pearsons also have a stake in BSkyB.

Since its creation from the merger of BSB and SKY, BSkyB has been marketing aggressively to try and win subscribers. There have been many sports deals in cricket, boxing and football, where BSkyB has bought the exclusive rights to major events, trying to attract the young C2 males who they hope will pay to see these events. In 1992 BSkyB paid £304 million, over a five-year period, for the exclusive right to show live Premier League football matches. The success of this tactic in gaining subscribers encouraged the company to then bid £674 million in 1996 to continue its exclusive rights to Premier League football. BSkyB has also signed exclusive deals for cricket matches abroad that feature England, for rugby, golf's Ryder Cup and boxing matches featuring Frank Bruno where 600 000 subscribers were asked to pay an extra 'pay-as-you-view' fee of £9.95 in addition to their normal subscription to see exclusive live coverage of the Bruno/Mike Tyson fight. (Figure 6.20.)

This strategy of expanding the satellite subscription market by buying up more and more sporting events seemed to have been successful, as BSkyB's numbers of subscribers increased from just over 2 million in 1993 to an estimated 5 million in 1996. BSkyB is estimated to be available, either by direct satellite or through cable services, in between 10 per cent and 15 per cent of homes in Britain, and to account for about 5–6 per cent of total television viewing, although in households with satellite or cable the percentage of 'non-terrestrial' viewing is usually considerably higher, at around 40 per cent of total viewing. (Figure 6.21.)

Estimates about the growth of satellite vary considerably, but it is assumed that by the year 2000 about 8.1 million households, or 45 per cent of homes in Britain, will have either satellite or cable services available. Despite the cost of these services there seems to be a perceived need among many people for 'more choice' or something different to the terrestrial diet on offer. (Figure 6.22.)

In the autumn of 1996, Granada television, in partnership with BSkyB, launched seven new satellite channels including Men and Motors aimed at a similar, young, male, audience as successful magazines like IPC's *Loaded* and EMAP's *FHM*, as well as a channel offering re-runs of *Coronation Street*.

The BBC is also expanding into satellite broadcasting. It shares two channels with Thames Television (owned by Pearsons, owners of the *Financial Times*) – UK Gold and UK Living – as well as sharing programmes such as *Breakfast with Frost* with SKY News and sporting events such as Wimbledon tennis with SKY Sports. It also offers its own,

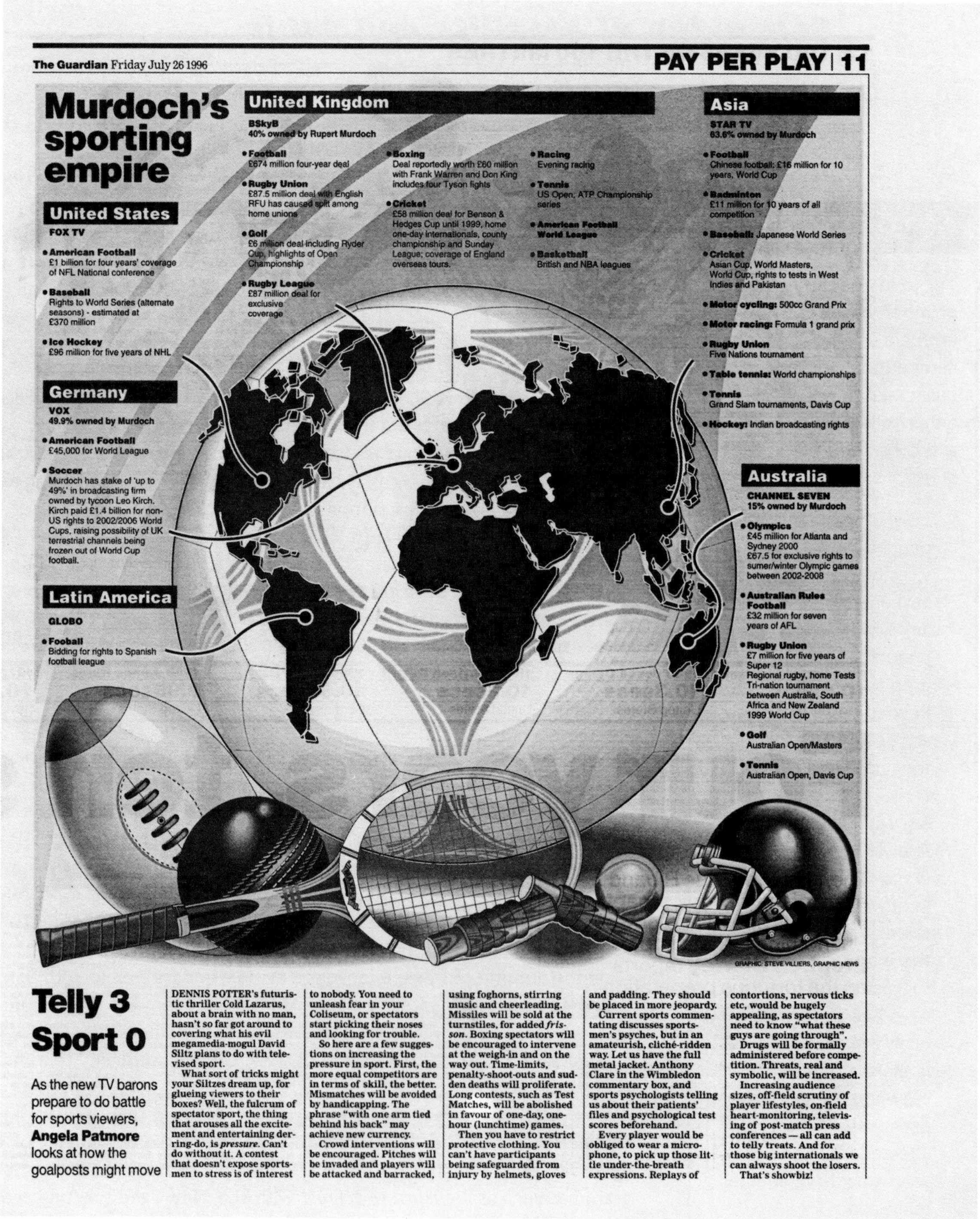

The Guardian Friday July 26 1996 — **PAY PER PLAY | 11**

Murdoch's sporting empire

United Kingdom

BSkyB
40% owned by Rupert Murdoch

- **Football** £674 million four-year deal
- **Rugby Union** £87.5 million deal with English RFU has caused split among home unions
- **Golf** £6 million deal including Ryder Cup, highlights of Open Championship
- **Rugby League** £87 million deal for exclusive coverage
- **Boxing** Deal reportedly worth £60 million with Frank Warren and Don King includes four Tyson fights
- **Cricket** £58 million deal for Benson & Hedges Cup until 1999, home one-day internationals, county championship and Sunday League; coverage of England overseas tours.
- **Racing** Evening racing
- **Tennis** US Open, ATP Championship series
- **American Football World League**
- **Basketball** British and NBA leagues

United States

FOX TV

- **American Football** £1 billion for four years' coverage of NFL National conference
- **Baseball** Rights to World Series (alternate seasons) - estimated at £370 million
- **Ice Hockey** £96 million for five years of NHL

Germany

VOX
49.9% owned by Murdoch

- **American Football** £45,000 for World League
- **Soccer** Murdoch has stake of 'up to 49%' in broadcasting firm owned by tycoon Leo Kirch. Kirch paid £1.4 billion for non-US rights to 2002/2006 World Cups, raising possibility of UK terrestrial channels being frozen out of World Cup football.

Latin America

GLOBO

- **Fooball** Bidding for rights to Spanish football league

Asia

STAR TV
63.6% owned by Murdoch

- **Football** Chinese football: £16 million for 10 years, World Cup
- **Badminton** £11 million for 10 years of all competition
- **Baseball:** Japanese World Series
- **Cricket** Asian Cup, World Masters, World Cup, rights to tests in West Indies and Pakistan
- **Motor cycling:** 500cc Grand Prix
- **Motor racing:** Formula 1 grand prix
- **Rugby Union** Five Nations tournament
- **Table tennis:** World championships
- **Tennis** Grand Slam tournaments, Davis Cup
- **Hockey:** Indian broadcasting rights

Australia

CHANNEL SEVEN
15% owned by Murdoch

- **Olympics** £45 million for Atlanta and Sydney 2000 £67.5 for exclusive rights to sumer/winter Olympic games between 2002-2008
- **Australian Rules Football** £32 million for seven years of AFL
- **Rugby Union** £7 million for five years of Super 12 Regional rugby, home Tests Tri-nation tournament between Australia, South Africa and New Zealand 1999 World Cup
- **Golf** Australian Open/Masters
- **Tennis** Australian Open, Davis Cup

GRAPHIC: STEVE VILLIERS, GRAPHIC NEWS

Telly 3 Sport 0

As the new TV barons prepare to do battle for sports viewers, **Angela Patmore** looks at how the goalposts might move

DENNIS POTTER's futuristic thriller Cold Lazarus, about a brain with no man, hasn't so far got around to covering what his evil megamedia-mogul David Siltz plans to do with televised sport.

What sort of tricks might your Siltzes dream up, for glueing viewers to their boxes? Well, the fulcrum of spectator sport, the thing that arouses all the excitement and entertaining derring-do, is *pressure*. Can't do without it. A contest that doesn't expose sportsmen to stress is of interest to nobody. You need to unleash fear in your Coliseum, or spectators start picking their noses and looking for trouble.

So here are a few suggestions on increasing the pressure in sport. First, the more equal competitors are in terms of skill, the better. Mismatches will be avoided by handicapping. The phrase "with one arm tied behind his back" may achieve new currency.

Crowd interventions will be encouraged. Pitches will be invaded and players will be attacked and barracked, using foghorns, stirring music and cheerleading. Missiles will be sold at the turnstiles, for added *frisson*. Boxing spectators will be encouraged to intervene at the weigh-in and on the way out. Time-limits, penalty-shoot-outs and sudden deaths will proliferate. Long contests, such as Test Matches, will be abolished in favour of one-day, one-hour (lunchtime) games.

Then you have to restrict protective clothing. You can't have participants being safeguarded from injury by helmets, gloves and padding. They should be placed in more jeopardy.

Current sports commentating discusses sportsmen's psyches, but in an amateurish, cliché-ridden way. Let us have the full metal jacket. Anthony Clare in the Wimbledon commentary box, and sports psychologists telling us about their patients' files and psychological test scores beforehand.

Every player would be obliged to wear a microphone, to pick up those little under-the-breath expressions. Replays of contortions, nervous ticks etc, would be hugely appealing, as spectators need to know "what these guys are going through".

Drugs will be formally administered before competition. Threats, real and symbolic, will be increased.

Increasing audience sizes, off-field scrutiny of player lifestyles, on-field heart-monitoring, televising of post-match press conferences — all can add to telly treats. And for those big internationals we can always shoot the losers.

That's showbiz!

Fig. 6.20

Worldwide picture of pay-as-you-view televised sports events

Source: Guardian, 26 July 1996

	Terrestrial only homes			Satellite dish homes			Cable homes		
	1991	1992	1993	1991	1992	1993	1991	1992	1993
BBC1	34	34	32	19	19	20	19	20	20
BBC2	14	13	15	7	7	8	6	8	7
Channel 3	39	39	39	24	26	24	25	25	23
Channel 4	13	13	15	7	9	8	7	9	8
Other	–	1	–	44	39	40	44	38	42
All channels	100	100	100	100	100	100	100	100	100

Fig. 6.21

Claimed channel shares of viewing

Source: B. Gunter, J. Sancho-Aldridge, P. Winstone, *Television: The Public's View*, John Libbey, 1994

commercially run, Worldwide Television Services. The BBC is also involved in delivering satellite services through the new digital multiplexes.

Digital future

In 1995 the Conservative government brought out a White Paper on digital broadcasting which would start in 1998 by offering up to 20 new television

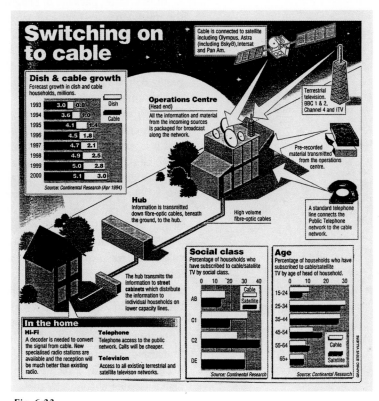

Fig. 6.22

Source: *Guardian*, 30 August 1994

ACTIVITY 6.11

Investigate the costs of the various satellite and/or cable packages that are on offer. Conduct a survey to try and discover who watches satellite, why, how much they pay, and what they feel satellite offers that terrestrial channels do not.

channels. Digital television will offer 'cinema-like' picture quality and CD sound quality on a screen that has over 1100 lines, double the present 625 lines; this will mean that a greater amount of 'information' can be sent with each picture frame, allowing for either better quality or extra information and a greater choice of programmes or different camera angles for the same programme. Viewers will need a set-top decoder box, expected to cost around £200, and will then be able to receive the new signals through their existing aerials.

Viewers will automatically be able to receive 'free' the existing terrestrial broadcasts from the BBC, C3, Channels 4 and 5, as well as the proposed BBC 24-hour news channel. These will be broadcast from three of the six digital 'multiplexes', or bundles of channels, to be made available.

In 1997 the other three multiplexes were auctioned in a manner similar to the C3 franchises in 1990 and were awarded to British Digital Broadcasting (BDB), a company backed by Carlton and Granada. Before awarding the licences to BDB the ITC insisted that BSkyB be dropped as a major shareholder in BDB because the ITC felt that Rupert Murdoch's company had too much dominance over the development of digital television in Britain. However, BSkyB will still be one of the main beneficiaries of the BDB licences as BSkyB 'owns' most of the rights to the films and premium sporting events that will be the main diet of BDB's subscription channels.

BDB's 'safer' package of programmes was chosen by the ITC instead of the more innovative offer of programming and interactive services offered by Digital Television Network (DTN), backed by United News and Media. Part of the reason for the ITC's decision can be seen as an attempt to ensure that the new 'digital revolution' is a success in Britain by guaranteeing BSkyB's proven diet of films and sport as one of its key selling points to consumers.

In Europe the digital television market is seen to present the greatest commercial opportunities by offering pay-per-view services via satellite and it is estimated that eventually there could be over 500 channels. In 1997 UFA, the television and radio branch of the German media group Bertelsmann, merged with Luxembourg-based CLT to form CLT-UFA, one of Europe's largest entertainment and media groups, with 19 television and 23 radio stations in ten European countries, including a share in Britain's Channel 5.

BSkyB and the German media group Kirch are developing a company called DF1 to spearhead digital pay-TV in Europe. Kirch already has a facilities agreement with Viacom, a US media company, for access to its library of programmes. Kirch's sports channel also has the exclusive TV rights to the 2002 and 2006 football World Cups; although as they are part of the 'listed events' in Britain, terrestial stations will have some access.

In 1997 a new consortium including BSkyB, BT, Midland Bank and Matsushita Electronics announced a new service called British Interactive Broadcasting (BIB), which plans to offer BSkyB subscribers more than 200 digital satellite channels by the spring of 1998. By the summer of 1998 BIB hopes to be able to offer another 200 channels plus, in partnership with companies such as Sainsburys, HMV and Thomas Cook, a wide range of digital shopping and other interactive services including holiday bookings, access to the Internet and video-on-demand.

BSkyB hope to sell over one million of their new set-top decoders costing around £200 each. This set-top box will be compatible with other decoders for digital terrestrial and cable services and so far viewers will be able to purchase additional set-top decoders for terrestrial digital services (which might again include BSkyB through the British Digital Broadcasting consortium) for around an extra £100.

Conclusion

The Conservative government claimed that its 1990 and 1996 Broadcasting Acts 'opened up', 'liberated' and 'deregulated' broadcasting in Britain; however, as figure 5.1 on p. 159 demonstrates, a look at the ownership of the television companies in the second half of the 1990s suggests that the opposite has occurred, and, particularly in television, ownership is limited to a small group of cross-media companies dominated by big-spenders such as BSkyB, Pearsons (which also has a stake in BSkyB, Channel 5 and Yorkshire/Tyne Tees Television), Granada (which has a stake in BSkyB, Yorkshire/Tyne Tees, ITN and GMTV as well as owning LWT), Carlton (which has stakes in Meridian/Anglia, ITN and GMTV as well as owning Central and Westcountry) and United News and Media (Meridian/Anglia as well as stakes in HTV, ITN, Channel 5 and Yorkshire/Tyne Tees, local newspapers and magazines). Other newspaper groups that are also involved in television ownership include the Guardian Media Group which also owns the *Observer* newspaper and has a stake in GMTV as well as ten local radio staions and DC Thompson, publishers of the *Beano* and the *Sporting Post*, with stakes in Carlton/Central/Westcountry.

Radio shows a similar concentration of ownership: Classic FM, originally owned by a consortium that included Time Warner, Associated Newspapers and Home Counties Newspapers, was taken over completely in 1996 by GWR. GWR, along with the Capital group, dominate the local radio sector. They have over 30 local radio licences including Cambridge, Reading, Swindon, Bristol, Bournemouth, Plymouth, Trent and Leicester, as well as joint ownership of London News Radio, the London FM station, with the *Daily Mail*, ITN and Reuters. EMAP Radio has 20 licences, including Kiss FM (as well as owning over 150 magazines including *Just Seventeen* and *Smash Hits*). Other large radio groups include Capital and Scottish Radio Holding. For more information on local radio, see the case study on *Community radio* in chapter 5.

The Conservative government's aim to raise quality through this process of deregulation is also questioned. A good deal of debate has involved differing definitions of what is meant by quality television (see Corner, 1995). Many commentators suggest that C3's programming has become less risk-taking, relying on proven genres such as police/flashing-

Fig. 6.23
Source: Jarrod Cripps

blue-lights series, established stars, more popularist imported mini-series and *Coronation Street* on four nights a week as a means of maintaining high audience ratings and enabling companies to meet the financial obligations of their 1993 franchise bids and pay for their expansion into new markets.

The BBC is again having difficulty trying to adjust to new markets, new competition and new concepts of both its function and audience, as well as in trying to justify the universality of its licence fee. The Director-General of the BBC, John Birt, outlined plans for the future of the BBC in 'the new broadcasting age' in the 1992 document *Extending Choice* (BBC, 1992). Birt characterised the BBC as offering a service that was 'distinctive' and 'innovative' but at the same time providing 'more real choice' and 'something for everyone'. *Extending Choice* also committed the BBC to providing a 'showcase for traditional and contemporary British culture', without clarifying what that meant, as well as continuing to offer programmes that 'help to educate and inform'. Central to any debate about the future of the BBC is the future of public service broadcasting, with its ethos of free access for all and quality not quantity. Notions of 'quality' and 'success' are increasingly being seen by the BBC as synonymous, and whether quality and success are achieved is being judged more and more by high audience viewing figures. The BBC under John Birt has gone through a considerable amount of restructuring, including the merging of some radio and television services such as news-gathering, and been the focus of considerable debate and criticism, much of it from within the BBC itself. In 1996 the Conservative government agreed that the licence fee could be increased at a rate above annual inflation for some years to allow the BBC to develop its digital services but then the rate of increase would be reduced below that of the rate of inflation, causing the corporation either to make more financial cuts or increase its commercial income.

For the commercial sector, 'success' increasingly means attracting the younger, affluent ABC1 audiences that the advertisers want; hence Channel 4's determination to keep programmes like *ER* and *Friends*. These audiences have the money to pay for 'quality' services. The danger is that other audiences, less desirable to advertisers or unable to pay for specialist programmes, will be relegated to the margins of broadcasting, such as much of daytime television. What is popular are sport, pop music and films; less popular are current affairs, documentaries and other minority programmes. This trend is already apparent with the move of *Highway*, a C3 version of *Songs of Praise* introduced by Harry Secombe, from the early evening 'God slot' on Sundays to make way for the 'family' films that are more attractive to younger audiences and advertisers. It is also the cause of the debate about the placing of *News at Ten*, which at present causes 'adult' films and drama programmes, that have to start after the 9 o'clock watershed, to have a half-hour break.

Reith's pre-war notion of a common broadcast 'national culture' and 'national voice' are not as popular with today's politicians as it was in the 1930s. It is true that the range of broadcast services available have increased considerably and perhaps now more accurately reflect the social diversification that exists in Britain. Radio and television have moved away

Fig. 6.24
Source: Channel 5

from the notion established in the 1920s of broadcasting to large homogenous audiences, united through their common participation in national events, *The Morecombe and Wise Christmas Show*, the wedding of Prince Charles and Lady Diana that attracted a television audience of 39 million or the 1966 World Cup Final with 32 million viewers. By contrast, television and radio seem to have moved towards a concept of 'narrowcasting' that reflects more the range and diversity of the magazine shelves of a newsagent's. Here audiences seem to have a wide choice of specialist products aimed at small but very specific markets, such as fly-fishing, home decoration and a vast range of consumer products such as cars, hi-fi equipment and computers. This range of choice, however, is only possible through advertising and the existence of consumers who are presumably prepared to pay more for their specialist products.

FURTHER ACTIVITIES

1 Read chapter 4 and then design and conduct surveys into the viewing habits of audiences. Correlate types of service and programme with particular types of audience. Identify and explain any particular patterns or variations that occur.

2 Identify ways in which the analysis of the history of radio or television helps to explain the present organisation and output.

3 Read chapter 5 and choose one media company to explore in more detail. Using sources of information such the *Guardian Media Guide* try to establish the particular media interests the company may have. Suggest how this media interpenetration benefits the company and consider to what extent it may also benefit the consumer.

4 How have changes in broadcasting organisation and legislation affected the forms and contents of programmes available today?

5 Define what is meant by 'public service broadcasting' and consider its future role in the provision of media information and entertainment services. Identify the parties involved in the debate about its future and list the arguments for and against the concept.

6 Summarise the debate surrounding the BBC's licence fee. Conduct research on attitudes to its continuation or replacement.

Further reading

General

Jenkins, K. 1991: *Re-thinking History*. Routledge.
Ward, K. 1989: *Mass Communications and the Modern World*. Macmillan.
Williams, K. 1997: '*Get Me a Murder a Day*': A History of Mass Communications in Britain. Arnold.

Press history

Boyce, G. *et al.* (eds). 1978. *Newspaper History: From the 17th Century to the Present Day*. Constable.

Cranfield, G.A. 1978: *The Press and Society*. Longman.

Curran, J. and Seaton, J. 1991: *Power Without Responsibility*. Routledge.

Harrison, S. 1974: *Poor Men's Guardians*. Lawrence & Wishart.

Lee, A.J. 1976: *The Origins of the Popular Press 1855–1914*. Croom Helm.

McNair, B. 1996: *News and Journalism in the UK*. Routledge.

Seymour-Ure, C. 1991: *The British Press and Broadcasting Since 1945*. Blackwell.

Thompson, E.P. 1968: *The Making of the English Working Class*. Penguin.

Cinema history

Armes, R. 1978: *A Critical History of British Cinema*. Oxford University Press.

Armes, R. 1988: *On Video*. Routledge.

Barnes, J. 1976: *The Beginnings of Cinema in Britain*. David & Charles.

Barr, C. 1986: *All Our Yesterdays*. BFI.

Chanan, M. 1980, 1995: *The Dream that Kicks: The Pre-History and Early Years of Cinema in Britain*. Routledge.

Curran, J. and Porter, V. (eds). 1983: *British Cinema History*. Weidenfeld & Nicolson.

Nelmes, J. (ed.) 1996: *An Introduction to Film Studies*. Routledge.

Robertson, J.C. 1989: *The Hidden Cinema: British Film Censorship 1913–1972*. Routledge.

Stead, P. 1989: *Film and the Working Class*. Routledge.

Walker, A. 1986: *Hollywood England*. Harrap.

Broadcasting history

Abercrombie, N. 1996: *Television and Society*. Polity Press.

Barnard, S. 1989: *On the Radio*. Open University Press.

Briggs, A. 1979: *The History of Broadcasting in the UK*, Vols 1–4. Oxford University Press.

Clarke, S. and Horrie, C. 1994: *Fuzzy Monsters: Fear and Loathing at the BBC*. Heinemann.

Corner, J. (ed.). 1991: *Popular Television in Britain*. BFI.

Crisell, A. 1994: *Understanding Radio*. Routledge.

Crisell, A. 1997: *An Introduction to the History of British Broadcasting*. Routledge.

Goodwin, A. and Whannel, G. (eds). 1990: *Understanding Television*. Methuen.

Gunter, B., Sancho-Aldridge, J. and Winstone, P. 1994: *Television: The Public's View 1993*. John Libbey.

Hood, S. (ed.). 1994: *Behind the Screens*. Lawrence & Wishart.

Kumar, K. 1977 'Holding the middle ground: The BBC, the public and the professional broadcaster', in J. Curran, M. Gurevitch and J. Woollacott (eds.) *Mass Communication and Society*. Edward Arnold.

Lewis, P. and Booth, J. 1989: *The Invisible Medium: Public, Commercial and Community Radio*. Macmillan.

O'Malley, T. 1994: *Closedown? The BBC and Government Broadcasting Policy, 1979–92*. Pluto.

Scannell, P. 1996: *Radio, Television and Modern Life*. Blackwell.

Scannell, P. and Cardiff, D. 1991: *A Social History of Broadcasting*. Blackwell.

Changing media worlds

The key theme in this chapter is change, and two main areas of study dominate the agenda. Each in turn deals with a specific series of questions about the changing nature of the media, in a changing, fluid and often unstable world. The first focus for study encourages you to assess some of the ways in which *new media technologies* are being harnessed and developed in the current phase. Central questions here are how they are destabilising or impacting on older and established forms of media production and consumption, and the extent to which, as is often claimed, they offer the potential for new and diverse kinds of cultural relationships to emerge.

The second focus of the chapter entails the analysis of worldwide media networks and the consequent emergence of what we should understand as international or *global culture*. This is a process which has deep historical roots but which many commentators have suggested has accelerated rapidly from the 1960s onwards. In part, this can be accounted for in terms of the development and potentials of certain 'new' media channels and communication technologies – notably satellite forms of extra-terrestrial broadcasting – and their abilities to cross national and international boundaries. However, it is not only at the global level that new media technologies are credited with the powers to effect radical forms of change in our social and cultural environments. The two areas contain some of the key dilemmas and debates involved in national media policy in the current phase. Changes in British media policy have in part been stimulated by the dynamics of new media technologies, but, as we shall suggest, there are other issues at stake here too.

New technologies for new times?

Fig. 7.1
Source: Paul Hickinbotham

Fig. 7.2
Source: Paul Hickinbotham

ACTIVITY 7.1

Map changes in media technologies and forms in your own household in recent years. Start with the most recent you can think of and work back. It may be useful to involve other, older members of the household in this activity and to develop a generational map. What was home life like before or in the early years of television, for instance? Refer back to figure 1.10 in chapter 1 and your research for activity 4.7 in chapter 4.

We are living in a period which has frequently been characterised as a 'communications revolution', a cycle of profound and accelerating social and cultural change often attributed to the impact of new media technologies. These technologies continue to play an important part in restructuring and changing certain aspects of the production, distribution and reception of 'old' media. Cable and satellite forms of broadcasting, video recorders, computer networks, word processors and digital technologies have all in recent years been developed and marketed, adding to the media saturation of modern life. Collectively, they have contributed to an important series of changes in many homes and domestic environments. These private spaces are increasingly 'multiscreen', 'multichannel', 'wired' or 'cabled' households, connected to the 'information super-highway', where the computer terminal, the fax, e-mail and the CD personal stereo operate alongside more established media machines and forms.

As well as having important consequences for private, leisure or 'non-work' time, the development and expansion of these technologies have also had important implications for public institutions and affairs – in the workplace, the college or the supermarket, for instance. In the face of these changes, it is important to bear in mind that all media – including the press, cinema, radio and television broadcasting – have relied on the development and regulation of 'new' media technologies. The printing press, the film projector, gramophone, 'wireless' and television have all, at one time, been regarded as rather strange, new, unfamiliar, 'one-way' machines for social and political communication. For many writers, these new machines have been defined as causal historical agents, capable of bringing about 'revolutionary' forms of social and political change. In the first chapter we suggested that the media, because of their public and private visibility and presence, have often operated to condense anxieties and debates about more general forms of change in the modern period.

As suggested in chapter 6, however, the history of the various media concerns the ways in which these 'machines' have been socially and commercially organised for the provision of information, entertainment and culture. This emphasis on the commercial or political forces which constrain or condition the social realisation of the technologies is an important counter to technological determinism. Such determinism is an oversim-

plified view that isolates and exaggerates the power of technologies themselves to cause effects directly, without sufficient understanding of the variety of factors which may govern the technologies' social applications and use (see Williams, 1990, and Heap *et al.*, 1995).

Recent debates about changing media technologies have focused on a series of general themes. These have been subject to optimistic and pessimistic forms of assessment and debate.

Computerisation and the computer chip are at the heart of many recent developments. Computers and the switched telecommunications networks that also carry telephone calls or faxes provide the technical basis for a massive growth in computer-mediated communications. These have given rise to increasingly sophisticated systems for information storage, management, access or distribution and have transformed many of the processes and practices involved in older generations of media production and consumption. Developments in what have become known as information technologies have, for instance, been central in the redesign of news rooms – for both press and broadcast production. At a general level, it is the convergence of these technologies within modern telecommunications industries and their networks that is responsible for a greatly increased speed and scale of information interchange. This shift in scale concerns not only the amount of information but also its reach and destination, via satellite links and worldwide networks. Cable systems, based on fibre-optic technologies, provide additional extensions to networks at local, regional or national levels. Furthermore, the goals of these kinds of development are ever more integrated digital systems which are capable of handling and linking up many types of information: written and spoken languages, music, still and moving visual images, data of all kinds. Previously discrete media are merging into new and hybrid, *multimedia* forms, including, for example, the worlds of the Internet and its virtual communities.

> So media is going to change and it will change profoundly. There will be 3000–5000 TV channels in the next three to five years due to digital technology. All newspapers and magazines will have interactive counterparts. All publishing companies will be involved in electronic publishing if they want to survive.
>
> *May (1996), p. 5*

Within these developments, much has been made of the *interactive* qualities of new media technologies. If older systems tended to the 'one-way' form of communication (see chapter 1), new media, it is claimed, allow for greatly increased plurality and interactivity, almost to the point that they challenge the old ideas of 'broadcasting' or 'mass' communication. Until recently, examples have tended to focus on changes in television. VCTV (viewer-controlled cable television) in the United States, for instance, has allowed viewers to create their own schedules. Some cable viewers in Britain have been offered sports programmes where they could choose channels with either different camera angles, replays or computer-generated information as accompaniments to their viewing of the live coverage. In October 1993, QVC, an American company, in conjunction with SKY television, became the first channel to offer 24-hour-a-day, all-year-round satellite shopping facilities. The channel pioneered the round-the-clock selling of a wide range of domestic, consumer and electrical goods to consumers 'at home', linked by phone and with the goods paid for by credit card in the UK. In 1996, various supermarket chains and other retail outlets in Britain also experimented with Internet shopping services. Home shopping, home banking and other

Fig. 7.4
Source: Tim O'Sullivan

Fig. 7.5
Source: Paul Hickinbotham

on-screen computer and video services and games are further examples of the ways in which the interactive potentials of new technologies are being developed and mobilised. Trials of interactive television are taking place all over the world as technology companies attempt to assess the commercial viability and potential of different services and their systems. In Cambridge, for example, the Acorn Online Media trial carries:

> ... video-on-demand and transactional services such as home shopping and banking to the homes of several hundred customers, via a special set-top box connected to the television. From the comfort of their armchairs they are able to access information on train times, watch programmes or the latest news, buy cinema tickets, check their bank accounts, listen to music, play games, do the shopping, get information from the library and find out about their local schools. Programmes can be watched with the facility to fast-forward, rewind or pause the action, just as on a video-recorder. This kind of wideband, video-on-demand service is however expensive to install; for each house having a direct high-speed connection to the 'server', the cost is well above £1,000. These costs have to be justified by the revenue expected by the service operator if they are ever to offer realistic commercial opportunities.
>
> *Wolffsohn (1996), p. 7*

In addition, interactivity allows for rapid viewer response: the computer terminal linked to the screen enables viewers to 'answer back', whether this is in the form of votes in a televised talent contest or of registering their opinions on matters of political or current affairs.

Interactivity, combined with increased number of channels for new information and entertainment services, gives rise to one of the most hotly debated issues, that of greater or expanded forms of *consumer choice*. For many writers, new media technologies have brought about the possibilities for much greater, more complex forms of choice and 'menu' (see, for example, the discussion of postmodernism in chapter 1). At one level, new technologies have had important consequences for the costs involved in many forms of media production and allowed for expansion or segmentation to take place in new media markets. At another, viewers, listeners and readers may now exercise choice across new, increasingly segmentalised or specialised 'narrowcast' channels and services, as for example in the case of sports, movie, home 'lifestyle' or children's channels, etc.

Fig. 7.6
Source: Tim O'Sullivan

Recent developments in cable services provide some useful examples. At the start of 1995, about 4.9 million UK homes (over one fifth of the total number) were able to subscribe to broad-band cable services, and over one million chose to do so (Zenith Media, 1995, p.43). As well as the four terrestrial channels – with a fifth channel launched in 1997 – and a wide mix of channels relayed from satellite, subscribers also have access to a menu of services provided exclusively by cable operators. The main source of income for most channels is on a pay-per-view basis plus advertising, or in some cases sponsorship. The development of digital broadcasting services promises to provide greatly expanded choice in a very short time, if commercial or other conditions allow.

There are two issues which need to be considered in this context. First, to what extent have video, satellite, cable and digital forms provided genuine *diversity* as opposed to a repackaging of old formats – 'more of the same'? This issue has been foregrounded in virtually all recent discussions of the changing nature of television in Britain. Secondly, we need to note related arguments concerning *access* to these new forms and services. Rather than operating as public services, open to all, the great majority of new information and entertainment channels require private investment or subscription. Individual spending power has increasingly become a key factor in determining whether one can or cannot afford to participate in the new media services and the new information society. Consumer 'choice' can be exercised, but at a price. Often shadowing and linked to a range of concerns for broadcasting quality in the 1990s, this has been one of the key issues in recent debates surrounding the future of public service broadcasting in Britain, discussed in the final case study in chapter 6.

ACTIVITY 7.2

Research the development and availability of cable services in your own area. What kinds of services are on offer at what kinds of prices? *The Cable and Telecom Year Book* is a good source for reference. *Spectrum*, the quarterly magazine of the Independent Television Commiss-ion, also contains useful articles on the expansion of cable services in the UK. Monitor the development of digital broadcast channels and programming in the UK.

In summary, the debates about the development of new media technologies in the 1990s are extensive, and more complicated and interwoven than they might appear at first sight. Advertisements for new media and their services tend to stress the ways in which they 'liberate' viewers and consumers and offer whole ranges of new and effortlessly exciting possibilities. The theme of consumer freedom or sovereignty has also been central in the policies promoting deregulation which have accompanied and fuelled their growth. All the 'old' media – press, cinema, radio and television – now face considerable challenges as they compete in changing markets and circumstances. Changes in media production – for instance, desk-top publishing (DTP), or the increasingly sophisticated portable video camera – as well as in the forms of what is produced and consumed are of considerable significance in any current analysis. As Curran and Seaton (1997) have argued, the major debates in this area are often posed between the *'neophiliacs'*, who welcome the new media technologies in optimistic terms, and the *'cultural pessimists'*, who view these developments with considerable disquiet and scepticism. The two, contrasting positions may be summarised as in figure 7.7.

Screen-based: video, cable, satellite, digital TV, High Definition TV, animation & effects, etc.
Screen-based print: DTP, digital printing, design & distribution, CD text systems, e-mail, Internet, electronic publishing.
Music: digital synthesisers, samplers, video, CD, DAT, etc.

Neophiliacs:	**Cultural pessimists:**
Questions of choice	
1 Many more channels – 'Communacopia'.	1 Market forces, especially when deregulated, squeeze out minority tastes, unless rich consumers. Competition for popular market ('wall-to-wall Dallas') restricts actual choice.
2 Segmentation and narrowcasting.	2 Rental and purchase costs lead to exclusion of poor and powerless.
3 Experimentation, growth and innovation.	3 Costs of production lead to more imports and cheaper forms of output.
Democracy	
1 More information and services available to consumers.	1 Increased control by media barons and multinational companies.
2 Interactive uses (voting, WWW sites, etc.).	2 Loss of public-service principles and public sphere, issues of regulations.
3 DIY and community production leads to autonomy.	3 Increasingly privatised culture, reliance on advertising revenue.
Demand	
1 Technological determinism?	1 Failure or low take-up of some new technologies, cost exclusion.
2 IT 'revolution', the 'wired' society.	2 Video growth and decline of terrestrial, public-service TV viewing (displacement).
3 Growth of private commercial culture.	3 Quality of existing services eroded.

Fig. 7.7
New media technologies: effects and consequences

The Internet

> Computer-mediated communications might become the next great escape medium, in the tradition of radio serials, Saturday matinees, soap-operas – which means that the new medium will be in some way a conduit for and reflector of our cultural codes, our social subconscious, our images of who 'we' might be, just as previous media have been. There are other reasons that ordinary non-technical citizens need to know something about this new medium and its social impact. Something big is afoot, and the final shape has not been determined.
>
> *Rheingold (1994), p. 11*

At the end of the twentieth century, and into the early stages of the twenty-first, any discussion of changing and emergent media technologies and their cultural forms is not complete without special consideration of the Internet – 'the Net' as it has become known. This is the label which since the late 1980s has been applied to the developing interconnected telecommunication computer networks that enable computer-mediated communications, 'Nets' and 'information super-highways to link people from around the world into public forms of discussion and interchange. As Frank Webster has noted:

> The scenario of networked computers is often compared to the provision of electricity: the 'information grid' is seen as analogous to the electrical supply. As the electricity grid links every home, office, factory and shop to provide energy, so the information grid offers information wherever it is needed. This is, of course, an evolutionary process, but with the spread of an ISDN (Integrated Services Digital Network) we have the foundational elements of an 'information society'.
>
> *Webster (1995), p. 7*

The Net gives rise to what have been referred to as virtual communities, the diverse collectivities and groups of dispersed users which emerge as a result of computer-mediated communication. These differ from both older 'face-to-face' communities and those established under traditional systems of 'mass' communication. The origins of the Net lie in American military research in the 1970s, and electronic mail and computer conferencing systems grew out of these early developments. The networks have grown dramatically, stimulated in part by the need for faster, global communication systems for financial or official forms of communication and data, and also by the growth of other diverse and sometimes unofficial groups of users. Howard Rheingold has outlined the basic principles involved in this growth, which has centrally involved the proliferation of Bulletin Board Systems (BBSs):

> The population of the grassroots part of the Net, citizen-operated BBSs, has been growing explosively as a self-financed movement of enthusiasts, without the benefit of Department of Defense funding. A BBS is the simplest, cheapest infrastructure for computer-mediated communication: you run special software, often available inexpensively, on a personal computer, and use a device known as a *modem* to plug the computer into your regular telephone line. The modem converts computer-readable information into audible beeps and boops that can travel over the same telephone wires that carry your voice; another modem at the other end decodes the beeps and boops into computer-readable bits and bytes. The BBS turns the bits and bytes into human-readable text. Other people use their computers to call your BBS, leave and retrieve messages stored in your personal computer, and you have a virtual community growing in your bedroom.
>
> *Rheingold (1994), pp. 8–9*

Fig. 7.8
Source: Tim O'Sullivan
Internet Book Shop

It is difficult to assess the full implications of the Internet for contemporary culture and social relations. It is still, as Rheingold and others have remarked, 'out of control' and volatile. What can be noted are the actual and likely impacts on existing media, short-circuiting, fragmenting and threatening to make obsolete in a variety of ways their previous formations, communities and networks. It is, however, important to counter the rather apocalyptic or utopian claims which have often accompanied the current stage of development. Celebrations of the expanding potentials of the Internet are currently countered by anxieties over its regulation and illicit use. Perhaps one of the key debates or claims to consider in this context concerns notions of a new 'electronic democracy', ushered in by the Internet. For Rheingold, there are three key social criticisms which need to be borne in mind when assessing the claimed democratic potentials of computer-mediated communication networks like the Internet.

The first issue concerns the degree to which electronic communications networks are simply continuing a process of 'commodification'. That is, turning political process into an advertised consumer product. This could act against the aspirations and hopes of online activists, who see the Net, in part, as a way of revitalising open and democratic discussion and access to a renewed, modernised public sphere, able to deal with the changing demands of modern times. Secondly, a number of writers have pointed to the ways in which the new interactive networks have a darker side, in terms of their involvement in processes of surveillance, control and disinformation. This theme sees an increase in the monitoring of network information comprising part of a modern assault on the personal and private liberties of citizens. The Net becomes a more ominous kind of modern entrapment. Finally, a number of writers, especially those who believe that we have entered a postmodern condition (refer back to discussion in chapter 1), have argued that the new information technologies have now reached a stage in their development whereby they have changed what used to be understood as reality into 'a slicked up electronic simulation' (Rheingold). This, ever more 'hyper-real', world is the product of the new technologies, which in fact produce a web of simulated illusion that grows more 'real' and 'lifelike' as more people invest in it and as the technologies, and the corporations which own them, become more powerful.

Fig. 7.9
Surfing the Net
Source: Cyberia Internet Cafe

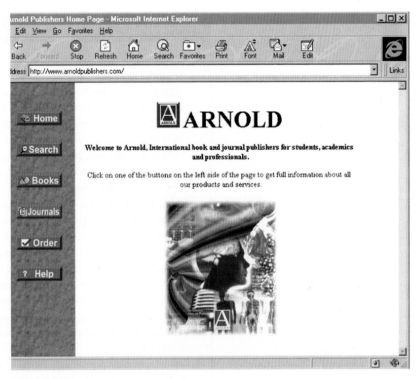

Fig. 7.10
Web site of publishers Arnold
Source: Arnold

Everywhere and nowhere: global culture

One recurrent theme in recent writing about the media, notably about television, has concerned the need for students and researchers to recognise the importance and growth of *worldwide* media networks. No longer can, or should, the study of the media be locked into an inward-looking, ethnocentric focus, fixed solely on the characteristics and dynamics of the domestic, particular, national situation.

Despite the fact that media institutions in Britain continue to be guided in a number of decisive ways by a framework of ideas and organisational considerations in which the 'imagined community' of the British nation – 'British' identity, experience, history, heritage and so on – continues to occupy a central place, changes in the last thirty years or so have altered things considerably. The British cultural economy as it moves into the

ACTIVITY 7.3

1 Do some general research work on the *Internet*. Surveys undertaken in 1997 indicate that 88 per cent of the UK population have now heard of the Internet – compared with 65 per cent in 1995 – and 11 per cent of the population have used it. If you have not yet tried it, make a point of doing so. How can it be understood as a new medium? Interview a range of regular Net users: how and where do they use the Net? What are their views on its development? Are they part of 'virtual communities'?

2 List some of the ways in which new media systems – *satellite, cable and video* – have changed the use of television in the home. Carry out some research interviews with people who subscribe to these services. What have been some of their main reasons for investing in them? How do they evaluate the services? How are digital services changing the shape of broadcasting in Britain?

3 How have new media technologies and networks changed conventional forms of media *production and consumption*? Have any alternative forms emerged as a result? You might focus on the camcorder, desk-top publishing, new musical technologies or the Internet.

4 What kinds of *interactivity* do new systems make available? Do these represent advances over previous systems?

5 Discuss the popularity of *computer games*. Have they changed patterns of leisure inside and outside the home? Who do they appeal to and why? How have computer games changed and how are they changing? What factors 'drive' these changes?

twenty-first century, more than ever before, is part of a wider set of global cultural relations. This encompasses both economic and cultural flows of international import and export, in businesses and cultural commodities, in media hardware and software.

Some evidence for this changing state of affairs can be found very readily in everyday forms of media consumption. British terrestrial forms of television, for example, regularly feature a mix of films and programmes which have been produced in other national locations around the world, originally for other audiences. Films from America, India, France and Canada are scheduled side-by-side with TV series and co-productions from the USA and Australia, and live or recorded sports coverage from Japan, New Zealand and Germany. The amount and typical content of imported programming has varied historically. Recent developments in satellite and cable TV channels have

ACTIVITY 7.4

Analyse the terrestial TV schedules for one week according to the percentages of 'home' and imported programmes shown. Break down imports into their national origins. Compare the patterns which emerge with a similar analysis of satellite or cable TV schedules for the same week. What kinds of programme are imported and from where? What conclusions might be drawn from these data overall?

added to these amounts of imported material, and digital transmissions may continue this pattern.

In British cinemas, the pattern of American dominance over the production of films appearing on British screens was established well before the Second World War. This pattern is still repeated, with some variations, and not just in current multiscreen cinemas; it also reappears in the video rental store and on satellite movie channels. In the case of music, MTV has been an interesting case. Film stars and television personalities, stars of music and sport, are mediated and merchandised to worldwide audiences, often in media spectaculars which involve simultaneous, live, global link-ups, performances or appeals. In terms of music, British charts and music radio also give access to a growing number of international forms, styles and crossovers. The emergence of the category of 'world music' in the 1980s, with its mission to introduce western ears to non-western styles of music, to provide a platform for many voices, and to allow instruments and traditions to communicate together irrespective of national boundaries and the dictates of the mainstream music industry, has been one development here worthy of discussion (see Burnett, 1996, and Negus, 1996).

Advertising campaigns and imagery have accompanied their products across national boundaries to the extent that the icons of Coca-Cola, Benetton, Del Monte, Marlboro and many others have become truly worldwide signs, part of the new 'global language'. 'Personalities' from Michael Jackson to Madonna, from Liam Gallagher to Mel Gibson, have been mediated to audiences on a worldwide basis. The contents of many newspapers, magazines and other print media are also tuned into these processes. In addition to relaying news and information from around the world, they may be coordinated for a number of national editions (*Cosmopolitan, Reader's Digest, National Geographic*) or aimed at international or pannational markets (*Time, Newsweek*, the *European, Financial Times*). Increasingly they are available in electronic formats for computer access.

The process and duty of mediating accounts of the 'world out there' into British public and private life has been a long-established function of the British media, particularly in fulfilling their public service remit (see chapter 6) and their consequent relations with domestic audiences. In broadcast news segments on radio and TV, in holiday feature or travel documentary programmes, we are effortlessly transported or moved around the world in live, recorded or 'virtual' time.

Fig. 7.11
Source: Jarrod Cripps

Fig. 7.12
Piccadilly Circus
Source: Jarrod Cripps

For many recent commentators, these and other aspects of modern culture are understood as part and parcel of the shift into *postmodern* conditions, whereby older forms of national identity and their historical 'securities' and divisions are being replaced, challenged or dislocated by new, multiple, cross-cutting allegiances derived from a diversity of local and global movements and imagery. As we noted in chapter 1, this is a version of ideas popularised by Marshall McLuhan in the 1960s, concerning the effects on the world of television and computerised media technologies and communication systems, and their potential to establish a 'global village'. In the 'global village', differences of time and space or geographical or national location are eroded as a result of the instantaneous nature of modern media and world communications. In this vision, as the speed, extent and complexity of communication systems accelerate, the world 'shrinks' and the media synchronise us into a randomised, or virtual, 'world time'. They also enable us to tune into a globally derived 'cocktail' or mix of places, events, personalities and locations.

Fig. 7.13
Source: Jarrod Cripps

The mediation of these two dimensions – of time and of space – is crucial in the construction of social identity at both public and private levels. A great deal of postmodern analysis has echoed and extended McLuhan's arguments on these themes. We have become, it is argued, dislocated and resynchronised into a new kind of simulated and decentralised world. There are now few limits or boundaries, it is suggested, in this new 'hyperspace' world with its excess of information and entertainment. (See Morley, 1991, Stevenson, 1995, and Webster, 1995, for useful discussion.)

In the face of these arguments and claims, it is important to recognise that *globalisation* is a process which has encompassed two linked levels of relationship. First of all, we need to recognise that a great deal of this process lies *behind* the growth in channels and technologies of images and information, whether on screen or on the page. Several writers have argued that internationalisation began, in fact, as a normal part of the commercial development of media markets in the twentieth century. The logic of this process has seen the emergence of multinational conglomerates, media companies with extensive networks of interests operating across national boundaries. One example is Rupert Murdoch's News International Corporation:

> It includes major press and publishing interests in the USA, UK and Australia, as well as America's fourth largest television network, Fox, and a controlling interest in Britain's direct satellite broadcasting service, British Sky Broadcasting. Other important examples include Sony of Japan which

owns CBS records and Columbia Pictures, and the Bertelsmann company of Germany, which controls RCA records and Doubleday books as well as a major domestic chain of newspapers and magazines.

Murdock and Golding (1991), p. 23

In the British context, internationalisation encompasses both the ways in which British companies have invested in operations outside the UK (Thorn–EMI, for example) and the ways in which American, other European, or Japanese companies have bought into British media concerns – the domestic market (USA or Canadian interests in UK cable TV, for example). Multinational conglomerates are geared to operate in and to develop worldwide cultural markets for information and entertainment facilities. Their activities concern the production and distribution of cultural commodities, not just for domestic national consumption, but for readers, listeners and viewers who inhabit a range of diverse national and international territories (see Hannerz, 1996).

If the first level of analysis here concerns the growth and development of worldwide multimedia conglomerates, their structures and transnational operations, the second, linked, level concerns the consequences of their growth and operation, the cultural flows of commodities – packaged programmes, films, images, etc. – and their reception by audiences in diverse situations worldwide. At the heart of current debates about globalisation are a number of key issues which concern contested interpretations of the increase in international forms and patterns of media operation.

For some writers, globalisation is a process which ultimately results in 'sameness' or *homogeneity* on an increasingly worldwide basis. As Hebdige has suggested in this context: 'The implication here is that we'll soon be able to watch *Dallas* or eat a Big Mac in any part of the inhabited world' (1989, p. 51). Put crudely, world culture and media have become relay stations for the most powerful multinational corporations and their forms of popular, profitable culture.

For others, these considerations of similarity or convergence have to confront the *diversity* and dynamism of world culture and the fragmentation of audiences, both within and across national boundaries. Emphasis on the power of the multinational media conglomerates and their products is counterbalanced by an emphasis on the potential and actual diversities of their creative origins and reception, the unpredictabilities

ACTIVITY 7.6

Analyse the data in figure 7.14 on ownership of radio, TV and VCR facilities worldwide. Compare the number of sets per head of population in different areas. What conclusions might be drawn from these data?

of their use and cultural impact. In order to develop this further, we need to step back from discussions of globalisation, and set them in the context of related studies of media or cultural imperialism. 'We' also need to remember the particular national point of view and part of the globe from which these issues are addressed.

One of the conclusions which might result from the analysis suggested in activity 7.6 is that access to the means of reception varies widely from country to country. For example, to look at two extreme cases, in Mali, West Africa, it has been calculated that there are seven radio sets and two TV sets per hundred population. This stands in stark contrast to the United Kingdom, where there are 148 radio sets and 72 TV sets per hundred population. Furthermore, although patterns

(all figures approximate)	Population ('000s)	Radio					Television				Number of VCRs ('000s)
		Number of radio sets (excluding wired receivers) ('000s)					Number of TV receivers (000s)				
	1991	1955	1965	1975	1985	1991	1965	1975	1985	1991	1991
World Figures	5 337 000	237 000	529 000	1 010 000	1 650 000	2 148 000	177 000	398 000	737 000	1 052 000	233 000
Europe											
Western Europe	851 000	65 310	116 500	186 000	297 800	575 000	49 400	103 400	162 900	366 800	79 700
USSR and Eastern Europe		20 260	59 700	92 600	164 300		24 000	87 000	130 100		
Arab World (inc. North Africa)	283 000	2 200	12 300	29 300	58 100	75 200	1 250	6 000	19 500	38 100	11 100
Africa											
South Africa	38 000	875	2 600	4 800	10 000	12 000	–	500	3 000	4 000	800
Other countries	453 000	360	4 800	18 500	42 600	61 300	100	600	7 900	14 300	2 300
South Asia and Far East											
Chinese P.R.	1 154 000	1 000	6 000	35 000	120 000	290 000	70	750	56 000	150 000	3 000
India	859 000	1 000	4 800	24 000	50 000	75 000	2	300	2 300	40 000	3 000
Japan	125 000	12 000	27 000	87 000	100 000	120 000	18 000	42 000	70 00	75 000	26 000
Other countries	823 000	1 800	13 300	49 700	111 600	129 200	700	8 950	31 000	64 900	14 400
North America and Caribbean											
USA	252 000	111 000	230 000	380 000	500 000	560 000	68 000	110 000	175 000	185 000	68 000
Canada	26 000	5 500	14 000	23 000	32 000	42 000	5 000	9 500	14 000	15 500	6 000
Caribbean	11 000	190	860	4 000	5 600	6 400	100	1 200	2 000	2 500	400
Latin America	432 000	12 600	29 400	62 800	133 500	171 100	7 400	22 600	54 900	86 200	13 300
Australasia and other ocean territories	29 000	2 760	7 800	13 000	24 700	30 600	3 200	5 000	8 600	9 800	4 700

Fig. 7.14

Radio and television receivers, worldwide, 1991

Source: International Broadcasting and Audience Research Library, June 1992

of ownership of television sets, video cassette recorders and radios worldwide may be a significant indicator of the relative availability of the hardware necessary for media reception, they tell us little about the ways in which these media may be used in context; equally they reveal little about the related questions of content – what is broadcast or available to watch or listen to within different international or national territories.

Modernisation and development

Historically, the data in figure 7.14 do provide some indication of the international growth and spread of radio, TV and the VCR in the last forty years or so. It is important to bear in mind the broad historical perspective, and recognise that the international growth and spread of organised systems of mass communication and broadcasting in the modern period has been part of broader political and economic processes of industrialisation and commercialisation.

Some historians and other writers suggest that the growth and diffusion of mass media did not just follow more general patterns of industrialisation and trade, but played an essential and active part in what was viewed as an overall process of 'modernisation' Early studies often emphasised the function and impact of media in what was perceived as an inevitable and worldwide development process. The media – particularly newspapers, films, radio and TV – were identified as key agencies for changing, 'modernising', the attitudes and values of populations experiencing phases of worldwide industrialisation. In particular, 'developing nations' – often newly independent from colonial rule – were the basis for studies in the 1950s and 1960s which sought to assess the ways in which the media might be used to change traditional ways and beliefs: for example, by means of educational or advertising campaigns and programmes. From this perspective, it is important to note that the media tended to be regarded as benign agencies capable of engineering positive social and cultural change, and assisting in the pursuit of greater industrial, technical, economic or social 'development'. Two key factors tended to be absent from this view: first, the power of the 'developed' nations, and second, the increasing dependency of 'developing' economies and nation states. These ideas have, however, formed the basis for more recent studies of international media relationships, and a series of debates concerning media or cultural imperialism.

ACTIVITY 7.7

Compare the structure and range of media sectors in Britain with those in any other countries that you can get access to. Make use of other material – TV and radio schedules, etc, from other countries (figures 7.15 and 7.16). Refer to the *Further reading* list at the end of the chapter for some useful sources.

TV today

12 noon: **Bugs Bunny Show**
12.25pm: **Police Academy 5: Assignment Miami**
1.50: **Great Experiments**
This programme shows how scientific experiments have proved to be milestones on technology developments and have helped shape the way we live today.
2.15: **Dream Machine**
Modern man would be lost without the computer. This series charts its origins, development and impact in a user-friendly way that make sense even to the most scientifically illiterate.
3.05: **Banana Joe**
Movie starring Bud Spencer as Banana Joe.
4.35: **My Two Dads**
5: **MASH**
5.25: **Hollywood Wives**
7pm: **Local News**
7.15: **ITN news**
7.40: **Beyond 2000**
8.25: **May to December**
Anton Rogers and Lesley Dunlop star in this comedy about an affable Scottish solicitor in his mid-fifties, romancing an attractive gym mistress half his age.
8.55: **Hill Street Blues**
9.45: **Local News**
10pm: **CBS news**
10.20: **BBC news**
10.35: **Wiseguy**
11.25: **Closedown (for West only)**
11.25: **Porridge (For Suva only)**
When a lack lustre show business soccer team play the inmates of Slade Prison, habitual prisoner Norman Stanley and his young cellmate Lennie Godber find themselves unexpectedly free and Fletcher's main problem is how to break into jail.
11.55: **Closedown (Suva only)**

TV tomorrow

12 noon: **Count Duckula**
12.25pm: **WKRP In Cincinnati**
Comedy in a radio station.
12.45: **Highway to Heaven**
A contemporary series starring Michael Landon as a probationary angel sent to earth. Along the way he teams up with an ex-cop and they travel the country helping and bringing people together.
1.30: **Carpenters Motors One World of Sport**
A sporting bonanza featuring top overseas sporting events. Today we have a Five Nations match between France and England and the second part of *More than a Game* documentary.
4pm: **Running on Empty**
5.55: **Sunday choir**
7pm: **Local news**
7.15: **ITN news**
7.40: **The Cosby Show**
8.35: **Supertots**
Can training children in sports from an early age produce super-athletes? A Californian coach, Marv Marinovich, believes it does. He has developed a highly successful training technique which he perfected by using his own children as guinea pigs. With the aid of a strict diet, a routine of physical exercise and a host of scientists, he has turned his 21-year-old son Todd into one of the hottest properties in American football with a career that could make him a millionaire.
9.05: **Trainer**
9.50: **Local news**
10.05: **CBS news**
10.25: **BBC news**
10.45: **Equal Justice**
11.30: **Porridge (for West viewers only)**
12 midnight: **Closedown (for West only)**
12.20: **Closedown (for Suva only)**

Fig. 7.15
Schedules from the Fiji Times, *16 January 1993*
Source: *Fiji Times*

Media imperialism

Fundamental to this view of international media relations is the general argument that capitalist, western media have dominated and controlled the cultures of many Third World and other developing nations. Far from any benign or neutral process of 'modernisation' taking place, western, especially American, communication systems and their values have 'invaded' and have established forms of worldwide control and influence in the production and supply of information and entertainment. This process is seen as historically systematic and linked to the more general economic and political processes of first colonial, and then imperial, developments in the twentieth century.

QTV		ABC	
5.00pm	SIMPSONS: "*Burns Verkaufen De Kraftwerk*". The nuclear power plant where Homer works is sold to a German company; Homer falls into a state of depression after he is the only one at the plant to lose his job. Stars: Dan Castellaneta, Julie Havner.	5.00pm	THE AFTERNOON SHOW WITH MICHAEL TUNN: (G)
		5.02	THE BABYSITTERS' CLUB: "*Dawn's Dream Boy*". (G)
		5.30	PRESS GANG: (Rpt)
		6.00	THE GOODIES: (G) (Rpt)
		6.30	TVTV: News and reviews of television programs. (G)
5.30	NEIGHBOURS: Lou is concerned by Lauren's strange behaviour. Doug jumps at a delivery job opportunity, paying thousand dollars a trip and Annalise catches Jeffrey in a compromising position at Lindy's flat. Starring Julie Mullins, Rebecca Ritters and Terence Donovan. (G)	7.00	ABC NEWS: (G)
		7.30	THE 7.30 REPORT: (G)
		8.00	A YEAR IN PROVENCE: "Bread Winner". The village baker's bread is very bad today – what is wrong? His wife has left him – and it's up to the Mayles to reunite them. Cast: John Thaw, Lindsay Duncan. (G)
6.00	EYEWITNESS NEWS: (G)		
7.00	HINCH: Derryn Hinch presents a hard-hitting half hour of top quality current affairs. (G)	8.28	NEWS UP-DATE: (G)
7.30	HEALTHY WEALTHY & WISE: (G)	8.30	FOUR CORNERS: (S)
EMTV		**ATI**	
5.00pm	MAGILLA GORILLA: Children's Cartoon. (G)	5.00pm	PALACE OF DREAMS: (G)
5.28	EMTV TOK SAVE: (G)	5.55	CONSUMING PASSION: (G)
5.29	EMTV NEWS BREAK: (G)	6.00	NEWS HEADLINES: (G)
5.30	HOME AND AWAY: Half-hour teenage drama (G)	6.05	PLAY SCHOOL: (G)
6.00	NATIONAL EMTV NEWS: (G)	6.30	SWAP SHOW: (G)
6.30	A CURRENT AFFAIR: (G)	7.00	MR SQUIGGLE: (G)
7.00	SALE OF THE CENTURY: Australia's richest and most popular quiz show. Hosted by Glenn Ridge. (G)	7.30	PLAYSCHOOL: (G)
		8.05	EARTH WATCH: (G)
7.30	LOTTO DRAW: (G)	8.30	INFANT MATCHES: (G)
7.32	CHM SUPERSON NEW RELEASE: (G)	9.05	WATCH! YOUR LANGUAGE (G)
7.35	NEIGHBOURS: Henry comes up with a double interesting wedding idea for the other two engaged couples. (G)	9.30	AUSTRALIA NEWS: (G)
		9.35	OPEN LEARNING – OUT OF EMPIRE: (G)
		10.05	QUESTION OF SURVIVAL: (G)
		10.30	NEWS HEADLINES: (G)

Fig. 7.16

Extracts from schedules in the Post Courier, *Papua New Guinea, 18 October 1993*
Source: Post Courier

'Imperialism' in this sense refers to the ways in which certain industrialised nation states have emerged as 'world powers', by extending their forms of control and rule over other political, economic and cultural communities and nations for the purposes of commercial advantage, military security, political or ideological 'mission', etc. Whereas colonialism is viewed as an early stage in this process, predominantly concerned with economic advantage and exploitation, imperialism results from wider and more complex forms of dominance, directed towards empire building at the global level. Imperialism is the systematic production of massive disparities in wealth, power and influence, on a worldwide scale. Dominant, 'First World' (a term usually referring to North America, Western Europe, Japan and Australia) economies are able to control supply and demand on world markets, and poorer countries are encouraged to import First World goods and commodities in exchange for raw materials or cheap labour.

Our concern here lies with the related but cultural aspects of these processes. Studies of international media flows and relations have consistently pointed to what Varis (1974), in the context of TV, has called a 'one-way traffic', *from* the relatively restricted centres of advanced commercial states, via multinational corporations, *to* world markets, especially the 'developing' markets of the 'Third World' (nation states in South America, Asia, Africa) and 'Second World' (the now ex-Soviet bloc and China). This traffic, it is argued, introduces the values and commodities of consumer capitalism. Media networks become vehicles for the worldwide dissemination of language, identity and aspirations, for cultivating values congruent with the dominant ideologies of western capitalism.

An early focus for work of this type was the Hollywood dominance of world film industries, although more recent studies have focused on later 'waves' of television, video (Alvarado, 1988), satellite, advertising, news and music (Malm and Wallis, 1984). In a study first published in 1969, entitled *Mass Communication and American Empire*, Schiller argued that American TV exports represented part of an imperialist policy to subjugate the world – world domination is the aim. Importantly, this type of analysis noted that the process did not solely concern the programmes, films, adverts and so on; it also embraced the changing technologies of production and reception, the practices of production, and the patterns of tastes, aspirations, fashions and lifestyles which are cultivated or 'transmitted' by these commodities. For writers like Schiller (see also his more recent writing, for example 1991), the media play an important part in a general process of cultural imperialism. In this view, traditional and indigenous cultures worldwide are 'penetrated' and transformed by American cultural influences, which act to 'spearhead' forms of global American consumerism. For developing nations, a major problem is to try to retain or preserve cultural autonomy in the face of external, often American, influence. From such a point of view, satellite broadcasting, with its abilities to cross national boundaries, has simply enabled this process to occur more rapidly and completely. Satellite forms of delivery threaten what has been referred to as the 'audiovisual space' (Mattelart *et al.*, 1984) or cultural autonomy of many nations, with significant consequences for cultural identities.

From the mid 1970s, these themes of cultural dependency and the global communications power of developed nations have been regularly debated and criticised under the auspices of

Fig. 7.17
Source: Paul Hickinbotham

UNESCO (United Nations Educational, Scientific and Cultural Organisation), which has had to deal with a series of demands for a New World Information Order, which would seek to redress the imbalance between information-rich and information-poor countries and nation states. Such proclamations, however, appear to have had limited material impact on subsequent global developments.

In recent years, the debate about media imperialism has developed in a number of ways (see the *Further reading* list at the end of the chapter). At the heart of these developments has been a reassessment of some of the evidence cited in favour of its operation. This has largely concerned television. One of the best guides to the general patterns of television distribution and flow worldwide has been provided by Varis (1984), in a long-term study sponsored by UNESCO which reported on amounts of imported programming in some 69 countries between 1973 and 1983. (Alvarado, 1988, provides a study of international flows in video.) The patterns indicated here suggest that, overall, imported programmes average about one third or more of total programming. The USA imports relatively little – between 2 and 5 per cent. Canada is a major importer of American-originated programmes (30 per cent), and Western European systems also import about this amount. Many Latin American stations have 50 per cent or more of their schedules filled by American output, and this pattern is repeated in many African, Asian, Pacific and other Third World sectors (see figures 7.15 and 7.16).

The study showed that some 20 per cent of programming in the former Soviet Union was imported. At a global level, most of the programme material imported originates from the USA, and to a lesser extent from Western Europe, Japan and Australia. It is important to note that these flows are mainly of a recreational kind: light entertainment, movies and sports programmes. These programmes can be bought in packages at a fraction of the price it would cost to produce 'home-grown' versions, and therefore the economic logic for purchasing them to fill schedules worldwide is clear and compelling. For example, a recent discussion of Zimbabwe TV notes:

> ZTV can only afford to produce about twelve hours of indigenous drama a year, albeit incredibly cheaply with the actors also doing day jobs and providing their own costumes. Drama series like *Ziva Kawakaba* (*Know Your Roots*) are very popular with the majority black audience, but the advertisers

know that they are going to get better value for money from imported programmes that appeal to the more affluent white or middle-class black audiences. And ZTV know that they can acquire an episode of *Miami Vice*, say, for the special 'Third World' rate of $500 – a fraction of the already minimal budget of an episode of *Ziva Kawakaba*.

Dowmunt (1993), pp. 6–7

More work is needed on these patterns in the age of video, satellite and digital, multichannel forms of delivery. We should also note that a significant dimension to this debate concerns not just popular programme formats like the 1980s American soap opera *Dallas* but also the mediation of news and other forms of information; for example, with the multinational operation of MTV or the Cable News Network (CNN). A series of studies have criticised the international operations of major western news agencies, and their abilities to set the global news agenda in this context (see Gurevitch, 1991).

Assessing imperialism

For some writers, the model of 'one-way flow' oversimplifies what is in fact a growing and more complex set of interrelationships, with significant internal patterns, reversals and regroupings occurring within different continental, linguistic and geographical regions. However, the main challenge to the media imperialism thesis in recent years has emerged in the form of a questioning of the limits to the evidence provided. In short, does the evidence of amounts of imported programming add up to the 'imperialist effect'? As one writer has observed:

There is an assumption that American TV imports do have an impact whenever and wherever they are shown, but actual investigation of this seldom occurs. Much of the evidence that is offered is merely anecdotal or circumstantial. Observations of New Guinean tribesmen clustered around a set in the sweltering jungle watching *Bonanza* or of Algerian nomads watching *Dallas* in the heat of the desert are often offered as sufficient proof.

Lealand (1984), pp. 6–7

Fig. 7.18
Traditional semi-nomadic ger dwelling in Arhangai, Outer Mongolia, complete with satellite dish
Source: Barbara Hind

What is centrally at stake here is the way in which increasingly mobile media audiences, in a diversity of national and other cultural locations, may make sense of and relate to imported programming. Those who support the ideas of media imperialism assume that American films and programmes 'blot out' authentic and original forms of indigenous culture, and replace them with the ideologies and values of American consumer capitalism. However, little actual evidence has been presented about the precise nature of the forms of reception or decoding which are in play in the worldwide situations confronted with such imported material. Some recent developments in this context are worth noting.

By the mid 1980s, many cultural critics and writers agreed with the then French Minister for Culture, Jack Lang, when he attacked the American soap opera *Dallas* as 'the symbol of American cultural imperialism'. Set in a world of Texan oil families and their private and public feuds and conflicts, the soap opera had enjoyed massive international popularity in over a hundred countries worldwide (see Ang, 1985, Silj, 1988). One study which set out to explore how *Dallas* was made sense of in a diversity of cultural and global locations was carried out by Katz and Liebes (1990). They studied a large number of groups, including, for example, newcomers to Israeli society from a diversity of ethnic and cultural contexts. They viewed the dispersed and different audience groups that formed the basis for their study as active, and as capable of negotiating a range of diverse positions with regard to the serial, its stories and characters, and its relevance to their own lives. The study offers some evidence for the need to reassess this aspect of the imperialism thesis. Audiences on the 'receiving end' of American cultural products like *Dallas* emerge as active agents, more complex, critical or resistant and certainly less predictable in their cultural responses than has been assumed. Certainly, as Tomlinson in his assessment points out, 'We clearly cannot assume that simply watching *Dallas* makes people want to be rich' (1991, p. 49). The detailed study of the uses made of television in diverse national and ethnic locations has recently been developed in a series of studies by Lull (1988). For discussion of some of these themes, refer back to chapter 4.

One final and related question has been posed in recent work. This first emerges in an account given by Pennachioni (1984) of some observations of television viewing she made in north-east Brazil. One of the situations she describes concerns a group of poor country people in this area who were laughing at a communally watched, televised Charlie Chaplin film. Pennachioni noted that she and they appeared to be

Fig. 7.19
Bollywood, Leicester
Source: Tim O'Sullivan

laughing at the same things, but that this was by no means necessarily the case. On the basis of this encounter, she suggested that western media researchers face formidable problems of understanding and interpretation. They and their research subjects, people in Third World settings, may appear to 'laugh at the same things' – the tramp character in Chaplin's films – but within very different, even irreconcilable frames of reference. Ultimately, her study poses some important questions about the assumptions often made about Third World audiences by western researchers and their methods.

The study also highlights some important issues about the 'universal' nature of the appeal and meanings of images like Chaplin or even more recently JR Ewing in *Dallas* or characters in the Australian soap opera *Neighbours*. Tracey (1985) has posed a number of provocative questions in this context by suggesting that the worldwide appeal of American popular culture must, in part, be explained not just by its imposition, but by understanding how it taps into certain *universal* feelings and 'common chords', which transcend national cultures and differences of lived, situated identity. As Tomlinson notes, however, this kind of argument comes dangerously close to ignoring the historical power of western media systems to saturate developing cultural economies with their types of material: 'One reason why Chaplin's humour can be plausibly seen as universal is that it is universally present' (1991, p. 53).

In summary, this section has suggested that there is considerable evidence available which points to the global concentration of power over media production and distribution. This has tended to be concentrated in western nations, states and corporations. Debates about the dynamics of media imperialism may need to address more directly questions of how international audiences for the films, channels, programmes, music, videos and so on make use of and interpret these cultural products in their daily lives. In so doing, they also need to deal with the arguments and ideas contained in recent accounts of 'globalisation'. Both of these issues are centrally linked with the emergence of more complex, new, multichannel media technologies, satellite, cable, digital and video being perhaps the prime examples of the moment. Media Studies has to move with these times and changes if it is to remain relevant and viable as a means of systematically participating in, challenging or changing the media enviroments of new times.

Further reading

Ang, I. 1996: *Living Room Wars: Rethinking Media Audiences for a Postmodern World*. Routledge.

Barker, C. 1997: *Global Television: An Introduction*. Blackwell.

Curran, J. and Seaton, J. 1997: *Power without Responsibility: The Press and Broadcasting in Britain*. Routledge.

Dowmunt, T. (ed.). 1993: *Channels of Resistance*. BFI/Channel 4.

Golding, P. and Harris, P. (eds) 1997: *Beyond Cultural Imperialism: Globalization, Communication and the New International Order*. Sage.

Hannerz, U. 1996: *Transnational Connections: Culture, People, Places*. Routledge.

Hayward, P. and Wollen, T. (eds.). 1993: *Future Visions: New Technologies of the Screen*. BFI.

Herman, E. and McChesney, R. 1997: *The Global Media: The New Missionaries of Corporate Capitalism*. Cassell.

Howes, D. (ed.). 1996: *Cross-Cultural Consumption: Global Markets, Local Realities*. Routledge.

Morley, D. and Robins, K. 1995: *Spaces of Identity: Global Media, Electronic Landscapes and Cultural Boundaries*. Routledge.

Murdock, G. and Golding, P. 1991: 'Culture, Communications and Political Economy' in J. Curran and M. Gurevitch (eds). *Mass Media and Society*. Edward Arnold.

Ostergaard, B. (ed.). 1997: *The Media in Western Europe*. Sage.

O'Sullivan, T. and Jewkes, Y. (eds). 1997: *The Media Studies Reader*. Arnold.

Reeves, G. 1993: *Communications and the 'Third World'*. Routledge.

Rheingold, H. 1994: *The Virtual Community: Finding Connection in a Computerised World*. Minerva.

Smith, A. 1993: *Books to Bytes. Knowledge and Information in the Postmodern Era*. BFI.

Sreberny-Mohammadi, A. 1991: 'The Global and the Local in International Communications' in J. Curran and M. Gurevitch (eds). *Mass Media and Society*. Edward Arnold.

Tomlinson, J. 1991: *Cultural Imperialism*. Pinter.

Webster, F. 1995: *Theories of the Information Society*. Routledge.

Williams, R. 1990: *Television: Technology and Cultural Form*. Routledge.

Winship, I. and McNab, A. 1996: *The Student's Guide to the Internet*. Library Association.

Media practice

Practice and theory in Media Studies cannot and should not really be separated. Their relationship is both complementary and integral to a full understanding of the subject area. Practical work plays an important part in many subject areas: for instance it is an established and well respected part of the science curriculum where students carry out 'practicals', often to 'test theory'. In English doing one's own work is both an opportunity to reinforce what has been taught but is also, perhaps more importantly, to develop one's own expressive, analytical or creative skills and abilities. Media Studies requires both the traditional skills of critical reflection and analysis but this is combined with some technical experience or production competence. Active involvement in media practice, producing short pieces for radio, video or magazines, etc., can help not only to reinforce and develop some of the ideas and issues in this and other books but also highlights and leads to a greater awareness of the difficulties and dilemmas associated with media production.

Media courses at every level usually try to integrate critical study with practical production and therefore expect students

Fig. 8.1
Source: Tim O'Sullivan

to carry out some kind of practical production work. At its best this should enable students to gain valuable, even vocationally relevant training and to develop technical, conceptual and working skills as well as building up a portfolio of work to show to those who 'gatekeep' – control access to – the next career stage, whether it be Higher Education or employment. Practical exercises are important because they show that the output of different media are the result of clear social, technical and economic contexts, the products of organisational requirements as well as men's and women's own individual actions. However, there is a danger that sometimes this emphasis on 'doing' can be rather crude and simplistic, merely providing students with a set of 'testable skills' that lack any reflective, critical or conceptual frameworks.

We will discuss how practical work can offer the opportunity to apply many of the key areas of knowledge and concepts that are discussed in this book, looking in particular at such areas as audiences, institutions and representations. Playing a part in the production of particular media texts can focus questions about the criteria by which professional media producers interpret 'reality' and how it is represented back to us and other audiences. These are rarely just technical questions and, for example, practice can help to illustrate the importance that the notion of 'audience' has as a determining factor in both the shape and content of a production. It also provides you with an opportunity to experience directly a version of the constraints, decisions and structures involved in media production and to understand the impact that these can have on the shape and outcome of the process and the final product itself.

As most media production involves working with others, there is also the value of working and negotiating with groups of people who may have different ideas, perspectives, ideologies and motives. The development of these skills can help prepare you for the life of an extended professional, a self-critical, flexible problem-solver, working in whatever industry or business you choose to make your career. Most importantly, this chapter considers the process of evaluation and self-reflection that should accompany any practical or production exercise and helps to identify the social and other organisational skills that can be 'transferred' across to a variety of different occupations and professions.

This first section of the chapter will look at the three main stages involved in creating a piece of media work: *pre-production,* including purpose and audience and considering the technology and resources required; *production,* including style and content, interviews and vox pops; and then *post-production*, which includes review and evaluation. Chapter 9 will then consider some of the issues involved in carrying out research for media productions.

Pre-production: purpose and audience

Purpose

Pre-production is perhaps the most time-consuming of the stages involved in media practice. Most productions start with an idea, an interest, a point of view or a topic that someone wants to explore, perhaps triggered by a news item or a particular piece of music. This may be in response to a given brief, where the producers have to work to a specification given to them by others, the 'client'; or the producers may have a free hand to work on an expressive or more creative piece of their own choice. Most practical work encountered in educational settings will usually begin with given exercises to help you to understand and develop confidence with certain techniques, equipment and procedures. At later stages, you may be given greater autonomy to decide what you want to produce, and how you would like to go about it.

As the ideas develop and the brief is interpreted, both the aims of the production and the sense of audience should be defined and clarified. Whatever the medium and the technologies being used, however long or short the production, all successful productions should be clearly thought out and should have a thoroughly researched and planned structure. Depending upon the medium used, and how ambitious the finished production is, this planning and preparation can take up to 50 per cent of the available time and effort. Start early and plan ahead in as much detail as possible.

As part of a team producing a media text, some of the questions that you will need to consider at this initial stage are:

- What are the key aims of the production?
- Which medium is most appropriate or available for it?
- What resources are available to fund and execute it?
- How can it be managed effectively to meet the deadline?

All media texts aim to produce some kind of meaning, whether it be explicitly informative or educational, or more open or entertaining. There may be a clear and unambiguous message to be presented, for instance in a video designed to promote to maximum advantage a college or local sports club, or there may be a more abstract and open-ended one, trying perhaps to convey an emotion or feeling, or simply hoping to elicit a variety of responses. As chapters 2 and 3 demonstrate, media texts and their meanings can sometimes be confusing, misinterpreted or even redundant, and many different criteria can be used in evaluating them.

Most productions should start by developing a sense of purpose and a clear set of aims that have to be defined and understood by all those involved in the production. You may need at this early stage to consider how your group will work, who will do and take responsibility for what aspects of the project. A common danger involves being too ambitious in deciding upon the aims of a production, particularly if there are limited resources. It is probably unrealistic, for example, if using video for the first time, to try to tell a general audience about the role and influence of the motor car in twentieth-century industrialised society. It might be a very interesting programme, or series of programmes, but are the resources required to make it realistically available? Be realistic as well as imaginative, in defining the scope and scale of your project.

A clearly defined set of aims provides one of the measures of the success or otherwise of a production and is an important part of the later review and evaluation process. It is therefore often useful to ask the question, 'At the end of watching/reading/listening to my piece of work the target audience should do, think, feel ... what?' Pinpoint exactly what it is you want to get across to the audience. For example, in the context of a short radio piece on a proposal for a local road bypass, should they:

- Understand the seriousness of the local traffic problem?
- Know what the local council's plans are?
- Understand the objections being raised by local conservation and other groups?
- Know how to get their own opinions heard?

Audience

For most productions, whether student or 'professional', audiences should be considered: the types of readers, listeners or viewers you want to communicate with. This helps focus the style and content of the work. For *Time* magazine the audience may be millions of readers throughout the world, for Classic

FM it may be three or four million listeners in Britain who enjoy particular types of classical music, whereas for the *Newbury Weekly News* (see chapter 5) it may only be a few thousand readers living in west Berkshire who share a more or less common interest in local events, news and personalities.

When thinking about your target audience it is important to try to be as specific as possible. Is the audience a specific group of people? If so, how would you categorise them? Are you trying to appeal to any particular subcultures, age groups, ethnic or gender groups, or other types of consituency? What else do they have in common – perhaps in terms of their interest in the media? Perhaps they all come from the same locality? Do they have similar hobbies and interests? It is important to be realistic when defining your audience too. Unmarried males over the age of 50 who live beside the sea and are interested in volleyball do exist, but it could be very difficult to reach a significant number of them.

It is important to spend time thinking how the audience is identified: for instance, is it an established and recognisable community or is it a new configuration created specifically for the project? There can be some difficulty in assessing what a new audience might want, particularly if the text is aimed not at meeting an existing need in competition with other products but at creating a new one. This is why many mainstream producers work with the concept of genre: because it provides some of the key rules and conventions which guide success and can help show producers what an audience wants and the ' formula' that has worked in the past. (See chapters 2 and 4.) In planning your production, it is helpful to consider how the target audience and their perceptions, needs and patterns of media consumption might affect the shape and content of your production and the audience's response to it. What assumptions have to be made about the audience's feelings, prejudices, and levels of prior knowledge and understanding, and how might this affect the way your message is presented or received – encoded and decoded?

The medium

A student production often starts with the idea of 'doing something on video' or 'producing a piece for radio'. However, it should only be after clarifying questions about aims, target audience, format and resources that the most appropriate medium is decided upon, if such choice is allowed by circumstances. The aims of a production will influence the medium used because some topics are more suited to certain media than

---

ACTIVITY 8.1

Using a production idea of your own, outline a profile of the people you aim to communicate with. Refer to chapter 4 on Audiences and Reception and consider the following categories: age; gender; social grade; location; lifestyle. Is there any other information or category that could be useful?

others. For example, if the topic is very visual, for instance the recording of a piece of student drama, then a medium which can encompass the visual would seem to be most appropriate. If the aim is to transmit a lot of facts and figures then a printed medium may be more successful than an audio one. If the production focuses on music, perhaps the history of a particular group, singer or type of music, then video or radio will probably work better than printed material. If the aim is to inform through the use of different points of view or experts, then radio or a printed medium may be more suitable than a visual one which might consist mainly of 'talking heads'.

The target audience may be a significant influence on the decision about the most appropriate medium, as groups of people have different preferences as to how they receive information, are engaged, persuaded or entertained. Different audiences consume the media in different social contexts, and whereas some groups are more willing to sit and read, perhaps privately, others prefer a visual or more active medium that they can share. (Recap some of the discussion in chapter 4 which looks in more detail at how different groups consume and relate to different media.)

ACTIVITY 8.2

There are several ways of investigating how existing conventions and patterns of consumption are affected by ideas of particular 'groups' of target audiences:

1 Take the front page of either a broadsheet newspaper or tabloid newspaper and 'reverse' it, rewriting the stories for a set of particular, different readers. Reselect and prioritise the stories, and redesign the page layout accordingly.
2 Compare and contrast the way advertisements on radio stations such as Classic FM and a local independent chart station are shaped and presented for their different audiences.
3 Choose a production in one particular medium, say, radio, and then consider how it would be modified if transposed into another medium, say, print or television.

Pre-production: technology and resources

One theme explored in chapters 5 and 6 was how media texts and output are produced under certain conditions: technical, organisational and other factors such as finance are important determinants. Your production will have to work to a budget, often decided by someone other than yourself. Often the budget limits the time, the equipment and the personnel available, and this may significantly affect the production values. This can include the technologies and expertise that you might use. If hi-tec equipment with lots of special effects is available there is often a strong temptation to use it irrespective of the time or cost. The temptation to use special effects as a substitute for content brings the danger that *what* is being said becomes less important than *how* it is being said. With most media becoming increasingly dependent upon new technologies, it is easy to become overawed or infatuated with new pieces of equipment that seem to do the same old tasks better, faster and more easily. Technical competence is not, however, the only criterion for success, and often the old, tried and tested methods can be more successful in producing the desired end result without the necessity of having to master new and unfamiliar technology in a short space of time. You, and the rest of your production team, therefore need to take careful stock of budget and technical possibilities and limits before proceeding too far in your production.

Increasingly the gap between the technology available in schools and colleges and that used by the 'professionals' is closing, as PC-based, electronic equipment becomes smaller,

ACTIVITY 8.3

To explore the effects of new technology:

1 Research how newspaper production has changed with the introduction of the computer. What are the main differences in the production methods known as 'hot lead' and 'cold type'? List what you consider to have been the main consequences of the introduction of these new production processes.

2 Research how developments in television technology have influenced the 'look' of programmes. Compare current television output with the output of the 1950s and early 1960s, looking in particular at the use of graphics and computer-generated special effects, and the number of angles of cameras being used. Sports programmes are a particularly interesting genre to look at, especially high-profile events like the Olympic Games or world championships. What changes are occurring now and under way for the near future?

more sophisticated and cheaper. In video it is now possible that the process and equipment used in a production may be virtually the same as that used by the mainstream production companies and it is only the tape format (SVHS instead of Betacam) that stops the production looking like the 'real thing'. In both journalism and radio the production process is centered around PC packages such as Quark Xpress, Photoshop and Wave cards and these have all stimulated a range of cheaper imitations.

The time and technologies that are available for your production may determine to a large extent the actual process of putting together the text. Despite what you, as a producer, may wish to do, it is quite likely that you will have to adjust your ideas to the equipment, budget and time available. It is easier to disguise a poor or inappropriate location if close-ups are used; perhaps an 'exotic' location can be suggested by music and a few simple close-ups rather than travelling to a location and taking long, panning shots. Television pictures are based upon a 'language' or 'grammar' (see chapter 2), where every type of shot carries a certain meaning and, when placed into a sequence, this builds up a story or message that can potentially be understood by people from many different cultures – a kind of visual Esperanto. As audiences become more tele-literate and increasingly share the same, usually American derived, production values, this style and language become more and more global, so that we all come to share an understanding of what a close-up or an establishing shot mean and when it is appropriate to use them. Cost and time, however, can often determine the type of shots used, how the grammar is put together and encoded.

ACTIVITY 8.4

- Record an extract from a television programme, list all the different shots and note how the 'grammar' is used, for instance by cutting from the outside of a building to a group of people talking indoors so that we assume that it is the same building. Try to find other examples.
- Compare and contrast programmes from different genres, for instance a police drama with a soap opera, to see if there are specific visual conventions and codes associated with different genres.

Guidelines for preparing a storyboard

- Decide what is to be shown.
- List the visuals in a logical order.
- Sketch the main elements and what will be in each shot.
- Describe the type of shot, e.g. long shot, close-up, etc.
- If possible give a rough idea of the length of each shot.
- Explain what sound or dialogue is going on at the same time, e.g. music, speech, etc.
- If someone else is involved in the shooting then make sure that they too can understand the storyboard.

ACTIVITY 8.5

1 Create a storyboard that shows the way 'real time' is condensed, for example when filming a journey or a simple household task like making a cup of coffee. What stages can be left out or shortened (the kettle coming to the boil?) How is this shortening of time indicated? How is one shot bridged with the next?

2 Plan and produce a storyboard for a video lasting no longer than three minutes. The video should aim to tell a story or create an atmosphere using only pictures – no sound or dialogue.

Checklist for planning a production:

● Estimate how much time is available and how it is going to be allocated. A timescale for all the different jobs, working back from the final deadline, is very useful.

● Make an action plan, listing all the research to be done, letters to be written, telephone calls to be made, interviews to be arranged, etc., and put beside each activity the name of the person who will be responsible for making sure that it is completed on time.

● Be realistic. How much money is there to spend? A rough costing needs to be worked out. Include the expenses incurred while undertaking research, any travelling expenses or photocopying, as well as the cost of any extra materials that may have to be purchased. Copyright is often overlooked, but it may also have to be paid for and can be very expensive, particularly for well-known pieces of music or film images and clips.

For video productions and projects, it is useful to prepare a storyboard as early as possible and to refine this with as much detail as possible as the project develops.

Production: style and content

Athough, as chapter 4 suggested, we often consume the media while paying very little direct attention, any successful production should aim to engage the audience so that, at the least, they will want to carry on watching, listening or reading. This can often mean compromising in favour of something that is short, sharp and to the point in content, rather than a production that is long, worthy but boring.

Every video production, for instance, has a certain style, and this will depend upon a number of factors. If the production is aimed at a youth audience, a short documentary about a local band or on the dangers of drugs, then the style usually borrows from current musical trends and includes fairly rapid editing, fast-moving visuals, graphics, loud soundtrack, special effects and a variety of messages all being broadcast simultaneously. This style has become well known and is often copied.

However, what looks easy and 'rough' is often difficult to do successfully with limited resources. It can be more worthwhile, successful and satisfying to try for a more original style that is within both your means and resources.

If the production has an older audience as its target, perhaps a publicity campaign about a local primary school aimed at parents of young children, then a more sedate style is often considered more appropriate; for example, a loud rock-music background is not likely to work effectively with this type of audience or topic. Some productions make a claim to be spontaneous, and some, like *Zoo TV* or *The Big Breakfast* on Channel 4, or Chris Evans' shows on radio and television and the *Chris Tarrant Breakfast Show* on Capital Radio, have aimed to be whacky and anarchic in their apparent lack of planning and rehearsal. Almost all radio and television shows, however, have a well-prepared script, and as part of 'mainstream' broadcasting, will have well-prepared playlists and fairly tightly controlled time schedules.

All media texts have some kind of *narrative* – a story to tell – and should have a structure that is appropriate for the purpose (see chapter 2). Producers and audiences both have ideas and expectations, sometimes articulated, often just assumed, as to what a particular production is about, where it should start from and how it should develop and finish. This will depend on such factors as whether or not the programme is part of a series, whether the characters or narrative are already familiar, or whether it is a one-off that has to create its characters' identities quickly and have a self-contained narrative within a given time-slot.

In chapter 2 the significance of *title sequences* was discussed. Most radio and television programmes are 'top-and-tailed', usually through the use of a theme tune, text or graphics. An effective start and introduction is sometimes made by using a sound or visual montage that not only introduces some of the main issues of the production but also hopefully attracts the audience's attention.

Most successful productions *vary their pace and content*, perhaps by following a 'talking head' segment with some action shots, or a piece of music with some speech. Each segment should lead naturally into the next. The American soap opera *Dallas,* which was exported worldwide in the 1980s, was particularly successful in working to a pattern where each scene started with an establishing shot (the Southfork Ranch or the front of the Ewing Oil office), moving through a series of mid to head-and-shoulder shots and ending with a close-up of someone's face to emphasise the emotion and drama. Each scene usually lasted for no more than two or three minutes and the pattern was repeated again and again throughout the programme. Each visual change of scene was 'bridged' by soft music that rose in volume as the camera closed in on someone's face for that scene's particular climax.

For video productions when both sound and vision have been planned and detailed on scripts and storyboard, they should be married together into a *shooting script*. Although this is a long and complex process, it is important for everyone involved in the project to understand exactly what is required of them and how their part fits into the overall production. If you are making a documentary, perhaps about some aspect of your local community, then two or three different voices can be used for voice-overs, perhaps varying between male and female, as one person's voice can quickly become monotonous. A commentary is often made to sound more realistic by using background noise, or 'actuality', such as traffic noises or birdsong, to give a sense of realism, involvement and of 'being there'.

ACTIVITY 8.6

- Choose a radio or television programme and study its main segments. How many are there? How long are they? How are they linked? Is there a pattern?
- Plan and produce a seven-minute radio feature for a 6.30pm magazine programme to be broadcast in your locality. Each segment should be no longer than 90 seconds and should include both an introduction and an 'outro', as well as a variety of different presenters.
- Using a piece of video recorded without sound, add contrasting types of musical soundtracks or different background sounds. Note how the different pieces of music or sounds can affect the 'meaning' of the visuals. A similar exercise can be done by putting different voices or different scripts to a piece of news footage, to highlight how the 'meaning' can be altered.
- Look at a recorded television programme and analyse one particular segment. Watch it to see how it has been constructed. Try to note every shot, giving its type and duration. Note also the use of any graphics or 'cutaways' – where the camera 'cuts' to a shot other than the main subject, often the interviewer. Look particularly for the ways that sound and pictures are linked. Working back, now transcribe the commentary and reconstruct the script, giving commentary, camera shots and other relevant information.

Guidelines for writing a script:

- Decide what is to be said.
- List the points in a logical or agreed order.
- Make sure that the opening is both interesting and informative.
- Try to visualise the individual listener or viewer. Remember that often we watch/listen or read alone or in small, intimate gatherings (often with our close family), so the production should have that same intimate feeling.
- Try out what is to be said by speaking the text aloud, then write it down if it sounds 'natural'. Some people have better speaking voices than others and it is important to make sure that the best voices are used.
- Try to write in short sentences or phrases but keep the language 'natural'. Some people immediately start to talk in an artificial, convoluted and rather pompous way when being recorded. This will usually detract from what is actually being said.
- If someone else is going to speak the text, make sure that they can understand it. Use clear punctuation and paragraphs and have the script typed with double spacing.
- Allow for rehearsals.

In an attempt at creating a sense of realism, documentaries often require the filming process to be as discreet at possible, frequently using the 'fly-on-the-wall' approach discussed in chapter 3. One method is to use a participant observer – someone who becomes one of the group or social situation under observation. These methods, although increasingly popular, have important ethical implications, particularly for individual privacy, and raise questions about the role of investigative journalism, particularly as technology improves and the recording equipment becomes smaller, more discreet and more sophisticated.

If you are working with printed material such as producing a local newspaper or magazine, the copy frequently has an 'inverted pyramid' structure, setting out a story with the five Ws (who, what, when, where and why) in the first paragraph, subsequent paragraphs being a mixture of additional information and background. Paragraph 3 or 4 usually contains a quotation. One advantage of writing a feature this way is that the end of the article should contain the least useful information and can therefore be most easily cut if there is a shortage of space.

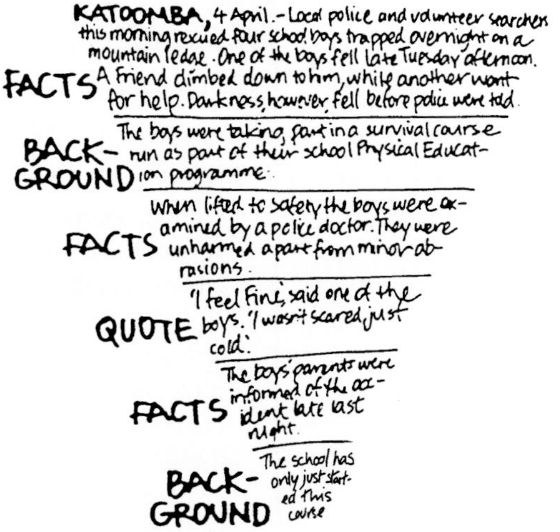

KATOOMBA, 4 April. - Local police and volunteer searchers this morning rescued four school boys trapped overnight on a mountain ledge. One of the boys fell late Tuesday afternoon.

FACTS A friend climbed down to him, while another went for help. Darkness, however, fell before police were told.

BACK-GROUND The boys were taking part in a survival course run as part of their school Physical Education programme.

FACTS When lifted to safety the boys were examined by a police doctor. They were unharmed apart from minor abrasions.

QUOTE 'I feel fine,' said one of the boys. 'I wasn't scared, just cold.'

FACTS The boys' parents were informed of the accident late last night.

BACK-GROUND The school has only just started this course

Fig. 8.2
Inverted pyramid structure of
newspaper/magazine story
Source: R. McRoberts, *Media Workshops: Vol. 1,*
Words, Macmillan, 1987

Production: interviews and vox pops

Interviews can play a large part in both the research and the production stages, particularly if the aim of your production is to inform or persuade. As edited parts of interviews are often included in the final programme, interviews are important not only as a means of acquiring information but also because they may affect the shape, content and style of a production as well as raise questions of 'balance' and impartiality (see the section on interviews in chapter 9).

If a production is investigating an issue of law and order, for example, drinking and driving or drug abuse, then the people most often interviewed are representatives of the police or related judicial, legal or medical professions. This is because they are relatively easy to contact, and usually have someone whose job it is to deal with the public and answer questions. They are often considered the 'experts' in matters of law and order, who mediate between 'us', society, and 'them', the criminals. It may well be in their own interest to gain media exposure, as they often have a point of view, some information or an appeal for information that they want to publicise. This dependence upon a quick and easy soundbite is often much more convenient than trying to obtain an interview with someone who represents the opposite – or an 'anti-establishment' – view. Not many people are willing to admit publicly that they drink and drive or take illegal drugs, although you may be able to get an interview with

ACTIVITY 8.7

Read the following information and write a newspaper story, following the 'pyramid' guidelines:

Fire brigade: Fire began at 7.05am today in Laing's Hotel, The Parade, Seamouth. Believed started in kitchen storeroom and spread rapidly by adjacent lift shaft to all three floors. Woman and man badly burned. Brought out by firemen.

Police: Four people taken to Axebridge Royal Infirmary by ambulances. Flames began to break through roof. Ambulance 1 took chef Alan Edwards, of 6, Langsett Road, Seamouth. Second contained hotel owner Alan Laing and wife, and a guest, Miss Irene Smollett of Exton.

Hospital: Miss Smollett and Mr Laing dead on arrival. Chef badly burned on face and hands: admitted. Wife treated for shock.

Hotel receptionist, Karen Broughton, said:
'Alan was preparing breakfast when he discovered the fire. He was burned trying to fight it. He told me, and I roused the Laings and we ran round the hotel warning the other staff and 17 guests. Everyone seemed to get out safely but when Mr Laing held a roll-call Miss Smollett was missing. He ran into the hotel. It was well alight by then. Then the fire brigade arrived.'

Chief fire officer, David Granville, said:
'My men found Mr Laing and a woman huddled at one of the top floor corridors. We got them out just before the roof collapsed. There was no hope of saving the building. Its age and the draught from the lift shaft meant it was certain to be destroyed once the fire had a good hold.'

Hotel built 1842. The Laing family have owned it for 53 years. Lived with wife, Anne, in hotel. Aged 63, wife 58. No children.

Media Techniques. Newspaper and Radio Journalism.
© *London Institute.*

someone who has 'reformed'. This unwillingness to 'confess' in public may be circumvented by offering someone anonymity, perhaps by appearing with the face blacked out or the voice distorted, but this is increasingly difficult to achieve without looking either cliché or humorous.

If you are planning to incorporate interviews in your finished production, you will need to arrange the interviews well in advance, as most people are unwilling or unable to stop what they are doing and immediately answer questions in any meaningful or useful way. They will probably want to know what the production is about and why they are being asked to appear in it. Interviewees may ask to see your questions in advance if they want time to prepare their answers. Some interviewers feel that this loses the spontaneity and excitement of an interview, but, although it may be considered unprofessional, it is common practice, especially if the interviewee is important to the content or style of the programme. Increasingly some people, particularly politicians and those in authority, also ask to see the finished, edited product, and can even ask for a right of veto in case they feel that they have been misrepresented. Most professionals would regard this as unacceptable, although in some cases producers do agree and then state in the programme that this has occurred. It is usual, however, to send a copy of the finished product to anyone who has helped in its construction.

When drafting your questions for an interview, it is helpful first to make a list of the key points that you need to cover. Good questions are simple and direct and you should be prepared to deviate from the prepared questions if other relevant issues come up. Wherever an interview takes place it should allow both the interviewer and the person being interviewed to relax, as it is usually when people are relaxed that they start to talk more volubly and naturally. Body language is a good indication of how people are feeling. People being interviewed often prefer to conduct the interview on familiar territory, frequently in their own offices, where they feel in control. If your interview is being recorded for use in a production, it is important to have an environment that does not have any disturbing background noises, such as roadworks or police car sirens. These may not be noticeable in the excitement of carrying out the actual interview, but can be very obvious and distracting when reviewing the material, and although sometimes they can be removed at the editing stage there can be difficult problems with continuity.

Guidelines for an interview:

- Check equipment, particularly the sound levels, as there may be only one opportunity to carry out a particular interview.
- Be prepared. Think about the type of interview and have a clear idea of its purpose. Will the person being interviewed be sympathetic and cooperative, or reticent and unwilling to impart the relevant information?

- Introduce yourself, say who you are, and state the purpose of the interview and its context.
- Ask 'open' questions: those that start with 'What', 'Where', 'Why', 'When', 'How' or 'Who'.
- Think about the 'shape' of the interview. Structure the questions, possibly around the past, the present and the future. 'What did you do before...?' 'What are you doing now...?' 'What are your plans for the future...?'
- Recap the main points and check dates and the spellings of names of people and places.
- Ask a 'bucket' question along the lines of 'Is there anything else you would like to say?' This allows the interviewee to drop in anything not covered so far.
- Close the gate. There was a famous reporter who during his career got a number of exclusives, and one of them concerned a vital witness in a notorious case. This witness, a woman, would not talk to any reporters, although hordes of them laid siege to her in her house. This reporter, like everyone else, got no reply when he called. However, he left a visiting card with a note saying that he would very much appreciate a chance to talk to the woman, and he promised that the interview would be on her terms. Later that day the woman rang him, saying that she did not want to talk to the entire press, so would he come that afternoon for an exclusive interview.

  Years later when they met again the woman asked the reporter if he knew why she had picked him rather than any of the others. 'Was it my little note on the back of the visiting card?' he asked. 'No,' she replied, 'lots of them tried that one... but you were the only one who closed my garden gate properly on the way out.'

  The lesson is that a little care and consideration can pay big dividends.

Most interviews on television are carried out with one camera, filming the interviewee, and the 'cutaways' (where the interviewer is asking the questions) and 'noddies' (where the interviewer nods in agreement) are filmed later. A more complicated way of conducting interviews on video without having to use cutaways is to use two cameras.

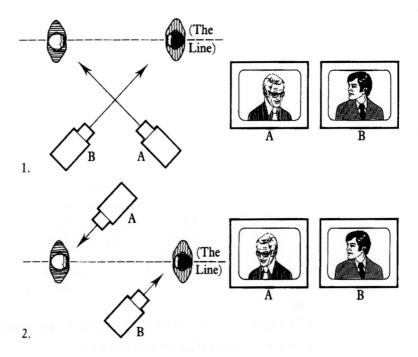

Fig. 8.3
*The positioning of cameras so as not to 'cross
the line'*

'Crossing the line'

When you are recording an interview, whether with one or two cameras, it is an important convention that the impression of two people talking to each other is achieved. This is done by setting up the cameras in such a way that they do not cross an invisible line but both stay on the same side of this line. The effect is that of one person looking to the left talking to the other who is looking to the right. In figure 8.3, cutting between cameras A and B on the same side of the line would be acceptable and give the impression of the two speakers facing each other as in a conversation. If, however, one camera crosses the line, the speakers no longer look as if they are talking to each other and this might confuse the audience, or at least be aesthetically unpleasing.

Vox pops

Vox pops, from *vox populi,* Latin for 'the voice of the people', are a common and widely used convention in much media output. Producers like them because they are fairly easy and cheap to produce and are popular with audiences, who like them because they are usually humorous as well as appearing to let 'the man or woman in the street' air his or her point of view. In television or radio the vox pop is usually a series of short reactions or comments from members of the public about a given topic, for instance a local traffic problem, often recorded in the local high street or shopping centre to give a sense of immediacy and context.

The reporter is rarely heard asking the question, except perhaps at the very beginning. On the finished package the public's answers are strung together to give a variety of voices and opinions or perhaps a common point of view. On television this device is frequently used to add some humour or as a more light-hearted alternative to 'talking heads'. In print, for instance in a local newspaper, it is presented as a series of interviews carried out 'on the streets' or under the banner of 'What our readers say'.

Post-production: evaluation and professionalism

Post-production, although the final stage, is possibly the most vital and valuable, because it contains two important operations: the editing or putting together of all the work, and an evaluation of how successful the whole exercise has been. This should include a review of what has been learnt about the

ACTIVITY 8.8

There are several exercises that you can do to improve your interviewing techniques:

- Try out some of the interviewing exercises that illustrate the effect of body language: for instance, conducting an interview sitting back to back where there is no eye contact, or across a desk with a physical barrier between the two people, or in unfamiliar surroundings.
- Think up a scenario and topic for an interview and ask someone to play the part of the interviewee. Try to conduct the interview as realistically as possible, with either pen and notebook, or audio or video equipment. Swap notes and discuss the interview afterwards and assess to what extent the interviewee was reassured and put at his or her ease. Are there any ways in which your interview manner could have been improved?

process of creating media products plus, wherever possible, feedback from listeners, readers or viewers.

Editing

Audio and video editing is necessary because, although some programmes may broadcast events or interviews 'live', generally very little of the raw material that has been filmed or recorded is tidy enough to be seen or read by audiences without going through some sort of editing process. Editing can be time-consuming, taking longer than the actual production stage, but for many people it is also the most enjoyable and creative part, as it is often at this stage that you, as a producer, can have the greatest impact.

Editing has four main functions: to make sure that the production is the required length or time; to remove unwanted material or mistakes; to alter, if necessary, the way or the sequence in which events will be portrayed; and finally, and perhaps most importantly, to establish the particular style and character of a production. There is still time to change ideas, and the editing stage offers you the opportunity to experiment with different combinations of media or sequences. Each combination will work in a slightly different way and each version may create distinctively different meanings.

As the producer, you will often have an ideal vision of the final production that may be carefully planned and written down in detail on paper or may just exist in your mind's eye. Sometimes this ideal works, sometimes it is unachievable, and the editing stage is often a process of experimentation and trial and error to see what works. Frequently, because of time and money constraints, the editing stage will often end in some sort of compromise between what is desirable and what is realistically achievable.

There are many criteria for assessing the success or effectiveness of media productions. For mainstream professional media producers these are often external or institutional and can be related to commercial or critical acclaim, ratings, and finishing within budget. For others, for example those working on projects within educational settings, the criteria for success are often more subjective, reflective and often largely personal, although still dependent to some extent on the opinion of others, such as peer group, tutors or audience. In many instances, the work produced may be graded or marked according to syllabus or course criteria, which should be clearly spelled out.

Review and evaluation

The process of review and evaluation should allow you the opportunity to stand back, reflect, and ask critical questions of the product and the processes involved in its production. The review also presents an opportunity for you to re-examine decisions you made earlier about the audience, the aims and the style and content of the production, and to see if, in retrospect, these were appropriate and fruitful. It is an opportunity, too, for you to assess how well the existing codes and conventions of mainstream media may have been assimilated, copied or challenged and what has been learnt about them.

For many productions, one of the most direct criteria for success is whether the audience liked it or not. Although not all productions are aimed at a specific audience, most productions, whatever their size or length, have some kind of target audience in mind. The review is an opportunity for you to consider whether your production has succeeded in engaging with the intended audience – the listener, viewer or reader – and whether the aims and objectives of the production overall have been realised. There are a variety of ways in which you can gather these responses, from formal questionnaires (see chapter 9) to less formally talking to people about their reactions.

Remember that a finished product is an achievement and that it is very much in the processes of producing it that the learning takes place. If you complete a finished product it should be shown or played to a sample of the target audience. Consider whether your audience had any preconceived ideas about how the production would (or should) look (or not look) like the 'real thing' and how this might have affected their expectations and responses.

You should use your log and notes to produce a written evaluation that should show to what extent, in your view, your production achieved its aims and whether anything else, perhaps unanticipated, happened as a bonus. Although not the only concern, it will be useful for you to consider the technical quality of the finished product. Did it affect the audience's responses? It is also important to consider your own reactions, as not all productions are necessarily purely audience-led.

The whole interwoven process of planning, preparation and production can be reviewed to see what particular aspects, in both the audience's and your opinion, were successful or unsuccessful. What seemed to work or did not work, what could be changed or kept in for any future work? Did the production attract and hold the audience's attention? If you were

ACTIVITY 8.9

Look at chapter 4 and consider what assumptions were made during your production process about the way certain groups or ideas should be handled; were any stereotypes used or how were they avoided? How were the decisions made in your group? Did you reach a consensus or was one opinion more dominant than the others? Was there any significant difference in the roles undertaken by different people in the group?

working in news, feature or documentary forms, was balance one of your objectives, and if so how far was it achieved? Did your own social or political standpoint or ideology affect the content? Were there any particular problems in carrying out interviews, perhaps technical issues or problems in gaining access to particular people? If you were to do it again, what would you change and why?

Most productions develop organically and their shape and emphasis changes during the production process, and adjustments are often made to the notional target audience, available material and to overall aims. What were the major problems in your production and how were they overcome? How did decisions about the conditions of production, the budget and the use of technologies affect the final form and content of the production?

Most productions are collective and collaborative enterprises, involving group and team work. It is useful therefore to consider how well everyone worked together and how tasks and roles were negotiated and allocated. If there was any conflict, what were the main causes and was it resolved? Was there, for instance, a gender bias that allowed males to dominate the technical hardware and the apparently more difficult technical tasks, while the females tended to be left with other roles, such as presenting or researching?

The process of creating media texts, whether large or small, individually or as part of a team, is usually an exciting, worthwhile and challenging experience. It should offer you insight into how individuals work as well as how 'professionals' and media institutions operate. The experience should provide you with a greater understanding of some of the choices, decisions and constraints that shape the form and content of media texts and output.

Professionalism

Producing a practical piece of work not only helps to illustrate in a very direct way the material and ideological implications of many of the dilemmas and constraints that 'professional' producers experience, but that media practice can also provide some direct experience of the problems and standards that 'professional' producers work with and to, and that audiences respond to.

There are some dangers associated with practical work, and perhaps one is thinking that what is produced in the 'professional' mainstream media is the one and only way of constructing media images and the standard by which all other work should be

ACTIVITY 8.10

You should now be familiar with the major stages in the production of a media text. Choose a television, radio or print text and outline the main stages in its production, with special consideration of the main pressures and constraints that the producers work under.

judged or measured. This view can often imply that what is produced outside of the mainstream can be dismissed as amateur and inferior. Although the level of technology may be different, usually below that of professional industry equipment, many of the processes and problems will nevertheless be similar.

Many first-time producers expect that their finished product will look like the 'real thing' and be of the same standard as those produced by mainstream media. A realistic 'product' is often emphasised by professionals and others, who are often keen to talk about ideas of 'standards' and 'expertise'. These can, however, lead to an exclusivity and a mystique associated with the professionals' status. There are in fact many instances where the opposite is the case and the 'professional' is keen to use new ideas or emulate the success of the 'amateur', particularly in the area of youth programmes on television, or in magazines, where the 'off-the-street' style of scratch videos or fanzines has an immediacy that the mainstream can only copy and try to incorporate into its own output.

The value of individual practical work carried out as part of a Media Studies syllabus is that it is not always necessary to replicate the professional or institutional patterns or constraints but that it may instead allow for the exploration of different, or alternative, experimental ways of presenting ideas and images. You can attempt to subvert or challenge the 'professional' notions of the correct way, and this professional aura can be demystified and examined. Working on practical exercises can involve 'deconstructing' what others have put together and learning to present alternatives – but first learn the rules and then break or bend them. Undertaking practical work is also likely to lead to a greater appreciation of some of the difficulties that professional media producers face in their everyday working lives, as well as to developing an interest in that work.

Conclusion

Practical work in Media Studies is not just about being trained in existing media practices nor merely replicating the production skills and standards of the current media industries, rather it is concerned with developing vocationally competent students who are self-critical, reflective and analytical but who also have the social and organisational skills and understanding that

Fig. 8.4
Source: Jarrod Cripps

are relevant in many different occupations, of which media may be only one option.

It is no longer the case that the only way into the media industries is by completing an Oxbridge degree and then moving to the BBC or a Fleet Street (or rather today, Canary Wharf) broadsheet. Today Media Studies courses have established an important presence in schools, colleges and universities, although many of these courses can be oversubscribed and competitive. Despite the fact that the media, information and cultural industries are now one of the largest employment sectors in Britain it is true that they will not be able to offer employment to all these graduates. However, studying the media – integrating applied practical experience with analytical and organisational skills – can make a prospective employee more desirable to an employer, not only in the 'glamorous' media industries, but also in other related areas such as management, marketing and public relations. It is these and other related organisations that represent some of the key growth industries for the twenty-first century.

As the study of broadcasting in chapter 6 illustrates, British radio and television industries are becoming increasingly fragmented, offering a broader range of choice for audiences. This choice is provided by an increasing range of channels and specialist services, served by a large and expanding number of independent production companies. Both the ITV companies and the BBC are required to have 25 per cent of their output produced by independent companies. This means that there is an increasing demand for people to work, albeit on a freelance, short-term or casual basis, in independent production houses or low-cost satellite and cable companies.

In magazine publishing there is an increasing range of publications aimed at specific, specialist markets and as media companies increasingly diversify into other areas, in both broadcasting and publishing, traditional boundaries and separate career paths are less rigid. Economic pressures also mean that some smaller organisations like local radio stations try to employ as few people as possible and that those who are employed are 'multi-skilled' and flexible so that the person who presented the drive-time show in the morning will put together advertising packages for a client in the afternoon and may also have to fit in some administrative tasks.

As audiences fragment towards increasingly specialist 'narrowcast' and niche markets there may be more opportunities for those other than the white middle-class male groups who have traditionally dominated the decision-making and production side of the industries. More people from under-represented groups may continue to be recruited into the industries to meet particular market or regulatory needs – new 'youth' and other markets or a local 'community' presence for some radio franchises.

Useful contacts

Association of Independent Radio Companies 77 Shaftesbury Avenue, London W1V 7AD. Has a computer database of radio training opportunities.

BBC Centre for Broadcast Skills Training Wood Norton, Evesham, Worcestershire WR11 4TB. Publishes 'Putting You in the Picture'.

British Film Institute 21 Stephen Street, London W1P 2LN. Has a reference library and publishes books on courses and careers.

Cyfle Gronant, Penrallt Isaf, Caernarfon, Gwynedd. Runs training for the Welsh television and film industries.

ITV Network Centre 200 Grays Inn Road, London WC1X 8HF. Publishes *The Official ITV Careers Handbook*.

National Council for the Training of Broadcast Journalists 188 Lichfield Court, Sheen Road, Richmond, Surrey TW9 1BB.

National Council for the Training of Journalists Latton Bush Centre, Southern Way, Harrow, Essex CM18 7BL
Both of the above organisations offer advice for potential entrants and are involved in the running of courses.

National Union of Journalists 314 Grays Inn Road, London WC1X 8DP. Publishes the booklet *Careers in Journalism*.

Newspaper Society 74 Great Russell Street, London WC1B 3DA. Runs the Newspaper in Education scheme and publishes the booklet *Making the Decision*.

Periodical Training Council Queens House, 28 Kingsway, London WC2B. Publishes the annual *Directory of Magazine Training*.

Scottish Daily Newspaper Society/Scottish Broadcast and Film Training 4 Park Gardens, Glasgow G3 7YE. The major training providers in Scotland.

Skillset 124 Horseferry Road, London SW1P 2TX. The industry training organisation for broadcasting, film, and video. Publishes a careers pack.

WAVES c/o London Women's Centre, 4 Wild Court, London WC2B 5AU. Provides training for women.

Further reading

Allen, J. 1990: *Careers in TV and Radio*. Kogan Page.

Boyd, A. 1988, 1994: *Broadcast Journalism. Techniques of Radio and TV News*. Heinemann (1st edn); Focal Press (3rd edn).

Brierley, S. 1995: *The Advertising Handbook*. Routledge.

Conroy, A. and Wilby, P. 1994: *The Radio Handbook*. Routledge.

Davis D. 1969: *The Grammar of Television Production*. Revised by Elliot; further revised by Wooller. Published under the auspices of the Society of Film and Television Arts. Barrie and Jenkins.

Dimbleby, N. Dimbleby, R. Whittington, K. 1994: *Practical Media*. Hodder & Stoughton.

Evans, H. 1986: *Pictures on a Page*. Heinemann.

Hedgecoe, J. 1991: *On Video*. Hamlyn.

Hodgson, F. 1987: *Modern Newspaper Editing and Production*. Heinemann.

Kaye, M. and Popperwell, A. 1992: *Making Radio*. Broadside Books.

Keeble, R. 1994: *The Newspapers Handbook*. Routledge.

Langham J. 1996: *Lights, Camera, Action!* BFI.

Medina, P and Donald, V. 1992: *Careers in Journalism*. Kogan Page.

Miller, J. 1990: *Broadcasting: Getting In and Getting On*. Butterworth.

Millersen, G. 1989: *Video Production Handbook*. Focal Press.

Niblock, S. 1996: *Inside Journalism*. Blueprint.

Quilliam, S. and Grove-Stephansan, I. 1990: *Into Print*. BBC.

Stafford, R. 1993: *Hands On*. BFI.

Watts, H. 1984: *On Camera*. BBC.

Watts, H. 1992: *Directing on Camera*. Aavo.

9

Media research and investigation

The purpose of this final chapter is twofold. It aims to provide you with some ideas and information which will help you both to think critically about *doing* some media research and also to assist in your *evaluation* of the different kinds of research evidence and data which you may encounter in a variety of published formats.

The social production of research

It is important to understand that research into the media and forms of mass communication, like many other areas of modern life, does not and has not occurred in a vacuum. In the twentieth century, which is when formal research into the media commenced, research has been shaped, guided and sponsored by many different forces and agencies. These include the commercial media industries themselves and their related networks, the state, government departments and military organisations, advertisers, public opinion analysts, universities and other educational bodies, as well as a range of pressure groups and 'moral entrepreneurs'. These have had important implications for the types of questions that researchers have been able to ask, and how they have tried to answer them. They have motivated and regulated the funding and direction of research in particular ways, towards answering some questions rather than others.

All research sets out to produce evidence, data or insight – answers to questions – and it falls into two parts: the *theory* and the *method*. The theoretical aspect of research concerns the

ACTIVITY 9.1

Make a list of all the different types of organisations that you can think of that have carried out research into the media in the twentieth century. What typical questions have they asked or sought answers to?

questions: how they come to be asked in the first place and what they are related to, especially in terms of an overall view of society or culture. Theories – or ideas, about the world, why and how it is as it is for instance, and how it might develop – require evidence or proof as a kind of test of their claims to truth. This evidence makes them credible and may give them legitimacy over other, competing claims and theories about the world. Theories tend to guide research in a variety of ways, not only suggesting the important questions to be asked but also the choice of research method and how the research results or 'data' will be interpreted and evaluated. A range of research methods have been deployed in the study of the media and cultural processes. These are best thought of as the specialised ways of observing, asking questions or analysing, which are used and applied to create and to interpret research evidence.

Types of research

Research into the various media has been influenced by a number of theories and their disciplines or subject areas. These include Sociology, Psychology, Economics, History and Politics as well as Literary and Cultural Studies or Media, Film and Communications Studies. In broad terms, two particular styles and traditions of research have emerged, often known as the *quantitative* and the *qualitative* approaches. As these titles imply, *quantitative* research seeks to systematically measure or 'quantify' the phenomenon under scrutiny and to express its results in terms of statistical data or tables. Its focus is often on the large-scale patterns which make up a particular population or activity, and its aims are to produce hard, numerical evidence about the world and the way it works. The typical methods used reflect this and would include large-scale surveys and questionnaires, structured opinion polls and interviews, structured forms of observation, content analysis and the analysis of secondary (i.e. from other sources) data and statistics. *Qualitative* research, on the other hand, aims less at measuring and more at understanding, often from 'the inside', the subjects under investigation. It tends to work on a much smaller scale, for instance with specific groups in particular contexts, and focuses on gaining insight into their meanings and values and how they may underpin aspects of social and cultural experience and action. These phenomena cannot, it is argued, simply be 'measured' and are not appropriate to statistical or numerical expres-

ACTIVITY 9.2

Revisit the initial notes you made in chapter 1 concerning cinema attendance in Britain in the post-war period and refer back to figures 1.6, 1.7, and 1.8 (see also figure 4.7, chapter 4). These are all examples of quantitative data and research. Write a short analysis of each table indicating what you think they tell us about the changing nature of cinema in Britain. What kinds of data, from what kinds of sources, have been used to construct them? How reliable and valid are they, in your view? Are there any further questions which you feel are implied or posed by these statistics? How might some qualitative research complement or develop the 'hard' evidence provided here?

sion. As a result, the typical methods involved include participant observation, less structured interviews and discussions, oral histories and forms of textual analysis. The two approaches and their different emphases are often thought of as polar opposites and characterised as mutually antagonistic traditions. In fact, as Bryman (1988), Alasuutari (1995), McNeill (1990) and others have noted, while there are important differences between them, there are also some common issues which bring them together in the interests of more adequate, critical forms of understanding.

In the first chapter of this book, we suggested that Media and Cultural Studies in general are focused on a number of linked stages in a cycle which encompasses production, texts and consumption. You may find it useful to review the discussion on p. 24 and the diagram in figure 1.21. In other words, media research has not only addressed large-scale questions and issues concerning the *overall* role and presence of the various media in society. It has also, in so doing, focused on the particular conditions and contexts of *media producers* and production; the forms of *media output* and discourse which result from their activities, in terms of the texts – programmes, images, front-page headlines, etc. – and their circulation; and finally their reception and use by *media audiences* and consumers. All three, and the interrelationships between them, have formed the basis for very different kinds of media research. Some of this has been *pragmatic*, largely industry-led, designed to provide definite answers to the problems of competition, marketing, sales, forecasting, and so on. Ien Ang (1991) has written a valuable account of the recent history and dilemmas of television companies and their attempts to measure and 'know' their audiences. Other research has been less pragmatic and more *critical* in design, carried out to make interventions into theoretical or policy debates (see for example, research summarised in Van Zoonen, 1994).

In what follows, we offer some tips on approaching research in the areas of media production, media texts and media audiences. You will find it useful to extend and supplement this discussion by consulting some of the general references on research and research methods presented in the *Further reading* section for this chapter.

Researching media production

An interest in the activities and practices of media producers and their working environments is an inescapable part of Media Studies. Not all of this interest is dedicated to learning the vocational skills and techniques of media production (see chapters 7 and 5 for related discussions), much of it simply seeks to understand how, and under what kinds of conditions and constraints, diverse forms of media output are assembled, how they assume the form they do, how they originate and how they change in the production process, and how they are evolving.

If you are interested in doing some research on an aspect of media production, one immediate research problem that you may encounter is *access*. Media organisations and institutions, like many others, are not easily open to researchers or students, especially in terms of the numbers of applications and requests for work experience or observation they often receive. They are more likely to respond positively, however, if you are able to clarify what it is that you are interested in. In this sense, direct approaches to media organisations, locally, as well as nationally (unless you have good contacts!), are likely to be unsuccessful if you have not done some prior research on your topic – on the structure and characteristics of the wider media sector as a whole. A number of trade or industry publications, often reporting quantitative data, can be useful sources here. These include: the annual *Guardian Media Guide*, *BRAD* (*British Rate & Data*), *Benn's Directory*, *Spectrum*, BPI Year Book, BBC and ITV annual reports, *Broadcast*, *Campaign* (see p. 30), *UK Press Gazette*, the *Financial Times*, and the *Zenith Media Guide*; and recently a number of CD-ROM and other databases have been developed. Consulting sources like these should enable you to contextualise your research effectively and to refine and clarify your research questions. Not all questions, however, can be answered from the 'outside' and some will require, ideally, access to the 'inside' worlds of media producers or managers themselves. This cannot be guaranteed, and when it is, may be variable in its terms and conditions.

An interesting study to read in this context is Philip Schlesinger's (1987) account of news production in the BBC in the 1970s. The research was designed to explore how BBC news programmes were put together and in particular how the constraints of time, impartiality and professionalism had consequences for what was reported and broadcast. Schlesinger used two principal methods in his research: direct observation, inside BBC radio and TV newsrooms (some 90 days of observation over a four-year period), and a combination of formal and less formal interviews and discussions (over 120 in all) with news staff.

We will look at interviewing techniques in more detail in a later section; for now, here are some issues to bear in mind about *observation*. As a research technique, it can be used for quantitative ends, for example in counting and classifying the number and types of story that an editor rejects from a particular issue of a magazine. However, it has been widely claimed that the real strengths of observation lie in its ability to provide qualitative insights. The researcher not only observes and records certain patterns and regularities but also gains access to the rules and meanings which both formally and informally comprise the working or producer culture. However, with all observational work, it is important to think about the position of the observer and, in particular, how the observer might affect the behaviour or responses of people being observed. Researchers themselves are seldom invisible, and their own 'appearance' can significantly intervene in, or complicate, the research process. Some researchers have attempted to overcome this problem by either 'participating' in the field – in a way camouflaging themselves as 'not researchers' and becoming part of the culture (a method known as **participant observation**) – or at least allowing sufficient time for people to get used to their presence and for them to fade into the background.

Researching media texts

A variety of approaches have been developed to study media texts and output and to try to investigate how they 'work' and how they 'carry' or activate meanings. In broad terms, these approaches and methods tend to be either quantitative or qualitative in their design and execution. That is, as suggested earlier in this chapter, they aim either to 'measure' media texts – systematically breaking them down into units, categories and frequencies – or they adopt a more qualitative emphasis on understanding and interpreting the interlinked levels or 'layers' of the text in question: the signs, codes and discourses which guide or 'prefer' particular meanings and representations. For those which set out to measure media texts and output such as *content analysis*, the investigation tends to be focused at the *manifest* or surface levels and features of media texts. For those which adopt a more qualitative or interpretative emphasis, as for example in *semiotic* approaches (see discussion in chapter 2), the analysis proceeds from these surface features to encompass latent or deeper-structure, underlying meanings which the texts draw upon and realise in relation to broader cultural formations.

A number of difficult methodological issues are posed in the study of media texts, and in undertaking your own work and in evaluating the work of others, you will find it useful to think through the following general questions.

1 We are all used to watching, listening to, reading and generally consuming media texts and media output as 'part and parcel' of our everyday lives. Interpreting media texts is something we all do as a matter of routine. How does analysis and research differ from these everyday activities? What about the researcher's own position and values? Don't we all have views and opinions about the meanings or significance of media images and output?

2 Often, studies of media texts make distinctions between different 'layers' or levels of meaning which make them up. The 'manifest' or surface features are contrasted with the 'latent' or deeper-structure meanings. One of the suggestions here is that while most people will understand surface meanings, relatively few may be aware of the underlying codes at work in them. Also, the further one goes beneath the surface of any given media text, the more possibilities there may be for multiple meanings and readings. Take some examples of current media output and use them to explore these ideas. How easy is it to distinguish between surface and deeper levels of meaning? Choose examples taken from a range of different media and different forms of output. Can some texts be regarded as more open than others? How do texts encourage or 'load' particular meanings? Review some of your work for activities in chapters 2 and 3.

3 How far can it be argued, and demonstrated, that media texts carry, 'prefer' or determine meanings? Recent work on media texts has tended to emphasise the 'polysemic' nature of much output – that is, in principle, capable of mobilising many meanings and readings. Studies of audiences and their use of media texts has also stressed the importance of recognising the active, plural and unpredictable roles played by people in interpreting media output and of taking into account their diverse contexts of reception and backgrounds in undertanding how meanings are made (review discussion in chapter 4). This emphasis has challenged the idea of the text as the sole bearer or carrier of meaning. To explore this, select some examples of current media output and discuss how they might have very different meanings for different types of audiences or groups of viewers, listeners or readers, depending upon such factors as context, background and identity.

In the remainder of this main section, we focus on content analysis. You should make a point of comparing this approach with that of semiotics, which is discussed in chapter 2.

Content analysis

Content analysis is part of the empirical, social scientific tradition, and it is a method which has been developed to investigate the patterns which characterise manifest or surface features of large quantities of media output. It can be carried out on a small scale, but given that its aims are to produce reliable, valid and generalisable information, the results of small-scale content analysis need to be treated with caution. It has been more typically employed on research projects investigating large-scale trends, changes or patterns, including for example the representation of women and men in a variety of media genres and forms – from country music to advertising, television news, television series and films. Other applications have included mapping the incidence and types of violence in TV programming, as well as studies focused on other social themes, such as media coverage of industrial relations, ethnic groups, crime, or environmental matters. As Lisbet Van Zoonen has suggested,

> In general its aim is to compare features of media output with concomitant features in reality. Thus, a typical conclusion of a content analysis study would be that the occurrence of violence on television grotesquely exaggerates the amount and type of violence one is likely to encounter in

real life. In feminist research, the exemplary conclusion is that media output fails to represent the actual numbers of women in the world (51 per cent) and their contribution to the labour force.

Van Zoonen (1994), p. 69

So, content analysis, in general, is a method which aims to provide a systematic and objective description of the surface features of media texts. It may be used to investigate the broad contours of media output – for instance in exploring the coverage of a given topic or theme: for example, how do the homeless, the disabled or the French appear in British TV news programmes? Figures 9.1 and 9.2 summarise the results of a study carried out in the early 1980s for the Commission for Racial Equality which monitored the number of appearances by actors of different ethnic origin.

Content analysis can also be used to make comparisons between different media – for instance in analysing the different types of content regularly featured in tabloid and broadsheet newspapers in Britain. It has also been employed to monitor or to map historical changes and trends, as for example in Ferguson's (1983) study of the dominant and sub-themes in the contents of large circulation women's magazines in the post-war period. Figure 9.3 presents the results for 1979–80.

Ethnic origin	BBC1					BBC2			
	Week 1	Week 2	Week 3	Total no. of actors	% of total no. of actors	Week 1	Week 2	Total no. of actors	% of total no. of actors
White* (British)	176	133	157	466	92.6	18	32	50	100
West Indian	1	–	1	2	0.4	–	–	–	–
Black (African)	–	1	1	2	0.4	–	–	–	–
Indian	1	1	5	7	1.4	–	–	–	–
White (except British)	8	2	5	15	3.0	–	–	–	–
Middle Eastern	–	–	5	5	1.0	–	–	–	–
Chinese	1	1	2	4	0.8	–	–	–	–
Japanese	1	1	–	2	0.4	–	–	–	–
Black (USA)	–	–	–	–	–	–	–	–	–
Totals	188	139	176	503	100	18	32	50	100

* *Includes Eire/N. Ireland*

Fig. 9.1

Total number of appearances of actors in BBC TV programmes monitored by ethnic origin

Source: Commission for Racial Equality, *Television in a Multi-racial Society*, 1982

Ethnic origin	London					Granada			
	Week 1	Week 2	Week 3	Total no. of actors	% of total no. of actors	Week 1	Week 2	Total no. of actors	% of total no. of actors
White* (British)	273	314	337	924	95.8	298	300	598	96.0
West Indian	6	4	10	20	2.1	6	4	10	1.6
Black (African)	1	1	–	2	0.2	1	1	2	0.3
Indian	1	–	–	1	0.1	1	1	2	0.3
White (except British)	4	6	2	12	1.2	4	6	10	1.6
Middle Eastern	–	–	–	–	–	–	–	–	–
Chinese	–	–	–	–	–	–	–	–	–
Japanese	–	1	–	1	0.1	–	1	1	0.2
Black (USA)	–	–	5	5	0.5	–	–	–	–
Totals	285	326	354	965	100	310	313	623	100

* Includes Eire/N. Ireland

Fig. 9.2
Total number of appearances of actors in ITV programmes monitored by ethnic origin
Source: Commission for Racial Equality, *Television in a Multi-racial Society*, 1982

Stages in content analysis

Content analysis can be applied to written, audio and visual forms of media texts and contents, although these different characteristics have implications for the basic mechanics of the analysis itself. Content analysis is also a method which has been developed to deal with large-scale amounts of media content and this has usually necessitated the use of trained teams of researchers, in recent years often using computers to compile and to analyse results.

The *first stage* of any content analysis should involve defining and 'pinning down' the research problem or question as clearly as possible. At this initial stage, you should be able to explain what it is that you are interested in and which basic patterns or frequencies of media content you are aiming to measure and why. You may even find it useful to think at this stage about how the results of your analysis might be interpreted. Make sure that your research question is one which is both amenable and appropriate to content analysis. Bear in mind, even at this early stage, the practicalities of what you are embarking on: for instance do you have the necessary time, resources and access to media content to manage the analysis you are proposing to carry out? If you do not have all these, you will need to rethink or redesign your proposals.

ACTIVITY 9.3

Prepare a brief summary of the main conclusions which might be drawn from, or argued for, on the basis of the data presented in figures 9.1 to 9.3. At this point, note down any questions which occur to you about the data and their collection.

Dominant themes	W	WO	WW	Total
Self-help: overcoming misfortune	35	32	40	36
Getting and keeping your man	11	10	15	12
Self-help: achieving perfection	13	14	6	11
The happy family	9	12	12	11
Heart versus head	12	8	12	10
The working wife is a good wife	9	13	7	10
Success equals happiness	11	8	8	9
Female state mysterious	–	–	–	–
Gilded youth	–	–	–	–
Other	–	3	–	1
n1	24	24	24	72

Sub-themes	W	WO	WW	Total
Getting and keeping your man	35	24	31	30
Self-help: overcoming misfortune	7	24	17	16
Heart versus head	26	8	14	16
The working wife is a good wife	18	15	15	16
The happy family	–	11	23	12
Self-help: achieving perfection	14	18	–	11
Female state mysterious	–	–	–	–
Gilded youth	–	–	–	–
Success equals happiness	–	–	–	–
Other	–	–	–	–
n2	14	17	12	43

*Excluding beauty
$n1$ = 1 per item, 3 items per issue, 4 issues per year;
$n2$ = open-ended
W = Woman; WO = Woman's Own; WW = Woman's Weekly

Fig. 9.3
*Dominant themes and sub-themes in women's magazines, all subjects, * all titles, 1979–80 (%)*
Source: M. Ferguson, *Forever Feminine: Women's Magazines and the Cult of Femininity*, Heinemann, 1983

This leads on to a *second stage* which involves more detailed planning and preparation. In spite of the fact that content analysis works most effectively when applied to large-scale or total amounts of media output, it is not always possible to cover everything. In fact, it is highly likely that you will need to construct a sample – a systematic selection from total output. If, for instance, you were interested in changes in content of *The Times* newspaper since 1900, it would prove too great a job to analyse every single edition. You would need to select a sample that was manageable but that was also representative, that is, adequately reflecting the overall picture of trends in content since 1900. For example, if you decide to select every edition of *The Times* published on a certain day – Saturdays for sake of argument – your sample may be biased as a result and this will compromise the subsequent analysis. One method used to try and overcome this problem is random sampling – selecting by chance a given number of texts for analysis. Some researchers prefer to use a system of quota sampling, where selection is guided by an agreed pattern: for example, in the case of a long-term newspaper study, you might choose to rotate your sample – starting with Monday's newspaper one week, Tuesday's the second, followed by Wednesday's the next, and so on. In this way the researcher tries to ensure more precisely that the sample will accurately reflect the whole. If your study deals with more than one medium, channel, or range of output, you will need to consider, in detail, precisely which combination of sources your analysis will be based upon.

Having defined your sample or the range of texts to be included in your analysis, you can then proceed to the *third stage* of measurement. The main point behind content analysis is to place parts of the text – the films, programmes, magazines, newspapers, adverts and so on – into certain categories. It sometimes helps to think of an old post office sorting room. Each piece of the text – measured in predefined units – is like a letter being placed or 'posted' into a pigeonhole or category. The idea is to see what kind of pattern is formed when all of the selected content has been divided into the available categories. Units will vary according to the medium, form and scale of the analysis. Words may be used, or pages, or other measures of text, for instance column centimetres. Photographs and components of images can equally form the basis for analysis. In broadcast or film forms, units of time are often employed as well as visual units of appearance or setting. Breaking the text down into units allows you to place it into categories, and these will vary depending on your focus and research question.

Defining the range of categories – the 'pigeonholes' in the sorting process – is of fundamental importance to the analysis. Categories should be very clearly defined and avoid ambiguity. How the categories are defined will directly affect final results. For example, if we were studying the typical contents of tabloid newspapers, we might use a range of categories including 'sports news' and 'news about celebrities' to measure the contents of an agreed sample of current tabloid papers. It would be important that these categories were clearly understood, and how the tabloids would deal with a report of a sports star misbehaving at a celebrity event might be one test of their application.

As with a great deal of research, before carrying out the full-scale analysis, it is a good idea to try out or 'pilot' your study, testing out the units and categories you have adopted, refining or amending them as necessary in the light of this rehearsal. You are then in a position to carry out your analysis.

The *fourth and final stage* takes place after you have completed your measurements and you are able to examine your results and review the analysis as a whole. You will find it useful to ask the following questions:

ACTIVITY 9.4

1 Refer back to your discussions of content analysis based on the data and figures used in the last activity. Discuss those studies in the light of the four stages outlined above. What key issues do they raise for you about content analysis as a research method?

2 Choose a question that interests you about an aspect of current media output or content. Using the four stages above, design and complete, to pilot stage only, a content analysis relevant to your question. Discuss, or give a short presentation on, your outline. After this, you may choose to extend this activity into a more developed or completed analysis if you wish.

- What kinds of patterns does your analysis reveal?
- Do your results provide evidence for, or answers to, your original research question?
- Are there any unexpected features?
- What problems did you encounter in carrying out the analysis?
- Are your results valid – do they reflect the real situation?
- What conclusions can be drawn from your data?

Researching media audiences

How can information about audiences be discovered? Much depends on the *type* of information collected and why it is required. There is a constant production of audience data gathered by market research organisations primarily for commercial purposes. These data are essentially quantitative in nature.

Tables like those reproduced in chapter 1 reveal the broad patterns of media consumption. National totals for television programmes watched (the 'ratings'), newspaper circulation figures, etc., help to inform those working in the various media industries about the relative success of their products in competitive market situations. Although these figures are quite crude in nature, they are still important indicators of cultural consumption. The fact that one in four people in Britain reads the *Sun* each day means it merits much more attention as a media text than, say, *The Times* with an average circulation of about 350 000.

One of the media industries' key motivations to research audiences is to supply data to potential advertisers who are

Programme (Day)	Channel	Week Ending 21 June		
		Production company	Audience share (%)	Audience (millions)
1 Through The Keyhole (Fri)	ITV	Yorkshire	56	9.23
2 Every Second Counts (Thurs)	BBC1	BBC Light Entertainment	42	7.69
3 That's Showbusiness (Sat)	BBC1	BBC North	44	5.43
4 Joker In The Pack (Fri)	BBC1	Action Time	29	5.17
5 Have I Got News For You? (Fri)	BBC2	Hat Trick	16	3.02
5 Fifteen-To-One (Tues)	C4	Regent Television	43	3.02
7 Fifteen-To-One (Wed)	C4	Regent Television	42	2.59
8 Crosswits (Wed)	ITV	Tyne Tees	77	2.55
8 Crosswits (Fri)	ITV	Tyne Tees	78	2.55
10 Fifteen-To-One (Fri)	C4	Regent Television	34	2.51

Fig. 9.4

Top ten quiz shows – adults
Source: *Television Week*, July 1992

Programme	Day/Time	Week Ending 21 June	
		Men (millions)	Women (millions)
Through The Keyhole	Fri (7pm)	3.32	5.91
Every Second Counts	Thurs (8pm)	2.56	5.13
That's Showbusiness	Sat (6.35pm)	2.49	2.95
Joker In The Pack	Fri (8.30pm)	2.13	3.05
Have I Got News For You?	Fri (10pm)	1.53	1.48
Fifteen-To-One	Wed (4.30pm)	1.31	1.71
Crosswits	Mon (9.26am)	0.72	1.84
The Crystal Maze	Thurs (8.30pm)	0.78	1.41
The Music Game	Fri (8.30pm)	0.61	0.94
Treasure Hunt	Tues (6pm)	0.46	0.54

Fig. 9.5

Quiz shows* – audience by gender
Source: *Television Week*, July 1992

Programme	Week Ending 21 June Audience (millions)					
	18–24	25–34	35–44	45–54	55–64	65+ yrs
Through The Keyhole	0.78	1.22	1.24	1.18	1.39	3.42
Every Second Counts	0.87	1.27	1.15	1.05	1.13	2.22
That's Showbusiness	0.69	0.94	0.96	0.68	0.80	1.36
Joker In The Pack	0.57	1.06	0.94	0.65	0.66	1.30
Have I Got News For You?	0.32	0.57	0.73	0.44	0.42	0.53
Fifteen-To-One	0.15	0.18	0.19	0.32	0.56	1.62
Crosswits	0.20	0.35	0.36	0.37	0.36	0.92
The Crystal Maze	0.37	0.45	0.51	0.24	0.26	0.36
The Music Game	0.30	0.35	0.21	0.16	0.15	0.38
Treasure Hunt	0.16	0.20	0.19	0.12	0.08	0.25

* Where programme is stripped (broadcast on several or many nights of the week), table shows highest rating single show in the week

Fig. 9.6

Quiz shows* – audience by age group
Source: *Television Week*, July 1992

looking to reach their target consumers in the most effective way. There has been an increasing trend towards monitoring the social profiles of media audiences. Such demographic data reveal how audiences are composed in terms of variables like social class, age and gender. This is valuable as a preliminary

Programme	AB	Week Ending 21 June Audience (millions)		
		C1	C2	DE
Through The Keyhole	1.21	2.07	2.10	3.85
Every Second Counts	0.85	1.81	2.09	2.95
That's Showbusiness	0.77	1.40	1.40	1.87
Joker In The Pack	0.56	1.04	1.44	2.13
Have I Got News For You?	0.94	0.89	0.73	0.46
Fifteen-To-One	0.32	0.55	0.76	1.40
Crosswits	0.18	0.51	0.59	1.27
The Crystal Maze	0.33	0.58	0.60	0.68
The Music Game	0.25	0.38	0.36	0.57
Treasure Hunt	0.08	0.22	0.31	0.38

What explanations could be offered to account for the patterns revealed in figures 9.4–9.7?

* Where programme is stripped, table shows highest rating single show in the week

Fig. 9.7

Quiz shows* – audience by social class
Source: Television Week, July 1992

point of reference for audience research which seeks to investigate patterns of use, and it then may go on to ask how and why social groups respond differently to the media (see figures 9.4 to 9.7). For instance, what conclusions might be drawn from the analysis of these tables, compiled in 1992?

Some audience research has relied almost exclusively on quantitative data. The correlation of television viewing figures and attitudinal surveys according to sociodemographic variables like age and family membership has been used in *cultivation analysis*. This is designed to test whether television viewing could be said to influence general attitudes to the world. For example, Gerbner and Gross (1976) argue that the more television you watch, the more likely you are to have a fearful or distrustful attitude to the world outside.

However, quantitative data do have serious limitations for media studies. In short, they reveal little about the meanings audiences produce from media texts and the context in which such texts are received. An example to illustrate this point is the television ratings figures compiled by the Broadcasters Audience Research Board (BARB). These measure the audience size via a sample of 4500 computer-linked homes in which meters are installed. When members of the household select a programme to view, the meter records their presence and which channel is chosen. What is not measured, though, is whether the set is actually being watched, the motivation for watching, how much social interaction is happening within the room, and the kind of meaningful response produced by the programme. Currently, the only supplementary information systematically gathered is audience appreciation statistics – an index of how interesting and/or enjoyable viewers found a particular programme.

Research questionnaires

Questionnaires are survey methods routinely used in the investigation of media consumption, although they can also be deployed to find out about aspects of media production or organisational policy and practice. They come through the letterbox, in newspapers and magazines, and they often form the basis for structured interviews in the street, shopping centre or over the telephone. Among the advantages sometimes claimed for them as research methods are their accuracy, their access to a wide range or dispersal of respondents and their flexibility. Disadvantages might include their expense, problems of no return or delayed response, and difficulties or ambiguities in design and response. Questionnaires are frequently employed to gather quantitative data and information about large-scale, representative populations, offering a choice of predetermined responses (the simplest being YES/NO tick boxes), although most will allow some space for more qualitative or open-ended forms of response. Questionnaires are usually administered by post or in written form, although they may also be the basis for telephone or other surveys where they operate as sequences of questions which are asked: the basis for more interactive and direct forms of survey.

Developing a questionnaire

As in the case of conducting a content analysis, outlined earlier in this chapter, there are a series of stages involved in developing and carrying out a research project based around the use of a questionnaire. This may be the sole method to be used, or it may be used to explore a particular part or phase of an overall research problem. Initially, it is useful to clarify, discuss and define which responses you are interested in, and why. There should be a clear point to your questionnaire and you should be able to make out a convincing case for using a questionnaire in your study.

In developing a questionnaire, you will need initially to identify your topic area carefully and develop a sequence of appropriate questions. The sequence or order of questions may be an important factor, what you ask first and so on, and you will need to plan the length of the questionnaire overall. You will also need to consider the *sample size*, in other words, how many respondents you are aiming for and why. You will also need to think carefully about the *type of respondents* you are

---

ACTIVITY 9.5

Gather together a number of questionnaires from magazines, newspapers or other media-related sources. Analyse and discuss their design and respective distribution methods. What kinds of information have they been constructed to collect and why? How might they be improved?

hoping to contact and elicit responses from. For instance, if your study is one which explores general patterns of radio use your questionnaire will be different from one which seeks to investigate the use of radio by young women in the home.

As Rothwell (1996) has suggested, most questionnaires are made up of a number of standard components, although these will vary depending on the purpose and scale of your project. The typical components include:

a A **title**

b An **identifying number.** This may be especially important where you wish to preserve the confidentiality of information collected. The number allows you to identify each individual respondent without necessarily revealing their name, status, etc.

c **Introductory remarks.** These may take the form of a covering letter supplied with the questionnaire or may be integrated into the opening section. This should explain the purpose of the survey, who is conducting it and why, and it is usual to provide assurances concerning the anonymity or confidentiality of data to be collected.

d **Instructions** for completing the questionnaire. Unless these are self-evident, they are usually provided just before the particular sections or questions to be answered. Typically they will explain the mode of response required – ticking boxes, circling numbers, etc. You may also need to indicate how the questionnaire should be returned for analysis.

e **Respondent details.** These may cover such matters as name, address, age, gender, occupation, etc. These details are often collected in an opening or closing section of the questionnaire. Remember to indicate that confidentiality will be preserved with regard to these and other details, as this may have a bearing on how your respondents answer your questions.

f **Focal data and questions.** These are questions or items which you will use to gather data on the attitudes, opinions or practices which lie at the heart of your investigation. These may take the form of what are known as *closed questions*, where the response is predetermined, typically the kinds which ask the respondent to tick boxes or circle numbers. For instance:

Do you own a compact disc player?   YES[ ]   NO[ ]

You can *list* a set of response *options*:

How long have you owned a personal stereo?
Less than 6 months [ ]
1 to 2 years [ ]
3 to 5 years [ ]
More than 5 years [ ]

You can also make use of questions which involve *scaling* or *ranking* where the respondent either chooses a point on a scale which you have predetermined, or is required to rank a number of given items or possibilities in order of preference, importance or significance. Examples of *scaled questions*:

How often do you listen to radio programmes in the evening?

Nearly always...Often...Seldom...Hardly ever
   1   2   3   4

Sometimes a statement may be used to stimulate a scaled response:

Television soap opera serials deal effectively with important social issues.

Agree strongly...Tend to agree...Tend to disagree...Disagree strongly
   1   2   3   4

In some cases, questionnaires may make use of the *semantic differential*, where words are used to establish the ends of a scaled dimension. For example:

Describe your favourite female film star by circling the numbers on the scales below which most closely correspond to your choice:

Strong	1 2 3 4 5 6 7	Weak
Active	1 2 3 4 5 6 7	Passive
Glamorous	1 2 3 4 5 6 7	Ordinary
Always the same	1 2 3 4 5 6 7	Varied performance
Like me	1 2 3 4 5 6 7	Not like me

Example of question using *ranked responses* to show preference:

Place a number from 1 to 7 in the left-hand column adjacent to each item to indicate your preferences for weekend television viewing.

[ ] Comedy programmes
[ ] Feature films
[ ] Cartoons
[ ] Sports programmes
[ ] Music programmes
[ ] Game shows
[ ] News and Documentary programmes

g **Open questions.** In contrast to closed questions, open-ended questions do not have predetermined options for the respondent and allow for a much greater range of unpredictable responses or answers. The main purpose of open questions is to allow the respondent to express their own views or ideas on the given topic. An example would be:

What do you think about the coverage of sport on television?

Responses to open questions like this one are more difficult to analyse because of their unpredictability. Usually, they will allow a space for the respondent to write their answer, and open questions are conventionally situated at the end, either of a given section or of the questionnaire as a whole.

h **Closing remarks.** You should always make a point of thanking your respondents and indicating how the questionnaire will be collected or should be returned to you.

As well as designing your questions and laying out your questionnaire to take account of these components, you should try to follow the following schedule and sequence in managing the overall project (adapted from Rothwell, 1996). Obviously, the sequence and times indicated may vary considerably, depending on the time available and the specific form and range of investigation aimed for.

a	Identify topic areas and develop initial questions and format	1 week
b	Discuss with tutor and revise	1 week
c	Try out or *pilot* questionnaire and revise	1 week
d	Print questionnaire and distribute	1 week
e	Wait for responses, possible follow-up	2 weeks
f	Collate, analyse and write up data	2 weeks
g	Review effectiveness of questionnaire and complete final report	1 week
	Total:	*9 weeks*

ACTIVITY 9.6

Choose a topic or an issue which you have encountered on your course in Media Studies which particularly interests you. Write some notes on how it might be researched using a questionnaire. Outline key questions and think about how you would interpret possible responses. If possible, discuss your outline notes with a tutor and other students.

If it is appropriate, design, pilot and carry out a small-scale questionnaire survey. You might choose, for instance, to compare aspects of large-scale, national or other patterns of media consumption with those which you research in particular, local circumstances.

Qualitative approaches: ethnographies and interviews

Qualitative research seeks to uncover audience interpretations and observations via in-depth personal interviews and discussions with individuals or small groups. At its best, it should allow subjects to express their responses freely in as natural a setting as possible. Such an approach is sometimes called 'ethnographic' to refer to an emphasis derived from anthropological studies where the researcher sometimes tries to fit in with, and be accepted by, the people, group or subculture being studied. It has been influential in much recent audience research, especially with respect to studies of television viewing. Nevertheless, ethnographic and other qualitative approaches in general are not without their problems. Reliance on subjects' own perceptions and accounts, for instance, assumes that they are fully conscious of how they are responding to a media text. Thus, there is a need for skilful interviewing to probe beyond glib or surface comments, while avoiding the temptation to put words in people's mouths:

> Eighteen families were interviewed in their own homes during the spring of 1985. Initially the two parents were interviewed, then later in each interview their children were invited to take part in the discussion along with their parents. The interviews, which lasted between one and two hours, were tape-recorded and then transcribed in full for analysis.
>
> The fact that the interviews were conducted *en famille* doubtless means that respondents felt a certain need to play

out accepted roles, and doubtless interviews with family members separately would bring out other responses. However, I was precisely interested in how they functioned *as families*, within (and against) their roles.

Moreover, the interviewing method (unstructured discussion for a period between one and two hours) was designed to allow a fair degree of probing. Thus on points of significance I returned the discussion to the same theme at different stages in the interview, from different angles. This means that anyone 'putting me on' (consciously or unconsciously) by representing themselves through an artificial/stereotyped *persona* which has no bearing on their 'real' activities would have to be able to sustain their adopted *persona* through what could be seen as quite a complex form of interrogation!

Morley (1986)

Research interviews: questions and answers

Interviews are a research method which can be employed to investigate a wide variety of research problems and projects. We may commonly encounter them in the street, supermarket, at the door, or on the telephone. They have become a major part of market research, public-opinion polling and other forms of social and commercial enquiry. In this section, we have assumed that you are interested in carrying out a study rather like Morley's, that is, small-scale and informal, aiming at insights into people's values and attitudes, *their* reasons and explanations for their media-related activities and forms of consumption or reception.

A consistent theme in discussions of interviewing as a research practice emphasises the basic point that if you want to find out something about people's activities, then the best way is to ask them. Research interviews, it is claimed, can give direct access to unique forms of experience and expression often denied by other methods. The strengths of interviews often include: their freedom (both the interviewer and interviewee are allowed to explore and negotiate the particular topic); their directness of contact, feedback and response; and their in-depth detail. Criticisms of projects which rely on interviews tend to include: questions of bias or distortion; their narrow and non-representative nature; and issues of interpretation and (mis)understanding.

The informal interview

If you opt for a project based on informal interviews, then you are probably interested in gaining qualitative insights or understanding of the meanings, interpretations, values and experiences of a small group of people. This may be the sole aim of the study, or you may choose to combine this approach with other methods, for example in linking textual analysis of a given item of media output to the study of its actual reception – how people respond to an advertising campaign, for instance. The task of the interviewer is to create and adapt to the conditions under which the interviewee will disclose or 'open up' their particular version or unique 'inside story' relevant to the topic under investigation. As a result, you will need to be alive to the multiple, often divergent perspectives, values and views held by people, and assume that you will encounter these. Informal interviews, in contrast to the more formal survey, adopt a conversational, flexible and more open-ended format, where the strict roles of interviewer and interviewee do not, ideally, intervene in the discussion. Rather than asking closed questions, researchers using this approach will employ open-ended, non-directed questions (see above under *Developing a questionnaire*). The interviewer will not work with a fixed schedule of questions, often preferring a loose sequence of themes or points to be covered in discussion. Informal interviews will also tend to be carried out in 'natural' settings – the home, household, workplace, club, or other social setting, on 'territory' familiar to the interviewee rather than to the interviewer.

In general terms, researchers using informal interviews often also draw on observation, in some cases participant observation. They should also pay more attention to the process of each interview – including their own part in it – and how this might have implications for the insights gathered as a result; this is termed 'reflexivity'. The aim is to act less as an 'interrogator' and more as a 'guide' in the conduct of the interview and in the mutual process of 'finding out about' the topics being researched.

Stages in the informal interview

There is no one correct way to conduct an informal interview, and the process will generally require more skill, patience and insight on the part of the interviewer than are involved in the survey situation. The steps in the research procedure can be summarised as follows (adapted from O'Sullivan, 1996):

1 **Specification.** This initial, preparatory, stage has much in common with the first stages of any research procedure. It should involve, as a result, the precise definition of the aims of the study, of research on any other sources of relevant

information, and a general clarification of goals. You will need to think through, and be able to defend, your choice of informal interviewing in terms of your chosen subject matter or topic selected for study. You should make a point of clearly establishing the limits to the study and clarifying your themes and questions for the interviews. How you will record the interviews is an issue which should be considered at this stage. Some piloting of your proposed sequence is also invaluable now, and you should discuss your research ideas with tutors and other students.

2 **Contact.** You will need to select and contact your potential interviewees. You may know them or not, they may be involved in a particular group or location. Think carefully about who and how you select for your interviews. When you make contact with them you should be able to briefly outline the nature of your research and the subjects you will want to cover in the interview. In general the interviewer will make her/himself available to suit the convenience of the interviewee, and it is the interviewee who usually nominates the meeting place. You, in turn, should be able to let them know approximately how long the interview will take and reassure them about the confidentiality of the proceedings.

3 **Interviewing.** There is considerable debate about the best ways to record informal types of interview. The attempt to put people at their ease, or to 'fit in' with social circumstances, is often undermined by the practice of recording what is said. Many people are put off by, or at least wary of, large microphones being waved under their noses, even when (or especially when) they have been told to 'relax'. Researchers can use either one or a combination of the following techniques:

- Notes written by the interviewer during the interview.
- Memory, with notes written up after the interview.
- Audio-tape recording, from which transcripts – written records – may be made.
- Video recording, from which transcripts may also sometimes be made.

All these have their relative merits and drawbacks. Note-taking or audio-tape recording are perhaps the two commonest methods, although the issue of how the act and means of recording may 'distort' the outcomes and conduct of the interview deserves important consideration. It is always useful to make a careful note of the date and circumstances of the interview, the name of the interviewee and any other details relevant to the project. It may be important to reiterate your reassurance to the interviewee about the confidential nature of the interview. In some circumstances it is also useful to ascertain, before beginning the interview, how much time is available so that you can pace the interview accordingly. About one hour is usually regarded as a rough guide for the minimum time needed to conduct a productive interview, although flexibility is needed here. The main questions and sequence of key themes may have been decided in advance, but discussion and follow-up questions cannot always be anticipated. Most interviewers have to 'think on their feet', and the use of prompt questions – to draw out or to follow up a particular response – can be very valuable in keeping the interview flowing along the right lines.

4 **Analysis.** Having completed as many interviews as possible or appropriate to your project, and depending on the method of recording, you will now have a mass of 'raw' information. Once a collection of interviews has been gathered, how can the material be analysed and organised? In general, analysis requires that you first thoroughly familiarise yourself with your information, 'immersing' yourself in the different interviewees' accounts. Wherever possible, common themes and patterns should be identified, for instance in classifying discourses or recurrent points of reference. You may also need to be alive to key similarities or differences of interpretation or response and deal with the problem of explaining the wider origins of these similarities or differences. In our media-saturated society (see chapter 1), responses to any single media text are bound to be influenced by exposure to previous related texts – what has been called intertextuality. For example, filmgoers viewing *Batman* may be influenced by having read the comics as children, seen the television series, been exposed to the publicity, had preconceptions about star performers like Jack Nicholson, and so on. Furthermore, individuals' frameworks of interpretation can always be seen as being partly a product of negotiating social determinants and identities such as class, gender, ages, nationality and ethnicity. This has formed a key theme and problem for much ethnographic audience research.

In the final stage of analysis, you will often have to write up your research report, and this will be supported by quotations or extracts from your interviews. In the context of the research problem that you began with, what have your interviewees told you about the topic under investigation?

Group interviews

As a basis for particular research projects, researchers have used interviews not only with individuals but also with groups of people. The benefits of this approach stem from the potential for discussion to develop among the group members and the value of this as a research resource. Market researchers, for instance, regularly employ 'focus groups' in their work. These are groups of consumers who are brought together by the interviewer to discuss and evaluate aspects of a product range, or an established or new brand. In a similar fashion, other recent forms of audience research have used family or household groups, groups of schoolchildren, women, or other groupings. Group interviews can be especially valuable when, in reality, it is the group or subculture which the researcher wants to investigate rather than the subject they are discussing. However, if you do use group interviews, you will need to manage and to be aware of the group dynamics in the conduct of the interview.

ACTIVITY 9.7

a Revisit the first chapter in this book. Plan and carry out an informal interview with a colleague, friend or family member about their everyday relationships with different types and forms of media. What conclusions might be drawn from this interview?

b Conduct a series of interviews as part of a local oral history project on either memories of cinema before the Second World War, or memories of early television. What do these interviews provide which you could not get from other research sources?

c Design and carry out a series of interviews with people to explore their attitudes to either satellite television (at least two with those who do have domestic access and two with those who do not), or a recent widespread advertising campaign. You may define and negotiate any other approved topic if appropriate. Summarise your main findings and present them to a group on your course.

Further reading

Alasuutari, P. 1995: *Researching Culture: Qualitative Method and Cultural Studies*. Sage.

Bell, J. 1987: *Doing Your Research Project*. Open University Press.

Berger, A. 1991: *Media Analysis Techniques*. Sage.

Bryman, A. 1988: *Quantity and Quality in Social Research*. Unwin Hyman.

Fairclough, N. 1995: *Media Discourse*. Arnold.

Hammersley, M. and Atkinson, P. 1983: *Ethnography: Principles in Practice*. Tavistock.

Jensen, K.B. and Jankowski, N.W. (eds). 1991: *A Handbook of Qualitative Methodologies for Mass Communication Research*. Routledge.

Krueger, R.A. 1994: *Focus Groups: A Practical Guide for Applied Research*. Sage.

McNeill, P. 1990: *Research Methods*. Routledge.

Morley, D. 1992: *Television, Audiences and Cultural Studies*. Routledge.

Oppenheim, A.N. 1992: *Questionnaire Design, Interviewing and Attitude Measurement*. Blackwell.

O'Sullivan, T. 1996: 'Research interviews', in B. Allison, T. O'Sullivan, A. Owen, J. Rice, A. Rothwell and C. Saunders (eds), *Research Skills for Students*. Kogan Page.

Rothwell, A. 1996: 'Questionnaire design', in Allison, B., *et al. Research Skills for Students*. Kogan Page.

Tolson, A. 1996: *Mediations: Text and Discourse in Media Studies*. Arnold.

Weber, R.P. 1990: *Basic Content Analysis*. Sage.

Note: Terms in italics are defined within the glossary.

Aberrant decoding – an interpretation which, rather than recognise the *preferred meaning* of a media text, produces instead a deviant or unanticipated reading.

Anchorage – the fixing or limiting of a particular set of meanings to an image, often a photograph or advert, usually through the use of a caption or other written text.

Audience positioning – the process whereby *media texts* work to situate the reader, spectator, etc. from a particular point of view or perspective.

Auteur – a film director who, it is claimed, is able to imbue his/her films with a recognisably distinctive personal vision or style.

Bricolage – the process of deliberately 'borrowing' or adapting signs or features from different styles or *genres* to create a new mixture of meanings; often associated with *postmodernism*.

Broadcasting flow – a reference to the continuous stream of television and radio output within which there is often a lack of distinctive programme boundaries.

Classical narrative structure – the dominant mode of storytelling found in Hollywood films, which involves three distinctive stages: a state of order or *equilibrium*, a disruption to that stability, and a climactic resolution which restores order and a new equilibrium and harmony.

Code – an organised cultural system of signs, language or symbols, and its rules, which govern and allow for the communication of meanings and interpretations.

Consensus – the set of ideas, beliefs and values that are shared and agreed by the majority of the population, the centre ground that by definition often excludes alternative positions.

Consumer society – modern complex *cultures* and societies which are defined by a dominant orientation towards the marketing and consumption of goods and services. These, it is argued, play central roles in the lifestyle cultures of modern times and in related processes which allow for the formation of identities. In consumer cultures, groups and individuals are increasingly defined in terms of their patterns of consumption, choice and expression, as related to leisure, clothing, music, food and many other goods and activities.

Content analysis – a research method used to systematically measure or compare the characteristics of selected samples of media output and content.

Convention – a widely accepted and recognised rule or device relating to aspects of *media texts* and their production and consumption.

Cropping – the process of cutting down an image, usually a photograph, to focus on one particular aspect or meaning and to eliminate superfluous detail.

Cultural capital/competence – the particular knowledge, experience, taste and skills possessed by audiences which shape their choice and interpretation of *media texts*. Cultural capital is related to social class and other divisions, especially to educational experience and career.

Culture – often understood as the 'whole way of life' which distinguishes a society or social group. Culture refers especially to the systems of ideas, beliefs and values which characterise and make up the world of the group and the systems which allow for communication, representation and meaning, from languages to computers, music and digital images. (See also *Mediated culture, Popular culture, Situated cultures* and *Surveillance culture*.)

Demographics – demographic data refers to the social characteristics of the population being studied, e.g. social class, gender and age. For the purposes of media analysis, it is particularly helpful in identifying the social profile of the audience.

Denotation/Connotation – different 'levels' of meaning within a text: the first level, **denotation**, represents only what the text shows whereas the second level, **connotation**, includes the additional associations (or information) that the reader (or producer) brings to the image or text and 'adds' to the denotative meaning.

Deregulation – relaxing the commercial controls and limitations on the media imposed by the state, usually focusing in particular on ownership and range or requirements of services and their quality.

Encoding/Decoding – the linked processes of constructing and interpreting *media texts* as they are conceived, transmitted and received, involving producers (who **encode** meanings) and receivers (who **decode** the meanings).

Equilibrium/Disequilibrium – the tensions of *narrative*. A secure and harmonious state is often used to begin many media narratives. This equilibrium or balance is conventionally followed and disturbed by tension or events which cause unpredictability or disequilibrium to occur. The typical 'happy ending' requires the restoration of the balance or equilibrium depicted at the beginning.

Ethnography – a research method which aims to understand the social perspective and cultural values of a particular group, from the 'inside', by participating with or getting to know their activities in depth and in detail.

Femme fatale – a seductive and powerful female character who is able to entrap and exploit men for personal gain.

Film noir – a *genre* of films characterised by a distinctive visual style – low-key and high-contrast lighting emphasising light and shadows, and a *narrative* focusing on the dark side of human life.

Fly-on-the-wall documentary – a television documentary form which is characterised by unobtrusively filming subjects in their natural settings, and representing them with a minimum of on-screen presenter or voice-over narration, as if the camera was not there.

Gatekeeper – a journalist, especially an editor, who filters the flow of news stories in order to select which stories will be presented to the audience. The term is also applied to other decision-makers within media and cultural industries.

Genre – a way of categorising texts by identifying certain common characteristics in style, *narrative* and structure.

Global culture (Globalisation) – the results of greatly increased, worldwide, media and communication systems and the activities of international cultural markets. The local and the national are now linked in many ways to a wider world culture. **Globalisation** refers to the international economic, political and cultural processes which have accelerated this growth post-1950.

Global village – a phrase which is used to describe the ways in which modern electronic media have spread around, interconnected and 'shrunk' the world, making possible seemingly immediate forms of communication and cultural relationships associated in the past with small-scale communities.

Hegemony – the theory that those in power maintain domination through cultural influence rather than force. Cultural agencies such as the media privilege dominant ideologies (that serve to disguise the realities of social injustice) which prevail over competing or alternative ideas through becoming accepted as 'commonsense' wisdom.

Hypodermic needle model – a theory which asserts that the media are powerful agents of influence, capable of 'injecting' ideas and behaviours directly into relatively passive audiences of isolated individuals.

Identification – the processes by which readers of a text negotiate a certain position with regard to its *narrative*, points of view and characters.

Ideology – a set of ideas, or a world view, which produces a partial and selective version of reality often to protect the interests of powerful social groups.

Independents – media producers who are free from control by larger media organisations and who are often more willing and able to engage in newer, less conservative forms of *media production*.

Integration – horizontal and vertical – horizontal integration occurs when a company takes over a competitor at the same level of production within the same market sector; **vertical integration** occurs when a company takes over another company which occupies a different stage of the manufacturing or distribution cycle.

International media flow – the patterns of import and export, *media production* and *media consumption* which result from the operation of worldwide media and cultural markets for films, television programmes, music, adverts, etc. Some countries and regions produce and export, others import and consume. Such patterns and relations of 'flow' have important consequences for identity and *globalisation*.

Internet – globally interconnected telecommunication and computer network systems which allow for diverse forms of interactivity and data interchange.

Intertextuality – the way in which *media texts* gain their meanings by referring to other media texts that the producers assume that the reader will be familiar with and recognise.

Male gaze – a term derived from feminist film theory which asserts that men are able to exercise control over women by representing them (through the camera lens) as passive sexual objects of male desire.

Manifest and latent meanings – different layers or levels of meaning within any one *media text* or item of media content. The distinction is associated with *content analysis*, which aims at the surface, unambiguous or manifest levels of meaning as opposed to the latent, deeper levels of interpretation.

Mass manipulation model – (see *Hypodermic needle model*)

Mass media (Mass communication) – organised and specialised modern *media institutions* such as the press, cinema and broadcasting, whose principal business involves the supply of the demand for forms of information and entertainment. *Mass communication* is used to describe what these agencies do, what they produce. Attached to both terms – and others, for example 'mass culture' or 'mass audience' – is the prefix 'mass'. This carries a series of one-dimensional assumptions about the homogeneity of the audience and the direct influence of the media.

Media concentration – a situation characterised by the domination of media markets by a small number (usually four or five) of large media corporations.

Media consumption – usually patterned activities of reading, watching, listening and buying which makes up interaction with media texts and output. These are consumed in the sense of being used, involving our time, attention, money and so on. In the process, this use contributes to and takes place within wider symbolic and cultural settings and contexts.

Media and cultural imperialism – the use of media and communication systems to establish worldwide influence and dominance. International media and their markets are significant networks for political and cultural values and forms of identity, playing a key role in relations of dominance or dependence. Many 'developing nations' face problems maintaining cultural autonomy and independent identity in the face of western and other forms of media export and output.

Media institutions – the historical organisations, routines and practices associated with the production and consumption of particular media forms such as television and cinema.

Media involvement – people's patterned and everyday involvement with the media. A distinction has been made between primary, secondary and tertiary forms of media involvement. These range from situations of high (**primary**) involvement, where listening, viewing or reading are the exclusive, focused activities, through those (**secondary**) where involvement accompanies other social or domestic activities, to the weakest, 'background' (**tertiary**) forms of interaction.

Media production – the organised processes and activities involved in making and distributing *media texts* and output. These usually require groups or teams of people working in a variety of commercial, technical and media settings and hierarchies.

Media reception – reading and making sense of *media texts* and output within particular locations and cultural contexts.

Media regulation – the laws, rules and guidelines which operate to define and restrict the parameters of what can be legitimately produced in the media. These may originate from state, government, commercial or other bodies and agencies.

Media saturation – a term used to describe the centrality and pervasiveness of the media and of mediated experience in modern, twenty-first-century cultures. This implies the increasing involvement of the media in public, national and global life, the growth of time and expenditure spent in private, everyday *media involvement*, and the popularity of media-related or media-derived activities. As a result, media are held to 'saturate' society, culture and identity.

Mediated culture and **Mediation** – the ideas, images, knowledge, values, and so on, which are derived from modern media. **Mediated culture** comes from beyond our individual, daily or immediate experience. It results from media organisations who produce and *encode* versions of events and issues in their output. These are **mediated** into our individual contexts and situations.

Media texts – the output of the media in general and in particular: programmes, films, magazines, advertisements and so on. Media texts may be written, as in the case of newspapers and magazines, but also assume many other combinations of written, audio and visual media forms.

Mise en scène – whatever appears in a film frame – the setting, characters, lighting, props, etc.

Mode of address – how a *media text* speaks to its particular audience, and in so doing, helps to form the nature of the relationship between producer and audience.

Multimedia – the convergence of previously discrete media systems – the camera, the typewriter, the audio and video recorder – into new computer- and digitally based systems capable of managing diverse forms of data and format.

Multinational multimedia conglomerates – very large commercial organisations whose operations involve competition in worldwide markets across a range of television, film, press, music and other information and cultural sectors.

Myth – a social and historically determined idea which has gained the status of accepted truth or naturalness.

Narrative – the organisation, structure and dynamics of 'stories' derived from media and other sources.

Narrowcasting – the opposite of broadcasting, where programmes are aimed at quite specific, special-interest or minority audiences.

Naturalism – a commitment to representing the world in a manner which reproduces the surface detail as accurately as possible.

New media technologies – the large-scale technical developments in communication systems of the moment and their cultural consequences. A term which is used to refer to cable, satellite, digital and other computer-based media in the current phase.

News values – the criteria employed by journalists when deciding which stories are most newsworthy.

Open/Closed text – an **open text** is one which lacks a clear *preferred meaning* and is capable of several different readings. A **closed text** is one in which there is little scope for differential readings (because its preferred meaning is overtly *anchored*).

Oppositional decoding – an interpretation of a *media text* which involves a conscious rejection and subversion of its *preferred meaning*.

Participant observation – a method of research where the researcher attempts to become part of the *culture*, group or activity under investigation and records the 'inside stories' which take place.

Pluralism – the theory that power is dispersed among a range of interest groups in society, and that no one group is able to exercise consistent dominance. This plurality of power, it is argued, is reflected in the diversity of ideas and views found in the media.

Polysemic – reflecting the idea that all signs and texts are capable of many potential meanings and readings, and can be *decoded* in a variety of ways according to many factors, including the particularities of the *situated culture* of the reader.

Popular culture – the everyday activities, styles and way of life of 'ordinary people, including media forms such as pop music and television. It is often dismissed as trashy and throwaway in contrast to the perceived superiority and demands of 'high' culture such as classical music or literature. Popular culture may articulate tensions or challenges to the dominant status quo, as well as endorsing it or reinforcing it.

Postmodernism – the cultural and social conditions which are claimed to have replaced and superseded earlier forms of modern twentieth-century life. These involve, and result from, the rapid growth of media and communications systems, of global *culture* and widespread insecurities concerning identity, history, progress and truth. Some *media texts* and output are said to be postmodern in style, mixing irony, parody and pastiche across conventional *genres*.

Preferred meaning/reading – the ways in which texts are constructed to encourage the reader towards a dominant or consensual interpretation.

Primary and Secondary sources – in terms of research, **primary** data are those which you generate yourself, through your own direct investigation of a topic. **Secondary** data are those which you read about or consult at various stages in the research process.

Private sphere – the household, home or domestic space and the *situated culture* which characterises it. Often contrasted or counterposed with the *public sphere*.

Propaganda – media images and campaigns which are designed and managed to promote – or discredit – a particular point of view, ideology or party line. This is achieved through emphasis, manipulation, partial selection or suppression of information and imagery, with the aim of persuading audiences.

Public opinion – in the modern period this has come to be associated with the views and debates articulated in news coverage and other forms of media coverage of issues defined as significant to modern, democratic citizens. Media coverage often represents public opinion, in the form of opinion polls, etc.

Public service broadcasting – the policy enshrined within the BBC under John Reith and carried into all aspects of broadcasting in the UK until the 1990 Broadcasting Act. The policy guaranteed broadcasters a degree of autonomy from both commercial pressures and political interests in their mission to provide services for the national audience that 'informed, educated and entertained'.

Public sphere – the world of political and cultural affairs and events associated with modern, especially democratic, societies. The media, in large part, construct, relay and *mediate* this in their operations and coverage.

Qualitative methods – research practices which aim at understanding and interpreting social and cultural relations rather than measuring them.

Quantitative methods – research practices which aim to measure and statistically analyse social and cultural phenomena, usually on the basis of large-scale, representative samples of people, opinions or data.

Radical press – a label applied particularly to the various wings of the working-class and oppositional newspaper press in Britain beginning in the late eighteenth century. It refers more generally to newspapers or other publications – pamphlets, magazines, etc. – which have been produced and written to challenge or change aspects of the social and political order.

Realism – the degree to which media representations accurately reflect the way things really are, and not as we would wish them to be. There is no one criterion by which the realism of a *media text* may be judged.

Reality television – those television programmes specifically designed to represent 'ordinary' experience, people in real-life situations, utilising actual or sometimes reconstructed scenes of real events.

Representation – the cultural activity of making and communicating meanings. Events, people and issues are represented in media output, and may be represented in diverse and contrasting ways.

Ritual media interaction – patterned and regular contacts with the media which have special and social symbolic value. For instance, identifying with certain musical styles, or the images of particular film stars or media personalities, may have a ritualised social significance.

Scheduling – the process by which broadcast programmes are sequenced to ensure each programme maximises its potential audience.

Semiotics – the study of signs, sign systems and their meanings.

Situated cultures – those familiar and everyday settings and the particular patterns, relationships, ideas and beliefs which characterise them. Media consumption and reception take place in particular situations, which are defined not only in terms of location, but also in terms of the identities and points of view of the people involved. Best understood in contrast to *mediated culture*.

Stereotype – an oversimplified representation which is used to categorise and evaluate all members of a particular social group.

Structuralism – a range of theories which are characterised by an emphasis on the underlying system or set of rules which determine how *media texts* produce meaning.

Surveillance culture – the results of modern security systems and other data systems using CCTV (closed-circuit television) or computer-based networks to monitor social and public spaces and people.

Synergy – the process by which media companies acquire and harness the relations between two or more elements of a *media production* and distribution process. The aim is to increase efficiency and avoid duplication of resources and may, for example, involve using the same local news-gathering resources for both a local radio station and a local newspaper. Another example is the selling of two or more compatible products simultaneously, as in the multimedia merchandising surrounding the release of a 'blockbuster' movie.

Technological determinism – an overemphasis on the role of technology and machines as the principal, if not the sole cause of social, cultural and historical change and development.

Uses and gratifications – the range of needs and pleasures fulfilled through audience consumption of the media.

Virtual Reality (Virtual communities) – computer-simulated worlds, models and versions of life encountered on-line and in cyberspace. **Virtual communities** result from computer-mediated communication systems based around web sites or bulletin boards on the *Internet*.

Voyeurism – the practice of gaining pleasure from looking at other people whilst remaining anonymous. It is most frequently associated with men deriving sexual pleasure from looking at women.

Bibliography

Abercrombie, N. 1996: *Television and Society*. Polity Press.

Alasuutari, P. 1995: *Researching Culture: Qualitative Method and Cultural Studies*. Sage.

Allen, J. 1990: *Careers in TV and Radio*. Kogan Page.

Allen, R. 1987: *Channels of Discourse*. Methuen.

Alvarado, M. 1988: *Video Worldwide*. John Libbey.

Alvarado, M., Gutch, R. and Wollen, T. 1987: *Learning the Media*. Macmillan.

Ang, I. 1985: *Watching Dallas – Soap Opera and the Melodramatic Imagination*. Methuen.

Ang, I. 1991: *Desperately Seeking the Audience*. Routledge.

Ang, I. 1996: *Living Room Wars: Rethinking Media Audiences for a Postmodern World*. Routledge.

Anwar, M. and Shang, A. 1982: *Television in a Multi-Racial Society: A Research Report*. Commission for Racial Equality.

Armes, R. 1978: *A Critical History of British Cinema*. Oxford University Press.

Armes, R. 1988: *On Video*. Routledge.

Baehr, H. and Dyer, G. (eds). 1987: *Boxed In: Women and Television*. Pandora.

Bandura, A. and Walters, R. 1963: *Social Learning and Personality Development*. Holt Rinehart and Winston.

Barker, C. 1997: *Global Television: An Introduction*. Blackwell.

Barker, M. 1989: *Comics, Ideology, Power and the Critics*. Manchester University Press.

Barker, M. and Petley, J. (eds). 1997: *Ill-Effects: The Media/Violence Debate*. Routledge.

Barnard, S. 1989: *On the Radio*. Open University Press.

Barnes, J. 1976: *The Beginnings of Cinema in Britain*. David & Charles.

Barnett, S. 1988: *The Listener Speaks*. Broadcasting Research Unit.

Barr, C. 1986: *All Our Yesterdays*. BFI.

Barthes, R. 1973: *Mythologies*. Paladin.

Barthes, R. 1975: *S/Z*. Cape.

Barthes, R. 1977: *Image–Music–Text*. Fontana.

Barwise, P. and Ehrenberg, A. 1988: *Television and its Audience*. Sage.

BBC. 1992: *Extending Choice: The BBC's Role in the New Broadcasting Age*. BBC Publications.

BBC International Broadcasting Audience Research. 1993: *World Radio and Television Receivers*. BBC.

Beharrell, M. 1993: *Protest, Press and Prejudice: RAF Greenham Common 1982–92*. Institute of Education, University of London.

Bell, J. 1987: *Doing Your Research Project*. Open University Press.

Berger, A. 1991: *Media Analysis Techniques*. Sage.

Berger, J. 1972: *Ways of Seeing*. Penguin.

Bignall, J. 1997: *Media Semiotics: An Introduction*. Manchester University Press.

Blanchard, S. and Morley, D. (eds). 1983: *What's This Channel Four? An Alternative Report*. Comedia.

Blumler, J. and Katz, E. (eds). 1974: *The Uses of Mass Communication*. Sage.

Boyce, G. *et al.* (eds). 1978: *Newspaper History: From the 17th Century to the Present Day*. Constable.

Boyd, A. 1988, 1994: *Broadcast Journalism. Techniques of Radio and TV News*. Heinemann (1st edn); Focal Press (3rd edn).

Branston, G. and Stafford, R. 1995: *The Media Student's Book*. Routledge.

Brierley, S. 1995: *The Advertising Handbook*. Routledge.

Briggs, A. 1979: *The History of Broadcasting in the UK*. Vols 1–4. Oxford University Press.

Briggs, S. 1981: *Those Radio Times*. Weidenfeld & Nicolson.

British Rate and Data (BRAD). Maclean Hunter Ltd.

Brunt, R. 1992: 'A Divine Gift to Inspire' in D. Strinati and S. Wagg (eds), *Popular Media Culture*. Routledge.

Bryman, A. 1988: *Quantity and Quality in Social Research*. Unwin Hyman.

Buckingham, D. 1987: *Public Secrets*: EastEnders *and its Audience*. BFI.

Burnett, R. 1996: *The Global Jukebox: The International Music Industry*. Routledge.

Burns, T. 1977: *The BBC: Public Institution and Private World*. Macmillan.

Burton, G. 1990, 1997: *More Than Meets the Eye: An Introduction to Media Studies*. Arnold.

Carr, E.H. 1961: *What is History?* Macmillan.

Carter, M.D. 1971: *An Introduction to Mass Communications.* Macmillan.

Cater, N. 1985: *Ten 8.* no. 19.

Chanan, M. 1980, 1995: *The Dream that Kicks: The Pre-History and Early Years of Cinema in Britain.* Routledge.

Channel 4. 1991: *This is Channel Four.* Channel 4.

Chater, K. 1989: *The Television Researcher's Guide.* BBC TV Training.

Chippendale, P. and Horrie, C. 1990: *Stick It Up Your Punter – The Rise and Fall of the Sun.* Heinemann.

Clarke, M. 1987: *Teaching Popular Television.* Heinemann.

Clarke, S. and Horrie, C. 1994: *Fuzzy Monsters: Fear and Loathing at the BBC.* Heinemann.

Clute, J. and Nicholls, P. (eds). 1993: *The Encyclopedia of Science Fiction.* Orbit.

Collett, P. 1986: 'The Viewers Viewed'. *The Listener.* 22 May.

Communications Research Group (Aston University). 1990: *Television Advertising and Sex Role Stereotyping.* Broadcasting Standards Council.

Conroy, A. and Wilby, P. 1994: *The Radio Handbook.* Routledge.

Constantine, S. 1986: *Buy and Build: The Advertising Posters of the Empire Marketing Board.* HMSO.

Cook, J. (ed.). 1982: 'Television Sitcom'. BFI Dossier no. 17. BFI.

Cook, P. (ed.). 1985: *The Cinema Book.* BFI.

Cooke, L. 1984: *Media Studies Bibliography.* BFI.

Corner, J. (ed.). 1991: *Popular Television in Britain.* BFI

Corner, J. 1995: *Television Form and Public Address.* Arnold.

Cranfield, G.A. 1978: *The Press and Society.* Longman.

Crisell, A. 1986, 1994: *Understanding Radio.* Methuen (1st edn); Routledge (2nd edn).

Cumberbatch, G., *et al.* 1990: *Television Advertising and Sex Role Stereotyping.* Broadcasting Standards Council.

Curran, J. and Porter, V. (eds). 1983: *British Cinema History.* Weidenfeld & Nicolson.

Curran, J. and Seaton, J. 1991, 1997 (5th edn): *Power without Responsibility: The Press and Broadcasting in Britain.* Routledge.

Curran, J., Gurevitch, M. and Woollacott, J. (eds). 1977: *Mass Communication and Society.* Edward Arnold.

Curtis, L. 1984: *Ireland: The Propaganda War.* Pluto Press.

Daniels, T. and Gerson, J. 1990: *The Colour Black.* BFI.

Davis, A. 1988: *Magazine Journalism Today.* Heinemann.

Davis, D. 1969: *The Grammar of Television Production*. Revised by Elliot; further revised by Wooller. Published under the auspices of the Society of Film and Television Arts. Barrie and Jenkins.

Donzelot, J. 1980: *The Policing of Families*. Hutchinson.

Dowmunt, T. (ed.). 1993: *Channels of Resistance*. BFI/Channel 4.

Du Gay, P., Hall, S., Janes, L., Mackay, H. and Negus, K. 1997: *Doing Cultural Studies: The Story of the Sony Walkman*. Open University/Stage.

Dimbleby, N., Dimbleby, R. and Whittington, K. 1994: *Practical Media*. Hodder & Stoughton.

Dutton, B. 1986, 1997: *The Media*. Longman.

Dutton, B. 1989, 1995: *Media Studies: An Introduction*. Longman.

Dyer, G. 1982: *Advertising as Communication*. Methuen.

Dyer, R. 1977: 'Entertainment and Utopia'. *Movie*, vol. 24.

Eco, U. 1981: *The Role of the Reader*. Hutchinson.

Eldridge, J., Kitzinger, J. and Williams, K. 1997: *The Mass Media and Power in Modern Britain*. Oxford University Press.

Ellis, J. 1982, 1992: *Visible Fictions: Cinema, Television, Video*. Routledge.

Evans, H. 1986: *Pictures on a Page*. Heinemann.

Fairclough, N. 1995: *Media Discourse*. Arnold.

Ferguson, M. 1983: *Forever Feminine: Women's Magazines and the Cult of Femininity*. Heinemann.

Fiske, J. 1982: *Introduction to Communication Studies*. Methuen.

Fiske, J. 1987: *Television Culture*. Routledge.

Fiske, J. 1989a: *Understanding Popular Culture*. Unwin Hyman.

Fiske, J. 1989b: *Reading the Popular*. Unwin Hyman.

Fiske, J. and Hartley, J. 1978: *Reading Television*. Methuen.

Fountain, N. 1988: *Underground: The London Alternative Press 1966–1974*. Comedia.

Franklin, B. 1994: *Packaging Politics*. Edward Arnold.

Franklin, B. and Murphy, D. 1991: *What News? The Market, Politics and the Local Press*. Routledge.

Frith, S. 1983: *Sound Effects*. Constable.

Frith, S. 1988: *Facing the Music*. Pantheon.

Frith, S. and Goodwin, A. (eds). 1990: *On Record*. Routledge.

Gallup Chart Services. 1993: *The UK Music Charts*.

Gamman, L. and Marshment, M. (eds). 1988: *The Female Gaze: Women as Viewers of Popular Culture*. The Women's Press.

Garfield, S. 1986: *Expensive Habits: The Dark Side of the Music Industry*. Faber and Faber.

Garnham, N. 1973, 1980: *Structures of Television*. BFI Television Monograph no. 1. BFI.

Geraghty, C. 1991: *Women and Soap Opera*. Polity Press.

Gerbner, G. and Gross, L. 1976: 'Living with Television: The Violence Profile'. *Journal of Communication*, vol.28, no. 3.

Gillett, C. 1983: *The Sound of the City*. Souvenir Press.

Glasgow University Media Group. 1976: *Bad News*. Routledge.

Glasgow University Media Group. 1985: *War and Peace News*. Open University Press.

Goldie, G. 1977: *Facing the Nation: Television and Politics, 1936–76*. Bodley Head.

Golding, P. 1974: *The Mass Media*. Longman.

Golding, P. and Harris, P. (eds). 1997: *Beyond Cultural Imperialism: Globalization, Communication and the New International Order*. Sage.

Goodhart, D. and Wintour, C. 1986: *Eddy Shah and the Newspaper Revolution*. Coronet.

Goodwin, A. 1987: *TV Studies Bibliography*. BFI.

Goodwin, A. 1993a: *Dancing in the Distraction Factory*. Routledge.

Goodwin, A. 1993b: 'Riding with Ambulances: Television and its Uses', *Sight & Sound*, vol.3, no.1.

Goodwin, A. and Whannel, G. (eds). 1990: *Understanding Television*. Routledge.

Gordon, P. and Rosenberg, D. 1989: *Daily Racism*. Runnymede Trust.

Grahame, J., Jempson, M. and Simons, M. 1995: *The News Pack*. English & Media Centre, London.

Gray, A. 1992: *Video Playtime*. Routledge.

Griffiths, T. 1976: *Comedians*. Faber and Faber.

Gunter, B., Sancho-Aldridge, J. and Winstone, P. 1994: *Television: The Public's View 1993*. Independent Television Commission Research Monographs series. John Libbey.

Gurevitch, M. 1991: 'The Globalisation of Electronic Journalism', in J. Curran and M. Gurevitch (eds), *Mass Media and Society*. Edward Arnold.

Hall, S. 1980: *Culture, Media, Language*. Hutchinson.

Halloran, J. 1970: *The Effects of Television*. Panther.

Hammersley, M. and Atkinson, P. 1983: *Ethnography: Principles in Practice*. Tavistock.

Hannerz, U. 1996: *Transnational Connections: Culture, People, Places*. Routledge.

Harcup, T. 1995: *A Northern Star – Leeds Other Paper and the Alternative Press 1974–1994*. Campaign for Press and Broadcasting Freedom.

Harris, R. 1983: *Gotcha: The Media, the Government and the Falklands Crisis*. Faber and Faber.

Harrison, S. 1974: *Poor Men's Guardians*. Lawrence & Wishart.

Hartley, J. 1982: *Understanding News*. Methuen.

Hartley, J., Goulden, H. and O'Sullivan, T. 1985: *Making Sense of the Media*. Comedia.

Hayward, P. and Wollen, T. (eds). 1993: *Future Visions: New Technologies of the Screen*. BFI.

Heap, N., Thomas, R., Einon, G., Mason, R. and Mackay, H. (eds). 1995: *Information Technology and Society*. Sage.

Hebdige, D. 1989: 'After the Masses'. *Marxism Today*, January.

Hedgecoe, J. 1991: *On Video*. Hamlyn.

Herman, E. and McChesney, R. 1997: *The Global Media: The New Missionaries of Corporate Capitalism*. Cassell.

Hetherington, A. 1985: *News, Newspapers and Television*. Macmillan.

HMSO 1966: *Sound and Television Broadcasting in Britain*. HMSO.

HMSO 1992: *Social Trends 22*. HMSO.

Hobson, D. 1982: *Crossroads: The Drama of a Soap Opera*. Methuen.

Hobson, D. 1985: 'Ladies' Men'. *The Listener*. 25 April.

Hodge, B. and Tripp, D. 1986: *Children and Television*. Polity Press.

Hodgson, F. 1984: *Modern Newspaper Practice*. Heinemann.

Hodgson, F. 1987: *Modern Newspaper Editing and Production*. Heinemann.

Hoggart, R. 1957: *The Uses of Literacy*. Pelican.

Hood, S. 1980: *On Television*. Pluto Press.

Hood, S. (ed.). 1994: *Behind the Screens*. Lawrence & Wishart.

Howes, D. (ed.). 1996: *Cross-Cultural Consumption: Global Markets, Local Realities*. Routledge.

Izod, J. 1989: *Reading the Screen*. Longman.

James, E. 1994: *Science Fiction in the 20th Century*. Oxford University Press.

James, L. 1976: *Print and the People 1819–1851*. Penguin.

Jenkins, K. 1991: *Re-thinking History*. Routledge.

Jensen, K.B. and Jankowski, N. (eds). 1991: *A Handbook of Qualitative Methodologies for Mass Communication Research*. Routledge.

Johnson, R. 1986: 'The Story So Far and Further Transformations?' in D. Punter (ed.), *Introduction to Contemporary Cultural Studies*. Longman.

Katz, E. and Liebes, T. 1986: 'Mutual Aid in the Decoding of *Dallas*' in P. Drummond and R. Paterson (eds), *Television in Transition*. BFI.

Katz, E. and Liebes, T. 1990: *The Export of Meaning*. Oxford University Press.

Kaye, M. and Popperwell, A. 1992: *Making Radio*. Broadside Books.

Keeble, R. 1994: *The Newspapers Handbook*. Routledge.

Keighron, P. 1993: 'Video Diaries: What's Up Doc?', *Sight & Sound*, October.

Kingsley, H. and Tibballs, G. 1989: *Box of Delights*. Macmillan.

Knightley, P. 1978: *The First Casualty*. Quartet.

Krueger, R.A. 1994: *Focus Groups: A Practical Guide for Applied Research*. Sage.

Kumar, K. 1977: 'Holding the Middle Ground: The BBC, the Public and the Professional Broadcaster', in J. Curran, M. Gurevitch and J. Woollacott (eds), *Mass Communication and Society*. Edward Arnold.

Langham, J. 1996: *Lights, Camera, Action!* BFI.

Lazarsfeld, P., Berelson, B. and Gaudet, H. 1944: *The People's Choice*. Duell, Sloan and Pearce.

Lealand, G. 1984: *American Television Programmes on British Screens*. Broadcasting Research Unit.

Lee, A.J. 1976: *The Origins of the Popular Press 1855–1914*. Croom Helm.

Levy, E. 1990: 'Social Attributes of American Movie Stars'. *Media Culture and Society*, vol. 12, no. 2.

Lewis, J. 1990: *Art, Culture and Enterprise*. Routledge.

Lewis, J. 1991: *The Ideological Octopus*. Routledge.

Lewis, P. 1994: *Community Radio – A Gateway to Employment*. Community Radio Association.

Lewis, P. and Booth, J. 1989: *The Invisible Medium: Public, Commercial and Community Radio*. Macmillan.

Local Radio Workshop. 1983: *Capital: Local Radio and Private Profit*. Comedia.

Longhurst, B. 1995: *Popular Music and Society*. Polity Press.

Lull, J. (ed.), 1988: *World Families Watch Television*. Sage.

Lusted, D. (ed.), 1991: *The Media Studies Book*. Routledge.

Madge, J. 1989: *Beyond the BBC*. Macmillan.

Malm, K. and Wallis, R. 1984: *Big Sounds from Small Peoples*. Constable.

Masterman, L. 1984: *Television Mythologies: Stars, Shows and Signs*. Comedia.

Mattelart, A., Delcourt, X. and Mattelart, M. 1984: *International Image Markets*. Comedia.

May, J. 1996: 'This is the Big One', *20/20*, Winter.

McDonald, M. 1995: *Representing Women*. Arnold.

McGuigan, J. 1992: *Cultural Populism*. Routledge.

McIntyre, I. 1993: *The Expense of Glory: A Life of John Reith*. HarperCollins.

McLuhan, M. 1964: *Understanding Media*. Routledge and Kegan Paul.

McMahon, B. and Quinn, R. 1986: *Real Images*. Macmillan.

McMahon, B. and Quinn, R. 1988: *Exploring Images*. Macmillan.

McNair, B. 1993, 1996: *News and Journalism in the UK*. Routledge.

McNair, B. 1995: *An Introduction to Political Communication*. Routledge.

McNair, B. 1996: *News and Journalism in the UK*. Routledge.

McNeill, P. 1990: *Research Methods*. Routledge.

McQuail, D. 1975: *Communication*. Longman.

McQuail, D. 1983, 1987, 1994: *Mass Communication Theory: An Introduction*. Sage.

McRobbie, A. 1994: *Postmodernism and Popular Culture*. Routledge.

McRobbie, A. 1996: 'More! New Sexualities in Girls' and Women's Magazines' in J. Curran, D. Morley and V. Walkerdine (eds), *Cultural Studies and Communications*. Arnold.

McRoberts, R. 1987: *Media Workshops: Vol. 1, Words*. Macmillan.

Media Monitoring Unit. 1990: *Broadcasting and Political Bias*. Hampden Trust.

Medina, P. and Donald, V. 1992: *Careers in Journalism*. Kogan Page.

Messenger Davies, M. 1989: *Television is Good for Kids*. Hilary Shipman.

Metz, C. 1974: *Film Language*. Oxford University Press.

Miller, J. 1990: *Broadcasting: Getting In and Getting On*. Butterworth.

Miller, W. 1992: 'I Am What I Read'. *The Listener*, 24 April.

Millersen, G. 1989: *Video Production Handbook*. Focal Press.

Monaco, J. 1977: *How to Read a Film: The Art, Technology, Language, History and Theory of Film and Media*. Oxford University Press.

Moores, S. 1993: *Interpreting Audiences*. Sage.

Morgan, J. and Welton, P. 1986, 1992: *See What I Mean*. Edward Arnold.

Morley, D. 1980: *The Nationwide Audience*. BFI.

Morley, D. 1986: *Family Television*. Comedia.

Morley, D. 1991: 'Where the Global Meets the Local: Notes from the Sitting Room'. *Screen*, vol. 32, no. 1.

Morley, D. 1992: *Television, Audiences and Cultural Studies*. Routledge.

Morley, D. and Robins, K. 1995: *Spaces of Identity: Global Media, Electronic Landscapes and Cultural Boundaries*. Routledge.

Morley, D. and Whitaker, B. (eds). 1983: *The Press, Radio and Television*. Comedia.

Mulvey, L. 1975: 'Visual Pleasure and Narrative Cinema'. *Screen*, vol. 16, no. 3.

Murdock, G. 1974: 'The Politics of Culture' in D. Holly (ed.). *Education or Domination*. Arrow Books.

Murdock, G. and Golding, P. 1991: 'Culture, Communications and Political Economy' in J. Curran and M. Gurevitch (eds). *Mass Media and Society*. Edward Arnold.

Negrine, R. 1989, 1994: *Politics and the Mass Media in Britain*. Routledge.

Negus, K. 1992: *Producing Pop*. Edward Arnold.

Negus, K. 1996: *Popular Music in Theory*. Polity Press.

Nelmes, J. (ed.). 1996: *An Introduction to Film Studies*. Routledge.

Niblock, S. 1996: *Inside Journalism*. Blueprint.

Nightingale, V. 1996: *Studying Audiences: The Shock of the Real*. Routledge.

Norman, B. 1984: *Here's Looking at You*. BBC.

O'Malley, T. 1994: *Closedown? The BBC and Government Broadcasting Policy, 1979–92*. Pluto.

Oppenheim, A.N. 1992: *Questionnaire Design, Interviewing and Attitude Measurement*. Blackwell.

Orwell, G. 1949: *1984*. Secker & Warburg.

Ostergaard, B. (ed.). 1997: *The Media in Western Europe: The Euromedia Handbook*. Sage.

O'Sullivan, T., Hartley, J., Saunders, D., Montgomery, M. and Fiske, J. 1994: *Key Concepts in Communication and Cultural Studies*. Routledge.

O'Sullivan, T. 1996: 'Research Interviews', in B. Allison, T. O'Sullivan, A. Owen, J. Rice, A. Rothwell and C. Saunders (eds), *Research Skills for Students*. Kogan Page.

O'Sullivan, T. 1997: 'What Lies Between Mechatronics and Medicine? The Critical Mass of Media Studies.' *Soundings*, issue 5, pp. 211–21.

O'Sullivan, T. and Jewkes, Y. (eds). 1997: *The Media Studies Reader*. Arnold.

Packard, V.I. 1957: *The Hidden Persuaders*. Longman.

Partridge, S. 1982: *Not the BBC/IBA – The Case for Community Radio*. Comedia/Minorities Press Group.

Paulu, B. 1981: *Television and Radio in the UK*. Macmillan.

Peacock, A. 1986: *Report of the Committee on Financing the BBC.* Cmnd 9824. HMSO.

Peak, S. and Fisher, P. (eds). (Annual:) *Guardian Media Guide.* Fourth Estate.

Pennachioni, I. 1984: 'The Reception of Television in North East Brazil.' *Media Culture and Society*, vol. 6, no. 4.

Perkins, T. 1979: 'Rethinking Stereotypes', in M. Barrett, P. Corrigan, A. Kuhn and V. Wolff (eds), *Ideology and Cultural Production.* Croom Helm.

Peterson, R.A. and Berger, D.G. 1975: 'Cycles in Symbolic Presentation: The Case of Popular Music'. *American Sociological Review*, vol.40.

Peterson, R.C. and Thurstone, L. 1933: *Motion Pictures and Social Attitudes.* Macmillan.

Pines, J. (ed.). 1992: *Black and White in Colour.* BFI.

Posener, J. 1982: *Spray it Loud.* Pandora.

Power, M. and Sheridan, G. (eds). 1984: 'Labour Daily? – Ins and Outs of a New Labour Daily and Other Media Alternatives'. Campaign for Press and Broadcasting Freedom.

Propp, V. 1968: *Morphology of the Folk Tale.* University of Texas Press.

Quilliam, S. and Grove-Stephansan, I. 1990: *Into Print.* BBC.

Real, M.R. 1996: *Exploring Media Culture: A Guide.* Sage.

Reeves, G. 1993: *Communications and the 'Third World'.* Routledge.

Reith, J. 1949: *Into the Wind.* Hodder & Stoughton.

Rheingold, H. 1994: *The Virtual Community: Finding Connection in a Computerised World.* Minerva.

Robertson, J.C. 1989: *The Hidden Cinema: British Film Censorship 1913–1972.* Routledge.

Rosen, M. and Widgery, D. 1991: *The Chatto Book of Dissent.* Chatto & Windus.

Ross, K. 1996: *Black and White Media.* Polity Press.

Rothwell, A. 1996: 'Questionnaire Design', in B. Allison, T. O'Sullivan, A. Owen, J. Rice, A. Rothwell and C. Saunders (eds), *Research Skills for Students.* Kogan Page.

Sales, R. 1986: 'An Introduction to Broadcasting History' in D. Punter (ed.), *An Introduction to Contemporary Cultural Studies.* Longman.

Scannell, P. 1987a: 'The State and Society: Broadcasting Rituals'. Open University D209.

Scannell, P. 1987b: *The Making of Britain: Mass Media, Mass Democracy.* Channel 4.

Scannell, P. 1996: *Radio, Television and Modern Life.* Blackwell.

Scannell, P. and Cardiff, D. 1991: *A Social History of British Broadcasting. Vol.1*. Blackwell.

Scannell, P. and Cardiff, D. 1981: 'Popular Culture: Radio in WW2'. Open University U203.

Schiller, H. 1969: *Mass Communication and American Empire*. Kelley.

Schiller, H. 1976: *Communication and Cultural Domination*. International Arts & Science Press.

Schiller, H. 1991: 'Not Yet the Post-Imperialist Era?' *Critical Studies in Mass Communication*, vol.8.

Schlesinger, P. 1987: *Putting 'Reality' Together – BBC News*. Methuen.

Schlesinger, P. 1991: *Media State and Nation*. Sage.

Schlesinger, P., Dobash, R.E., Dobash, R.P. and Weaver, C. 1992: *Women Viewing Violence*. BFI.

Seymour-Ure, C. 1991: *The British Press and Broadcasting Since 1945*. Blackwell.

Shippey, T. (ed.). 1991: *Fictional Space: Essays on Contemporary Science Fiction*. Oxford University Press.

Silj, A. (ed.). 1988: *East of Dallas*. BFI.

Smith, A. 1993: *Books to Bytes: Knowledge and Information in the Postmodern Era*. BFI.

Smith, J. 1990: *Misogynies*. Faber and Faber.

Snagge, J. and Barsley, M. 1972: *Those Vintage Years of Radio*. Pitman.

Sontag, S. 1977: *On Photography*. Penguin.

Sreberny-Mohammadi, A. 1991: 'The Global and the Local in International Communications', in J. Curran and M. Gurevitch (eds), *Mass Media and Society*. Edward Arnold.

Stafford, R. 1993: *Hands On*. BFI.

Stead, P. 1989: *Film and the Working Class*. Routledge.

Stevenson, N. 1995: *Understanding Media Cultures: Social Theory and Mass Communication*. Sage.

Stokes, P. 1992: *No Apology Needed: The Story of the N.W.N.*. Blacket Turner.

Strinati, D. and Wagg, S. (eds). 1992: *Come On Down: Popular Media Culture in Post War Britain*. Routledge.

Swanson, G. 1991: 'Representations', chapter 6 in D. Lusted (ed.), *The Media Studies Book*. Routledge.

Tasker, Y. 1993: *Spectacular Bodies: Gender, Genre and the Action Cinema*. Routledge.

Taylor, A.J.P. 1965: *English History 1914–45*. Clarendon Press.

Taylor, J. 1991: *War Photography*. Comedia.

Taylor, P. 1992: *Propaganda and Persuasion in the Gulf War*. Manchester University Press.

Thompson, E.P. 1968: *The Making of the English Working Class*. Penguin.

Thompson, J.B. 1988: 'Mass Communication and Modern Culture: Contribution to a Critical Theory of Ideology'. *Sociology*, vol. 22, no. 3.

Thompson, J.B. 1995: *The Media and Modernity*. Polity Press.

Tilley, A. 1991: 'Narrative', chapter 3 in D. Lusted (ed.), *The Media Studies Book*. Routledge.

Todorov, T. 1973: *The Fantastic: Towards a Structural Approach*. Case Western Reserve University Press.

Tolson, A. 1996: *Mediations: Text and Discourse in Media Studies* Arnold.

Tomlinson, J. 1991: *Cultural Imperialism*. Pinter.

Tracey, M. 1985: 'The Poisoned Chalice? International Television and the Idea of Dominance'. *Daedalus*, vol. 114, no. 4.

Trowler, P. 1989, 1996: *Investigating the Media*. Tavistock (1st edn); HarperCollins (2nd edn).

Tunstall, J. 1983: *The Media in Britain*. Constable.

Tunstall, J. 1996: *Newspaper Power: The New National Press in Britain*. Clarendon Press.

Turkle, S. 1984: *The Second Self: Computers and the Human Spirit*. Granada.

Turner, G. 1996: *British Cultural Studies: An Introduction*. Routledge.

Van Zoonen, L. 1994: *Feminist Media Studies*. Sage.

Varis, T. 1974: 'Global Traffic in Television'. *Journal of Communication*, vol. 24.

Varis, T. 1984: 'The International Flow of Television Programmes'. *Journal of Communication*, vol. 34, no. 1.

Walker, A. 1986: *Hollywood England*. Harrap.

Ward, K. 1989: *Mass Communications and the Modern World*. Macmillan.

Watson, J. and Hill, A. 1996: *A Dictionary of Communication and Media Studies*. Arnold.

Watts, H. 1984: *On Camera*. BBC.

Watts, H. 1992: *Directing on Camera*. Aavo.

Weber, R.P. 1990: *Basic Content Analysis*. Sage.

Webster, F. 1995: *Theories of the Information Society*. Routledge.

Wenden, D.J. 1974: *The Birth of the Movies*. Dutton.

Whitaker, B. (ed.). 1984: *News Ltd: Why You Can't Read All About It*. Comedia.

Williams, K. 1997: *'Get Me a Murder a Day': A History of Mass Communications in Britain*. Arnold.

Williams, R. 1965: *The Long Revolution*. Pelican.

Williams, R. 1966: *Communications*. Chatto & Windus.

Williams, R. 1974, 1990: *Television, Technology and Cultural Form*. Fontana (1st edn); Routledge (2nd edn).

Williams, R. 1976: *Keywords: A Vocabulary of Culture and Society*. Fontana.

Williams, R. 1990: *Television: Technology and Cultural Form*. Routledge.

Williamson, J. 1978: *Decoding Advertisements: Ideology and Meaning in Advertising*. Marion Boyars.

Willings Press Guide. Vol. I. Reed Information Services.

Winn, M. 1977: *The Plug-in Drug*. Penguin.

Winship, I. and McNab, A. 1996: *The Student's Guide to the Internet*. Library Association.

Winship, J. 1987: *Inside Women's Magazines*. Pandora.

Wolffsohn, A. 1996: 'Shaping the Future', *Spectrum*, 23, Autumn. Independent Television Commission.

Woolf, M. and Holly, S. 1994: *Employment Patterns and Training Needs 1993/4: Radio Survey*. Skillset.

Zenith Media. 1995: *UK Media Handbook*. Zenith.